ISBN 978-1-333-49056-0
PIBN 10511061

This book is a reproduction of an important historical work. Forgotten Books uses
state-of-the-art technology to digitally reconstruct the work, preserving the original format
whilst repairing imperfections present in the aged copy. In rare cases, an imperfection in
the original, such as a blemish or missing page, may be replicated in our edition. We do,
however, repair the vast majority of imperfections successfully; any imperfections that
remain are intentionally left to preserve the state of such historical works.

1 MONTH OF
FREE
READING

at
www.ForgottenBooks.com

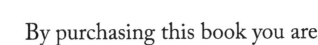

By purchasing this book you are eligible for one month membership to ForgottenBooks.com, giving you unlimited access to our entire collection of over 1,000,000 titles via our web site and mobile apps.

To claim your free month visit:

www.forgottenbooks.com/free511061

THE LIFE OF LUDWIG VAN BEETHOVEN

VOLUME I

The Life of
Ludwig van Beethoven

By Alexander Wheelock Thayer

Edited, revised and amended from the original
English manuscript and the German editions
of Hermann Deiters and Hugo Riemann, concluded, and all the documents newly translated

By
Henry Edward Krehbiel

Volume I

Published by
The Beethoven Association
New York

SECOND PRINTING

From the press of G. Schirmer, Inc., New York
Printed in the U. S. A.

IN PROFOUND REVERENCE THIS WORK

IS DEDICATED BY THE EDITOR

TO THE MEMORY OF

𝔄lexander 𝔚heelock 𝔗hayer and 𝔇r. 𝔥ermann 𝔇eiters

ALSO IN GRATEFUL APPRECIATION

TO

THE BEETHOVEN ASSOCIATION

AND WITH A LARGE MEASURE OF GRATITUDE AND AFFECTION

TO HIS FRIEND AND COLLEAGUE

RICHARD ALDRICH

Introduction

IF for no other reasons than because of the long time and monumental patience expended upon its preparation, the vicissitudes through which it has passed and the varied and arduous labors bestowed upon it by the author and his editors, the history of Alexander Wheelock Thayer's Life of Beethoven deserves to be set forth as an introduction to this work. His work it is, and his monument, though others have labored long and painstakingly upon it. There has been no considerable time since the middle of the last century when it has not occupied the minds of the author and those who have been associated with him in its creation. Between the conception of its plan and its execution there lies a period of more than two generations. Four men have labored zealously and affectionately upon its pages, and the fruits of more than four score men, stimulated to investigation by the first revelations made by the author, have been conserved in the ultimate form of the biography. It was seventeen years after Mr. Thayer entered upon what proved to be his life-task before he gave the first volume to the world—and then in a foreign tongue; it was thirteen more before the third volume came from the press. This volume, moreover, left the work unfinished, and thirty-two years more had to elapse before it was completed. When this was done the patient and self-sacrificing investigator was dead; he did not live to finish it himself nor to see it finished by his faithful collaborator of many years, Dr. Deiters; neither did he live to look upon a single printed page in the language in which he had written that portion of the work published in his lifetime. It was left for another hand to prepare the English edition of an American writer's history of Germany's greatest tone-poet, and to write its concluding chapters, as he believes, in the spirit of the original author.

Under these circumstances there can be no vainglory in asserting that the appearance of this edition of Thayer's Life of Beethoven deserves to be set down as a significant occurrence

in musical history. In it is told for the first time in the language
of the great biographer the true story of the man Beethoven—
his history stripped of the silly sentimental romance with which
early writers and their later imitators and copyists invested it so
thickly that the real humanity, the humanliness, of the composer
has never been presented to the world. In this biography there
appears the veritable Beethoven set down in his true environ-
ment of men and things—the man as he actually was, the man as
he himself, like Cromwell, asked to be shown for the information
of posterity. It is doubtful if any other great man's history
has been so encrusted with fiction as Beethoven's. Except
Thayer's, no biography of him has been written which presents
him in his true light. The majority of the books which have
been written of late years repeat many of the errors and falsehoods made current in the first books which were written about
him. A great many of these errors and falsehoods are in the
account of the composer's last sickness and death, and were either
inventions or exaggerations designed by their utterers to add
pathos to a narrative which in unadorned truth is a hundred-
fold more pathetic than any tale of fiction could possibly be.
Other errors have concealed the truth in the story of Beethoven's
guardianship of his nephew, his relations with his brothers, the
origin and nature of his fatal illness, his dealings with his publishers and patrons, the generous attempt of the Philharmonic
Society of London to extend help to him when upon his deathbed.

   In many details the story of Beethoven's life as told here
will be new to English and American readers; in a few cases the
details will be new to the world, for the English edition of Thayer's
biography is not a translation of the German work but a presentation of the original manuscript, so far as the discoveries made
after the writing did not mar its integrity, supplemented by the
knowledge acquired since the publication of the first German
edition, and placed at the service of the present editor by the
German revisers of the second edition. The editor of this English
edition was not only in communication with Mr. Thayer during
the last ten years of his life, but was also associated to some extent with his continuator and translator, Dr. Deiters. Not only
the fruits of the labors of the German editors but the original manuscript of Thayer and the mass of material which he accumulated
came into the hands of this writer, and they form the foundation
on which the English "Thayer's Beethoven" rests. The work
is a vastly different one from that which Thayer dreamed of when
he first conceived the idea of bringing order and consistency into

the fragmentary and highly colored accounts of the composer's life upon which he fed his mind and fancy as a student at college; but it is, even in that part of the story which he did not write, true ·to the conception of what Beethoven's biography should be. Knowledge of the composer's life has greatly increased since the time when Thayer set out upon his task. The first publication of some of the results of his investigations in his "Chronologisches Verzeichniss" in 1865, and the first volume of the biography which appeared a year later, stirred the critical historians into activity throughout Europe. For them he had opened up a hundred avenues of research, pointed out a hundred subjects for special study. At once collectors of autographs brought forth their treasures, old men opened up the books of their memories, librarians gave eager searchers access to their shelves, churches produced their archives, and hieroglyphic sketches which had been scattered all over Europe were deciphered by scholars and yielded up chronological information of inestimable value. To all these activities Thayer had pointed the way, and thus a great mass of facts was added to the already great mass which Thayer had accumulated. Nor did Thayer's labors in the field end with the first publication of his volumes. So long as he lived he gathered, ordered and sifted the new material which came under his observation and prepared it for incorporation into later editions and later volumes. After he was dead his editors continued the work.

Alexander Wheelock Thayer was born in South Natick, Massachusetts, on October 22nd, 1817, and received a liberal education at Harvard College, whence he was graduated in 1843. He probably felt that he was cut out for a literary career, for his first work after graduation was done in the library of his *Alma Mater*. There interest in the life of Beethoven took hold of him. With the plan in his mind of writing an account of that life on the basis of Schindler's biography as paraphrased by Moscheles, and bringing its statements and those contained in the "Biographische Notizen" of Wegeler and Ries and a few English accounts into harmony, he went to Europe in 1849 and spent two years in making researches in Bonn, Berlin, Prague and Vienna. He then returned to America and in 1852 became attached to the editorial staff of "The New York Tribune." It was in a double sense an attachment; illness compelled him to abandon journalism and sever his connection with the newspaper within two years, but he never gave up his interest in it. He read it until the day of his death, and his acquaintance with the member of the Tribune's staff who was destined to have a part in the completion of his lifework began when, a little more than a generation after he had gone to Europe for the second time, he opened a correspondence with him on a topic suggested by one of this writer's criticisms. In 1854 he went to Europe again, still fired with the ambition to rid the life-history of Beethoven of the defects which marred it as told in the current books. Schindler had sold the *memorabilia* which he had received from Beethoven and Beethoven's friend Stephan von Breuning to the Prussian Government, and the precious documents were safely housed in the Royal Library at Berlin. It was probably in studying them that Thayer realized fully that it was necessary to do more than rectify and harmonize current accounts of Beethoven's life if it were correctly to be told. He had already unearthed much precious ore at Bonn, but he lacked the money which alone would enable him to do the long and large work which now loomed before him. In 1856 he again came back to America and sought employment, finding it this time in South Orange, New Jersey, where Lowell Mason employed him to catalogue his musical library. Meanwhile Dr. Mason had become interested in his great project, and Mrs. Mehetabel Adams, of Cambridge, Massachusetts, also. Together they provided the funds which enabled him again to go to Europe, where he now took up a permanent residence. At first he spent his time in research-travels, visiting Berlin, Bonn, Cologne, Düsseldorf (where he found material of great value in the archives of the old Electoral Courts of Bonn and Cologne), Frankfort, Paris, Linz, Graz, Salzburg, London and Vienna. To support himself he took a small post in the Legation of the United States at Vienna, but exchanged this after a space for the U. S. Consulship at Trieste, to which office he was appointed by President Lincoln on the recommendation of Senator Sumner. In Trieste he remained till his death, although out of office after October 1st, 1882. To Sir George Grove he wrote under date June 1st, 1895: "I was compelled to resign my office because of utter inability longer to continue Beethoven work and official labor together." From Trieste, when his duties permitted, he went out on occasional exploring tours, and there he weighed his accumulations of evidence and wrote his volumes.

In his travels Thayer visited every person of importance then living who had been in any way associated with Beethoven or had personal recollection of him—Schindler, the composer's factotum and biographer; Anselm Hüttenbrenner, in whose arms he died; Caroline van Beethoven, widow of Nephew Karl; Charles Neate and Cipriani Potter, the English musicians who had been his pupils; Sir George Smart, who had visited him to learn the proper interpretation of the Ninth Symphony; Moscheles, who had been a professional associate in Vienna; Otto Jahn, who had undertaken a like task with his own, but abandoned it and turned over his gathered material to him; Mähler, an artist who had painted Beethoven's portrait; Gerhard von Breuning, son of Beethoven's most intimate friend, who as a lad of fourteen had been a cheery companion of the great man when he lay upon his fatal bed of sickness;—with all these and many others he talked, carefully recording their testimony in his note-books and piling up information with which to test the correctness of traditions and printed accounts and to amplify the veracious story of Beethoven's life. His industry, zeal, keen power of analysis, candor and fairmindedness won the confidence and help of all with whom he came in contact except the literary charlatans whose romances he was bent on destroying in the interest of the verities of history. The Royal Library at Berlin sent the books in which many of Beethoven's visitors had written down their part of the conversations which the composer could not hear, to him at Trieste so that he might transcribe and study them at his leisure.

In 1865, Thayer was ready with the manuscript for Volume I of the work, which contained a sketch of the Courts of the Electors of Cologne at Cologne and Bonn for over a century, told of the music cultivated at them and recorded the ancestry of Beethoven so far as it had been discovered. It also carried the history of the composer down to the year 1796. In Bonn, Thayer had made the acquaintance of Dr. Hermann Deiters, Court Councillor and enthusiastic musical littérateur, and to him he confided the task of editing and revising his manuscript and translating it into German. The reason which Thayer gave for not at once publishing his work in English was that he was unable to oversee the printing in his native land, where, moreover, it was not the custom to publish such works serially. He urged upon his collaborator that he practise literalness of translation in respect of his own utterances, but gave him full liberty to proceed according to his judgment in the presentation of documentary evidence. All of the material in the volume except the draughts from Wegeler, Ries and Schindler, with which he was frequently in conflict, was original discovery, the result of the labors begun in Bonn in 1849. His principles he set forth in these words: "I fight for no theories, and cherish no prejudices; my sole point of view is the truth. . . . . . I have resisted the temptation to discuss the character of his (Beethoven's) works and to make such a discussion the foundation of historical speculation, preferring to leave such matters to those who have a greater predilection for them. It appears to me that Beethoven the *composer* is amply known through his works and in this assumption the long and wearisome labors of so many years were devoted to Beethoven the *man*." The plan to publish his work in German enabled Thayer to turn over all his documentary evidence to Deiters in its original shape, a circumstance which saved him great labor, but left it for his American editor and continuator. The first German volume appeared in 1866; its stimulative effect upon musical Europe has been indicated. Volume II came from the press in 1872, Volume III in 1879, both translated and annotated by Deiters. They brought the story of Beethoven's life down to the end of the year 1816, leaving a little more than a decade still to be discussed.

The health of Thayer had never been robust, and the long and unintermittent application to the work of gathering and weighing evidence had greatly taxed his brain. He became subject to severe headaches and after the appearance of the third volume he found it impossible to apply himself for even a short time to work upon the biography. In July, 1890, he wrote a letter to Sir George Grove which the latter forwarded to this writer. In it he tells in words of pathetic gratitude of the unexpected honors showered upon him at Bonn when at the invitation of the Beethoven-Haus Verein he attended the exhibition and festival given in Beethoven's birthplace a short time before. Then he proceeds: "Of course the great question was on the lips of all: When will the fourth volume appear? I could only say: When the condition of my head allows it. No one could see or have from my general appearance the least suspicion that I was not in mental equal to my physical vigor. In fact, the extreme excitement of these three weeks took off for the time twenty years of my age and made me young again; but afterwards in Hamburg and in Berlin the reaction came. Spite of the delightful musical parties at Joachim's, Hausmann's, Mendelssohn's . . . . my head broke down more and more, and since my return hither, July 3rd, has as yet shown small signs of recuperation. The extreme importance of working out my fourth volume is more than ever impressed upon my mind and weighs upon me like an incubus. But as yet it is still utterly impossible for me to really work. Of course I only live for that great purpose and do not despair. My general health is such that I think the brain must in time recover something of its vigor and power of labor. What astonishes me and almost creates envy is to see this wonderful power of labor as exemplified by you and my neighbor, Burton. But from boyhood I have had head troubles, and what I went through with for thirty years in supporting myself and working on Beethoven is not to be described and excites my wonder that I did not succumb. Well, I will not yet despair." Thayer's mind, active enough in some things, refused to occupy itself with the Beethoven material; it needed distraction, and to give it that he turned to literary work of another character. He wrote a book against the Baconian authorship of Shakespeare's works; another on the Hebrews in Egypt and their Exodus (which Mr. E. S. Willcox, a friend of many years, published at his request in Peoria, Illinois). He also wrote essays and children's tales. Such writing he could do and also attend to his consular duties; but an hour or two of thought devoted to Beethoven, as he said in a letter to the present writer, brought on a racking headache and unfitted him for labor of any kind.

Meanwhile year after year passed by and the final volume of the biography was no nearer its completion than in 1880. In fact, beyond the selection and ordination of its material, it was scarcely begun. His friends and the lovers of Beethoven the world over grew seriously concerned at the prospect that it would never be completed. Sharing in this concern, the editor of the present edition developed a plan which he thought would enable Thayer to complete the work notwithstanding the disabilities under which he was laboring. He asked the coöperation of Novello, Ewer & Co., of London, and got them to promise to send a capable person to Trieste to act as a sort of literary secretary to Thayer. It was thought that, having all the material for the concluding volume on hand chronologically arranged, he might talk it over with the secretary, but without giving care to the manner of literary presentation. The secretary was then to give the material a proper setting and submit it to Thayer for leisurely revision. Very hopefully, and with feelings of deep gratitude to his friends, the English publishers, the American editor submitted his plan; but Thayer would have none of it. Though unable to work upon the biography for an hour continuously, he yet clung to the notion that some day he would not only finish it but also rewrite the whole for English and American readers. From one of the letters placed at my disposal by Sir George Grove, it appears that subsequently (in 1892) there was some correspondence between an English publisher and Mr. Thayer touching an English edition. The letter was written to Sir George on June 1st, 1895. In it he says: "I then hoped to be able to revise and prepare it (the Beethoven MS.) for publication myself, and was able to begin the labor and arrange with a typewriting woman to make the clean copy. How sadly I failed I wrote you. Since that time the subject has not been renewed between us. I am now compelled to relinquish all hope of ever being able to do the work. There are two great difficulties to be overcome: the one is that all letters and citations are in the original German as they were sent to Dr. Deiters; the other, there is much to be condensed, as I always intended should be for this reason: From the very first chapter to the end of Vol. III, I am continually in conflict with all previous writers and was compelled, therefore, to show in my text that I was right by so using my materials that the reader should be taken along step by step and compelled to see the truth for himself. Had all my arguments been given in notes nine readers out of ten would hardly have read them, and I should have been involved in numberless and endless controversies. Now the case is changed. A. W. T's novelties are now, with few if any exceptions, accepted as facts and can, in the English edition, be used as such. Besides this, there is much new matter to be inserted and some corrections to be made from the appendices of the three German volumes. The prospect now is that I may be able to do some of this work, or, at all events, go through my MS. page by page and do much to facilitate its preparation for publication in English. I have no expectation of ever receiving any pecuniary recompense for my 40 years of labor, for my many years of poverty arising from the costs of my extensive researches, for my—but enough of this also." In explanation of the final sentence in this letter it may be added that Thayer told the present writer that he had never received a penny from his publisher for the three German volumes; nothing more, in fact, than a few books which he had ordered and for which the publisher made no charge.

Thus matters rested when Thayer died on July 15th, 1897. The thought that the fruits of his labor and great sacrifices should be lost to the world even in part was intolerable. Dr. Deiters, with undiminished zeal and enthusiasm, announced his willingness to revise the three published volumes for a second edition and write the concluding volume. Meanwhile all of Thayer's papers had been sent to Mrs. Jabez Fox of Cambridge, Massachusetts, the author's niece and one of his heirs. There was a large mass of material, and it became necessary to sift it in order that all that was needful for the work of revision and completion might be placed in the hands of Dr. Deiters. This work was done, at Mrs. Fox's request, by the present writer, who, also at Mrs. Fox's request, undertook the task of preparing this English edition. Dr. Deiters accomplished the work of revising Volume I, which was published by Weber, the original publisher of the German volumes, in 1891. He then decided that before taking up the revision of Volumes II and III he would bring the biography to a conclusion. He wrote, not the one volume which Thayer had hoped would suffice him, but two volumes, the mass of material bearing on the last decade of Beethoven's life having grown so large that it could not conveniently be comprehended in a single tome, especially since Dr. Deiters had determined to incorporate critical discussions of the composer's principal works in the new edition. The advance sheets of Volume IV were in Dr. Deiters's hands when, full of years and honors, he died on May 1st, 1907. Breitkopf and Härtel had meanwhile purchased the German copyright from Weber, and they chose Dr. Hugo Riemann to complete the work of revision. Under Dr. Riemann's supervision Volumes IV and V were brought out in 1908, and Volumes II and III in 1910–1911.

Not until this had been accomplished could the American collaborator go systematically to work on his difficult and voluminous task, for he had determined to use as much as possible of Thayer's original manuscript and adhere to Thayer's original purpose and that expressed in his letter to Sir George Grove. He also thought it wise to condense the work so as to bring it within three volumes and to seek to enhance its readableness in other ways. To this end he abolished the many appendices which swell the German volumes, and put their significant portions into the body of the narrative; he omitted many of the hundreds of foot-notes, especially the references to the works of the earlier biographers, believing that the special student would easily find the sources if he wished to do so, and the general reader would not care to verify the statements of one who has been accepted as the court of last resort in all matters of fact pertaining to Beethoven, the man; he also omitted many letters and presented the substance of others in his own words for the reason that they can all be consulted in the special volumes which contain the composer's correspondence; of the letters and other documents used in the pages which follow, he made translations for the sake of accuracy as well as to avoid conflict with the copyright privileges of the publishers of English versions. Being as free as the German editors in respect of the portion of the biography which did not come directly from the pen of Thayer, the editor of this English edition chose his own method of presentation touching the story of the last decade of Beethoven's life, keeping in view the greater clearness and rapidity of narrative which, he believed, would result from a grouping of material different from that followed by the German editors in their adherence to the strict chronological method established by Thayer.

A large number of variations from the text of the original German edition are explained in the body of this work or in footnotes. In cases where the German editors were found to be in disagreement with the English manuscript in matters of opinion merely, the editor has chosen to let Mr. Thayer's arguments stand, though, as a rule, he has noted the adverse opinions of the German revisers also. A prominent instance of this kind is presented by the mysterious love-letter found secreted in Beethoven's desk after his death. Though a considerable literature has grown up around the "Immortal Beloved" since Thayer advanced the hypothesis that the lady was the Countess Therese Brunswick, the question touching her identity and the dates of the letters is still as much an open one as it was when Thayer, in his characteristic manner, subjected it to examination. This editor has, therefore, permitted Thayer not only to present his case in his own words, but helped him by bringing his scattered pleadings and briefs into sequence. He has also outlined in part the discussion which followed the promulgation of Thayer's theory, and advanced a few fugitive reflections of his own. The related incident of Beethoven's vain matrimonial project has been put into a different category by new evidence which came to light while Dr. Riemann was engaged in his revisory work. It became necessary, therefore, that the date of that incident be changed from 1807, where Thayer had put it, to 1810. By this important change Beethoven's relations to Therese Malfatti were made to take on a more serious attitude than Thayer was willing to accord them.

In this edition, finally, more importance is attached to the so-called Fischer Manuscript than Thayer was inclined to give it, although he, somewhat grudgingly we fear, consented that Dr. Deiters should print it with critical comments in the Appendix of his Vol. I. The manuscript, though known to Thayer, had come to the attention of Dr. Deiters too late for use in the narrative portion of the volume, though it was thus used in the second edition. The story of the manuscript, which is now preserved in the museum of the Beethoven-Haus Verein in Bonn, is a curious one. Its author was Gottfried Fischer, whose ancestors for four generations had lived in the house in the Rheingasse which only a few years ago was still, though mendaciously, pointed out to strangers as the house in which Beethoven was born. Fischer, who lived till 1864, was born in the house which formerly stood on the site of the present building known as No. 934, ten years after Beethoven's eyes opened to the light in the Bonngasse. At the time of Fischer's birth the Beethoven family occupied a portion of the house and Fischer's father and the composer's father were friends and companions. There, too, had lived the composer's grandfather. Gottfried Fischer had a sister, Cäcilia Fischer, who was born eight years before Beethoven; she remained unmarried and lived to be 85 years old, dying on May 23rd, 1845. The festivities attending the unveiling of the Beethoven monument in 1838 brought many visitors to Bonn and a natural curiosity concerning the relics of the composer. Inquirers were referred to the house in the Rheingasse, then supposed to be the birthplace of the composer, where the Fischers, brother and sister, still lived. They told their story and were urged by eager listeners to put it into writing. This Gottfried did the same year, but, keeping the manuscript in hand, he added to it at intervals down to the year 1857 at least. He came to attach great value to his revelations and as time went on embellished his recital with a mass of notes, many of no value, many consisting of iterations and reiterations of incidents already recorded, and also with excerpts from books to which, in his simplicity, he thought that nobody but himself had access. He was an uneducated man, ignorant even of the correct use of the German language; it is, therefore, not surprising that much of his record is utterly worthless; but mixed with the dross there is much precious metal, especially in the spinster's recollection of the composer's father and grandfather, for while Gottfried grew senile his sister remained mentally vigorous to the end. Thayer examined the document and offered to buy it, but was dissuaded by the seemingly exorbitant price which the old man set upon it. It was finally purchased for the city's archives by the Oberbürgermeister and thus came to the notice of Dr. Deiters. His use of it has been followed by the present editor.

HENRY EDWARD KREHBIEL.

Blue Hill, Maine, U. S. A.
    July, 1914.

Postscript

The breaking out, in August, 1914, of the war between Austria and Servia which eventually involved nearly all the civilized nations of the world, led the publishers, who had originally undertaken to print this Work as brought to a conclusion by the American Editor, indefinitely to postpone its publication.   In the spring of 1920 the Beethoven Association, composed of musicians of high rank, who had given a remarkably successful series of concerts of Beethoven's chamber-music in New York in the season 1919-20, at the suggestion of O. G. Sonneck and Harold Bauer resolved to devote the proceeds of the concerts to promoting the publication of Thayer's biography.   To this act of artistic philanthropy the appearance of the work is due.

Blue Hill, Maine, U. S. A.   H. E. K.
    September, 1920.

Contents of Volume I

Chapter I

Introductory—The Electors of Cologne in the Eighteenth Century—Joseph Clemens, Clemens August and Max Friedrich—The Electoral Courts and Their Music—Musical Culture in Bonn at the Time of Beethoven's Birth—Appearance of the City in 1770.

ONE of the compensations for the horrors of the French Revolution was the sweeping away of many of the petty sovereignties into which Germany was divided, thereby rendering in our day a union of the German People and the rise of a German Nation possible. The first to fall were the numerous ecclesiastical-civil members of the old, loose confederation, some of which had played no ignoble nor unimportant part in the advance of civilization; but their day was past. The people of these states had in divers respects enjoyed a better lot than those who were subjects of hereditary rulers, and the old German saying: "It is good to dwell under the crook," had a basis of fact. At the least, they were not sold as mercenary troops; their blood was not shed on foreign fields to support their princes' ostentatious splendor, to enable mistresses and ill-begotten children to live in luxury and riot. But the antiquated ideas to which the ecclesiastical rulers held with bigoted tenacity had become a barrier to progress, the exceptions being too few to render their farther existence desirable. These members of the empire, greatly differing in extent, population, wealth and political influence, were ruled with few or no exceptions by men who owed their positions to election by chapters or other church corporations, whose numbers were so limited as to give full play to every sort of intrigue; but they could not assume their functions until their titles were confirmed by the Pope as head of the church, and by the Emperor as head of the confederation. Thus the subject had no voice in the matter, and it hardly need be said that his welfare and prosperity were never included among the motives and considerations on which the elections turned.

[1]

The sees, by their charters and statutes, we think without exception, were bestowed upon men of noble birth. They were benefices and sinecures for younger sons of princely houses; estates set apart and consecrated to the use, emolument and enjoyment of German John Lacklands. In the long list of their incumbents, a name here and there appears, that calls up historic associations;—a man of letters who aided in the increase or diffusion of the cumbrous learning of his time; a warrior who exchanged his robes for a coat of mail; a politician who played a part more or less honorable or the reverse in the affairs and intrigues of the empire, and, very rarely, one whose daily walk and conversation reflected, in some measure, the life and principles of the founder of Christianity. In general, as they owed their places wholly to political and family influences, so they assumed the vows and garb of churchmen as necessary steps to the enjoyment of lives of affluence and pleasure. So late as far into the eighteenth century, travelling was slow, laborious and expensive. Hence, save for the few more wealthy and powerful, journeys, at long intervals, to a council, an imperial coronation or a diet of the empire, were the rare interruptions to the monotony of their daily existence. Not having the power to transmit their sees to their children, these ecclesiastics had the less inducement to rule with an eye to the welfare of their subjects: on the other hand, the temptation was very strong to augment their revenues for the benefit of relatives and dependents, and especially for the gratification of their own tastes and inclinations, among which the love of splendor and ostentatious display was a fruitful source of waste and extravagance.

Confined so largely to their own small capitals, with little intercourse except with their immediate neighbors, they were far more dependent upon their own resources for amusement than the hereditary princes: and what so obvious, so easily obtained and so satisfactory as music, the theatre and the dance! Thus every little court became a conservatory of these arts, and for generations most of the great names in them may be found recorded in the court calendars. One is therefore not surprised to learn how many of the more distinguished musical composers began life as singing boys in cathedral choirs of England and Germany. The secular princes, especially those of high rank, had, besides their civil administration, the stirring events of war, questions of public policy, schemes and intrigues for the advancement of family interests and the like, to engage their attention; but the ecclesiastic, leaving the civil administration, as a rule, in the hands of ministers, had little to occupy him officially but a tedious routine of religious forms and ceremonies; to him therefore the theatre, and music for the mass, the opera, the ball-room, and the salon, were matters of great moment—they filled a wide void and were cherished accordingly.

The three German ecclesiastical princes who possessed the greatest power and influence were the Archbishops of Mayence, Trèves and Cologne—Electors of the Empire and rulers of the fairest regions of the Rhine. Peace appears hardly to have been known between the city of Cologne and its earlier archbishops; and, in the thirteenth century, a long-continued and even bloody quarrel resulted in the victory of the city. It remained a free imperial town. The archbishops retained no civil or political power within its walls, not even the right to remain there more than three days at any one time. Thus it happened, that in the year 1257 Archbishop Engelbert selected Bonn for his residence, and formally made it the capital of the electorate, as it remained until elector and court were swept away in 1794.

Of the last four Electors of Cologne, the first was Joseph Clemens, a Bavarian prince, nephew of his predecessor Maximilian Heinrich. The choice of the chapter by a vote of thirteen to nine had been Cardinal Fürstenberg; but his known, or supposed, devotion to the interests of the French king had prevented the ratification of the election by either the Emperor or the Pope. A new one being ordered, resulted in favor of the Bavarian, then a youth of eighteen years. The Pope had ratified his election and appointed a bishop to perform his ecclesiastical functions *ad interim*, and the Emperor invested him with the electoral dignity December 1, 1689. Vehse says of him:

Like two of his predecessors he was the incumbent of five sees; he was Archbishop of Cologne, Bishop of Hildesheim, Liège, Ratisbon and Freisingen. His love for pomp and splendor was a passion which he gratified in the magnificence of his court. He delighted to draw thither beautiful and intellectual women. Madame de Raysbeck, and Countess Fugger, wife of his chief equerry, were his declared favorites. For seventeen years, that is, until the disastrous year 1706, when Fénelon consecrated him, he delayed assuming his vows. He held the opinion, universal in the courts of those days, that he might with a clear conscience enjoy life after the manner of secular princes. In pleasing the ladies, he was utterly regardless of expense, and for their amusement gave magnificent balls, splendid masquerades, musical and dramatic entertainments, and hunting parties.

St. Simon relates that several years of his exile were passed at Valenciennes, where, though a fugitive, he followed the same

round of costly pleasures and amusements. He also records one
of the Elector's jests which in effrontery surpasses anything related of his contemporary, Dean Swift. Some time after his consecration, he caused public notice to be given, that on the approaching first of April he would preach. At the appointed time he
mounted the pulpit, bowed gravely, made the sign of the cross,
shouted "Zum April!" (April fool!), and retired amid a flourish of
trumpets and the rolling of drums.

Dr. Ennen labors energetically to prove that Joseph Clemens's
fondness in later years for joining in all grand church ceremonies
rested upon higher motives than the mere pleasure of displaying
himself in his magnificent robes; and affirms that after assuming
his priestly vows he led a life devoted to the church and worthy
of his order; thenceforth never seeing Madame de Raysbeck,
mother of his illegitimate children, except in the presence of a
third person. It seems proper to say this much concerning a
prince whose electorship is the point of departure for notices of
music and musicians in Bonn during the eighteenth century; a
prince whose fondness for the art led him at home and in exile to
support both vocal and instrumental bands on a scale generous
for that age; and who, moreover, made some pretensions to the
title of composer himself, as we learn from a letter which under
date of July 20, 1720, he wrote to a court councillor Rauch to
accompany eleven of his motets. It is an amusingly frank letter,
beginning with a confession that he was an *Ignorant* who knew
nothing about notes and had absolutely no knowledge of *musique*,
wherefore he admits that his manner of composing is "very odd,"
being compelled to sing anything that came into his head to a
composer whose duty it was to bring the ideas to paper. Nevertheless he is quite satisfied with himself. "At all events I must
have a good ear and *gusto*, for the public that has heard has always
approved. But the *methodum* which I have adopted is that of
the bees that draw and collect the honey from the sweetest flowers;
so, also, I have taken all that I have composed from good masters
whose *Musikalien* pleased me. Thus I freely confess my pilfering,
which others deny and try to appropriate what they have taken
from others. Let no one, therefore, get angry if he hears old
arias in it, for, as they are beautiful, the old is not deprived of its
praise. . . . I ascribe everything to the grace of God who
enlightened me, the unknowing, to do these things." Not all
"composers," royal or mean, are as honest as the old Elector!

It is fortunate for the present purpose, that the portion of
the electoral archives discovered after a lapse of nearly seventy

years and now preserved at Düsseldorf, consists so largely of documents relating to the musical establishment of the court at Bonn during the last century of its existence. They rarely afford information upon the character of the music performed, but are sufficiently complete, when supplemented by the annual Court Calendars, to determine with reasonable correctness the number, character, position and condition of its members. The few petitions and decrees hereafter to be given in full because of their connection with the Beethovens, suffice for specimens of the long series of similar documents, uniform in character and generally of too little interest to be worth transcription.

In 1695 a decree issued at Liège by Joseph Clemens, then in that city as titular bishop, though not consecrated, adds three new names to the "Hoff-Musici," one of which, Van den Eeden, constantly reappears in the documents and calendars down to the year 1782. From a list of payments at Liège in the second quarter of 1696, we find that Henri Vandeneden (Heinrich Van den Eeden) was a bass singer, and that the aggregate of vocalists, instrumentists, with the organ-blower (*calcant*), was eighteen persons.

Returned to Bonn, Joseph Clemens resumed his plan of improving his music, and for those days of small orchestras and niggardly salaries he set it upon a rather generous foundation. A decree of April 1, 1698, put in force the next month, names 22 persons with salaries aggregating 8,890 florins.

After the death of Maximilian Heinrich the government passed into the hands of Cardinal Fürstenberg, his coadjutor, who owed the position to the intrigues of Louis XIV, and now used it by all possible means to promote French interests. The king's troops under French commanders, he admitted into the principal towns of the electorate, and, for his own protection, a French garrison of 10,000 men into Bonn. War was the consequence; an imperial army successfully invaded the province, and, advancing to the capital, subjected its unfortunate inhabitants to all the horrors of a relentless siege, that ended October 15, 1689, in the expulsion of the garrison, now reduced to some 3900 men, of whom 1500 were invalids. Yet in the war of the Spanish Succession which opened in 1701, notwithstanding the terrible lesson taught only eleven years before, the infatuated Joseph Clemens embraced the party of Louis. Emperor Leopold treated him with singular mildness, in vain. The Elector persisted. In 1702 he was therefore excluded from the civil government and fled from Bonn, the ecclesiastical authority in Cologne being empowered by the Emperor to rule in his stead. The next year, the great success of the French armies against the allies was celebrated by Joseph Clemens with all pomp in Namur, where he then was; but his triumph was short.   John Churchill, then Earl of Marlborough, took the field as commander-in-chief of the armies of the allies.   His foresight, energy and astonishing skill in action justified Addison's simile—whether sublime or only pompous—of the angel riding in the whirlwind and directing the storm.   He was soon at Cologne, whence he despatched Cochorn to besiege Bonn.   That great general executed his task with such skill and impetuosity, that on May 15 (1703) all was ready for storming the city, when d'Allègre, the French commander, offered to capitulate, and on the 19th was allowed to retire.   "Now was Bonn for the third time wrested from the hands of the French and restored to the archbishopric, but alas, in a condition that aroused indignation, grief and compassion on all sides," says Müller.

Leopold was still kindly disposed toward Joseph Clemens, but he died May 5, 1705, and his successor, Joseph I, immediately declared him under the ban of the Empire.   This deprived him of the means and opportunities, as Elector, for indulging his passion for pomp and display, while his neglect hitherto, under dispensations from the Pope, to take the vows necessary to the performance of ecclesiastical functions, was likewise fatal to that indulgence as archbishop.   But this could be remedied; Fénelon, the famous Archbishop of Cambray, ordained him subdeacon August 15, 1706; the Bishop of Tournay made him deacon December 8, and priest on the 25th; on January 1, 1707, he read his first mass at Lille, and indulged his passion for parade to the full, as a pamphlet describing the incident, and silver and copper medals commemorating it, still evince.   "Two years later, May 1, 1709, Joseph Clemens received from Fénelon in Ryssel (Lille) episcopal consecration and the pallium."—(Müller.)   Upon the victory of Oudenarde by Marlborough, and the fall of Lille, he took refuge in Mons.   The treaty of Rastadt, March, 1714, restored him to his electoral dignities and he returned to the Rhine; but Dutch troops continued to hold Bonn until December 11, 1715.   On the morning of that day they evacuated the city and in the afternoon the Elector entered in a grand, solemn procession commemorated by an issue of silver medals.

During all these vicissitudes Joseph Clemens, from whatever source he derived the means, did not suffer his music to deteriorate and, returned to Bonn, no sooner was the public business regulated and restored to its former routine than he again turned his attention to its improvement.

Joseph Clemens died November 12, 1723, having previously secured the succession to his nephew Clemens August, last of the five Electors of Cologne of the Bavarian line. The new incumbent, third son of Maximilian Emanuel, Elector of Bavaria and his second wife, a daughter of the celebrated John Sobieski of Poland, was born August 17, 1700, at Brussels, where his father resided at the time as Governor General. From his fourth to his fifteenth year he had been held in captivity by the Austrians at Klagenfurt and Gratz; then, having been destined for the church, he spent several years at study in Rome. As a child in 1715 he had been appointed coadjutor to the Bishop of Regensburg; in 1719 he was elected to the two sees of Paderborn and Münster made vacant by the death of his brother Moritz, was chosen coadjutor to his uncle of Cologne in 1722, made his solemn entry into Bonn as elector May 15, 1724, was the same year also elected Bishop of Hildesheim, in 1725 Provost of the Cathedral at Liège, 1728 Bishop of Osnabrück, and, finally, in 1732 reached the dignity of Grand Master of the Teutonic Order.

His rule is distinguished in the annals of the electorate for little else than the building, repairing, renewing and embellishing of palaces, hunting-seats, churches, convents, and other edifices. At Bonn he erected the huge pile the foundation of which had been laid by his uncle, now the seat of the university. The handsome City Hall was also his work; the villa at Poppelsdorf was enlarged by him into a small palace, Clemensruhe, now the University Museum of Natural History. In Brühl, the Augustusburg, now a Prussian royal palace, dates from his reign, and Münster, Mergentheim, Arnsberg and other places show similar monuments of his prodigality in the indulgence of his taste for splendor. "Monstrous were the sums," says Dr. Ennen, "squandered by him in the purchase of splendid ornaments, magnificent equipages, furniture costly for its variety, and of curious works of art; upon festivities, sleighing-parties, masquerades, operas, dramas and ballets; upon charlatans, swindlers, female vocalists, actors and dancers. His theatre and opera alone cost him 50,000 thalers annually and the magnificence of his masked balls, twice a week in winter, is proof sufficient that no small sums were lavished upon them."

The aggregate of the revenues derived from the several states of which Clemens August was the head nowhere appears; but the civil income of the electorate alone had, in his later years, risen from the million of florins of his predecessor to about the same number of thalers—an increase of some 40 per centum;

added to this were large sums derived from the church, and subsidies from Austria, France and the sea-coast states amounting
to at least 14,000,000 francs; indeed, during the Elector's last
ten years the French subsidies alone made an aggregate of at
least 7,300,000 francs; in 1728 Holland paid on account of the
Clemens Canal 76,000 thalers.   At the centennial opening of
the strong-box of the Teutonic Order he obtained the fat accumulations of a hundred years; and 25 years later he opened it again.
Yet, though during his rule peace was hardly interrupted in his
part of Europe, he plunged ever deeper and more inextricably
into debt, leaving one of large proportions as his legacy to his successor.   He was a bad ruler, but a kindly, amiable and popular
man.   How should he know or feel the value of money or the
necessity of prudence?   His childhood had been spent in captivity, his student years in Rome, where, precisely at that period,
poetry and music were cultivated, if not in very noble and manly
forms, at least with a Medicean splendor.   The society of the
Arcadians was in full activity.   True, both Clemens August and
his brother were under the age which enabled them to be enrolled
as "Shepherds," and consequently their names appear neither in
Crescembini nor in Quadrio; but it is not to be supposed that two
young princes, already bishops by election and certain of still higher
dignities in the future, were excluded from the palaces of Ruspoli
and Ottoboni, from those brilliant literary, artistic and luxurious
circles in which, only half a dozen years before, their young
countryman, the musician Handel, had found so cordial a welcome.   Those were very expensive tastes, as the citation from
Ennen shows, which the future elector brought with him from
Rome.   Italian palaces, Italian villas, churches, gardens, music,
songstresses, mistresses, an Italian holy staircase on the Kreuzberg
(leading to nothing); Italian pictures, mosaics and, what not?
All these things cost money—but must he not have them?

This elector is perhaps the only archbishop on record to
whose epitaph may truthfully be added: "He danced out of this
world into some other";—which happened in this wise: Having,
in the winter of 1760-61, by some unexpected stroke of good fortune, succeeded in obtaining from the usually prudent and careful
bankers of Holland a loan of 80,000 thalers, he embraced the
opportunity of making a long-desired visit to his family in Munich.
Owing to a sudden attack of illness he was once on the point of
turning back soon after leaving Bonn.   He persevered, however,
reached Coblenz and crossed over to the palace of the Elector
of Trèves at Ehrenbreitstein, where he arrived at 4 P.M.

February 5, 1761. At dinner an hour later he was unable to eat; but at the ball, which followed, he could not resist the fascination of the Baroness von Waldendorf—sister of His Transparency of Trèves—and danced with her "eight or nine turns." Of course he could not refuse a similar compliment to several other ladies. The physical exertion of dancing, joined to the excitement of the occasion and following a dreary winter-day's journey, was too much for the enfeebled constitution of a man of sixty years. He fainted in the ballroom, was carried to his chamber and died next day.

It seems to have been the etiquette, that when an elector breathed his last, the musical chapel expired with him. At all events, no other explanation appears of the fact that so many of the petitions for membership, which are still preserved, should be signed by men who had already been named in the Court Calendars. It is also to be remarked that some of the petitioners receive appointments "without salary." These seem to have been appointments of the kind, which in later years were distinguished in the records and in the calendars by the term "accessist," and which, according to the best lights afforded by the archives, may be considered as having been provisional, until the incumbent had proved his skill and capacity, or until a vacancy occurred through the death or resignation of some old member. There are indications that the "accessists," though without fixed salary, received some small remuneration for their services; but this is by no means certain. It would seem that both vocalists and instrumentists who received salaries out of the state revenues were limited to a fixed number; that the amount of funds devoted to this object was also strictly limited and the costs incurred by the engagement of superior artists with extra salaries, or by an increase of the number, were defrayed from the Elector's privy purse; that the position of "accessist" was sought by young musicians as a stepping-stone to some future vacancy which, when acquired, insured a gradually increasing income during the years of service and a small pension when superannuated; that the etiquette of the court demanded, even in cases when the Elector expressly called some distinguished artist to Bonn, that the appointment should be apparently only in gracious answer to an humble petition, and that, with few exceptions, both singers and members of the orchestra were employed in the church, the theatre and the concert-room.

Clemens August made his formal entry into Bonn, May 15, 1724. A number of petitions are passed over, but one granted "without salary" on February 18, 1727, from Van den Eeden must be given in its entirety:

Supplique tres humble a S. A. S. E. de Cologne
        pour Gille Vandeneet.

BONN, d. 18 Feb., 1727.

Prince Serenissime,
    Monsigneur.
    Vandeneet vient avec tout le respect qui luy est possible se mettre aux pieds de V. A. S. E. luy representer qu'ayant eu l'honneur d'avoir estre second organiste de feu S. A. S. E. d'heureuse memoire, elle daigne luy vouloir faire la même grace ne demendant aucun gage si long tems qu'il plaira a V. A. S. E. promettant la servire avec soin et diligence.
            Quoi faisant etc. etc.

On the same date Van den Eeden received his appointment as second court organist. June 8, 1728, a decree is issued granting him a salary of 100 florins. To a third petition the next year, signed Van den Enden, the answer is an increase of his salary to 200 thalers, and thus a future instructor of Ludwig van Beethoven becomes established in Bonn. The records need not concern us now until we reach the following, which forms part of the history of the grandfather of the subject of this biography:

March, 1733,

DECRETUM

For Ludovicum van Beethoven as Electoral Court Musician.

Cl. A. Whereas His Serene Highness Elector of Cologne, Duke Clemens August in Upper and Lower Bavaria, etc. Our Gracious Lord having, on the humble petition of Ludovico van Beethoven, graciously declared and received him as Court Musician, and assigned him an annual salary of 400 florins Rhenisb, the present decree under the gracious hand of His Serene Electoral Highness and the seal of the Privy Chancellor, is granted to him, and the Electoral Councillor and Paymaster Risack is herewith commanded to pay the said Beethoven the 400 fl. *quartaliter* from the beginning of this year and to make a proper accounting thereof. B. . . . . March, 1733.

Thirteen years later we find this:

Allowance of an additional 100 Thalers annually to the
Chamber Musician van Beethoven.

Inasmuch as His Serene Highness Elector of Cologne, Duke Clement August of Upper and Lower Bavaria, our most Gracious Lord has increased the salary of his Chamber Musician van Beethoven by the addition of 100 thalers annually which became due through the death of Joseph Kayser, instrument maker, the Court Chamber Councillor and Paymaster Risach is hereby informed and graciously commanded to pay to him the said Beethoven the 100 fl. a year in quarterly installments against voucher from the proper time and to make the proper accounting. Witness, etc.   Poppelsdorf, August 22, 1746.

On May 2, 1747, Johann Ries became Court Trumpeter with a salary of 192 thalers.   This is the first representative we have met of a name which afterwards rose to great distinction, not only in the orchestra of the Elector but also in the world at large.   On March 5, 1754, he was formally appointed Court Musician (violinist) having set forth in his petition that instead of confining himself to the trumpet he had made himself serviceable in the chapel by singing and playing other instruments. Later he took ill and was sent to Cologne.   We shall presently meet his two daughters and his son Franz Ries, the last of whom will figure prominently in the life-history of Beethoven.   Under date March 27, 1756, occur several papers which have a double interest.   They relate to the Beethoven family and are so complete as to exhibit the entire process of appointment to membership in the electoral chapel.   The original documents are not calculated to give the reader a very exalted idea of the orthographical knowledge of the petitioner or the Chamber Music Director Gottwaldt; but that fault gives us the clue to the correct pronunciation of the name Beethoven—the English "Beetgarden."

To His Electoral Serenity of Cologne, etc.   My most Gracious Lord
the humble petition and prayer of
Joan van Biethoffen.

Most Reverend, most Serene Elector,
Most Gracious Lord, Lord, etc.

May it please your Electoral Serenity graciously to hear the humble representations how in the absence of voices in Your Highness's Court Chapel my insignificant self took part in the music for at least four years without the good fortune of having allotted by Your Serene Electoral Highness a small *salario.*

I therefore pray Your Serene Electoral Highness most humbly that it graciously please you (in consideration of my father's faithful service for 23 years) to rejoice me with a decree as court musician, which high grace will infuse me with zeal to serve Your Serene Highness with the greatest fidelity and zealousness.

Your
Serene Electoral Highness's
Most humble-obedient-faithful servant,
Joan van Biethoffen.

To the Music Director Gottwaldt for a report of his humble
      judgment.   Attestation by the most gracious
      sign manual and seal of the privy chancellary.
Bonn, March 19, 1756.

(Signed) Clemens August (L.S.)

Most reverend, most serene Elector,
      Most gracious Lord, Lord, etc.
Your Serene Electoral Highness has referred to my humble judgment the petition of Joan van Piethoffen, the supplicant prays Your
Electoral Highness for a gracious decree as accessist in the court music,
he has indeed served for two years with his voice on the Duc Sall
(doxal), hopes in time to deserve the good will of Your Serene Highness
by his industry, and his father who enjoys the grace of serving Your
Highness as bass singer prays his appointment, I pray most humbly and
obediently for instruction concerning your Highness's good will in the
matter, submit myself humbly and obediently to Your Serene Highness's
grace and remain in greatest humility.

Your Serene and Electoral Highness's
Most Humble and obedient servant
Gottwaldt, Director of the
Chamber Music.

A further report was made to the Elector as follows:

BONN, March 27, 1756.

Coloniensis gratiosa.
Chamber Music Director Gottwaldt *ad supplicam* of Joan van
Betthoffen has served two years on the docsal and hopes through his
industry to serve further to the satisfaction of Your Electoral Highness,
to which end his father who through Your Highness's grace serves as
bass singer will seek completely to qualify him which may it please Your
Serene Highness to allow.

Idem Gottwaldt *ad supplicam* Ernest Haveckas, accessist in the
court music, reports that suppliant, though not fully capable as yet
hopes by special diligence to make himself worthy of Your Highness's
service and would be encouraged and rejoiced in his efforts if Your Serene
Highness would graciously deign to grant him a *decreto*, humbly praying
to be informed as to Your Highness's wishes in the matter.

DECRETUM

Court Musician's Decree for Johan van Biethofen.

Clm. A.   Whereas His Serene Electoral Highness of Cologne,
Duke Clement August in Upper and Lower Bavaria etc.   Our Gracious
Lord on the humble petition of Johan van Biethofen and in consideration of his skill in the art of singing, also the experience in the same
already gained, having graciously declared and accepted him as court
musician, appoint and accept him by this writing; therefore the said

Biethofen receives this decree with the gracious sign manual and seal of the Privy Chancellary, and those who are concerned to recognize him hereafter as an Electoral court musician and to pay him such respect as the position deserves. Bonn, March 25, 1756.

Johann van Beethoven was 16 years old at this time. Why he should appear in the Court Calendar as an *accessist* four years after the publication of this decree appointing him Court Musician does not appear.

But slender success has rewarded the search for means of determining the character and quality of that opera and music, upon which, according to Ennen, Clemens August lavished such large sums. The period embraced in that elector's rule (1724–1761) was precisely that in which the *old* Italian opera, the oratorio and the sacred cantata reached their extreme limits of development through the genius of Handel and J. S. Bach. It closes at the moment when Gluck, C. P. E. Bach and Joseph Haydn were laying the immovable foundations of a new operatic, orchestral and pianoforte music, and before the perfected sonata-form, that found universal adoption in all compositions of the better class, not vocal. Little music comparatively was issued from the press in those days, and consequently new forms and new styles made their way slowly into vogue. Another consequence was that the offices of composer for the chamber, the church, the comedy, or however they were named, were by no means sinecures—neither at the imperial court of Maria Theresia, nor at the court of any petty prince or noble whose servants formed his orchestra. Composers had to furnish music on demand and as often as was necessary, as the hunter delivered game or the fisherman fish. What a volume of music was produced in this manner can be seen in the case of Joseph Haydn at Esterhaz, whose fruitfulness did not, in all probability, exceed that of many another of his contemporaries. The older Telemann furnished compositions to the courts of Bayreuth and Eisenach as well as the Gray Friars at Frankfort-on-the-Main, and also performed his duties as musical director and composer at Hamburg. He wrote music with such ease that, as Handel said, he could write for eight voices as rapidly as an ordinary man could write a letter. Under such conditions did the men write who are mentioned as official composers in our narrative. It is probable that not a note of theirs remains in existence, and equally probable that the loss is not at all deplorable except as it leaves the curiosity of an antiquary unsatisfied. A few text-books to vocal pieces performed on various occasions during this reign have been preserved, their titles being

"Componimento per Musica," music by Giuseppe dall'Ábaco, Director of the Chamber Music (1740); "La Morte d'Abel" (no date is given, but "il Signor Biethoven" sang the part of *Adamo*); "Esther" ("From the Italian of S. F. A. Aubert," the text partly in German, partly in Italian); "Anagilda" (*Drama per Musica*).

After the unlucky ball at Ehrenbreitstein the crook and sceptre of Cologne passed from the Bavarian family which had so long held them into the hands of Maximilian Friedrich of the Suabian line Königsegg- (or Königseck-) Rothenfels. For a century or more this house had enjoyed fat livings in the church at Cologne, in which city the new elector was born on May 13, 1708. He was the fourth of his race who had held the important office of Dean of the Cathedral, from which post he was elevated to the electorship on April 6, 1761, and to the ecclesiastical principality of Münster the next year; with which two sees he was fain to be content. He was by nature an easy, good-tempered, indolent, friendly man, of no great force of character—qualities which in the incumbent of a rich sinecure just completing his fifty-third year, would be too fully confirmed and developed by habit to change with any change of circumstances; and which, says Stramberg, made him unusually popular throughout the land despite the familiar little verse:

> Bei Clemens August trug man blau und weiss,
> Da lebte man wie im Paradeis;
> Bei Max Friedrich trug man sich schwarz und roth,
> Da litt man Hunger wie die schwere Noth.

The condition of the finances had become such through the extravagant expenditures of Clemens August that very energetic measures were necessary, and to the effects of these, during the first few years of Max Friedrich's rule, in throwing many persons out of employment, these doggerel lines doubtless owe their origin. It was fortunate for the Elector's subjects that his indolence was made good by the activity and energy of a prime minister who found his beau ideal of a statesman in Frederick II of Prussia, whom, in his domestic policy, he imitated as far as the character of the two governments allowed. This was equally if not more true in the principality of Münster. To the respect which one must feel for the memory of Belderbusch, the all-powerful minister at Bonn, is added, in the case of Fürstenberg, the equally powerful minister at Münster, admiration and regard for the man. The former was respected, feared, but not loved in the electorate; the latter was respected and very popular in the principality.

To Kasper Anton von Belderbusch the new Elector owed his elevation; to his care he entrusted the state; to his skill and strength of character he was indebted for release from the pecuniary difficulties which beset him and for the satisfaction, as the years rolled by, of seeing his states numbered among the most prosperous and flourishing in Germany. Belderbusch's first care was to reduce the expenditure. "He put a stop to building," says Ennen, "dismissed a number of the actors, restricted the number of concerts and court balls, dispensed with the costly hunts, reduced the salaries of court officials, officers and domestics, lessened the *état* for the kitchen, cellar and table of the prince, turned the property left by Clemens August into money and comforted the latter's creditors with the hope of better times." But though economy was the rule, still, where the Elector considered it due to his position, he could be lavish. Whatever opinions may be entertained as to the wisdom and expediency of clothing ecclesiastics with civil power, it would be unjust not to give the bright as well as the dark side of the picture. This is well put by Kaspar Risbeck in relation to the Rhenish states whose princes were churchmen, and his remarks are in place here, since they relate in part to that in which the childhood and youth of Beethoven were spent.

The whole stretch of the country from here to Mayence is one of the richest and most populous in Germany. Within this territory of 18 German miles there are 20 cities lying hard by the shore of the Rhine and dating, for the greater part, from the period of the Romans. It is still plainly to be seen that this portion of Germany was the first to be built up. Neither morasses nor heaths interrupt the evidences of cultivation which stretch with equal industry far from the shores of the river over the contiguous country. While many cities and castles built under Charlemagne and his successors, especially Henry I, in other parts of Germany have fallen into decay, all in this section have not only been preserved but many have been added to them. . . . . . The natural wealth of the soil in comparison with that of other lands, and the easy disposition of its products by means of the Rhine, have no doubt contributed most to these results. Nevertheless, great as is the prejudice in Germany against the ecclesiastical governments, they have beyond doubt aided in the blooming development of these regions. In the three ecclesiastical electorates which make up the greater part of this tract of land nothing is known of those tax burdens under which the subjects of so many secular princes of Germany groan. These princes have exceeded the old assessments but slightly. Little is known in their countries of serfdom. The appanage of many princes and princesses do not force them to extortion. They have no inordinate military institution, and do not sell the sons of their farmers; and they have never taken so active a part in the domestic and foreign wars of Germany as

the secular princes. Though they are not adept in encouraging their
subjects in art culture, varied agriculture has been developed to a high
degree of perfection throughout the region. Nature does of its own
accord what laws and regulations seek to compel, as soon as the rocks
of offence are removed from the path.[1]

Henry Swinburne, whose letters to his brother were published
long after his death under the title of "The Courts of Europe,"
writes under date of November 29, 1780:

Bonn is a pretty town, neatly built, and its streets tolerably well
paved, all in black lava. It is situated in a flat near the river. The
Elector of Cologne's palace faces the South entry. It has no beauty
of architecture and is all plain white without any pretensions.
  We went to court and were invited to dine with the Elector (Königsegge). He is 73 years old, a little, hale, black man, very merry and
affable. His table is none of the best; no dessert wines handed about,
nor any foreign wines at all. He is easy and agreeable, having lived
all his life in ladies' company, which he is said to have liked better than
his breviary. The captains of his guard and a few other people of the
court form the company, amongst whom were his two great-nieces,
Madame de Hatzfeld and Madame de Taxis. The palace is of immense
size, the ball-room particularly large and low. . . . The Elector goes
about to all the assemblies and plays at Tric-trac. He asked me to be
of his party but I was not acquainted with their way of playing. There
is every evening an assembly or play at court. The Elector seems very
strong and healthy, and will, I think, hold the Archduke a good tug yet.

This Archduke was Max Franz, youngest son of Maria
Theresia, whose acquaintance Swinburne had made in Vienna,
and who had just been chosen coadjutor to Max Friedrich. A
curious proof of the liberality, not to say laxity, of the Elector's
sentiments in one direction is given by Stramberg in his "Rheinischer Antiquarius," to wit, the possession of a mistress in common
by him and his minister Belderbusch—the latter fathering the
children—and this mistress was the Countess Caroline von
Satzenhofen, Abbess of Vilich!
  The reduction which was made by Belderbusch upon the
accession of Max Friedrich in the expenses of the theatre and
other amusements does not appear, except in the case of the chapelmaster, to have extended to the court music proper, nor to have
been long continued in respect to the "operetta and comedy."
The first in order of the documents and notices discovered relating to the musical establishment of this Elector are of no common
interest, being the petition of a candidate for the vacant office of

chapelmaster and the decree appointing him to that position. They are as follows:

Very Reverend Archbishop and Elector
most gracious Lord Lord!

May it please Your Electoral Grace to permit a representation of my faithfully and dutifully performed services for a considerable space as vocalist as well as, since the death of the chapelmaster, for more than a year his duties *in Dupplo,* that is to say by singing and wielding the baton concerning which my demand still remains *ad referendum* much less have I been assured of the position. Inasmuch as because of particular *recommendation* Dousmoulin was preferred over me, and indeed unjustly, I have been forced hitherto to submit to fate.

But now, gracious Elector and Lord, that because of the reduction in salaries Chapelmaster Dousmoulin has already asked his demission or will soon do so, and I at the command of Baron Belderbusch am to begin *de novo* to fill his office, and the same must surely be replaced,—Therefore

There reaches Your Electoral Grace my humble petition that you may graciously be pleased (: inasmuch as the "Toxal" must be sufficiently supplied with *musique,* and I must at all events take the lead in the occurring church ceremonies *in puncto* the chorales:) to grant me the justice of which I was deprived on the death of Your Highness's *antecessori* of blessed memory, and appoint me chapelmaster with some augmentation of my lessened salary because of my services performed in *Duplo.* For which highest grace I shall pour out my prayers to God for the long continuing health and government of your Electoral Grace, while in deepest submission I throw myself at your feet.

> Your
> Electoral Grace's
> most humble servant
> Ludwig van Beethoven
> "Passist."

M. F. Whereas We, Maximilian Friedrich, Elector of Cologne, on the demission of our former chapelmaster Touche Moulin, and the humble petition of our bass singer Ludwig van Beethoven have appointed the latter to be chapelmaster with the retention of his position as bass singer, and have added 97 rthlr. *species* 40 alb. to his former salary of 292 rthlr. *species* 40 alb. per annum divided in *quartalien,* which appointment is hereby made and payment ordered by our grace, our exchequer and all whom it may concern are called on to observe the fact and do what is required under the circumstances.

Attest, etc. Bonn, July 16, 1761.

Next in order, at an interval of rather more than a year, is the following short paper in reply to a petition, not preserved, of the new chapelmaster's son:

Supplicanten is hereby graciously assured that in the event of a *vacatur* of a court musician's salary he shall have special consideration.

Attest our gracious sign manual and the impress of the seal of the Privy Chancellary.

Bonn, November 27, 1762.   Max Fried. Elector.
                                              v. Belderbusch, (:L. S.:)

About December, 1763, a singer, Madame Lentner, after some four and a half years of service, threw up her appointment, giving occasion, through the vacancy thus caused, for the following petition, report and decrees:

Most Reverend Elector, Most Gracious
            Lord, Lord.
Will Your Electoral Grace deign to receive the representation that by the acceptance of service elsewhere of Court Musician Dauber there ,has fallen to the disposition of Your Reverend Electoral Grace a salary of 1,050 rth., wherefore I, Joannes van Beethoven, having graciously been permitted for a considerable time to serve as court musician and have been graciously assured by decree of appointment to the first vacancy, and have always faithfully and diligently performed my duties and graciously been permitted to be in good voice, therefore my prayer is made to Your Reverend and Electoral Grace for a grant of the aforesaid 1,050 rth. or a gracious portion thereof, which act of highest grace I shall try to merit by fidelity and zeal in the performance of my duties.

                                    Your
                          Reverend Electoral Grace's
                             most obedient servant
                             Joannes van Beethoven,
                                  vocalist.

This petition was seconded by the father in the following manner:

Most Reverend Archbishop and Elector,
        Most gracious Lord, Lord.
Your Electoral Grace having graciously been pleased to submit for my humble report the humble petition of Your Highness's court musician Joann Ries that his daughter be appointed to the place in the court music of Your Highness made vacant by the discharged soprano Lentner *sub Litt. A.*

Humbly obeying Your gracious command I submit an impartial report that for about a year the daughter of the court musician Ries has frequented the "Duc sahl" (doxal) and sung the soprano part and that to my satisfaction.

But now that my son Joannes van Beethoven has already for 13 years sung soprano, contralto and tenor in every emergency that has arisen on the "Duc sahl," is also capable on the violin, wherefore Your Reverend Electoral Grace *27 Novembris 1762* granted the accompanying decree graciously bearing your own high sign manual *sub Litt. B.*

My humble and obedient but not anticipatory opinion is that the court singer Lentner's vacated salary *ad* 300 fl. (: who went away without the gracious permission of Your Highness over a quarter of a year ago and reported to me *in specie* she was going without permission and would not return :) be graciously divided so that my son be decreed to receive 200 florins and the daughter of Court Musician Ries 100 fl.

Zu Ewr. Churfürst. gnaden beständige hulden und gnaden mich unter-thänigst erlassendt in tieffester submission ersterbe.

Your Reverend Electoral Grace's
most humble and obedient
Ludwig van Beethoven,
Chapel Master.

Increase of salary of 100 rthr. for Court Musician Beethoven.

M. F.

Whereas We, Maximilian Friedrich. Elector of Cologne, on the humble petition of our court musician Johann van Beethoven, have shown him the grace to allow him 100 rthr. out of the salary vacated by the departure of the singer Lentner to be paid annually in *quartalien* we hereby confirm the allowance; for which this decree is graciously promulgated to be observed by our Electoral exchequer which is to govern itself accordingly.

Attest p. Bonn, April 24, 1764.

Under the same date a decree was issued appointing Anna Maria Ries, daughter of Johann Ries, Court Singer, with a salary of 100 th. also out of that of the Lentner. A few days later the following action was taken:

M. F. E.

To the Electoral Exchequer touching the appointment of Court Musician Beethoven and the Singer Ries.

You are hereby graciously informed that our court musician Beethoven junior and the singer Ries will soon lay before you two decrees of appointment. Now inasmuch as with this the salary of the former singer Lentner is disposed of but since she received an advance of 37½ rth. from our Master of Revenues and 18 rth. *spec.* was paid to her creditors we graciously command you herewith so to arrange the payment of the two salaries that the advance from the Revenues and then the payment to the creditors be covered from the Lentner's salary; and that until this is done the salaries of the beforementioned Ries and Bethoven do not begin.

We etc. Bonn, April 27, 1764.

On April 3, 1778, Anna Maria Ries received an additional 100 fl. A few more documents lead us to the family of Johann Peter Salomon:

ad Supplicam Philip Salomon.

To inform our chapelmaster van Betthoven appointed on his humble petition that we are not minded to grant the letter prayed for to the Prince v. Sulkowsky, but in case his son is not returned by the beginning of the coming month 8bris, we are graciously determined to make disposition of his place and salary.

Attest. Münster, August 8, 1764.
Sent, the 22 *dito.*

In spite of this order on July 1, 1765, the Elector gave a document to the son, Johann Peter Salomon, certifying that he had served him faithfully and diligently and had "so conducted himself as to deserve to be recommended to every one according to his station."[1] On petition of Philipp Salomon, the father, he , and his daughter were appointed Court Musicians by decree dated August 11, 1764.

Several papers, dated April 26, 1768, although upon matters of very small importance, have a certain interest as being in part official communications from the pen of Chapelmaster van Beethoven, and illustrating in some measure his position and duties. They show, too, that his path was not always one bordered with roses. Being self-explanatory they require no comment:

I.

Most Reverend Archbishop and Elector,
Most Gracious Lord, Lord.

Will Your Electoral Grace deign to listen to the complaint that when Court Singer Schwachhofer was commanded in obedience to an order of His Excellency Baron von Belderbusch to alternate with Jacobina Salomon in the singing of the solos in the church music as is the custom, the said Schwachhofer in the presence of the entire chapel impertinently and literally answered me as follows: I will not accept your *ordre* and you have no right to command me.

Your Electoral Grace will doubtless recall various *disordre* on the part of the court chapel indicating that all respect and *ordonance* is withheld from me, each member behaving as he sees fit, which is very painful to my sensibilities.

Wherefore my humble prayer reaches Your Electoral Highness that the public affront of the Schwachhofer be punished to my deserved *satisfaction* and that a decree issue from Your Highness to the entire

---

[1]This was the beginning of the career of Salomon. He became concertmaster to Prince Henry of Prussia, played in Paris, and in 1781 took up a residence in London where, as violinist and conductor, he became brilliantly active and successful. He made repeated visits to Bonn, once in 1790, when he was on his way to London accompanied by Haydn.

chapel that at the cost of Your Gracious displeasure or punishment according to the offence my *ordre* shall not be evaded.

Your Electoral Grace's
Humble and Most Obedient Servant
Ludovicus van Beethoven.

II.

To Chapelmaster van Beethoven
Concerning the Court Musicians.

M. F. E.

Receive the accompanying Command to the end that its contents be conveyed to all of our court musicians or be posted on the "toxal." We remain, etc.

Bonn, April 26, 1768.

III.

Command respecting the Court Musicians.

Having learned with displeasure that several of our court musicians have tried to evade the *ordre* issued by our Chapel Master or refused to receive them from him, and conduct themselves improperly amongst themselves, all of our court musicians are hereby earnestly commanded without contradiction to obey all the commands given by our Chapel Master in our name, and bear peaceful relations with each other, since we are determined to proceed with rigor against the guilty to the extent of dismissal in certain cases.

Sig. Bonn, April 26, 1768.

On November 17, 1769, Johann van Beethoven submits a petition in which he exhibits anew his genius for devising methods for varying the spelling of his own name. That he could no longer live on 100 th. salary is evident when it is remembered that he has now been married two years; but as there were several applicants for the salary which had fallen to the disposal of the Elector, it was divided among the four most needy. Beethoven's memorial contains a fact or two in regard to his duties as Court Musician which are new:

To
His Electoral Grace
of Cologne, etc., etc.

The Humble Supplication
and Prayer

of
Johann Bethof, Court Musician.

Most Reverend Archbishop and Elector,
Most Gracious Lord, Lord.

May Your Most Reverend Electoral Grace, graciously permit the presentation of this humble *supplicando*, how for many years I have served Your Highness faithfully and industriously on the "Duc saahl" and the theatre, and also have given instruction in various *supjecta* concerning the aforesaid service to the entire satisfaction of Your Electoral Grace, and am engaged now in study to perfect myself to this end.

My father also joins in this *supplic* in his humble capacity of the *theatri* and will participate in the gladness should Your Electoral Grace graciously grant the favor; as it is impossible for me to live on the salary of 100 th. graciously allowed me, I pray Your Electoral Grace to bestow upon me the 100 th. left at Your gracious disposal by the death of Your court musician Philip Haveck; to merit this high grace by faithful and diligent service shall be my greatest striving.

Your Electoral Grace's
most humble
Joannes Bethof,
Court Musician.

In answer to this there came the following decree:

Whereas we, Max. Frid. p. on the death of Court Musician Philipp Haveck and the submissive petition of our court musician Philipp Salomon bestowed upon him the grace of adding 50 fl. for his two daughters to the salary which he already enjoys out of the salary of the above mentioned Haveck per year; we confirm the act hereby; wherefore we have graciously issued, this decree, which our Electoral Court Exchequer will humbly observe and make all necessary provisions.

Attest. p. Münster, 17th 9bris 1769.

(On the margin:) "Gracious addition of 50 fl. for the court musician Philipp Salomon" and, besides Brandt and Meuris, also *"in simili* for Court Musician Joann Bethoff 25 fl."

There need be no apology for filling a few more pages with extracts from documents found in the Düsseldorf archives; for now a period has been reached in which the child Ludwig van Beethoven is growing up into youth and early manhood, and thrown into constant contact with those whose names will appear. Some of these names will come up many years later in Vienna; others will have their parts to play in the narrative of that child's life. Omitting, for the present, a petition of Johann van Beethoven, we begin them with that of Joseph Demmer, of date January 23, 1773, which first secured him his appointment after a year's service and three months' instruction from "the young Mr. van Beethoven."

Most Reverend Archbishop and Elector,
Most Gracious Lord, etc., etc.

I have been accepted as chorister in the cathedral of this city at a salary of 80 th. per year, and have so practised myself in music that

I humbly flatter myself of my ability to perform my task with the highest satisfaction.

It being graciously known that the bass singer van Beethoven is incapacitated and can no longer serve as such, and the contra-bassist Noisten can not adapt his voice: therefore this my submissive to Your Reverend Electoral Grace that you graciously be pleased to accept me as your bass singer with such gracious salary as may seem fit; I offer should it be demanded to attend the operettas also and qualify myself in a short time. It depends upon a mere hint from Your Electoral Grace alone; that it shall not be burdensome to the cantor's office of the cathedral to save the loss of the 80 th. yearly which it has bestowed upon me.

I am in most dutiful reverence
Your Electoral Grace's
most obedient
Joseph Demmer.

Pro Memoria.

Cantor Demmer earned at the utmost 106 rth. per year if he neglected none of the greater or little *Horis*.

Pays the Chamber Chancellor Kügelgen
for board, annually, 66 rth.
for *quartier* (lodging) 12 rth.

moreover, he must find himself in clothes and washing since his father, the sub-sacristan in Cologne, is still overburdened with 6 children.

He has paid 6 rth. to young Mr. Beethoven for 3 months.

In response to another petition after the death of L. van Beethoven the following decree was issued:

Decree as Court vocal bass for Joseph Demmer.

Whereas His Electoral Grace of Cologne, M. F. our most gracious Lord, on the humble petition of Joseph Demmer has graciously appointed and accepted him as His Highness's vocal bass on the Electoral Toxal, with a yearly salary of 200 fl. divided in *quartalien* to begin with the current time, the appointment is confirmed hereby and a decree granted to the same Demmer, of which, for purposes of payment, the Electoral Chancellary will take notice and all whom it may concern will respect and obey the same and otherwise do what is necessary in the premises. Attest. p. Bonn, May 29, 1774.

Two years later leave of absence, but without salary, was granted to Joseph Demmer to visit Amsterdam to complete his education in music. Further notes from documentary sources:

1774. May 26. Andreas Lucchesi appointed Court Chapelmaster in place of Ludwig van Beethoven, deceased, with a salary of 1,000 fl.

May 29. Salary of Anna Maria Ries raised from 250 fl. to 300 fl. On May 13, 1775, together with Ferdinand Trewer (Drewer), violinist, she receives leave of absence for four months, to

begin in June with two quarters' pay in advance. In the
Court Calendar for 1775, which was printed about seven
months in advance, she is already described as Madame
Drewers, née Ries. She was considered the best singer in
the chapel.

November 23. Franz Anton Ries has granted him 25 th.
payable quarterly.

1775. March 23. Nicolas Simrock appointed on petition "Court Hornist
on the Electoral Toxal, in the cabinet and at table," and a
salary of 300 fl. was granted April 1. This is the first appearance in these records of a name which afterwards rose into
prominence.

1777. April 20. B. J. Mäurer, violoncellist, "who has served in the
court chapel from the beginning of the year till now on a
promise of 100 th.," prays for an appointment as court 'cellist
at a salary of 400 th. Appointed at a salary of 200 th.; we
shall have occasion to recur to him presently in connection
with notices touching Beethoven.

Under date May 22, 1778, J. van Beethoven informs the
Elector that "the singer Averdonck, who is to be sent to Chapelmaster Sales at Coblenz, is to pay 15 fl. per month for board and
lodging but that only a *douceur* is to be asked for her instruction
and that to take her thither will cost 20 th." There followed
upon this the following document:

To the humble announcement of Court Musician Beethoven
touching the singer Averdonck.

Electoral Councillor Forlivesi is to pay to the proper authorities
for a year beginning next month, 15 fl. a month and for the travelling
expenses 20 rth. once and for all as soon as the journey is begun. Attest.
p. Bonn, May 22, 1778.

This pupil of Johann van Beethoven, Johanna Helena Averdonk, born in Bonn on December 11, 1760, and brought forward
by her teacher at a concert in Cologne, received 120 th. "as a
special grace" on July 2, and was appointed Court Singer on
November 18, 1780, with a salary of 200 th." She died nine
years later, August 13, 1789.

The petitions sent in to the Elector were rarely dated and
were not always immediately attended to; therefore the date of
a *decretum* is not to be taken as conclusive in regard to the date of
facts mentioned in a petition. An illustration is afforded by a
petition of Franz Ries. He has returned from a tour to Vienna
and prays for a salary of 500 fl. "not the half of what he can earn
elsewhere." The petition is dated March 2. Two months passing
without bringing him an answer, he petitions again and obtains

a decree on May 2 that in addition to his salary of 28 th. 2 alb. 6, he shall receive "annoch so viel,"—again as much,—i. e., 400 fl.

1780. August. Court Organist Van den Eede prays that in consideration of his service of 54 years he be graciously and charitably given the salary vacated by the death of Court Musician Salomon. Eighteen others make the same prayer. The decision of the privy council is in these words: "To be divided between Huttenus and Esch. A decree as musical vocalist must first be given to the latter."

1781. February 15. The name of C. G. Neefe is now met with for the first time. He petitions for appointment to the position of organist in succession to Van den Eede, obviously aged and infirm. A decree was issued "*placet et expediatur* on the death of Organist Van den Eede," and a salary of 400 fl. granted.

1782. May 16. Johann van Beethoven petitions for "the three measures (*Malter*) of corn."

The archives of Düsseldorf furnish little more during the time of Max Frederick save certain papers relating to the Beethoven family, which are reserved for another place.

The search for means to form some correct idea of the character of the musical performances at the Elector's court during this reign has been more successful than for the preceding; but much is left to be desired down to the year 1778, when the theatre was placed upon a different basis and its history is sufficiently recorded. Such notices, however, in relation to the operatic entertainments as have been found scattered, mostly in the newspapers of Bonn, in those years, are numerous enough to give an idea of their character; while the remarks upon the festivities of the court, connected with them, afford a pretty lively picture of social amusement in the highest circle. We make room for some of the most significant occurrences, in chronological order:

1764. January 3. Galuppi's opera "Il Filosofo di Campagna," given in the Electoral Theatre with great applause.

January 8. A grand assembly at the palace in the afternoon, a magnificent supper in the grand gallery at which many spectators were present, and finally a masked ball.

March 23. Second performance of "La buona Figliuola," music by Piccini.

May 13. Elector's birthday; "Le Nozze," music by Galuppi, and two ballets.

May 20. "Il Filosofo" again, the notice of which is followed by the remark that the Elector is about removing to Brühl for the summer but will visit Bonn twice a week "on the days when operas are performed."

September 21. "La Pastorella al Soglio" (composer not named, probably Latilla), and two ballets.

December 16. "La Calamità di cuori," by Galuppi, and two ballets. This was "the first performance by the Mingotti company under the direction of Rizzi and Romanini."

1765. January 6. "Le Aventure di Rodolfo" (Piccini?), given by the same company together with a pantomime, "L'Arlequino fortunato per la Maggia." After the play there was a grand supper at which the Pope's nuncio was a guest, and finally a masked ball kept up till 6 o'clock in the morning.

1767. May 13. The Archbishop's birthday. Here is the programme condensed from the long description of the festivities in the "Bonnischer Anzeiger": 1, Early in the morning three rounds from the cannon on the city walls; 2, The court and public graciously permitted to kiss His Transparency's hand; 3, solemn high mass with salvos of artillery; 4, Grand dinner in public, the pope's nuncio, the foreign ministers and the nobility being the guests and the eating being accompanied by "exquisite table-music"; 5, After dinner "a numerously attended assembly"; 6, "A serenata composed especially for this most joyful day" and a comic opera in the palace theatre; 7, Supper of 130 covers; 8, *Bal masqué* until 5 a. m. The two dramatic pieces were "Serenata festivale, tra Bacco, Diana ed il Reno," the authors unnamed, and "Schiava finta," *drama giocoso dal celebre don Francesco Garzia, Spagnuolo,* the music probably by Piccini; "Giovanni van Beethoven" sang the part of *Dorindo.*

1768. May 16. "On the stage of the Court Theatre was performed with much applause a musical poem in German, specially written for the birthday of His Highness, and afterward an Italian intermezzo entitled 'La Nobiltà delusa.'"

1769. The festivities in honor of the birthday of the Elector took place May 17th, when, according to the "Anzeiger," "an Italian musical drama written expressly for this occasion was performed"—but the title suggests the possibility of a mistake; "Il Riso d'Apolline," with music by Betz, had been heard in 1701.

1771. A single discovery only for this year has rewarded search, that of a text-book, one of particular interest: "Silvain," comédie en une acte, mêlée d'ariettes, représentée, etc. Text by Marmontel, music by Grétry. *Dolmon père,* Mons. Louis van Beethoven, *Maître de Chapelle; Dolmon, fils ainé,* Jean van Beethoven, etc.

1772. February 27. "Le Donne sempre Donne," music by Andreas Lucchesi.

In March, on occasion of the opening of the Estates, "La Contadine in Corte," music by Sacchini.

The pieces given on the birthday this year were "Il Natal di Giove," music by Lucchesi, and "La buona Figliuola," music by Piccini. On the 17th the latter was repeated on the arrival of the French ambassador.

1773. May 30. The Elector's birthday; "L'Inganno scoperto, overo il Conte Caramella," music by Lucchesi, in which Ludovico van Beethoven sang the part of *Brunoro, contadino e tamburino*.

There are three more operettas which evidently belong to the succeeding winter when the Bonn company had the aid of two singers from the electoral court of Trèves. Their titles are "L'Improvvisata, o sia la Galanteria disturbata," by Lucchesi, "Li tre Amanti ridicoli," by Galuppi, and "La Moda," by Baroni. Ludwig van Beethoven did not sing in them. The means are still wanting to fill up the many gaps in the annals of this period or to carry them on during the next three years. Perhaps, however, the loss is not of much importance, for the materials collected are sufficient to warrant certain conclusions in regard to the general character of the court music. The musicians, both vocal and instrumental, were employed in the church, concert-room and theatre; their number remained without material change from the days of Christopher Petz to the close of Chapelmaster van Beethoven's life; places in this service were held to be a sort of heritage, and of right due to the children of old incumbents, when possessed of sufficient musical talent and knowledge; few if any names of distinguished virtuosos are found in the lists of the members, and, in all probability, the performances never rose above the respectable mediocrity of a small band used to playing together in the light and pleasing music of the day.

The dramatic performances appear to have been confined to the operetta; and the vocalists, who sang the Latin of the mass, seem to have been required to be equally at home in German, Italian and French in the theatre. Two visits of the Angelo Mingotti troupe are noted; and one attempt, at least, to place the opera upon a higher basis by the engagement of Italian song-stresses, was evidently made in the time of Clemens August.; it may be concluded that no great improvement was made—it is certain that no permanent one was; for in the other case the Bonn theatrical revolution of 1778 had not been needed. This must be noticed in detail.

Chronologically the following sketch belongs to the biography of Ludwig van Beethoven, as it embraces a period which happens in his case to be of special interest, young as he was;—the period from his 8th to his 14th year. But the details given, though of great importance for the light which they throw upon the musical life in which he moved and acted, would hardly be of so much interest to most readers as to justify breaking with them the course of the future narrative.

It was a period of great awakening in theatrical matters. Princes and courts were beginning everywhere in Germany to patronize the drama of their mother tongue and the labors of Lessing, Gotter and other well-known names, in the original production of German, or in the translation of the best English, Italian and French plays, were justifying and giving ever new impulse to the change in taste. From the many itinerant troupes of players performing in booths, or, in the larger cities, in the play-houses, the better class of actors were slowly finding their way into permanent companies engaged and supported by the governments. True, many of the newly established court theatres had but a short and not always a very merry life; true, also, that the more common plan was merely to afford aid and protection to some itinerant troupe; still the idea of a permanent national theatre on the footing of the already long-existing court musical establishments had made way, and had already been carried out in various places before it was taken up by the elector at Bonn. It can hardly be supposed that the example of the imperial court at Vienna, with the immense means at its disposal, could exert any direct influence upon the small court at Bonn at the other extremity of Germany; but what the Duke of Gotha and the elector at Mannheim had undertaken in this direction, Max Friedrich may well have ventured and determined to imitate. But there was an example nearer home—in fact in his own capital of Münster, where he, the prince primate, usually spent the summer. In 1775, Dobbler's troupe, which had been for some time playing in that city, was broken up.

The Westhus brothers in Münster built up their own out of the ruins; but it endured only a short time. Thereupon, under the care of the minister, H. von Fürstenberg (one of those rare men whom heaven elects and equips with all necessary gifts to cultivate what is good and beautiful in the arts), a meeting of the lovers of the stage was arranged in May and a few gentlemen of the nobility and a few from the parterre formed a council which assumed the direction. The Elector makes a considerable contribution. The money otherwise received is to be applied to the improvement of the wardrobe and the theatre. The actors receive their honoraria every month.[1]

At Easter, 1777, Seyler, a manager famous in German theatrical annals, and then at Dresden, finding himself unable to compete with his rival, Bondini, left that city with his company to try his fortunes in Frankfort-on-the-Main, Mayence, and other cities in that quarter. The company was very large—the Theatre

[1] Reichardt, "Theaterkalender, 1778," p. 99.

Lexicon (Article "Mainz") makes it, including its orchestra, amount to 230 individuals!—much too large, it seems, in spite of the assertion of the Theatre Lexicon, to be profitable. Be that as it may, after an experience of a year or more, two of the leading members, Grossmann and Helmuth, accepted an engagement from Max Friedrich to form and manage a company at Bonn in order that "the German art of acting might be raised to a school of morals and manners for his people." Taking with them a pretty large portion of Seyler's company, including several of the best members, the managers reached Bonn and were ready upon the Elector's return from Münster to open a season. "The opening of the theatre took place," says the Bonn "Dramaturgische Nachrichten," "on the 26th of November, 1778, with a prologue spoken by Madame Grossmann, 'Wilhelmine Blondheim,' tragedy in three acts by Grossmann, and 'Die grosse Batterie,' comedy in one act by Ayrenhofer." The same authority gives a list of all the performances of the season, which extended to the 30th of May, 1779, together with débuts, the dismissals and other matters pertaining to the actors. The number of the evenings on which the theatre was open was 50. A five-act play, as a rule, occupied the whole performance, but of shorter pieces usually two were given; and thus an opening was found occasionally for an operetta. Of musical dramas only seven came upon the stage and these somewhat of the lightest order except the first—the melodrama "Ariadne auf Naxos," music by Benda. The others were:

1779. February 21. "Julie," translated from the French by Grossmann, music by Desaides.
February 28. "Die Jäger und das Waldmädchen," operetta in one act, music by Duni.
March 21. "Der Hofschmied," in two acts, music by Philidor.
April 9. "Röschen und Colas," in one act, music by Monsigny.
May 5. "Der Fassbinder," in one act, music by Oudinot.
May 14. A prologue "Dedicated to the Birthday Festivities of His Electoral Grace of Cologne, May 13, 1779, by J. A. Freyherrn vom Hagen."

The selection of dramas was, on the whole, very creditable to the taste of the managers. Five of Lessing's works, among them "Minna von Barnhelm" and "Emilia Galotti," are in the list and some of the best productions of Bock, Gotter, Engel and their contemporaries; of translations there were Colman's "Clandestine Marriage" and "Jealous Wife," Garrick's "Miss in her Teens," Cumberland's "West Indian," Hoadly's "Suspicious Husband," Voltaire's "Zaire" and "Jeannette," Beaumarchais's "Eugénie," two or three of the works of Molière, and Goldoni, etc.;—in short, the list presents much variety and excellence.

Max Friedrich was evidently pleased with the company, for the "Nachrichten" has the following in the catalogue of performances: "On the 8th (of April) His Electoral Grace was pleased to give a splendid breakfast to the entire company in the theatre. . . . The company will occupy itself until the return of His Electoral Grace from Münster, which will be in the middle of November, with learning the newest and best pieces, among which are 'Hamlet,' 'King Lear' and 'Macbeth,' which are to be given also with much splendor of costume according to the designs of famous artists."

It may be remarked here that the "Bonn Comedy House" (for painting the interior of which Clemens August paid 468 thalers in 1751, a date which seems to fix the time at which that end of the palace was completed), occupied that portion of the present University Archæological Museum room next the Coblenz Gate, with large doors opening from the stage into the passageway so that this space could be used as an extension of the stage in pieces requiring it for the production of grand scenic effects. Above the theatre was the "Redouten-Saal" of Max Franz's time. The Elector had, of course, an entrance from the passages of the palace into his box. The door for the public, in an angle of the wall now built up, opened out upon the grove of horsechestnuts. The auditorium was necessarily low, but spacious enough for several hundred spectators. Though much criticized by travellers as being unworthy so elegant a court, not to say shabby, it seems to have been a nice and snug little theatre.

Meanwhile affairs with Seyler were drawing to a crisis. He had returned with his company from Mannheim and reopened at Frankfort, August 3, 1779. On the evening of the 17th, to escape imprisonment as a bankrupt, whether through his own fault or that of another—the Theatre Lexicon affirms the latter case—he took his wife and fled to Mayence. The company was allowed by the magistrates to play a few weeks with a view of earning at least the means of leaving the city; but on October 4, its members began to separate; Benda and his wife went to Berlin, but C. G. Neefe, the music director, and Opitz, descended the Rhine to Bonn and joined the company there—Neefe assuming temporarily the direction of the music in the theatre—of which more in another place.

No record has been found of the repertory of the Bonn theatre for the season 1779–1780, except that the opening piece on

December 3, on the evening after the Elector's return from Mün-ster, was a prologue, "Wir haben Ihn wieder!" text by Baron vom Hagen, with airs, recitatives and choruses composed by Neefe; that the "Déserteur" was in the list, and finally Hiller's "Jagd." In June, 1781, the season being over, the company migrated to Pyrmont, from Pyrmont to Cassel, and thence, in October, back to Bonn.

The season of 1781–'82 was a busy one; of musical dramas alone 17 are reported as newly rehearsed from September, 1781, to the same time in 1782, viz:

"Die Liebe unter den Handwerkern"
("L'Amore Artigiano").............Music by Gassmann
"Robert und Calliste"................ " " Guglielmi
"Der Alchymist"........ : .... " " Schuster.
"Das tartarische Gesetz"............ " " d'Antoine (of Bonn)
"Der eifersüchtige Liebhaber"
("L'Amant jaloux")............... " " Grétry
"Der Hausfreund"
("L'Ami de la Maison")........... " " Grétry
"Die Freundschaft auf der Probe"
("L'Amitié à l'Épreuve").......... " " Grétry
"Heinrich und Lyda"................ " " Neefe
"Die Apotheke"..................... " " Neefe
"Eigensinn und Launen der Liebe"..... " " Deler (Teller, Deller?)
"Romeo und Julie"................... " " Benda
"Sophonisba" (Deklamation mit Musik) " " Neefe
"Lucille"........................... " " Grétry
"Milton und Elmire"................ " " Mihl (or Mühle)
"Die Samnitische Vermählungsfeier"
("Le Marriage des Samnites")....... " " Grétry
"Ernst und Lucinde".................. " " Grétry
"Günther von Schwarzburg".......... " " Holzbauer

It does not follow, however, that all these operas, operettas and plays with music were produced during the season in Bonn. The company followed the Elector to Münster in June, 1782, and removed thence to Frankfort-on-the-Main for its regular series of performances at Michaelmas. It came back to Bonn in the Autumn.

The season 1782–'83 was as active as the preceding. Some of the newly rehearsed spoken dramas were "Sir John Falstaff," from the English, translations of Sheridan's "School for Scandal," Shakespeare's "Lear," and "Richard III," Mrs. Cowley's "Who's the Dupe?" and, of original German plays, Schiller's "Fiesco" and "Die Räuber," Lessing's "Miss Sara Sampson," Schroeder's "Testament," etc., etc. The number of newly rehearsed musical

dramas—in which class are included such ballad operas as General
Burgoyne's "Maid of the Oaks"—reached twenty, viz:

"Das Rosenfest"....................	Music by	Wolf (of Weimar)	
"Azalia"	" "	Johann Küchler	
		(Bassoonist in the	
		Bonn chapel)	
"Die Sklavin" (*La Schiava*)..........	" "	Piccini	
"Zémire et Azor"....................	" "	Grétry	
"Das Mädchen im Eichthale"	"		
("Maid of the Oaks")..............	" "	d'Antoine (Captain	
		in the army of the	
		Elector of Cologne)	
"Der Kaufmann von Smyrna".........	" "	J. A. Juste (Court	
		Musician in The	
		Hague)	
"Die seidenen Schuhe"..............	" "	Alexander Frizer (or	
		Fridzeri)	
"Die Reue vor der That".............	" "	Desaides	
"Der Aerndtetanz"..................	" "	J. A. Hiller	
"Die Olympischen Spiele" (*Olympiade*)	" "	Sacchini	
"Die Lügnerin aus Liebe"............	" "	Salieri	
"Die Italienerin zu London".........	" "	Cimarosa	
"Das gute Mädchen" (*La buona figliuola*)	" "	Piccini	
"Der Antiquitäten-Sammler".........	" "	André	
"Die Entführung aus dem Serail".....	" "	Mozart	
"Die Eifersucht auf der Probe"			
(*Il Geloso in Cimento*)..............	" "	Anfossi	
"Rangstreit und Eifersucht auf dem			
Lande" (*Le Gelosie villane*).........	" "	Sarti	
"Unverhofft kommt oft" (*Les Évène-*			
ments imprévus)....................	" "	Grétry	
"Felix, oder der Findling" (*Félix ou*			
l'Enfant trouvé).....................	" "	Monsigny	
"Die Pilgrimme von Mekka".........	" "	Gluck	

But a still farther provision has been made for the Elector's
amusement during the season of 1783–'84, by the engagement of
a ballet corps of eighteen persons. The titles of five newly rehearsed ballets are given in the report from which the above
particulars are taken, and which may be found in the theatrical
calendar for 1784.

With an enlarged company and a more extensive repertory,
preparations were made for opening the theatre upon the Elector's
return, at the end of October, from Münster to Bonn. But the
relations of the company to the court have been changed. Let
the "Theater-Kalender" describe the new position in which the
stage at Bonn was placed:

Bonn. His Electoral Grace, by a special condescension, had graciously determined to make the theatrical performances gratuitous and to that end has closed a contract with His Highness's Theatrical Director Grossmann according to which besides the theatre free of rent, the illumination and the orchestra he is to receive an annual subvention for the maintenance of the company. On His Highness's command there will be two or three performances weekly. By particular grace the director is permitted to spend several summer months in other places.

The advantages of this plan for securing a good repertory, a good company and a zealous striving for improvement are obvious; and its practical working during this, its only, season, so far as can now be gathered from scanty records, was a great success. It will hereafter be seen that the boy Ludwig van Beethoven was often employed at the pianoforte at the rehearsals—possibly also at the performances of the company of which Neefe was the musical director. That a company consisting almost exclusively of performers who had passed the ordeal of frequent appearance on the stage and had been selected with full knowledge of the capacity of each, and which, moreover, had gained so much success at the Bonn court as to be put upon a permanent footing, must have been one of more than the ordinary, average excellence, at least in light opera, needs no argument. Nor need comments be made upon the influence which daily intercourse with it, and sharing in its labors, especially in the direction of opera, must have exerted upon the mind of a boy of twelve or thirteen years possessed of real musical genius.

The theatrical season, and with it the company, came to an untimely end. Belderbusch died in January, 1784. Madame Grossmann died in childbed on March 28, and on April 15 the Elector followed them to another world. After the death of the Elector Maximilian Friedrich the Court Theatre was closed for the official mourning and the company dismissed with four weeks' salary.

It is consonant to the plan of this introductory chapter that some space be devoted to sketches of some of the principal men whose names have already occurred and to some notes upon the musical amateurs of Bonn who are known, or may be supposed, to have been friends of the boy Beethoven. These notices make no claim to the credit of being the result of original research; they are, except that of Neefe, little more than extracts from a letter, dated March 2, 1783, written by Neefe and printed in Cramer's "Magazin der Musik" (Vol. I, pp. 337 et seq.). At that time the "Capelldirector," as Neefe calls him, was Cajetano Mattioli,

born at Venice, August 7, 1750, whose appointments were concertmaster and musical director in Bonn, made on May 26, 1774
and April 24, 1777.

He studied in Parma, says Neefe, with the first violinist Angelo
Moriggi, a pupil of Tartini, and in Parma, Mantua and Bologna conducted grand operas like "Orfeo," "Alceste," etc., by the Chevalier Gluck
with success.   He owed much to the example set by Gluck in the matter
of conducting.   It must be admitted that he is a man full of fire, of
lively temperament and fine feeling.   He penetrates quickly into the
intentions of a composer and knows how to convey them promptly and
clearly to the entire orchestra.   He was the first to introduce accentua-
tion, instrumental declamation, careful attention to forte and piano,
or all the degrees of light and shade in the orchestra of this place.   In
none of the qualifications of a leader is he second to the famed Cannabich
of Mannheim.   He surpasses him in musical enthusiasm, and, like him,
insists upon discipline and order.   Through his efforts the musical repertory of this court has been provided with a very considerable collection
of good and admirable compositions, symphonies, masses and other
works, to which he makes daily additions; in the same manner he is
continually striving for the betterment of the orchestra.   Just now he
is engaged in a project for building a new organ for the court chapel.
The former organ, a magnificent instrument, became a prey of the flames
at the great conflagration in the palace in 1777.   His salary is 1,000 fl.

The chapelmaster (appointed May 26, 1774) was Mr. Andrea
Lucchesi, born May 28, 1741, at Motta in Venetian territory.   His teachers
in composition were, in the theatre style, Mr. Cocchi of Naples; in
the church style, Father Paolucci, a pupil of Padre Martini at Bologna,
and afterwards Mr. Seratelli, Chapelmaster of the Duke of Venice.   He
is a good organist and occupied himself profitably with the instrument
in Italy.   He came here with Mr. Mattioli as conductor of an Italian
opera company in 1771.   Taken altogether he is a light, pleasing and
gay composer whose part-writing is cleaner than that of most of his
countrymen.   In his church-works he does not confine himself to the
strict style affected by many to please amateurs.   Neefe enumerates
Lucchesi's compositions as follows: 9 works for the theatre, among
them the opera "L'Isola della Fortuna" (1765), "Il Marito geloso" (1766),
"Le Donne sempre Donne," "Il Matrimonio per astuzia" (1771) for
Venice, and the two composed at Bonn, "Il Natal di Giove" and "L'inganno scoperto," various intermezzi and cantatas; various masses,
vespers and other compositions for the church; six sonatas for the pianoforte and violin; a pianoforte trio, four pianoforte quartets and several
pianoforte concertos.   His salary was 1,000 fl.

The organist of the Court Chapel was Christian Gottlob
Neefe, son of a poor tailor of Chemnitz in Saxony, where he was
born February 5, 1748.   He is one of the many instances in musical
history in which the career of the man is determined by the beauty
of his voice in childhood.   At a very early age he became a
chorister in the principal church, which position gave him the

best school and musical instruction that the small city afforded—advantages so wisely improved as to enable him in early youth to gain a living by teaching. At the age of 21, with 20 thalers in his pocket and a stipend of 30 thalers per annum from the magistrates of Chemnitz, he removed to Leipsic to attend the lectures of the university, and at that institution in the course of time he passed his examination in jurisprudence. Upon this occasion he argued the negative of the question: "Has a father the right to disinherit a son for devoting himself to the theatre?" In Chemnitz Neefe's teachers in music had been men of small talents and very limited acquirements, and even in Leipsic he owed more to his persevering study of the theoretical works of Marpurg and C. P. E. Bach than to any regular instructor. But there he had the very great advantage of forming an intimate acquaintance with, and becoming an object of special interest to, Johann Adam Hiller, the celebrated director of the Gewandhaus Concerts, the then popular and famous composer, the introducer of Handel's "Messiah" to the German public, the industrious writer upon music, and finally a successor of Johann Sebastian Bach as Cantor of the Thomas School. Hiller gave him every encouragement in his power in his musical career; opened the columns of his musical "Wöchentliche Nachrichten" to his compositions and writings; called him to his assistance in operatic composition; gave him the results of his long experience in friendly advice; criticized his compositions, and at length, in 1777, gave him his own position as music director of Seyler's theatrical company, then playing at the Linkische Bad in Dresden. Upon the departure of that troupe for Frankfort-on-the-Main, Neefe was persuaded to remain with it in the same capacity. He thus became acquainted with Fräulein Zinck, previously court singer at Gotha but now engaged for Seyler's opera. The acquaintance ripened into a mutual affection and ended in marriage not long afterward. It is no slight testimony to the high reputation which he enjoyed that at the moment of Seyler's flight from Frankfort (1779) Bondini, whose success had driven that rival from Dresden, was in correspondence with Neefe and making him proposals to resign his position under Seyler for a similar but better one in his service. Pending the result of these negotiations Neefe, taking his wife with him, temporarily joined Grossmann and Helmuth at Bonn in the same capacity. Those managers, who knew the value of his services from their previous experience as members of the Seyler troupe, paid a very strong, though involuntary, tribute to his talents and personal character by adopting such unfair measures as to compel the musician to remain in Bonn until Bondini was forced to fill his vacancy by another candidate. Having once got him, Grossmann was determined to keep him—and succeeded.

As long as the Grossmann company remained undivided Neefe accompanied it in its annual visits to Münster and other places;—thus the sketch of his life printed sixteen years later in the first volume of the "Allgemeine Musikzeitung" of Leipsic bears date "Frankfort-on-the-Main, September 30, 1782"; but from that period save, perhaps, for a short time in 1783, he seems not to have left Bonn at all.

There were others besides Grossmann and Helmuth who thought Neefe too valuable an acquisition to the musical circles of Bonn not to be secured. Less than a year and a half after his arrival there the minister Belderbusch and the countess Hatzfeld, niece of the Elector, secured to him, though a Protestant, an appointment to the place of court organist. The salary of 400 florins, together with the 700 florins from Grossmann, made his income equal to that of the court chapelmaster. It is difficult now to conceive of the forgotten name of C. G. Neefe as having once stood high in the list of the first North German composers; yet such was the case. Of Neefe's published compositions, besides the short vocal and clavier pieces in Hiller's periodical, there had already appeared operettas in vocal score, "Die Apotheke" (1772), "Amor's Guckkasten" (1772), "Die Einsprüche" (1773) and "Heinrich und Lyda" (1777); also airs composed for Hiller's "Dorf-Barbier" and one from his own republished opera "Zemire und Azor"; twelve odes of Klopstock—sharply criticized by Forkel in his "Musikalisch-Kritische Bibliothek," much to the benefit of the second edition of them; and a pretty long series of songs. Of instrumental music he had printed twenty-four sonatas for pianoforte solo or with violin; and from Breitkopf and Härtel's catalogues, 1772 and 1774, may be added the following works included neither in his own list nor that of Gerber: a partita for string quartet, 2 horns, 2 oboes, 2 flutes and 2 bassoons; another for the same instruments minus the flutes and bassoons; a third for the string quartet and 2 oboes only, and two symphonies for string quartet, 2 horns, 2 oboes and 2 flutes. The "Sophonisbe" music was also finished and twenty years later, after Mozart had given a new standard of criticism, it was warmly eulogized in the "Allgemeine Musikzeitung" of Leipsic. At the date of his letter to Cramer (March 2, 1783) he had added to his published works "Sechs Sonaten am Clavier zu singen," "Vademecum für Liebhaber des Gesangs und Clavier," the clavier score of "Sophonisbe,"

and a concerto for clavier and orchestra.   His manuscripts, he adds
(Cramer's "Magazine," I; p. 382), consist of (a) the scores of the
operettas which had appeared in pianoforte arrangements; (b) the
score of his opera "Zemire und Azor"; (c) the score of his opera
"Adelheit von Veltheim"; (d) the score of a bardic song for the
tragedy "The Romans in Germany"; (e) the scores of theatrical
between-acts music; (f) the score of a Latin "Pater noster";
(g) various other smaller works.   He had in hand the composition
of the operetta "Der neue Gutsherr," the pianoforte score of
which, as also that of "Adelheit von Veltheim," was about to be
published by Dyck in Leipsic.   A year before at a concert for
amateurs at the house of Mr. von Mastiaux he had produced an
ode by Klopstock, "Dem Unendlichen," for four chorus voices
and a large orchestra, which was afterwards performed in Holy
Week in the *Fräuleinstiftskirche*.   In short, Neefe brought to
Bonn a high-sounding reputation, talent, skill and culture both
musical and literary, which made him invaluable to the managers
when new French and Italian operas were to be prepared for the
German stage; great facility in throwing off a new air, song,
entr'acte or what not to meet the exigencies of the moment; very
great industry, a *cacoethes scribendi* of the very highest value to
the student of Bonn's musical history in his time and a new element
into the musical life there.   This element may have seemed somewhat formal and pedantic, but it was solid, for it was drawn from
the school of Handel and Bach.

Let us return to Neefe's letter to Cramer again for some
notices of music outside the electoral palace:

Belderbusch, the minister, retained a quintet of wind-instruments,
2 clarinets, 2 horns and a bassoon.

The Countess von Belderbusch, wife of a nephew of the minister,
whose name will come up again, "plays skilfully upon the clavier."

The Countess von Hatzfeld, niece of the Elector, was "trained in
singing and clavier playing by the best masters of Vienna to whom,
indeed, she does very much honor.   She declaims recitatives admirably
and it is a pleasure to listen to her sing arias *di parlante*. She plays the
fortepiano brilliantly and in playing yields herself up completely to her
emotions, wherefore one never hears any restlessness or uneveness of
time in her *tempo rubato*.   She is enthusiastically devoted to music
and musicians."[1]

Chancellor and Captain von Schall "plays clavier and violin.
Though not adept on either instrument he has very correct musical
feeling.   He knows how to appreciate the true beauties of a composition,
and how to judge them, and has large historical and literary knowledge
of music." .

[1]To her Beethoven dedicated his Variations on "Venni Amore."

Frau Court Councillor von Belzer "plays the clavier and sings. She has a strong, masculine contralto of wide range, particularly downwards."

Johann Gottfried von Mastiaux, of the Finance Department and incumbent of divers high offices, is a self-taught musician. He plays several instruments himself and has given his four sons and a daughter the best musical instruction possible in Bonn. All are pianists and so many of them performers on other instruments that the production of quintets is a common family enjoyment. He is a devoted admirer of Haydn, with whom he corresponds, and in his large collection of music there are already 80 symphonies, 30 quartets and 40 trios by that master. His rare and valuable instruments are so numerous "that he could almost equip a complete orchestra. Every musician is his friend and welcome to him."

Count Altstädter: "in his house one may at times hear a very good quartet."

Captain Dantoine, "a passionate admirer and knower of music; plays the violin and the clavier a little. He learned composition from the books of Marpurg, Kirnberger and Riepel. Formed his taste in Italy. In both respects the reading of scores by classical masters has been of great service to him." Among his compositions are several operettas, symphonies and quartets "in Haydn's style."

The three Messrs. Facius, "sons of the Russian agent here, are soundly musical; the two elder play the flute and the youngest plays the violoncello." (According to Fischer the members of this family were visitors at the house of the Beethovens.)

There are many more music-lovers here, but the majority of them are too much given to privacy, so far as their musical practice goes, to be mentioned here. Enough has been said to show that a stranger fond of music need never leave Bonn without nourishment. Nevertheless, a large public concert institution under the patronage of His Electoral Grace is still desirable. It would be one more ornament of the capital and a promoter of the good cause of music.

What with the theatre, the court music, the musical productions in the church and such opportunities in private it is plain that young talent in those days in Bonn was in no danger of starvation for want of what Neefe calls "musikalische Nahrung."

So much upon the *dramatis personæ*, other than the principal figure and his family. Let an attempt follow to describe the little city as it appeared in 1770—in other words, to picture the scene. By an enumeration made in 1789, the population of Bonn was 9,560 souls, a number which probably for a long series of years had rarely varied beyond a few score, more or less—one, therefore, that must very nearly represent the aggregate in 1770. For the town had neither manufactures nor commerce beyond what its own wants supported; it was simply the residence of the Elector—the seat of the court, and the people depended more or less directly upon that court for subsistence—as a wag expressed it, "all Bonn was fed from the Elector's kitchen." The old city walls—(the "gar gute Fortification, dass der Churfürst sicher genug darinnen Hof halten kann" of Johann Hübner's description) —were already partially destroyed. Within them the whole population seems to have lived. Outside the city gates it does not appear that, save by a chapel or two, the eye was impeded in its sweep across gardens and open fields to the surrounding villages which, then as now hidden in clusters of walnut and fruit trees, appeared, when looked upon from the neighboring hills, like islands rising upon the level surface of the plain. The great increase of wealth and population during the last 150 years in all this part of the Rhine valley under the influence of the wise national economy of the Prussian government, has produced corresponding changes in and about the towns and villages; but the grand features of the landscape are unchanged; the ruins upon the Drachenfels and Godesberg looked down, as now, upon the distant roofs and spires of Bonn; the castle of Siegburg rose above the plains away to the East; the chapel crowned the Peters-berg, the church with the marble stairs the nearer Kreuzberg.

The fine landing place with its growing trees and seats for idlers, the villas, hotels, coffee-houses and dwellings outside the old walls, are all recent; but the huge ferryboat, the "flying bridge," even then was ever swinging like a pendulum from shore to shore. Steam as a locomotive power was unknown, and the commerce of the Rhine floated by the town, gliding down with the current on rafts or in clumsy but rather picturesque boats, or impelled against the stream by the winds, by horses and even by men and women. The amount of traffic was not, however, too great to be amply provided for in this manner; for population was kept down by war, by the hard and rude life of the peasant class, and by the influences of all the false national-economic principles of that age, which restrained commerce by every device that could be made to yield present profit to the rulers of the Rhine lands. Passengers had, for generations, no longer been plundered by mail-clad robbers dwelling upon a hundred pictur-esque heights; but each petty state had gained from the Em-peror's weakness "vested rights" in all sorts of custom-levies and taxes. Risbeck (1780) found nine toll-stations between May-ence and Coblenz; and thence to the boundary of Holland, he declares there were at least sixteen, and that in the average each must have collected 30,000 Rhenish florins per annum.

To the stranger, coming down from Mayence, with its narrow dark lanes, or up from Cologne, whose confined and pestiferously dirty streets, emitting unnamed stenches, were but typical of the bigotry, superstition and moral filth of the population—all now happily changed, thanks to a long period of French and Prussian rule—little Bonn seemed a very picture of neatness and comfort.   Even its ecclesiastical life seemed of another order. The men of high rank in the church were of high rank also by birth; they were men of the world and gentlemen; their manners were polished and their minds enlarged by intercourse with the world and with gentlemen; they were tolerant in their opinions and liberal in their views.   Ecclesiastics of high and low degree were met at every corner as in other cities of the Rhine region; but absence of military men was a remarkable feature. Johann Hübner gives the reason for this in few and quaint words: —"In times of war much depends upon who is master of Bonn, because traffic on the Rhine can be blockaded at this pass.   Therefore the place has its excellent fortification which enables the Elector to hold his court in ample security within its walls.   But he need not maintain a garrison there in time of peace, and in time of war troops are garrisoned who have taken the oath to the Emperor and the empire.   This was settled by the peace of Ryswick as well as Rastatt."

While the improvement in the appearance of the streets of Bonn has necessarily been great, through the refitting or rebuilding of a large portion of the dwelling-houses, the plan of the town, except in those parts lying near the wall, has undergone no essential change, the principal one being the open spaces, where in 1770 churches stood.   On the small triangular Römer-Platz was the principal parish church of Bonn, that of St. Remigius, standing in such a position that its tall tower looked directly down the Acherstrasse.   In 1800 this tower was set on fire by lightning and destroyed; six years later the church itself was demolished by the French and its stones removed to become a part of the fortifications at Wesel.   On the small, round grass plot as one goes from the Münster church toward the neighboring city gate (Neuthor) stood another parish church—a rotunda in form—that of St. Martin, which fell in 1812 and was removed; and at the opposite end of the minster, separated from it only by a narrow passage, was still a third, the small structure dedicated to St. Gangolph.   This, too, was pulled down in 1806.   Only the fourth parish church, that of St. Peter in Dietkirchen, is still in existence and was, at a later date, considerably enlarged.   After the demolition of these buildings a new division of the town into parishes was made (1806).

The city front of the electoral palace, now the university, was more imposing than now, and was adorned by a tall, handsome tower containing a carillon, with bells numerous enough to play, for instance, the overture to Monsigny's "Deserter." This part of the palace, with the tower and chapel, was destroyed by fire in 1777.

The town hall, erected by Clemens August, and the other churches were as now, but the large edifice facing the university library and museum of casts, now occupied by private dwellings and shops, was then the cloister and church of the Franciscan monks. A convent of Capuchin nuns stood upon the Kesselgasse; its garden is now a bleaching ground.

Let the fancy picture, upon a fine Easter or Pentecost morning in those years, the little city in its holiday attire and bustle. The bells in palace and church tower ringing; the peasants in coarse but picturesque garments, the women abounding in bright colors, come in from the surrounding villages, fill the market-place and crowd the churches at the early masses. The nobles and gentry —in broad-flapped coats, wide waistcoats and knee-breeches, the entire dress often of brilliant colored silks, satins and velvets, huge, white, flowing neckcloths, ruffles over the hands, buckles of silver or even of gold at the knees and upon the shoes, huge wigs becurled and bepowdered on the heads, and surmounted by the cocked hat, when not held under the arm, a sword at the side, and commonly a gold-headed cane in the hand (and if the morning be cold, a scarlet cloak thrown over the shoulders)—are daintily picking their way to the palace to kiss His Transparency's hand or dashing up to the gates in heavy carriages with white wigged and cocked-batted coachmen and footmen. Their ladies wear long and narrow bodices, but their robes flow with a mighty sweep; their apparent stature is increased by very high-heeled shoes and by piling up their hair on lofty cushions; their sleeves are short, but long silk gloves cover the arms. The ecclesiastics, various in name and costume, dress as now, save in the matter of the flowing wig. The Elector's company of guards is out and at intervals the thunder of the artillery on the walls is heard. On all sides, strong and brilliant contrasts of color meet the eye, velvet and silk, purple and fine linen, gold and silver—such were the fashions of the time—costly, inconvenient in form, but imposing, magnificent and marking the differences of rank and class. Let the imagination picture all this, and it will have a scene familiar to the boy Beethoven, and one in which as he grew up to manhood he had his own small part to play.

Chapter II

The Ancestral van Beethoven Family in Belgium—Removal
of the Grandfather to Bonn—His Activities as Singer
and Chapelmaster — Birth and Education of Johann
van Beethoven—The Parents of the Composer.

A
T the beginning of the seventeenth century a family named
van Beethoven lived in a village of Belgium near Louvain.
A member of it removed to and settled in Antwerp about
1650. A son of this Beethoven, named William, a wine dealer,
married, September 11, 1680, Catherine Grandjean and had issue,
eight children. One of them, baptized September 8, 1683, in the
parish of Notre Dame, now received the name Henry Adelard, his
sponsors being Henry van Beethoven, acting for Adelard de Re-
dincq, Baron de Rocquigny, and Jacqueline Grandjean. This Henry
Adelard Beethoven, having arrived at man's estate, took to wife
Maria Catherine de Herdt, who bore him twelve children—the
third named Louis, the twelfth named Louis Joseph. The latter,
baptized December 9, 1728, married, November 3, 1773, Maria
Theresa Schuerweghs, and died November 11, 1808, at Ooster-
wyck. The second daughter, named like her mother Maria
Theresa, married, September 6, 1808, Joseph Michael Jacobs and
became the mother of Jacob Jacobs, in the middle of the nineteenth century a professor of painting in Antwerp, who supplied
in part the materials for these notices of the Antwerp Beethovens,
although the principal credit is due to M. Léon de Burbure of
that city.[1]

The certificate of baptism of Louis van Beethoven, third
son of Henry Adelard, is to this effect:

Antwerp, December 23, 1712—*Baptizatus*, Ludovicus.

Parents: Henricus van Beethoven and Maria Catherine de
Hert.

---

[1] In Fétis' "Biographie universelle" (new ed.) several of these names are mis-
printed. They are corrected here from Mr. Jacobs' letter to A. W. T.

Sponsors: Petrus Bellmaert and Dymphona van Beethoven.

It is a family tradition—Prof. Jacobs heard it from his mother —that this Louis van Beethoven, owing to some domestic difficulties (according to M. Burbure they were financial), secretly left his father's house at an early age and never saw it again, although in later years an epistolary correspondence seems to have been established between the fugitive and his parents. Gifted with a good voice and well educated musically, he went to Louvain and applied for a vacant position as tenor to the chapter ad Sanctum Petrum, receiving it on November 2, 1731.[1] A few days later the young man of 18 years was appointed substitute for three months for the singing master (*Phonascus*), who had fallen ill, as is attested by the minutes of the Chapter, under date November 2, 1731.[2]

The young singer does not seem to have filled the place beyond the prescribed time. By a decree of Elector Clemens August, dated March, 1733 (the month of Joseph Haydn's birth), he became Court Musician in Bonn with a salary of 400 florins, a large one for those days, particularly in the case of a young man who only three months before had completed his 20th year. Allowing the usual year of probation to which candidates for the court chapel were subjected, Beethoven must have come to Bonn in 1732. This corresponds to the time spent at Louvain as well as to a petition of 1774, to be given hereafter, in which Johann speaks of his father's "42 years of service." There is another paper of date 1784 which makes the elder Beethoven to have served about 46 years, but this is from another hand and of less authority than that written by the son.

What it was that persuaded Ludwig van Beethoven to go to Bonn is unknown. Gottfried Fischer, who owned the house in the Rheingasse in which two generations of Beethovens lived, professed to know that Elector Clemens August learned to know him as a good singer at Liège and for that reason called him to

---

[1]Thayer's account of this period in the life of Beethoven's grandfather has here been extended from an article by the Chevalier L. de Burbure, published in the "Biographie nationale publiée par l'Académie Royale des sciences, des lettres et des beaux arts de Belgique." Tome II, p. 105. (Brussels, 1868.) From this it further appears that two other members of the Antwerp branch of the family were devoted to the fine arts, viz.: Peter van Beethoven, painter, pupil of Abr. Genoel, jr., and Gerhard van Beethoven, sculptor, accepted in the guild of St. Luke about 1713. Director Vollmer, of Brussels, in a communication to Dr. Deiters gave information of a branch of the family in Mechlin and of still another in Brabant where, in the village of Wambeke, there was a curé van Beethoven who must either have died or been transferred between 1729 and 1732.

[2]The original entry is printed in full in the German edition of this biography.

Bonn. That is not impossible, whether the Elector went to Louvain or Ludwig introduced himself to him at Liège. But it is significant that another branch of the Beethoven family was already represented at Bonn. Michael van Beethoven was born in Malines in February, 1684. He was a son of Cornelius van Beethoven and Catherine Leempoel, and beyond doubt, as the later associations in Bonn prove, closely related to the Antwerp branch of the family. Michael van Beethoven married Maria Ludovica Stuykers (or Stuykens) on October 8, 1707. His eldest son also bore the name of Cornelius (born in September, 1708, in Malines) and there were four other sons born to him during his stay in Malines, among them two who were named Louis, up to 1715. At a date which is uncertain, this family removed to Bonn. There Cornelius, on February 20, 1734, married a widow named Helena de la Porte (née Calem), in the church of St. Gangolph, Ludwig van Beethoven, the young court singer, being one of the witnesses. In August of the same year Cornelius was proxy for his father (who, evidently, had not yet come to Bonn), as godfather for Ludwig's first child. Later, after his son had established a household, he removed to Bonn, for Michael van Beethoven died in June, 1749, in Bonn, and in December of the same year Maria Ludovica Stuykens (*sic*), "the Widow van Beethoven." Cornelius became a citizen of Bonn on January 17, 1736, on the ground that he had married the widow of a citizen, and in 1738 he stands alone as representative of the name in the list of Bonn's citizens. He seems to have been a merchant, and is probably the man who figures in the annual accounts of Clemens August as purveyor of candles. He lost his wife, and for a second married Anna Barbara Marx, *virgo*, on July 5, 1755, who bore him two daughters (1756 and 1759), both of whom died young and for both of whom Ludwig van Beethoven was sponsor. Cornelius died in 1764 and his wife in 1765, and with this the Malines branch of the family ended. Which one of the two cousins (for so we may in a general way consider them) came to Bonn, Ludwig or Cornelius, must be left to conjecture. There is evidence in favor of the former in the circumstance that Cornelius does not appear as witness at the marriage of Ludwig in 1733. If Ludwig was the earlier arrival, then the story of his call by the Elector may be true; he was not disappointed in his hope of being able to make his way by reason of his knowledge of music and singing.

The next recorded fact in his history may be seen in the ancient register of the parish of St. Remigius, now preserved in the town hall of Bonn. It is the marriage on September 7, 1733,

of Ludwig van Beethoven and Maria Josepha Poll, the husband
not yet 21 years of age, the wife 19.   Then follows in the records
of baptisms in the parish:

1734, August 8.
Parents:	Baptized:	Sponsors:
Ludwig van Beethoven,	Maria	Maria Bernardina Menz,
Maria Josepha Poll.	Bernardina	Michael van Beethoven;
	Ludovica.	in his place Cornelius van
		Beethoven.

The child Bernardina died in infancy, October 17, 1735.   Her
place was soon filled by a son, Marcus Josephus, baptized April
15, 1736, of whom the parents were doubtless early bereaved, for
no other notice whatever has been found of him.   After the lapse
of some four years the childless pair again became parents, by
the birth of a son, whose baptismal record has not been discovered.
It is supposed that this child, Johann, was baptized in the Court
Chapel, the records of which are not preserved in the archives
of the town and seem to be lost; or that, possibly, he was born
while the mother was absent from Bonn.   An official report upon
the condition and characters of the court musicians made in 1784,
however, gives Johann van Beethoven *born in Bonn* and aged
forty-four—thus fixing the date of his birth towards the end of
1739 or the beginning of 1740.

The gradual improvement of the elder Beethoven's condition
in respect of both emolument and social position, is creditable to
him alike as a musician and as a man.   Poorly as the musicians
were paid, he was able in his last years to save a small portion of
his earnings; his rise in social position is indicated in the public
records;—thus, the first child is recorded as the son of L. v. Beethoven "musicus"; as sponsor to the eldest daughter of Cornelius
van Beethoven, he appears as "Dominus" van Beethoven;—to the
second as "Musicus Aulicus"; in 1761 he becomes "Herr Kapellmeister," and his name appears in the Court Calendar of the
same year, third in a list of twenty-eight "Hommes de chambre
honoraires." Of the elder Beethoven's appointment as head of
the court music no other particulars have been obtained than
those to be found in his petition and the accompanying decree
printed in Chapter I.   From these papers it appears that the
bass singer has had the promise of the place from Clemens August
as successor to Zudoli, but that the Elector, when the vacancy
occurred, changed his mind and gave it to his favorite young

violinist Touchemoulin, who held the position for so short a time,
however, that his name never appears as chapelmaster in the
Court Calendar, he having resigned on account of the reduction
of his salary by Belderbusch, prime minister of the new Elector
who just at that period succeeded Clemens August. The elevation of a singer to such a place was not a very uncommon event
in those days, but that a chapelmaster should still retain his
place as singer probably was. Hasse and Graun began their
careers as vocalists, but more to the point are the instances of
Steffani, Handel's predecessor at the court of Hanover, and of
Righini, successively chapelmaster at Mayence and Berlin. In
all these cases the incumbents were distinguished and very successful composers. Beethoven was not. Wegeler's words, "the
chapelmaster and bass singer had at an earlier date produced
operas at the National Theatre established by the Elector," have
been rather interpreted than quoted by Schindler and others
thus: "it is thought that under the luxury-loving Elector Clemens
August, he produced operas of his own composition"—a construction which is clearly forced and incorrect. Strange that so
few writers can content themselves with exact citations! Not
only is there no proof whatever, certainly none yet made public,
that Chapelmaster van Beethoven was an author of operatic
works, but the words in his own petition, "inasmuch as the
Toxal must be sufficiently supplied with *musique*," can hardly
be otherwise understood than as intended to meet a possible
objection to his appointment on the ground of his not being a
composer. Wegeler's words, then, would simply mean that he
put upon the stage and conducted the operatic works produced,
which were neither numerous nor of a very high order during his
time. His labors were certainly onerous enough without adding
musical composition. The records of the electoral court which
have been described and in part reproduced in the preceding
chapter, exhibit him conducting the music of chapel, theatre and
"Toxal," examining candidates for admission into the electoral
musical service, reporting upon questions referred to him by the
privy council and the like, and all this in addition to his services
as bass singer, a position which gave him the principal bass parts
and solos to sing both in chapel and theatre. Wegeler records
a tradition that in Gassmann's operetta "L'Amore Artigiano"
and Monsigny's "Déserteur" he was "admirable and received
the highest applause." If this be true it proves no small degree
of enterprise on his part as chapelmaster and of well-conserved
powers as a singer; for these two operas were first produced, the

one in Vienna, the other in Paris, in 1769, when Beethoven had already entered his fifty-eighth year.

The words of Demmer in his petition of January 23, 1773, "the bass singer van Beethoven is incapacitated and can no longer serve as such," naturally suggest the thought that the old gentleman's appearance as *Brunoro* in Lucchesi's "L'Inganno scoperto" in May, 1773, was a final compliment to his master, the Elector, upon his birthday. He did not live to celebrate another; the death of "Ludwig van Beethoven, Hoffkapellmeister," is recorded at Bonn under date of December 24, 1773—one day after the sixty-first anniversary of his baptism in Antwerp.

At home the good man had his cross to bear. His wife, Josepha, who with one exception had buried all her children, and possibly on that very account, became addicted to the indulgence of an appetite for strong drink, was at the date of her husband's death living as a boarder in a cloister at Cologne. How long she had been there does not appear, but doubtless for a considerable period. The son, too, was married, but though near was not in his father's house. The separation was brought about by his marriage, with which the father was not agreed. The house in which the chapelmaster died, and which he occupied certainly as early as 1765, was that next north of the so-called Gudenauer Hof, later the post-office in the neighboring Bonngasse, and bore the number 386. The chapelmaster appears, upon pretty good evidence, to have removed hither from the Fischer house in the Rheingasse, where he is said to have lived many years and even to have carried on a trade in wine, which change of dwelling may have taken place in 1767.

When one recalls the imposing style of dress at the era the short, muscular man, with dark complexion and very bright eyes, as Wegeler describes him[1] and as a painting by Courtpainter Radoux, still in possession of his descendants in Vienna, depicts him, presents quite an imposing picture to the imagination.

Of the early life of Johann van Beethoven there are no particulars preserved except such as are directly or indirectly conveyed in the official documents. Such of these papers as came from his own hand, if judged by the standard of our time, show a want of ordinary education; but it must not be forgotten that the orthography of the German language was not then fixed; nor that many a contemporary of his, who boasted a university

[1] "The grandfather was a man short of stature, muscular, with extremely animated eyes, and was greatly respected as an artist" Fischer's description is different, but Wegeler is the more trustworthy witness of the two.

education, or who belonged to the highest ranks of society, wrote in a style no better than his. This is certain: that after he had received an elementary education he was sent to the *Gymnasium*, for as a member of the lowest class (*infima*) of that institution he took part in September, 1750, as singer in the annual school play which it was the custom of the *Musæ Bonnenses* to give. It would seem, therefore, that his good voice and musical gifts were appreciated at an early period. Herein, probably, is also to be found the reason why his stay at the gymnasium was not of long duration. The father had set him apart for service in the court music, and himself, as appears from the statements already printed, undertook his instruction; he taught him singing and clavier playing. Whether or not he also taught him violin playing, in which he was "capable," remains uncertain. In 1752, at the age of 12, as can be seen from his petition of March, 1756, and his father's of 1764, he entered the chapel as soprano. According to Gottwald's report of 1756 he had served "about 2 years"; the contradiction is probably explained by an interruption caused by the mutation of his voice. At the age of 16, he received his *decretum* as "accessist" on the score of his skill in singing and his experience already acquired, including his capability on the violin, which was the basis of the decree of April 24, 1764, granting him a salary of 100 rth. per annum.

So, at the age of 22, the young man received the promise of a salary, and at 24 obtained one of 100 thalers. In 1769, he received an increase of 25 fl., and 50 fl. more by the decree of April 3, 1772. He had, moreover, an opportunity to gain something by teaching. Not only did he give lessons in singing and clavier playing to the children of prominent families of the city, but he also frequently was called on to prepare young musicians for service in the chapel. Thus Demmer, says the memorandum heretofore given, "paid 6 rth. to young Mr. Beethoven for 3 months"; and a year later the following resolve of the privy council was passed:

Ad Suppl. Joan Beethoven

The demands of the suppliant having been found to be correct, the Electoral Treasury is commanded to satisfy the debt by·the usual withdrawal of the sum from the salary of the defendant.

Bonn, May 24, 1775.   Attest. P.

which probably refers to a debt contracted by one of the women of the court chapel. A few years later, as we have seen, he seems

to have been intrusted with the training of Johanna Helena
Averdonck, whom he brought forward as his pupil in March, 1778,
and the singer Gazzenello was his pupil before she went elsewhere.
It was largely his own fault that the musically gifted man was
unfortunate in both domestic and official relations.   His intem-
perance in drink, probably inherited from his mother but attributed by old Fischer to the wine trade in which his father embarked,
made itself apparent at an early date, and by yielding to it more
and more as he grew older he undoubtedly impaired his voice and
did much to bring about his later condition of poverty.   How it
finally led to a catastrophe we shall see later.   According to the
testimony of the widow Karth, he was a tall, handsome man, and
wore powdered hair in his later years.   Fischer does not wholly
agree with her: "of medium height, longish face, broad forehead,
round nose, broad shoulders, serious eyes, face somewhat scarred,
thin pigtail."   Three and a half years after obtaining his salary
of 100 th. he ventured to marry.   Heinrich Kewerich, the father
of his wife, was head cook in that palace at Ehrenbreitstein in
which Clemens danced himself out of this world, but he died before
that event took place.[1]   His wife, as the church records testify,
was Anna Clara Daubach.   Her daughter Maria Magdalena,
born December 19, 1746, married a certain Johann Laym, valet
of the Elector of Trèves, on January 30, 1763.   On November
28, 1765, the husband died, and Maria Magdalena was a widow
before she had completed her 19th year.   In a little less than two
years the marriage register of St. Remigius, at Bonn, was enriched
by this entry:

*12ma 9bris.   Praevia Dispensatione super 3bus denuntiationibus
copulavi D. Joannem van Beethoven, Dni. Ludovici van Beethoven et
Mariae Josephae Poll conjugum filium legitimum, et Mariam Magdalenam
Keferich viduam Leym ex Ehrenbreitstein, Henrici Keferich et annae clarae
Westorffs filiam legitimam.   Coram testibus Josepho clemente Belseroski
et philippo Salomon.*

That is, Johann van Beethoven has married the young
widow Laym.

How it came that the marriage took place in Bonn instead of
the home of the bride we are told by Fischer.   Chapelmaster van
Beethoven was not at all agreed that his son should marry a

[1]The church records at Ehrenbreitstein say that he died August 2, 1759, in Molzberg,
at the age of 58; his funeral took place in Ehrenbreitstein.   A Frau Eva Katharina
Kewerich, who died at Ehrenbreitstein on October 10, 1753, at the age of 89 years, was
probably his mother.

woman of a lower station in life than his own.   He did not continue
his opposition against the fixed determination of his son; but it
is to be surmised that he would not have attended a ceremony in
Ehrenbreitstein, and hence the matter was disposed of quickly
in Bonn.   After the wedding the young pair paid a visit of a few
days' duration to Ehrenbreitstein.

Fischer describes Madame van Beethoven as a "handsome,
slender person" and tells of her "rather tall, longish face, a nose
somewhat bent (gehöffelt, in the dialect of Bonn), spare, earnest
eyes."   Cäcilia Fischer could not recall that she had ever seen
Madame van Beethoven laugh; "she was always serious."   Her
life's vicissitudes may have contributed to this disposition:—
the early loss of her father, and of her first husband, and the
death of her mother scarcely more than a year after her second
marriage.   It is difficult to form a conception of her character
because of the paucity of information about her.   Wegeler lays
stress upon her piety and gentleness; her amiability and kindliness
towards her family appear from all the reports; nevertheless,
Fischer betrays the fact that she could be vehement in controversies with the other occupants of the house.   "Madame van
Beethoven," Fischer continues, "was a clever woman; she could
give converse and reply aptly, politely and modestly to high and
low, and for this reason she was much liked and respected.   She
occupied herself with sewing and knitting.   They led a righteous
and peaceful married life, and paid their house-rent and baker's
bills promptly, quarterly, and on the day.   She[1] was a good, a
domestic woman, she knew how to give and also how to take in a
manner that is becoming to all people of honest thoughts."   From
this it is fair to assume that she strove to conduct her household
judiciously and economically; whether or not this was always
possible in view of the limited income, old Fischer does not seem
to have been informed.   She made the best she could of the
weaknesses of her husband without having been able to influence
him; her care for the children in externals was not wholly sufficient.
Young Ludwig clung to her with a tender love, more than to the
father, who was "only severe"; but there is nothing anywhere to
indicate that she exerted an influence upon the emotional life
and development of her son, and in respect of this no wrong will
be done her if the lower order of her culture be taken into consideration.   Nor must it be forgotten that in all probability she was

[1]Some notes by Fischer contain the characteristic addition: "Madame van Beethoven once remarked that the most necessary things, such as house-rent, the baker,
shoemaker and tailor must first be paid, but she would never pay drinking debts."

naturally delicate and that her health was still further weakened by her domestic troubles and frequent accouchements. The "quiet, suffering woman," as Madame Karth calls her, died in 1787 of consumption at the age of 40 years. Long years after in Vienna Beethoven was wont, when among his intimate friends, to speak of his "excellent" (vortreffliche) mother.[1]

At the time when Johann van Beethoven married, there was quite a colony of musicians, and other persons in the service of the court, in the Bonngasse, as that street is in part named which extends from the lower extremity of the market-place to the Cologne gate. Chapelmaster van Beethoven had left the house in the Rheingasse and lived at No. 386. In the adjoining house, north, No. 387, lived the musical family Ries. Farther down, the east house on that side of the way before the street assumes the name Kölnerstrasse was the dwelling of the hornist, afterward publisher, Simrock. Nearly opposite the chapelmaster's the second story of the house No. 515 was occupied (but not till after 1771) by the Salomons; the parterre and first floor by the owner of the house, a lace-maker or dealer in laces, named Clasen. Of the two adjoining houses the one No. 576 was the dwelling of Johann Baum, a master locksmith, doubtless the Jean Courtin, "serrurier," of the Court Calendar for 1773. In No. 617 was the family Hertel, twelve or fifteen years later living under the Beethovens in the Wenzelgasse, and not far off a family, Poll, perhaps relations of Madame Beethoven the elder. Conrad Poll's name is found in the Court Calendars of the 1770's as one of the eight Electoral "Heiducken" (footmen). In 1767 in the rear of the

[1]In the collection of Beethoven relics in the Beethoven House in Bonn there is a portrait which is set down as that of Beethoven's mother. The designation, however, rests only on uncertain tradition and lacks authoritative attestation. It is certainly difficult to see in it the representation of a consumptive woman only 40 years old. Moreover, it is strange that Beethoven should have sent from Vienna for the portrait of his grandfather and not for that of his dearly loved mother had one been in existence. It is only because of a resemblance between this picture and another that the belief exists that portraits of both of the parents of Beethoven are in existence. In 1890 two oil portraits were found in a shed in Cologne and restored by the painter Kempen, who recognized in them the handiwork of the painter Beckenkamp, who, like Beethoven's mother, was born in Ehrenbreitstein, was a visitor at the Beethoven home in Bonn and died in Cologne in 1828. The female portrait agrees with that in Bonn; they are life-size, finely executed pictures, but they are certainly not Beethoven's parents. Enough has been said about the portrait of the mother. In the case of that of the father the first objection is that it also lacks authentication. Fischer's description does not wholly fit the picture; the old man would not have forgotten the protruding lower lip. But the entire expression of the face, serious, it is true, but fleshy and vulgar, and the gray perruque, do not conform to what we know of the easy-going musician. It will be difficult, too, to trace any resemblance of expression between it and the familiar one of Beethoven from which a conclusion might be drawn. So long as proofs are wanting, scientific biography will have no right to accept the portraits as those of Beethoven's parents. Reproductions of them may be found in the "Musical Times" of London, December 15, 1892.

Clasen house, north,[1] there was a lodging to let; and there the newly married Beethovens began their humble housekeeping. Their first child was a son, Ludwig Maria, baptized April 2, 1769, whose sponsors, as may be read in the register of St. Remigius parish, were the grandfather Beethoven and Anna Maria Lohe, wife of Jean Courtin, the next-door neighbor. This child lived but six days. In two years the loss of the parents was made up by the birth of him who is the subject of this biography.

[1]The house is now owned by the Beethoven-Haus Verein, and maintained as a Beethoven museum.

Chapter III

The Childhood of Beethoven—An Inebriate Grandmother and a Dissipated Father—The Family Homes in Bonn —The Boy's Schooling—His Music Teachers—Visits Holland with his Mother.

THERE is no authentic record of Beethoven's birthday. Wegeler, on the ground of custom in Bonn, dates it the day preceding the ceremony of baptism—an opinion which Beethoven himself seems to have entertained. It is the official record of this baptism only that has been preserved. In the registry of the parish of St. Remigius the entry appears as follows:

Parentes:	Proles:	Patrini:
D: Joannes van Beethoven & Helena Keverichs, conjuges	17ma Xbris. Ludovicus	D: Ludovicus van Beethoven & Gertrudis Müllers dicta Baums

The sponsors, therefore, were Beethoven's grandfather the chapelmaster, and the wife of the next-door neighbor, Johann Baum, secretary at the electoral cellar. The custom obtaining at the time in the Catholic Rhine country not to postpone the baptism beyond 24 hours after the birth of a child, it is in the highest degree probable that Beethoven was born on December 16, 1770.[1]

Of several certificates of baptism the following is copied in full for the sake of a remark upon it written by the master's own hand:

[1]In one of Beethoven's conversation books his nephew writes on December 15, 1823: "To-day is the 15th of December, the day of your birth, but I am not sure whether it is the 15th or 17th, inasmuch as we can not depend on the certificate of baptism and I read it only once when I was still with you in January." The nephew, it will be observed, does not appeal to a family tradition but to the baptismal certificate, and the uncertainty, therefore, is with reference to the date of baptism, not of birth. Hence the deduction which Kalischer makes ("Vossische Zeitung," No. 17, 1891) that Beethoven was born on December 15. Hesse calls to witness a clerk employed in Simrock's establishment with whom Beethoven had business transactions, and who had written on the back of the announcement of Beethoven's death, "L. v. Beethoven was born on December 16, 1770."

Department de Rhin et Moselle
Mairie de Bonn.

Extrait du Registre de Naissances de la Paroisse
de St. Remy à Bonn.

Anno millesimo septingentesimo septuagesimo, de decima septima Decembris baptizatus est Ludovicus. Parentes D: Joannes van Beethoven et Helena[1] Keverichs, conjuges. Patrini, D: Ludovicus van Beethoven et Gertrudis Müllers dicta Baums.

Pour extrait conforme
délivré à la Mairie de Bonn.
Bonn le 2 Juin, 1810.
[*Signatures and official seals.*]

On the back of this paper Beethoven wrote:

, 1772

"Es scheint der Taufschein nicht richtig, da noch ein Ludwig vor mir. Eine Baumgarten war glaube ich mein Pathe.
Ludwig van Beethoven."[2]

The composer, then, even in his fortieth year still believed the correct date to be 1772, which is the one given in all the old biographical notices, and which corresponds to the dates affixed to many of his first works, and indeed to nearly all allusions to his age in his early years. Only by keeping this fact in mind, can the long list of chronological contradictions, which continually meet the student of his history during the first half of his life, be explained or comprehended. Whoever examines the original record of baptism in the registry at Bonn, sees instantly that the certificate, in spite of Beethoven, is correct; but all possible doubt is removed by the words of Wegeler:

Little Louis clung to this grandfather . . . with the greatest affection, and, young as he was when he lost him, his early impressions always remained lively. He liked to speak of his grandfather with the friends of his youth, and his pious and gentle mother, whom he loved much more than he did his father, who was only severe, was obliged to tell him much of his grandfather.

Had 1772 been the correct date the child could never have retained personal recollections of a man who died on December 24, 1773. A survey of the whole ground renders the conclusion irresistible that at the time when the boy began to attract notice

---

[1]The mistake in the mother's name is sufficiently explained by the use of Lena as the contraction of both Helena and Magdalena.

[2]"The baptismal certificate seems to be incorrect, since there was a Ludwig born before me. A Baumgarten was my sponsor, I believe. Ludwig van Beethoven."

by his skill upon the pianoforte and by the promise of his first attempts in composition, his age was purposely falsified, a motive for which may perhaps be found in the excitement caused in the musical world by the then recent career of the Mozart children, and in the reflection that attainments which in a child of eight or ten years excite wonder and astonishment are considered hardly worthy of special remark in one a few years older.   There is, unfortunately, nothing known of Johann van Beethoven's character which renders such a trick improbable.   Noteworthy is it that, at first, the falsification rarely extends beyond one year; and, also, that in an official report in 1784 the correct age is given. Here an untruth could not be risked, nor be of advantage if it had been.

Dr. C. M. Kneisel, who championed the cause of the house in the Bonngasse in a controversy conducted in the "Kölnische Zeitung" in 1845, touching the birthplace of Beethoven, remarks that the mother "was, as is known, a native of the Ehrenbreitstein valley and separated from her relatives; he (Johann van Beethoven) was without relatives and in somewhat straitened circumstances financially.   What, then, was more natural than that he should invite his neighbor, Frau Baum, a respected and well-to-do woman, *in whose house the baptismal feast was held*, to be sponsor for his little son?"   This last fact indicates clearly the narrowness of the quarters in which the young couple dwelt. Does it not also hint that the grandfather was now a solitary man with no home in which to spread the little feast?   Let Johann van Beethoven himself describe the pecuniary condition in which he found himself upon the death of his father:

Most Reverend Archbishop,
Most Gracious Elector and Lord, Lord.

Will Your Electoral Grace graciously be pleased to hear that my father has passed away from this world, to whom it was granted to serve his Electoral Grace Clemens August and Your Electoral Grace and gloriously reigning Lord Lord 42 years, as chapelmaster with great honor, whose position I have been found capable of filling, but nevertheless I would not venture to offer my capacity to Your Electoral Grace, but since the death of my father has left me in needy circumstances my salary not sufficing and I compelled to draw on the savings of my father, my mother still living and in a cloister at a cost of 60 rth. for board and lodging each year and it is not advisable for me to take her to my home.   Your Electoral Grace is therefore humbly implored to make an allowance from the 400 rth. vacated for an increase of my salary so that I may not need to draw upon the little savings and my mother may receive the pension graciously for the few years which she

may yet live, to deserve which high grace it shall always be my
striving.

Your Electoral Grace's
Most humble and obedient
Servant and musicus jean van Beethoven.

There is something bordering on the comic in the coolness
of the hint here given that the petitioner would not object to an
appointment as his father's successor, especially when it is remembered that Lucchesi and Mattioli were already in Bonn and the
former had sufficiently proved his capacity by producing successful operas, both text and music, for the Elector's delectation.
The hint was not taken; what provision was granted him, however, may be seen from a petition of January 8, 1774, praying
for an addition to his salary from that made vacant by the death
of his father, and a pension to his mother who is kept at board
in a cloister. A memorandum appears on the margin to the effect
that the Elector graciously consents that the widow, so long as
she remains in the cloister, shall receive 60 rth. quarterly.
Another petition of a year later has been lost, but its contents are
indicated in the response, dated June 5, 1775, that Johann van
Beethoven on the death of his mother shall have the enjoyment
of the 60 rth. which had been granted her. The death of the
mother followed a few months later and was thus announced in
the "Intelligenzblatt" of Bonn on October 3, 1775: "Died, on
September 30, Maria Josepha Pals (*sic*), widow van Beethoven,
aged 61 years." In a list of salaries for 1776 (among the papers
at Düsseldorf) for the "Musik Parthie" the salary of Johann van
Beethoven is given at 36 rth. 45 alb. payable quarterly. The
fact of the great poverty in which he and his family lived is manifest from the official documents (which confirm the many traditions to that effect) and from the more important recollections of
aged people of Bonn brought to light in a controversy concerning the birthplace of the composer. For instance, Dr. Hennes,
in his unsuccessful effort to establish the claims of the Fischer
house in the Rheingasse, says: "The legacy left him (Johann van
Beethoven) by his father did not last long. That fine linen,
which, as I was told, could be drawn through a ring, found its way,
piece by piece, out of the house; even the beautiful large portrait
showing the father wearing a tasseled cap and holding a roll of
music, went to the second-hand shop." This is an error, though
the painting may have gone for a time to the pawnbroker.

From the Bonngasse the Beethovens removed, when, is uncertain, to a house No. 7 or No. 8 on the left as one enters the

Dreieckplatz in passing from the Sternstrasse to the Münsterplatz. They were living there in 1774, for the baptism of another son on the 8th of April of that year is recorded in the register of the parish of St. Gangolph, to which those houses belonged. This child's name was Caspar Anton Carl, the first two names from his sponsor the Minister Belderbusch, the third from Caroline von Satzenhofen, Abbess of Vilich. Was this condescension on the part of the minister and the abbess intended to soothe the father under the failure of his hopes of advancement? From the Dreieckplatz the Beethovens migrated to the Fischer house, No. 934 in the Rheingasse, so long held to be the composer's birthplace and long thereafter distinguished by a false inscription to that effect. Whether the removal took place in Ludwig's fifth or sixth year is not known; but at all events it was previous to the 2nd of October, 1776, for upon that day another son of Johann van Beethoven was baptized in the parish of St. Remigius by the name of Nicholas Johann. Dr. Hennes in his letter to the "Kölnische Zeitung" lays much stress upon the testimony of Cäcilia Fischer. He says: "the maiden lady of 76 years, Cäcilia Fischer, still remembers distinctly to have seen little Louis in his cradle and can tell many anecdotes about him, etc." The mistake is easily explained without supposing any intentional deception:—62 years afterwards she mistook the birth of Nicholas Johann for that of Ludwig. According to Fischer's report the family removed from this house in 1776 for a short time to one in the Neugasse, but returned again to the house in the Rheingasse after the palace fire in 1777. One thought which suggests itself in relation to these removals of Johann van Beethoven may, perhaps, be more than mere fancy: that in expectation of advancement in position upon the death of his father he had exchanged the narrow quarters of the lodging in the rear of the Clasen house for the much better dwelling in the Dreieckplatz; but upon the failure of his hopes had been fain to seek a cheaper place in the lower part of the town down near the river.

There is nothing decisive as to the time when the musical education of Ludwig van Beethoven began, nor any positive evidence that he, like Handel, Haydn or Mozart, showed remarkable genius for the art at a very early age. Schlosser has something on this point, but he gives no authorities, while the particulars which he relates could not possibly have come under his own observation. Müller[1] had heard from Franz Ries and

---

[1] "Allg. Mus.-Ztg.," May 23. 1827.

Nicholas Simrock that Johann van Beethoven gave his son instruction upon the pianoforte and violin "in his earliest childhood.
. . . To scarcely anything else did he hold him." In the
dedication of the pianoforte sonatas (1783) to the Elector, the
boy is made to say: "Music became my first youthful pursuit
in my fourth year," which might be supposed decisive on the point
if his age were not falsely given on the title-page. This much is
certain: that after the removal to the Fischer house the child
had his daily task of musical study and practice given him and in
spite of his tears was forced to execute it. "Cäcilia Fischer,"
writes Hennes (1838), "still sees him, a tiny boy, standing on a
little footstool in front of the clavier to which the implacable severity of his father had so early condemned him. The patriarch of
Bonn, Head Burgomaster Windeck, will pardon me if I appeal to
him to say that he, too, saw the little Louis van Beethoven in this
house standing in front of the clavier and weeping." To this
writes Dr. Wegeler:

> I saw the same thing. How? The Fischer house was, perhaps
> still is, connected by a passage-way in the rear with a house in the
> Giergasse, which was then occupied by the owner, a high official of the
> Rhenish revenue service, Mr. Bachen, grandfather of Court Councillor
> Bachen of this city. The youngest son of the latter, Benedict, was my
> schoolmate, and on my visits to him the doings and sufferings of Louis
> were visible from the house.

It must be supposed that the father had seen indications of
his son's genius, for it is difficult to imagine such an one remaining
unperceived; but the necessities of the family with the failure
of the petition for a better salary—sent in just at the time when
the Elector was so largely increasing his expenditures for music
by the engagement of Lucchesi and Mattioli and in other ways—
are sufficient reasons for the inflexible severity with which the
boy was kept at his studies. The desire to say something new
and striking on the part of many who have written about Beethoven has led to such an admixture of fact and fancy that it is
now very difficult to separate them. One (Schlosser) tells his
readers that "the greatest joy of the lad was when his father took
him upon his knees and permitted him to accompany a song on
the clavier with his tiny fingers," while others tell the tale of
his childhood in a manner to convey the idea that the father was
a pitiless tyrant, the boy a victim and a slave—an error which
a calm consideration of what is really known of the facts in the
case at once dispels. There is but one road to excellence, even
for the genius of a Handel or a Mozart—unremitted application.

To this young Ludwig was compelled, sometimes, no doubt, through the fear or the actual infliction of punishment for neglect; sometimes, too, the father, whose habits were such as to favor a bad interpretation of his conduct, was no doubt harsh and unjust. And such seems to be the truth. At any rate, the boy at an early date acquired so considerable a facility upon the clavier that his father could have him play at court and when he was seven years old produce him with one of his pupils at a concert in Bonn. Here is the announcement of the concert as it was reproduced in the "Kölnische Zeitung" of December 18, 1870, from the original:

AVERTISSEMENT

To-day, March 26, 1778, in the musical concert-room in the Sternengasse the Electoral Court Tenorist, Beethoven, will have the honor to produce two of his scholars, namely, Mlle. Averdonck, Court Contraltist, and his little son of six years. The former will have the honor to contribute various beautiful arias, the latter various clavier concertos and trios. He flatters himself that he will give complete enjoyment to all ladies and gentlemen, the more since both have had the honor of playing to the greatest delight of the entire Court.

Beginning at five o'clock in the evening.

Ladies and gentlemen who have not subscribed will be charged a florin. Tickets may be had at the aforesaid Akademiesaal, also of Mr. Claren auf der Bach in Mühlenstein.

Unfortunately we learn nothing concerning the pieces played by the boy nor of the success of his performance. That the violin as well as the pianoforte was practised by him is implicitly confirmed by the terms in which Schindler records his denial of the truth of the well-known spider story: "The great Ludwig refused to remember any such incident, much as the tale amused him. On the contrary, he said it was more to be expected that everything would have fled from his scraping, even flies and spiders."

The father's main object being the earliest and greatest development of his son's musical genius so as to make it a "marketable commodity," he gave him no other school education than such as was afforded in one of the public schools. Fischer says he first attended a school in the Neugasse taught by a man named Huppert[1] and thence went to the Münsterschule. Among the lower grade schools in Bonn was the so-called Tirocinium, a Latin school, which prepared pupils for the gymnasium but was not

---

[1]There was no teacher of this name in Bonn at the time. There was a Rupert, however, who may have been the one meant by Fischer.

directly connected with it, but had its own corps of teachers, like
the whole educational system of the period, under the supervision
of the Academic Council established by Max Friedrich in 1777.
The pupils learned, outside of the elementary studies (arithmetic
and writing are said to have been excluded), to read and write
Latin up to an understanding of Cornelius Nepos. Johann Krengel,
a much respected pedagogue, was teacher at the time and was
appointed municipal schoolmaster in 1783 by the Academic
Council. In 1786 he transferred the school to the Bonngasse.
To this school young Beethoven was sent; when, is uncertain.
His contemporary and schoolfellow Wurzer, Electoral Councillor
and afterwards president of the Landgericht, relates the following
in his memoirs:[1]

> One of my schoolmates under Krengel was Luis van Beethoven,
> whose father held an appointment as court singer under the Elector.
> Apparently his mother was already dead at the time,[2] for Luis v. B. was
> distinguished by uncleanliness, negligence, etc. Not a sign was to be
> discovered in him of that spark of genius which glowed so brilliantly
> in him afterwards. I imagine that he was kept down to his musical
> studies from an early age by his father.

Wurzer entered the gymnasium in 1781; Beethoven did not.
This, therefore, must have been the time at which all other studies
were abandoned in favor of music. _In what manner his education was otherwise pieced out is not to be learned. The lack of
proper intellectual discipline is painfully obvious in Beethoven's
letters throughout his life. In his early manhood he wrote a
fair hand, so very different from the shocking scrawl of his later
years as to make one almost doubt the genuineness of autographs
of that period; but in orthography, the use of capital letters,
punctuation and arithmetic he was sadly deficient all his life long.
He was still able to use the French tongue at a later period, and
of Latin he had learned enough to understand the texts which
he composed; but even as a schoolboy his studies appear to have
been made second to his musical practice with which his hours
out of school were apparently for the most part occupied. He
was described by Dr. Müller as "a shy and taciturn boy, the necessary consequence of the life apart which he led, observing more
and pondering more than he spoke, and disposed to abandon
himself entirely to the feelings awakened by music and (later)

---

[1]These memoirs are in manuscript. They were formerly in the possession of Dr.
Bodifée of Bonn, later in the Town Hall.

[2]Error; Beethoven's mother did not die until 1787, long after he had left school.

by poetry and to the pictures created by fancy." Of those who were his schoolfellows and who in after years recorded their reminiscences of him, not one speaks of him as a playfellow, none has anecdotes to relate of games with him, rambles on the hills or adventures upon the Rhine and its shores in which he bore a part. Music and ever music; hence the power of clothing his thoughts in words was not developed by early culture, and the occasional bursts of eloquence in his letters and recorded conversations are held not to be genuine, because so seldom found. As if the strong mind, struggling for adequate expression, should not at times break through all barriers and overcome all obstacles![1] Urged forward thus by the father's severity, by his tender love for his mother and by the awakening of his own tastes, the development of his skill and talents was rapid; so much so that in his ninth year a teacher more competent than his father was needed.

The first to whom his father turned was the old court organist van den Eeden, who had been in the electoral service about fifty years and had come to Bonn before the arrival there of Ludwig van Beethoven, the grandfather. One can easily imagine his willingness to serve an old and deceased friend by fitting his grandson to become his successor; and this might account for Schlosser's story that at first he taught him gratis, and that he continued his instructions at the command and expense of the Elector. The story may or may not be true, but nothing has been discovered in the archives at Düsseldorf confirming the statement; in fact concerning the time, the subjects and the results of van den Eeden's instruction we are thrown largely upon conjecture. "In his eighth year," says Mäurer in his notices, "Court Organist van den Eeden took him as a pupil; nothing

---

[1]Thayer's characterization of the joyless boyhood of Beethoven may submit to a slight modification, at least so far as his childhood is concerned, without violence to the verities of history. Fischer would have us believe that the lad took part with his brother Carl in boyish capers which were not always of a harmless character. In a letter to Simrock, Court Councillor Krupp relates: "My father, who died in 1847, was a youthful friend and schoolmate of Ludwig and Carl van Beethoven, and distantly related to the godmother of the former. Thursdays were holidays for the schoolboys, and the brothers Beethoven, L. and C., were then wont to come to the house of my grandparents, No. 28 Bonngasse (now belonging to my sister and me), and amuse themselves, among other things, with target shooting. There was a wall between the garden of our house and the gardens of the adjoining houses in the Wenzelgasse against which the target was placed at which the boys shot arrows; a hit in the centre brought forth a *Stuber* (about 4 pfennigs) for the lucky marksman. Garden and wall are now (1890) in the same condition as then. In the evening the Beethoven brothers went home through the Gudenauergässchen. The family lived at the time in the Wenzelgasse back of our house." Here is an inaccuracy, for Ludwig van Beethoven no longer went to school when the Beethoven family changed their house in the Rheingasse for that in the Wenzelgasse—which was probably about 1785. The letter continues: "Ludwig's father treated him harshly, especially when he was intoxicated, and sometimes shut him up in the cellar."

has been learned of his progress." This, if Mäurer was correct in stating his age, would have been about 1778. It is after this that Mäurer refers to his study under Pfeiffer. Independently of all this Fischer says: "His father not being able to teach him more in music, and suspecting that he had talent for composition, took him at first to an aged master named Santerrini who instructed him for a while; but the father thought little of this teacher, did not consider him the right man and desired a change." This desire resulted in securing Pfeiffer through the mediation of Grossmann. There was no musician Santerrini in the court chapel, but an actor, named Santorini, was a member of Grossmann's troupe; he cannot be considered in this connection. There is evidently a confusion of names, and the whole context, especially the reference to the "aged master," shows that no other than van den Eeden was meant by the teacher who gave instruction for a short time before Pfeiffer.

Schlosser does not say that this instruction was on the organ and it is unlikely that the boy, who was destined for a more systematic instruction in pianoforte playing, was put at the organ at so early an age. It was a deduction, probably, from the fact that van den Eeden was an organist and that later Beethoven displayed a great deal of dexterity upon that instrument. It is noteworthy that Wegeler (p. 11) says nothing definite as to whether or not Beethoven took lessons from van den Eeden; he merely thought it likely, because he knew no one else in Bonn from whom Beethoven could have learned the technical handling of the organ. But there were several such in Bonn irrespective of Neefe. Schindler makes certainty out of Wegeler's conjecture and relates that Beethoven often spoke of the old organist when discoursing upon the proper position and movement of the body and hands in organ and pianoforte playing, he having been taught to hold both calm and steady, to play in the connected style of Handel and Bach. This may have been correct so far as pianoforte playing is concerned; but Schindler had little knowledge of Beethoven's Bonn period, and the possibility of a confusion of names is not excluded even on the part of Beethoven himself, who received hints from several organists. Mäurer, after speaking of Pfeiffer, continues as follows: "Van den Eeden remained his only teacher in thorough-bass. As a man of seventy he sent the boy Louis, between eleven and twelve years old, to accompany the mass and other church music on the organ. His playing was so astonishing that one was forced to believe he had intentionally concealed his gifts. While preluding for the *Credo* he

took a theme from the movement and developed it to the amazement of the orchestra so that he was permitted to improvise
longer than is customary. That was the opening of his brilliant
career." Mäurer seems to know nothing of Neefe when he says
that van den Eeden was Beethoven's only teacher in thoroughbass. What he says, too, about the lad's performance at the
organ as substitute obviously rests upon a confounding of van
den Eeden with another of Beethoven's organ teachers—most
likely Neefe.

It is our conjecture that van den Eeden taught the boy chiefly
and perhaps exclusively pianoforte playing, he being a master
in that art; but his influence was small. It must be remembered
that van den Eeden was a very old man, as whose successor
Neefe had been chosen in 1781, and who died in June, 1782.
Nowhere does he, like the other teachers of Beethoven, disclose
individual traits; he is a totally colorless picture in the history
of Beethoven's youth. Nor does it appear that there was any
intimacy between him and the Beethoven family, since otherwise he would not have been missing in the notices of Fischer,
who does not even know his name. The judgment of the father
that his instruction was inefficient was probably correct.

A fitter master, it was thought, was obtained in Tobias
Friedrich Pfeiffer, who came to Bonn in the summer of 1779, as
tenor singer in Grossmann and Helmuth's theatrical company.
Mäurer, the violoncellist, in some reminiscences of that period communicated to this work by Professor Jahn, says that Pfeiffer was
a skillful pianist and gave the boy lessons, but not at any regular
hours. Often when he came with Beethoven, the father, from
the wine-house late at night, the boy was roused from sleep and
kept at the pianoforte until morning;—a course not particularly
favorable to his progress at school, but one which may be readily
credited in the light of what is known of Pfeiffer and Johann Beethoven, and one, moreover, which would cause the lessons to make
an enduring impression upon the memory. There is some reason
to think that the former was an inmate of the latter's family,
which adds probability to the story. Although Pfeiffer was in
Bonn but one year, Wegeler affirms that "Beethoven owed most
of all to this teacher, and was so appreciative of the fact that
he sent him financial help from Vienna through Simrock." To
what extent Wegeler's opinion as to Beethoven's obligations is
correct, it would be difficult to decide; but the utter improbability that a single year's lessons from this man would profit a
boy eight and a half to nine and a half years old, more than those

from any other of his teachers, much longer and systematically continued, is manifest. About this time the young court musician Franz Georg Rovantini lived in the same house with Beethoven. He was the son of a violinist Johann Conrad Rovantini who had been called to Bonn from Ehrenbreitstein and who died in 1766. He was related to the Beethoven family. The young musician was much respected and sought after as teacher. According to the Fischer document the boy Beethoven was among his pupils, taking lessons on the violin and viola. But these lessons, too, came to an early end; Rovantini died on September 9, 1781, aged 24.

A strong predilection for the organ was awakened early in the lad and he eagerly sought opportunities to study the instrument, apparently even before he became Neefe's pupil. In the cloister of the Franciscan monks at Bonn there lived a friar named Willibald Koch, highly respected for his playing and his expert knowledge of organ construction. We have no reason to doubt that young Ludwig sought him out, received instruction from him and made so much progress that Friar Willibald accepted him as assistant. In the same way he made friends with the organist in the cloister of the Minorites and "made an agreement" to play the organ there at 6 o'clock morning mass. It would seem that he felt the need of familiarity with a larger organ than that of the Franciscans. On the inside of the cover of a memorandum book which he carried to Vienna with him is found the note: "Measurements (*Fussmass*) of the Minorite pedals in Bonn." Plainly he had kept an interest in the organ. Still another tradition is preserved in a letter to the author from Miss Auguste Grimm, dated September, 1872, to the effect that Heinrich Theisen, born in 1759, organist at Rheinbreitbach near Honneck on the Rhine, studied the organ in company with Beethoven under Zenser, organist of the Münsterkirche at Bonn, and that the lad of ten years surpassed his fellow student of twenty. The tradition says that already at that time Ludwig composed pieces which were too difficult for his little hands. "Why, you can't play that, Ludwig," his teacher is said to have remarked, and the boy to have replied: "I will when I am bigger."

When Beethoven's studies with van den Eeden began and ended, whether they were confined to the organ or pianoforte, or partook of both—these are undecided points. It does not appear that any instruction in composition was given him until he became the pupil of Neefe. In the *facsimile* which follows the part devoted to thorough-bass in the so-called "Studien," the composer says: "Dear Friends: I took the pains to learn this only that I might write the figures readily and later instruct others; for myself I never had to learn how to avoid errors, for from my childhood I had so keen a sensibility that I wrote correctly without knowing it had to be so, or could be otherwise." This lends plausibility, at least, to another anecdote related by Mäurer concerning an alleged precocious composition by Beethoven:

About this time the English Ambassador to the Elector's court, named Kressner, who had extended help to the Beethoven family, living scantily on a salary of 400 fl. [?], died. Louis composed a funeral cantata to his memory—his first composition. He handed his score to Lucchesi and asked him to correct the errors. Lucchesi gave it back with the remark that he could not understand it, and therefore could not comply with his request, but would have it performed. At the first rehearsal there was great astonishment at the originality of the composition, but approval was divided; after a few rehearsals the approbation grew and the piece was performed with general applause.

George Cressener came to Bonn in the autumn of 1755, and died there January 17, 1781, in the eighty-first year of his age. The "about this time" in Mäurer's story agrees, therefore, well enough with that date; it is, however, a suspicious circumstance that Mäurer had left the service and returned to Cologne in the Spring of 1780 and, therefore, was not eye-witness to the fact; and another that the circumstance was not remembered by other members of the court chapel, not even by Franz Ries, nor by Neefe, who, though not then a member, was already in Bonn. "In 1780," continues Mäurer, "Beethoven got acquainted with Zambona, who called his attention to his neglected education, gave him lessons daily in Latin, Louis continuing a year (in six weeks he read Cicero's letters!)—also logic, French and Italian—until Zambona left Bonn in order to become bookkeeper for Bartholdy in Mühlheim." In the "Geheime Staats-Conferenz Protocollen," May 20, 1787, one reads: "Stephan Zambona prays to be appointed, *Kammerportier*, etc.," to which is appended the remark: "the request not granted." Zambona is a name, too, which, half a dozen years later, often appears in the Bonn "Intelligenzblatt," as that of a shopkeeper in the Market Place of that town. If the story of the cantata be doubtful, that of these private studies on the part of a boy in Beethoven's position, only in his tenth year and a schoolboy then if ever, like Hamlet's possible dreams in the sleep of death, must "give us pause."

Mother and son undertook a voyage to Holland in the beginning of the winter of 1781. The widow Karth, one of the Hertel family, born in 1780 and still living in Bonn in 1861, passed her childhood in the house No. 462 Wenzelgasse in the upper story of which the Beethovens then lived. One of her reminiscences is in place here. She distinctly remembered sitting, when a child, upon her own mother's knee, and hearing Madame van Beethoven— "a quiet, suffering woman"—relate that when she went with her little boy Ludwig to Holland it was so cold on the boat that she had to hold his feet in her lap to prevent them from being frostbitten; and also that, while absent, Ludwig played a great deal in great houses, astonished people by his skill and received valuable presents. The circumstance of the cold feet warmed in the mother's lap, is precisely one to fasten itself in the memory of a child and form a point around which other facts might cluster.[1]

Another incident related in connection with this journey to Holland—not as a fact, but as one which she had heard spoken of in her childhood—and one very difficult to comprehend, is, that some person, whether an envious boy or a heartless adult she could not tell, drew a knife across the fingers of Ludwig to disable him from playing!

[1] There seems to have been no knowledge on the part of Beethoven's biographers of this visit to Holland until Thayer brought the incident to notice. It is, therefore, highly significant that the Fischer family also recalled the circumstance and, besides, knew what brought it about. The sister of young Rovantini, who died in September, 1781, was employed as governess in Rotterdam, and on receiving intelligence of the death of her brother came to Bonn, together with her mistress (whose name has not been preserved), to visit his grave. For a month she was an inmate of the Beethoven house; there was a good deal of music-making and some excursions to neighboring places of interest, including Coblenz. The visitors invited the Beethoven family to make a trip to Holland. Inasmuch as Johann van Beethoven could not get away, the mother went with the lad, and, a party of five, they embarked upon the voyage. This must have been in October or November, 1781, which agrees with the story of the extreme cold encountered on the voyage. They remained a considerable time, but whether or not Ludwig gave a concert as he had intended, is not known. Despite the attentions showered upon him by the wealthy lady from Rotterdam and the many honors, the pecuniary results were disappointing. To Fischer's question how he had fared Beethoven is reported to have answered: "The Dutch are skinflints (*Pfennigfuchser*); I'll never go to Holland again."

Chapter IV

Beethoven a Pupil of Neefe—His Talent and Skill Put to
Use—First Efforts at Composition—Johann van Beethoven's Family—Domestic Tribulations.

CHRISTIAN GOTTLOB NEEFE succeeded the persons mentioned as Beethoven's master in music. When this tutorship
began and ended, and whether or not it be true that the Elector engaged and paid him for his services in this capacity, as affirmed
by divers writers—here again positive evidence is wanting. Neefe
came to Bonn in October, 1779; received the decree of succession
to the position of Court Organist on February 15, 1781, and was
thus permanently engaged in the Elector's service. The unsatisfactory nature of the earlier instruction, as well as the high reputation of Neefe, placed in the strongest light before the Bonn
public by those proceedings which had compelled him to remain
there, would render it highly desirable to Johann van Beethoven
to transfer his son to the latter's care. It would create no surprise
should proof hereafter come to light that this change was made
even before the issue of the decree of February 15, 1781;—that
even then the pupil was profiting by the lessons of the zealous
Bachist. Whether this was so or not, it was more than ever
necessary that the boy's talents should be put to profitable use,
for the father found his family still increasing. The baptism
of a daughter named Anna Maria Franciska after her sponsors
Anna Maria Klemmers, *dicta* Kochs, and Franz Rovantini, court
musician, is recorded in the St. Remigius register February 23,
1779, and her death on the 27th of the same month. The baptism
of August Franciscus Georgius van Beethoven—Franz Rovantini,
Musicus Aulicus and Helene Averdonk, *patrini,* follows nearly
two years later—January 17, 1781. There is no minister of
State now to lend his name to a child of Johann van Beethoven,
nor any lady abbess. Rovantini, one of the youngest members
of the orchestra (relative and friend of the family), and a Frau
Kochs, the young contralto, whose musical education the father

had superintended, take their places—another indication that the head of the family is gradually sinking in social position.

It is Schlosser who states that "the Elector urged Neefe to make it his particular care to look after the training of the young Beethoven." How much weight is to be attached to this assertion of a man who hastily threw a few pages together soon after the death of the composer, and who begins by adopting the old error of 1772 as the date of his birth, and naming his father "Anton," may safely be left to the reader. That the story may possibly have some foundation in truth is not denied; but the probabilities are all against it. Just in these years Max Friedrich is busy with his tric-trac, his balls, his new operettas and comedies, and with his notion of making the theatre a school of morals. The truth seems to be (and it is the only hypothesis that suggests itself, corresponding to the established facts), that Johann van Beethoven had now determined to make an organist of his son as the surest method of making his talents productive. The appointment of Neefe necessarily destroyed Ludwig's hope of being van den Eeden's successor; but Neefe's other numerous employments would make an assistant indispensable, and to this place the boy might well aspire. It will be seen in the course of the narrative that Beethoven never had a warmer, kinder and more valuable friend than Neefe proved throughout the remainder of his Bonn life; that, in fact, his first appointment was obtained for him through Neefe, although this is the first hint yet published that the credit does not belong to a very different personage. What, then, so natural, so self-evident as that Neefe, foreseeing the approaching necessity of some one to take charge of the little organ in the chapel at times when his duties to the Grossmann company would prevent him from officiating in person, should gladly undertake the training of the remarkable talents of van den Eeden's pupil with no wish for any other remuneration than the occasional services which the youth could render him?

Dr. Wegeler remarks: "Neefe had little influence upon the instruction of our Ludwig, who frequently complained of the too severe criticisms made on his first efforts in composition." The first of these assertions is evidently an utter mistake. In 1793 Beethoven himself, at all events, thought differently: "I thank you for the counsel which you gave me so often in my progress in my divine art. If I ever become a great man yours shall be a share of the credit. This will give you the greater joy since you may rest assured," etc. Thus he wrote to his old teacher. As to the complaint of harsh criticism it may be remarked that

Neefe, reared in the strict Leipsic school, must have been greatly dissatisfied with the direction which the young genius was taking under the influences which surrounded him, and that he should labor to change its course. He was still a young man, and in his zeal for his pupil's progress may well have criticized his childish compositions with a severity which, though no more than just and reasonable, may have so contrasted with injudicious praise from other quarters as to wound the boy's self-esteem and leave a sting behind; especially if Neefe indulged in a tone at all contemptuous, a common fault of young men in like cases. Probably, in some conversation upon this point Beethoven may have remarked to Wegeler that Neefe had criticized him in his childhood rather too severely.

But to return from the broad field of hypothesis to the narrow path of facts. "On this day, June 20, 1782," Neefe writes of himself and the Grossmann company, "we entered upon our journey to Münster, whither the Elector also went. The day before my predecessor, Court Organist van den Eeden, was buried; I received permission, however, to leave my duties in the hands of a vicar and go along to Westphalia and thence to the Michaelmas fair at Frankfort." The Düsseldorf documents prove that this vicar was Ludwig van Beethoven, now just eleven and a half years of age. In the course of the succeeding winter, Neefe prepared that very valuable and interesting communication to 'Cramer's Magazine" which has been so largely quoted. In this occurs the first printed notice of Beethoven, one which is honorable to head and heart of its author. He writes, under date of March 2, 1783:

Louis van Beethoven, son of the tenor singer mentioned, a boy of eleven years and of most promising talent. He plays the clavier very skilfully and with power, reads at sight very well, and—to put it in a nutshell—he plays chiefly "The Well-Tempered Clavichord" of Sebastian Bach, which Herr Neefe put into his hands. Whoever knows this collection of preludes and fugues in all the keys—which might almost be called the *non plus ultra* of our art—will know what this means. So far as his duties permitted, Herr Neefe has also given him instruction in thoroughbass. He is now training him in composition and for his encouragement has had nine variations for the pianoforte, written by him on a march—by Ernst Christoph Dressler—engraved at Mannheim. This youthful genius is deserving of help to enable him to travel. He would surely become a second Wolfgang Amadeus Mozart were he to continue as he has begun.

This allusion to Mozart, who had not then produced those immortal works upon which his fame now principally rests, speaks

well for the insight of Neefe and renders his high appreciation of
his pupil's genius the more striking.   Had this man then really
so little influence upon its development as Wegeler supposed?
That C. P. E. Bach's works were included in Neefe's course
of instruction is rendered nearly certain by the following facts:
he was himself a devout student of them; the only reference to
his father made by Beethoven in all the manuscripts examined
for this work, an official document or two excepted, is upon an
unfinished copy of one of Bach's cantatas in these words: "Written
by my dear father;"[1] and one of the works most used by him in
compiling his "Materialien für Contrapunkt" in 1809 was Bach's
"Versuch über die wahre Art das Clavier zu Spielen."   The unlucky remark of Wegeler, founded, too, possibly upon some expression of Beethoven's in a moment of spleen, but certainly not
in justice, has cast a shadow upon the relation between Neefe
and his pupil.   Writer after writer has copied without examining
it.   Does it bear examination?   Possibly, if it be supposed to
relate only to execution upon the pianoforte and organ; but in
no other case.   It is self-evident that serious study in the severe
school of the Bachs was necessary to counteract the influence of
the light and trivial music of the Bonn stage upon the young
genius; and to Neefe the credit of seeing this and acting accordingly must be given.   The reader's attention is called particularly to the words "He is now training him in composition, and
for his encouragement has had nine variations for the pianoforte
written by him on a march by Dressler engraved at Mannheim,"
in Neefe's notice of Beethoven above cited, and the date of the
article from which it is taken—March 2, 1783.   Is it not perfectly clear that these variations have been recently composed,
and very recently printed?   Yet upon the title stands, "Par un
jeune amateur, Louis van Beethoven, âgé de dix ans."   If this
were a solitary case of apparent discrepancy between the boy's
age and the year given it would attract and deserve no notice;
but it is one of many and adds its weight to the evidence of that
falsification already spoken of.[2]

[1] "Morgengesang am Schöpfungstage."

[2] As given by Nottebohm in his catalogue (p. 154) the title of the original publication of the Variations by Goetz of Mannheim ran as follows: *Variations pour le Clavecin
sur une Marche de Mr. Dressler, composées et Dediées à son Excellence Madame la Comtesse
de Wolfmetternich, née Baronne d'Assebourg, par un jeune amateur Louis van Beethoven,
âgé de dix ans. 1780."*   Inasmuch as Nottebohm's Notes on Thayer's "Chronologisches
Verzeichniss" do not give the date 1780, it was probably appended by mistake.   In the
delle Sinfonie, etc., che si trovanno in manoscritto nella officina de Breitkopf in Lipsia, under
the compositions of 1782, 1783 and 1784: *Variations da Louis van Beethoven, âgé de dix
ans, Mannheim,* with the theme in notation.   The Countess Wolff-Metternich, to whom

A second work belonging to this period is a two-part fugue in D for the organ.[1]

To return to the young organist, who, since the publication of Wegeler's "Notizen," has always been supposed to have been placed at that instrument by the Elector Max Franz in the year 1785, as a method of giving him pecuniary aid without touching his feelings of pride and independence. The place of assistant to Neefe was no sinecure; although not involving much labor, it brought with it much confinement. The old organ had been destroyed by the fire of 1777, and a small chamber instrument still supplied its place. It was the constantly recurring necessity of being present at the religious services which made the position onerous.

On all Sundays and regular festivals (says the Court Calendar) high mass at 11 a.m. and vespers at 3 (sometimes 4) p. m. The vespers will be sung throughout in *Capellis solemnibus* by the musicians of the electoral court, the middle vespers will be sung by the court clergy and musicians chorally as far as the *Magnificat*, which will be performed music-ally. On all Wednesdays in Lent the *Miserere* will be sung by the chapel at 5 p.m. and on all Fridays the *Stabat mater*. Every Saturday at 3 p.m. the Litanies at the altar of Our Lady of Loretto. Every day throughout the year two masses will be read, the one at 9, the other at 11—on Sundays the latter at 10.

Such a programme gave the organist something at least to do, and when Neefe left Bonn for Münster, June 20, 1782, he left his pupil no easy task. Before the close of the theatrical season of the next winter (1782–'83) the master was obliged to call upon the boy for still farther assistance. "In the winter of 1784," writes the widow Neefe, "my husband of blessed memory was tempo-rarily entrusted with the direction of the church music as well as other music at court while the Electoral Chapelmaster L. was absent on a journey of several months." The date is wrong, for Lucchesi's petition for leave of absence was granted April 26, 1783. Thus overwhelmed with business, Neefe could no longer conduct at the pianoforte the rehearsals for the stage, and Ludwig van

the variations are dedicated, was the wife of Count Ignaz von Wolff-Metternich, "Kon-ferenzmeister" and president of the High Court of Appeals, who died in Bonn, March 15, 1790. Ernst Christoph Dressler, composer of the theme varied by Beethoven, was an opera singer in Cassel.

[1]The Bagatelles for Pianoforte, Op. 33, included by Thayer in his MSS. and his "Chronologisches Verzeichniss" as also belonging to this period on the strength of their superscription on a manuscript copy, "Louis van Beethoven . . . 1782," were, as Notte-bohm has shown, not composed at this time. One of them was composed in 1802 and another sketched between 1799 and 1801. See Nottebohm ("Zweite Beethoveniana," p. 250). Nottebohm conjectures that the organ fugue was composed at his trial for the post of second court organist. In view of the fact that his age was falsified by his father at this time, it is likely that the work was composed in 1783.

Beethoven, now 12 years old, became also "cembalist in the orchestra." In those days every orchestra was provided with a harpsichord or pianoforte, seated at which the director guided the performance, playing from the score. Here, then, was in part the origin of that marvellous power, with which in later years Beethoven astonished his contemporaries, of reading and playing the most difficult and involved scores at first sight. The position of cembalist was one of equal honor and responsibility. Handel and Matthison's duel grew out of the fact that the former would not leave the harpsichord on a certain occasion before the close of the performance. Gassmann placed the young Salieri at the harpsichord of the Imperial Opera House as the best possible means of training him to become the great conductor that he was. This was the high place of honor given to Haydn when in London. In Ludwig van Beethoven's case it was the place in which he, as Mosel says of Salieri, "could make practical use of what he learned from books and scores at home." Moreover, it was a place in which he could, even in boyhood, hear to satiety the popular Italian, French and German operas of the day and learn to feel that something higher and nobler was necessary to touch the deeper feelings of the heart; a place which, had the Elector lived ten years longer, might have given the world another not merely great but prolific, nay inexhaustible, operatic composer. The cembalist's duties doubtless came to an end with the departure of the Elector for Münster in May or June, and he then had time for other pursuits, of which composition was one. A song, "Schilderung eines Mädchens," by him was printed this year in Bossler's "Blumenlese für Liebhaber," and a Rondo in C for pianoforte, anonymous, which immediately follows, was also of his composition. A more important work, which before the close of the year was published by Bossler with a magniloquent dedication to Max Friedrich, was the three sonatas for pianoforte, according to the title, if true, "composed by Ludwig van Beethoven, aged 11 years."[1] The reader can judge whether or not the 11 should be 12.

To turn for a moment to the Beethoven family matters. This summer (1783) had brought them some sorrow again. The child Franz Georg, now just two and a half years old, died

---

[1]Title of the original publication: "Drei Sonaten für Klavier, dem Hochwürdigsten Erzbischofe und Kurfürsten zu Koln, Maximilian Friedrich meinem gnädigsten Herrn gewidmet und verfertigt von Ludwig van Beethoven, alt eilf Jahr." Beethoven wrote on a copy of the sonatas: "These Sonatas and the Variations of Dressler are my first works." He probably meant his first published works. See Thayer's "Chronologisches Verzeichniss," p. 2, 183.

August 16th. This was another stroke of bad fortune which not only wounded the heart but added to the pecuniary difficulties of the father, who was now losing his voice and whose character is described in an official report made the next summer by the words "of tolerable conduct." If the duties of Neefe during the last season had been laborious, in the coming one, 1783-'84, they were still more arduous. It was the first under the new contract by which the Elector assumed all the costs of the theatre, and a woman, Mme. Grossmann, had the direction. It was all-important to singers, actors and whoever was concerned that the result of the experiment should be satisfactory to their employer; and as the opera was more to his taste than the spoken drama, so much the more difficult was Neefe's task. Besides his acting as chapelmaster in the place of Lucchesi, still absent, there was "every forenoon rehearsal of opera," as Mme. Grossmann wrote to Councillor T., at which, of course, Neefe had to be present. There was ever new music to be examined, arranged, copied, composed—what not?—all which he must attend to; in short, he had everything to do which could be imposed upon a theatrical music director with a salary of 1,000 florins. It therefore became a busy time for his young assistant, who still had no recognition as member of the court chapel, not even as "accessist"—the last "accessist" organist was Meuris (1778)—and consequently no salary from the court. But he had now more than completed the usual year of probation to which candidates were subjected, and his talents and skill were well enough known to warrant his petition for an appointment. The petition has not been dis-covered; but the report made upon it to the privy council has been preserved, together with the following endorsement: "High Lord Steward Count von Salm, referring to the petition of Ludwig van Beethoven for the position of Assistant Court Organist, is of the humble opinion that the grace ought to be bestowed upon him, together with a small compensation." This endorsement is dated "Bonn, February 29, 1784." The report upon the petition is as follows:

Most Reverend Archbishop and Elector,
Most Gracious Lord, Lord.

Your Electoral Grace has graciously been pleased to demand a dutiful report from me on the petition of Ludwig van Beethoven to Your Grace under date the 15th inst.

Obediently and without delay (I report) that suppliant's father was for 29 years, his grandfather for 46, in the service of Your Most Reverend Electoral Grace and Your Electoral Grace's predecessors; that the suppliant has been amply proved and found capable to play the court

organ as he has done in the absence of Organist Neefe, also at rehearsals
of the plays and elsewhere and will continue to do so in the future; that
Your Grace has graciously provided for his care and subsistence (his
father no longer being able to do so).   It is therefore my humble judgment that for these reasons the suppliant well deserves to have graciously
bestowed upon him the position of assistant at the court organ and an
increase of remuneration.   Commending myself to the good will of Your
Most Reverend Electoral Grace I am Your Most Reverend Grace's

most humble and obedient servant

Bonn, February 23, 1784.   Sigismund Altergraff zu
Salm und Reifferscheid.

The action taken is thus indicated:

Ad Sup.
> Ludwig van Beethoven.
> On the obedient report the suppliant's submissive prayer,
granted. (*Beruhet.*)

Bonn, February 29, 1784.

Again, on the cover:

Ad sup.
> Lud. van Beethoven,
Granted. (*Beruhet.*)   Sig. Bonn, February 29, 1784.

The necessity of the case, the warm recommendation of
Salm-Reifferscheid, very probably, too, the Elector's own knowledge of the fitness of the candidate, and perhaps the flattery in
the dedication of the sonatas—for these were the days when dedications but half disguised petitions for favor—were sufficient
inducements to His Transparency at length to confirm the young
organist in the position which Neefe's kindness had now for nearly
two years given him.   Opinions differ as to the precise meaning
of the word *Beruhet* (translated "granted" in the above tran-
scripts); but this much is certain: Beethoven was not appointed
assistant organist in 1785 by Max Franz at the instance of Count
Waldstein, but at the age of 13 in the spring of 1784 by Max
Friedrich, and upon his own petition supported by the influence
of Neefe and of Salm-Reifferscheid.

The appointment was made, but the salary had not been
determined on when an event occurred which wrought an entire
change in the position of theatrical affairs at Bonn:—the Elector
died on April 15, and the theatrical company was dismissed
with four weeks' wages.   There was no longer a necessity for
a second organist; and fortunate it was for the assistant that
his name came before Max Friedrich's successor (in the reports
soon to be copied) as being a regular member of the court chapel,
although "without salary."   Lucchesi returned to Bonn; Neefe

had nothing to do but play his organ, cultivate his garden outside the town and give music lessons. It was long before such a conjunction of circumstances occurred as would have led the economical Max Franz to appoint an organist adjunct. Happy was it, therefore, that one of the deceased Elector's last acts secured young Beethoven the place.

The excellent Frau Karth, born in 1780, could not recall to memory any period of her childhood down to the death of Johann van Beethoven, when he and his family did not live in the lodging above that of her parents. This fact, together with the circumstance that no mention is made of the Beethovens in the account of the great inundation of the Rhine in February, 1782, when all the families dwelling in the Fischer house of the Rheingasse were rescued in boats from the windows of the first story, added to the strong probability that Beethoven's position was but the first formal step of the regular process of confirming an appointment already determined upon;—these points strongly suggest the idea that to Ludwig's advancement his father owed the ability to dwell once more in a better part of the town, i.e., in the pleasant house No. 462 Wenzelgasse. The house is very near the Minorite church, which contained a good organ, concerning the pedal measurements of which, as we have seen, Beethoven made a memorandum in a note-book which he carried with him to Vienna.[1] In the "Neuen Blumenlese für Klavierliebhaber" of this year, Part I, pp. 18 and 19, appeared a Rondo for Pianoforte, in A major, "dal Sig.ᵉ van Beethoven"[2]; and Part II, p. 44, the Arioso "An einen Säugling, von Hrn. Beethoven."[3] "Un Concert pour le Clavecin ou Fortepiano composé par Louis van Beethoven âgé de douze ans," 32 pp. manuscript written in a boy's hand, may also belong to this year[4]; and, judging by the handwriting, to the

---

[1]The editor has here thought it advisable to permit Thayer's original text to stand in the body of the book, although Dr. Deiters made a radical correction in his revision of the first volume of the biography. On the basis of the Fischer manuscript Dr. Deiters relates that the Beethoven family lived in the house in the Rheingasse at the time of the inundation; that Beethoven's mother sought to stay the alarm of the inmates with encouraging words, but at the last had to make her escape with the others into the Giergasse over boards and down ladders. Admitting that there are many inaccuracies in the recital, Dr. Deiters nevertheless accepts it in this particular and conjectures that Beethoven lived in the house in the Rheingasse until 1785.

[2]B. and H. Ges. Ausg. Serie 18, No. 196.

[3]B. and H. Ges. Ausg. Serie 23, No. 229.

[4]The manuscript contains the solo part complete with the orchestral preludes and interludes in transcription for pianoforte. There are indications that it was scored for small orchestra—strings, flutes and horns only. The composition was long unknown. Thayer included it in his "Chronologisches Verzeichniss" under No. 7, giving the themes. Guido Adler edited it at a much later date, and it has been published in the supplement to the collected works of Beethoven.

period may also be assigned a movement in three parts of four pages, formerly in the Artaria collection, without title, date or remark of any kind.[1]

The widow Karth perfectly remembered Johann van Beethoven as a tall, handsome man with powdered head. Ries and Simrock described Ludwig to Dr. Müller "as a boy powerfully, almost clumsily built."[2] How easily fancy pictures them—the tall man walking to chapel or rehearsal with the little boy trotting by his side, through the streets of Bonn, and the gratified expression of the father as the child takes the place and performs the duties of a man!

[1]Nottebohm conjectured that the movement referred to by Thayer was that for a musical clock, No. 29, in Thayer's chronological catalogue, there described as a duo. Dr. Deiters thinks that it was a fragment of a composition for pianoforte and violin, No. 131 in the catalogue of the Artaria collection. It contains suggestions of Beethoven's style, but the manuscript is a copy, not an autograph, and its authenticity is not proven.

[2]In the Fischer MS.: "Short of stature, broad shoulders, short neck, large head, round nose, dark brown complexion; he always bent forward slightly when he walked. In the house he was called der Spagnol (the Spaniard)."

Chapter V

Maria Theresia—Appearance and Character of Elector
Max Franz—Musical Culture in the Austrian Im-
perial Family—A Royal Violinist—His Admiration for
Mozart—His Court Music.

Maria Theresia was a tender mother, much concerned to see all her
children well provided for in her lifetime and as independent as possible
of her eldest son, the heir to the throne. This wish had already been
fulfilled in the case of several of them. . . . The youngest son, Maximilian (born in Vienna, December 8, 1756), was already chosen coadjutor
to his paternal uncle, Duke Karl of Lorraine, Grand Master of the Teutonic Order. But to provide a more bountiful and significant support,
Prince Kaunitz formulated a plan which pleased the maternal heart of
the monarch, and whose execution was calculated to extend the influence
of the Court of Vienna in the German Empire. It was to bestow more
ecclesiastical principalities upon the Archduke Maximilian. His eyes
fell first upon the Archbishopric and Electorate of Cologne and the Archbishopric and Principality of Münster. These two countries had one
and the same Regent, Maximilian Friedrich, descended from the Suabian
family of Königseck-Rothenfels, Counts of the Empire. In view of the
advanced age of this ruler his death did not seem far distant; but it was
thought best not to wait for that contingency, but to secure the right of
succession at once by having the Archduke elected Coadjutor in Cologne
and Münster. Their possession was looked upon as a provision worthy
of the son of an Empress-Queen. As Elector and Lord of the Rhenish
shore, simultaneously co-director of the Westphalian Circuit (a dignity
associated with the archbishopric of Münster), he could be useful to his
house, and oppose the Prussian influence in the very part of Germany
where it was largest.

THUS Dohm begins the seventh chapter of his "Denkwürdig-
keiten" where, in a calm and passionless style, he relates the
history of the intrigues and negotiations which ended in the
election of Maria Theresia's youngest son on August 7, 1780, as
coadjutor to the Elector of Cologne and, on the 16th of the same
month, to that of Münster, and secured him the peaceful and immediate succession when Max Friedrich's functions should cease.
The news of the election at Cologne reached Bonn on the same
day about 1 o'clock p. m. The Elector proceeded at once to the

Church of the Franciscans (used as the chapel since the conflagration of 1777), where a "musical 'Te Deum' " was sung, while all the city bells were ringing.   Von Kleist's regiment fired a triple salvo, which the cannon on the city walls answered.   At noon a public dinner was spread in the palace, one table setting 54, another 24 covers.   In the evening at 8 1-2 o'clock, followed the finest illumination ever seen in Bonn, which the Elector enjoyed riding about in his carriage.   After this came a grand supper of 82 covers, then a masked ball "to which every decently clad subject as well as any stranger was admitted, and which did not come to an end till nearly 7 o'clock."

Max Franz was in his twenty-eighth year when he came to Bonn.   He was of middle stature, strongly built and already inclining to that corpulence which in his last years made him a prodigy of obesity.   If all the absurdities of his eulogists be taken for truth, the last Elector of Cologne was endowed with every grace of mind and character that ever adorned human nature. In fact, however, he was a good-looking, kindly, indolent, somewhat choleric man; fond of a joke; affable; a hater of stiff ceremony; easy of access; an honest, amiable, conscientious ruler, who had the wisdom and will to supply his own deficiencies with enlightened and skilful ministers, and the good sense to rule, through their political foresight and sagacity, with an eye as much to the interests of his subjects as his own.

In his boyhood he was rather stupid.   Swinburne dismisses him in two lines: "Maximilian is a good-natured, neither here-nor-there kind of youth."   The brilliant, witty, shrewdly observant Mozart wrote to his father (Nov. 17, 1781): "To whom God gives an office he also gives an understanding.   This is really the case with the Archduke.   Before he became a priest he was much wittier and more intellectual and talked less, but more sensibly. You ought to see him now!   Stupidity looks out of his eyes; he talks eternally, always in falsetto; he has a swollen neck—in a word, the man is completely transformed."   His mother had supplied him with the best instructors that Vienna afforded, and had sent him travelling pretty extensively for an archduke in those days.   One of his journeys was to visit his sister Marie Antoinette in Paris, where his awkwardness and breaches of etiquette caused as much amusement to the anti-Austrian party as they did annoyance to the Queen, and afterwards to his brother Joseph, when they came to his ears.

In 1778 he was with Joseph in the campaign in Bavaria.   An injury to his knee, caused by a fall of his horse, is the reason alleged for his abandonment of a military career; upon which he was prevailed upon, so the "Historisches Taschenbuch" (II, Vienna, 1806) expresses it, to become a candidate for the Coadjutorship of Cologne. If he had to be "prevailed upon" to enter the church, the more to his credit was the course he pursued when once his calling and election were sure.

The rigid economy which he introduced at court immediately after his accession in 1784 gave rise to the impression that he was penurious. It may be said in his defence that the condition of the finances required retrenchment and reform; that he was simple in his tastes and cared nothing for show and magnificence, except upon occasions when, in his opinion, the electoral dignity required them. Then, like his predecessors, he was lavish. His personal expenses were not great, and he waited until his revenues justified it before he indulged to any great extent his passion for the theatre, music and dancing (stout as he was, he was a passionate dancer), and his table. He was, through the nature of his physical constitution, an enormous eater, though his drink was only water.

The influence of a ruler upon the tone and character of society in a small capital is very great. A change for the better had begun during the time of Max Friedrich, but under his successor a new life entered Bonn. New objects of ambition were offered to the young men. The church and cloister ceased to be all in all. One can well understand how Wegeler in his old age, as he looked back half a century to the years when he was student and professor— and *such* a half-century, with its revolutionary and Napoleonic wars, its political, religious and social changes!—should write ("Notizen," p. 59): "In fact, it was a beautiful and in many ways active period in Bonn, so long as the genial Elector, Max Franz, Maria Theresia's youngest son and favorite, reigned there." How strongly the improved tone of society impressed itself upon the characters of the young is discernible in the many of them who, in after years, were known as men of large and liberal ideas and became distinguished as jurists, theologians and artists, or in science and letters. These were the years of Beethoven's youth and early manhood; and though his great mental powers were in the main exercised upon his art, there is still to be observed through all his life a certain breadth and grandeur in his intellectual character, owing in part, no doubt, to the social influences under which it was developed.

It is highly honorable to the young Max Franz that he refused to avail himself of a privilege granted him in a Papal bull obtained for him by his mother—that of deferring the assumption of priestly vows for a period of ten years—but chose rather, as soon as he had leisure for the step, to enter the seminary in Cologne to fit himself for consecration. He entered November 29, rigidly submitted himself to all the discipline of the institution for the period of eight days, when, on December 8, the nuntius, Bellisoni, ordained him sub-deacon; after another eight days, on the 16th, deacon; and on the 21st, priest; thus showing that if there be no royal road to mathematics, there is a railway with express train for royal personages in pursuit of ecclesiastical science. Returning to Bonn, he read his first mass on Christmas eve in the Florian Chapel.

The cause of science and education the Elector had really at heart. In 1785 he had established a botanic garden; now he opened a public reading room in the palace library and sent a message to the theological school in Cologne, that if the improved course of instruction adopted in Austria was not introduced, he should found other seminaries. On the 26th of June he was present at the opening of a normal school; and on August 9th came the decree raising the Bonn Hochschule to the rank of a university by authority of an Imperial diploma.

Upon the suppression of the Jesuits in 1774, Max Friedrich devoted their possessions and revenues to the cause of education. New professorships were established in the gymnasium and in 1777 an "Academy" was formed. This was the first step; the second was to found an independent institution called the Lyceum; and at his death an application was before the Emperor for a university charter. Max Franz pushed the matter, obtained the charter from his brother, and Monday, the 20th of November, 1786, was the day appointed for the solemn inauguration of the new institution. The Court Calendar for the next year names six professors of theology, six of jurisprudence, civil and ecclesiastical, four of medicine, and ten of philology and other branches of learning. In later editions new names are added; in that of 1790, Wegeler is professor of midwifery.

Though economical, Max Franz drew many a man of superior abilities—men of letters and artists—to Bonn; and but for the bursting of the storm which was even then gathering over the French border, his little capital might well have had a place in German literary history not inferior to that of Weimar. Nor are instances wanting in which he gave generous aid to young talent struggling with poverty; though that he did so much for Beethoven as is usually thought is, at least, doubtful.

This man, not a genius, not overwhelmingly great mentally, nor, on the other hand, so stupid as the stories told of his boyhood seem to indicate, but honest, well-meaning, ready to adopt and enforce wise measures devised by skilful ministers; easy, jocose and careless of appearances, very fond of music and a patron of letters and science,—this man, to whom in that period of vast intellectual fermentation the Index Expurgatorius was a dead letter, gave the tone to Bonn society.

That solid musical education which she had received from her father, Maria Theresia bestowed upon her children, and their attainments in the art seem to have justified the time and labor spent. In 1749, at the age of seven and six, Christina and Maria Elizabeth took part in one of the festive musical pieces; Marie Antoinette was able to appreciate Gluck and lead the party in his favor in later years at Paris. Joseph is as much known in musical as in civil and political history. When Emperor he had his daily hour of music in his private apartments, playing either of several instruments or singing, according to the whim of the moment; and Maximilian, the youngest, acquired a good degree of skill both in singing and in the treatment of his favorite instrument, the viola. Beethoven once told Schindler that the Elector thought very highly of Mattheson. In his reminiscences of a visit to Vienna in 1783, J. F. Reichardt gives high praise to the musical interest, skill and zeal of Emperor Joseph and his brother Archduke Maximilian, and a writer in "Cramer's Magazine," probably Neefe, tells of a "remarkable concert" which took place at court in Bonn on April 5, 1786, at which the Elector played the viola, Duke Albrecht the violin, "and the fascinating Countess Belderbusch the clavier most charmingly."

Maximilian had become personally acquainted with Mozart in Salzburg in 1775, where the young composer had set Metastasio's "Il Re pastore" to music to be performed in his honor (April 23rd); from which time, to his credit be it said, he ever held the composer and his music in kindest remembrance. When in 1781 Mozart determined to leave his brutal Archbishop of Salzburg and remain in Vienna, the Archduke showed at all events a desire to aid him.

Yesterday (writes the composer November 17, 1781) the Archduke Maximilian summoned me to him at 3 o'clock in the afternoon. When I entered he was standing before a stove in the first room awaiting me. He came towards me and asked if I had anything to do to-day? "Nothing, Your Royal Highness, and if I had it would always be a grace to wait upon Your Royal Highness." "No; I do not wish to constrain anyone." Then he said that he was minded to give a concert in the evening for the Court of Wurtemberg. Would I play something and accompany the aria? I was to come to him again at 6 o'clock. So I played there yesterday.

Mozart was everything to him (continues Jahn); he signalized him at every opportunity and said, if he were Elector of Cologne, Mozart would surely be his chapelmaster. He had also suggested to the Princess (of Wurtemberg) that she appoint Mozart her music teacher, but received the reply that if it rested with her she would have chosen him; but the Emperor—"for him there is nobody but Salieri!" cries out Mozart peevishly—had recommended Salieri because of the singing, and she had to take him, for which she was sorry.

Jahn gives no reason why Mozart was not engaged for Bonn. Perhaps he would have been had Lucchesi resigned in consequence of the reduction of his salary; but he kept his office of chapelmaster and could not well be dismissed without cause. Mattioli's resignation was followed by the call of Joseph Reicha to the place of concertmaster; but for Mozart no vacancy occurred at that time. Maximilian was in Vienna during most of the month of October, 1785, and may have desired to secure Mozart in some way, but just at that time the latter was, as his father wrote, "over head and ears busy with the opera 'Le Nozze di Figaro.'" Old Chapelmaster Bono could not live much longer; which gave him hope, should the opera succeed, of obtaining a permanent appointment in Vienna; and, in short, his prospects seemed just then so good that his determination—if he should really receive an offer from the Elector—to remain in the great capital rather than to take his young wife so far away from home and friends as the Rhine then was, and, in a manner, bury himself in a small town where so few opportunities would probably be given him for the exercise of the vast powers which he was conscious of possessing, need not surprise us.

Was it the good or the ill fortune of the boy Beethoven that Mozart came not to Bonn? His marvellous original talents were thus left to be developed without the fostering care of one of the very greatest of musical geniuses, and one of the profoundest of musical scholars; but on the other hand it was not oppressed, perhaps crushed, by daily intercourse with that genius and scholarship.

Maximilian, immediately after reaching Bonn as Elector, ordered full and minute reports to be made out concerning all branches of the administration, of the public and court service and of the cost of their maintenance. Upon these reports were based his arrangements for the future. Those relating to the court music are too important and interesting to be overlooked, for they give us details which carry us instantly into the circle which young Beethoven has just entered and in which, through his father's connection with it, he must from earliest childhood have moved. They are three in number, the first being a list of all the individuals constituting the court chapel; the second a detailed description of the singers and players, together with estimates of their capabilities; the third consists of recommendations touching a reduction in salaries. A few paragraphs may be presented here as most intimately connected with significant personages in our history; they are combined and given in abstract from the first two documents. Among the tenors we find

J. van Beethoven, age 44, born in Bonn, married; his wife is 32 years old, has three sons living in the electorate, aged 13, 10 and 8 years, who are studying music, has served 28 years, salary 315 fl. "His voice has long been stale, has been long in the service, very poor, of fair deportment and married."

Among the organists:

Christian Gottlob Neefe, aged 36, born at Chemnitz; married, his wife is 32, has served 3 years, was formerly chapelmaster with Seiler; salary 400 fl. "Christian Neffe, the organist, in my humble opinion might well be dismissed, inasmuch as he is not particularly versed on the organ, moreover is a foreigner, having no *Meritten* whatever and of the Calvinistic religion."
Ludwig van Beethoven, aged 13, born at Bonn, has served 2 years, no salary. "Ludwig Betthoven, a son of the Betthoven *sub* No. 8, has no salary, but during the absence of the chapelmaster Luchesy he played the organ; is of good capability, still young, of good and quiet deportment and poor."

One of the items of the third report, proposing reductions of salaries and removals, has a very special interest as proving that an effort was made to supplant Neefe and give the post of court organist to young Beethoven. It reads:

Item. If Neffe were to be dismissed another organist would have to be appointed, who, if he were to be used only in the chapel could be had for 150 florins, the same is small, young, and a son of a court *musici*, and in case of need has filled the place for nearly a year very well.

The attempt to have Neefe dismissed from the service failed, but a reduction of his salary to the pittance of 200 florins had already led him to look about him to find an engagement for himself and wife in some theatre, when Maximilian, having become acquainted with his merits (notwithstanding his Calvinism), restored his former allowance by a decree dated February 8, 1785. When Joseph Reicha came to Bonn in Mattioli's place is still undetermined with exactness; but a decree raising him from the position of concertmaster to that of concert director, and increasing his salary to 1,000 florins, bears date June 28, 1785. In the general payroll of this year Reicha's salary is stated to be 666 thalers 52 alb., "tenorist Beethoven's" 200 th., "Beethoven jun." 100 th.

Chapter VI

Beethoven Again—The Young Organist—A First Visit to
Vienna—Death of Beethoven's Mother—Sympathetic
Acquaintances—Dr. Wegeler's "Notizen"—Some Questions of Chronology.

SCHINDLER records—and on such points his testimony is
good—that he had heard Beethoven attribute the marvellous
development of Mozart's genius in great measure to the "consistent instruction of his father," thus implying his sense of the disadvantages under which he himself labored from the want of regular
and systematic musical training through the period of his childhood and youth.[1] It is, however, by no means certain that had
Ludwig van Beethoven been the son of Leopold Mozart, he would
ever have acquired that facility of expression which enabled
Wolfgang Mozart to fill up the richest and most varied scores
almost as rapidly as his pen could move, and so as hardly to need
correction—as if the development of musical idea was to him a
work of mere routine, or perhaps, better to say, of instinct. *Poeta
nascitur, non fit*, not only in respect to his thoughts but to his
power of clothing them in language. Many a man of profoundest ideas can never by any amount of study and practice acquire
the art of conveying them in a lucid and elegant manner. On
the other hand there are those whose thoughts never rise above
the ordinary level, but whose essays are very models of style.
Handel said of the elder Telemann, that he could compose in
eight parts as easily as he (Handel) could write a letter; and
Handel's own facility in composition was something astonishing.
Beethoven, on the contrary, as his original scores prove, earned
his bread by the sweat of his brow. But no amount of native
genius can compensate for the want of thorough training. If,
therefore, it be true that nature had in some degree limited his

[1]Czerny also related that Beethoven had spoken to him of the harsh treatment
and insufficient instruction received from his father. "But," he added, "I had talent
for music." From a note by Otto Jahn. Also see Cock's "Musical Miscellany."

powers of expressing his musical as well as his intellectual ideas, so much greater was the need that, at the age which he had now reached, he should have opportunity to prosecute uninterruptedly a more profound and systematic course of study. Hence, the death of Maximilian Friedrich, which must have seemed to the Beethovens at first a sad calamity, proved in the end a blessing in disguise; for while it did not deprive the boy of the pecuniary benefits of the position to which he had just been appointed, it gave him two or three years of comparative leisure, uninterrupted save by his share of the organist's duties, for his studies, which there is every reason to suppose he continued under the guidance of his firm friend Neefe.

These three years were a period of theatrical inactivity in Bonn. For the carnival season of 1785, the Elector engaged Böhm and his company, then playing alternately at Cologne, Aix-la-Chapelle and Düsseldorf. This troupe during its short season may have furnished the young organist with valuable matter for reflection, for in the list of newly studied pieces, from October 1783 to the same month 1785—thus including the engagement in Bonn—are Gluck's "Alceste" and "Orpheus," four operas of Salieri (the "Armida" among them), Sarti's "Fra due Litiganti" and "L'Incognito" in German translation, Holzbauer's "Günther von Schwarzburg" and five of Paisiello's operas. These were, says the report in the "Theater-Kalender" (1786), "in addition to the old and familiar French operettas, 'Zémire et Azor,' 'Sylvain,' 'Lucile,' 'Der Prächtige,' 'Der Hausfreund,' etc., etc." The three serious Vienna operas, "Alceste," "Orpheus" and "Armida," in such broad contrast to the general character of the stock pieces of the Rhenish companies, point directly to Maximilian and the Bonn season. The elector of Hesse-Cassel, being then in funds by the sale of his subjects to George III for the American Revolutionary War just closed, supported a large French theatrical company, complete in the three branches of spoken and musical drama and ballet. Max Franz, upon his return from Vienna in November, 1785, spent a few days in Cassel, and, upon the death of the Elector and the dismissal of the actors, a part of this company was engaged to play in Bonn during January and February, 1786. The performances were thrice a week, Monday, Wednesday and Saturday, and, with but two or three exceptions, consisted of a comedy, followed by a light opera or operetta. The list contains eight of Grétry's compositions, three by Desaides, two by Philidor, and one each by Sacchini, Champein, Pergolesi, Gossec, Frizieri, Monsigny and

Schwarzendorf (called Martini)—all of light and pleasing character, and enjoying then a wide popularity not only in France but throughout the Continent.

Meantime Grossmann had left Frankfort and with Klos, previously a manager in Hamburg, had formed a new company for the Cologne, Bonn and Düsseldorf stages. This troupe gave the Carnival performances in 1787, confining them, so far as appears, to the old round of familiar pieces.

Each of these companies had its own music director. With Böhm was Mayer, composer of the "Irrlicht" and several ballets; with the French company Jean Baptiste Rochefort was "music-master"; and Grossmann had recently engaged Burgmüller, of the Bellomo company, composer of incidental music for "Macbeth." Hence, during these years, Neefe's public duties extended no farther than his service as organist, for Lucchesi and Reicha relieved him from all the responsibilities of the church and concert-room.

That the organ service was at this time in part performed by the assistant organist is a matter of course; there is also an anecdote, related by Wegeler on the authority of Franz Ries, which proves it. On Tuesday, Friday and Saturday of Holy Week, portions of the Lamentations of Jeremiah were included in the chapel service, recited by a single voice, accompanied on the pianoforte (the organ being interdicted) to the familiar Gregorian chant tune.

On one occasion, in the week ending March 27, 1785, the vocalist was Ferdinand Heller, too good a musician to be easily disconcerted, the accompanist Ludwig van Beethoven, now in his fifteenth year.' While the singer delivered the long passages of the Latin text to the reciting note the accompanist might indulge his fancy, restricted only by the solemnity fitted to the service. Wegeler relates that Beethoven

asked the singer, who sat with unusual firmness in the tonal saddle, if he would permit him to throw him out, and utilized the somewhat too readily granted permission to introduce so wide an excursion in the accompaniment while persistently striking the reciting note with his little finger, that the singer got so bewildered that he could not find the closing cadence. Father Ries, the first violinist, then Music Director of the Electoral Chapel, still living, tells with details how Chapelmaster Lucchesi, who was present, was astonished by Beethoven's playing. In his first access of rage Heller entered a complaint against Beethoven with the Elector, who commanded a simpler accompaniment, although the spirited and occasionally waggish young prince was amused at the occurrence. Schindler adds that Beethoven in his last years remembered the circumstance, and said that the Elector had "reprimanded him very graciously and forbidden such clever tricks in the future."

The date is easily determined: In Holy Week, 1784, neither Maximilian nor Lucchesi was in Bonn; in 1786 Beethoven's skill would no longer have astonished the chapelmaster. Of the other characteristic anecdotes related of Beethoven's youth there is not one which belongs to this period (May, 1784–April, 1787), although some have been attributed to it by previous writers.

Nothing is to be added to the record already made except that, on the authority of Stephan von Breuning, the youth was once a pupil of Franz Ries on the violin, which must have been at this time; that, according to Wegeler, his composition of the song "Wenn Jemand eine Reise thut"[1] fell in this period, and that he wrote three pianoforte quartets, the original manuscript of which bore the following title: "Trois Quatuors pour Clavecin, violino, viola e basso. 1785. Composé par (de L.) Louis van Beethoven, âgé 13 ans."[2] The reader will remark and understand the discrepancy here between the date and the author's age. Were these quartets intended for publication and for dedication to Max Franz, as the sonatas had been for Max Friedrich? During their author's life they never saw the light, but their principal themes, even an entire movement, became parts of future works. They were published in 1832 by Artaria and appear as Nos. 75 and 77, Series 10, in the Complete Works.

One family event is recorded in the parish register of St. Remigius—the baptism of Maria Margaretha Josepha, daughter of Johann van Beethoven, on May 5, 1786.

There is a letter from Bonn, dated April 8, 1787, in "Cramer's Magazine" (II, 1385), which contains a passing allusion to Beethoven. It affords another glimpse of the musical life there:

Our residence city is becoming more and more attractive for music-lovers through the gracious patronage of our beloved Elector. He has a large collection of the most beautiful music and is expending much every day to augment it. It is to him, too, that we owe the privilege of hearing often virtuosi on various instruments. Good singers come seldom. The love of music is increasing greatly among the inhabitants. The pianoforte is especially liked; there are here several *Hammerclaviere* by Stein of Augsburg, and other correspondingly good instruments. . . . The youthful Baron v. Gudenau plays the pianoforte right bravely, and besides young Beethoven, the children of the chapelmaster deserve

---

[1] "Urian's Reise um die Welt," Op. 52, No. 1, published in 1805.

[2] The manuscript formerly owned by Artaria is now (1907) in the possession of Dr. E. Prieger in Bonn. The figure indicating the composer's age was first written "14" and then changed.

to be mentioned because of their admirable and precociously developed talent. All of the sons of Herr v. Mastiaux play the clavier well, as you already know from earlier letters of mine.

"This young genius deserves support to enable him to travel," wrote Neefe in 1783. In the springtime of 1787 the young "genius" was at length enabled to travel. Whence or how he obtained the means to defray the expenses of his journey, whether aided by the Elector or some other Mæcenas, or dependent upon the small savings from his salary and—hardly possible—from the savings from his music lessons painfully and carefully hoarded for the purpose, does not appear. The series of papers at Düsseldorf is at this point broken; so that not even the petition for leave of absence has been discovered. The few indications bearing on this point are that he had no farther aid from the Elector than the continued payment of his salary. What is certain is that the youth, now sixteen, but passing for a year or two younger, visited Vienna, where he received a few lessons from Mozart (Ries, in "Notizen," page 86); that his stay was short, and that on his way home he was forced to borrow some money in Augsburg.

When he made the journey is equally doubtful. Schindler was told by some old acquaintances of Beethoven "that on the visit two persons only were deeply impressed upon the lifelong memory of the youth of sixteen years: the Emperor Joseph and Mozart." If the young artist really had an interview with the Emperor it must have occurred before the 11th of April, or after the 30th of June, for those were the days which began and ended Joseph's absence from Vienna upon his famous tour to the Crimea with the Russian Empress Catharine; if before that absence, then Beethoven was at least three months in the Austrian capital and had left Bonn before the date of Neefe's letter to "Cramer's Magazine"; in which case how could the writer in speaking of his young colleague have omitted all mention of the fact? How, too, could so important a circumstance have been unknown to or forgotten by Dr. Wegeler and have found no place in his "Notizen," which moreover, were prepared under the eyes of both Franz Ries and Madame von Breuning? It will soon be seen that Beethoven was again in Bonn before July 17—a date which admits the bare possibility of the reported meeting with Joseph after his return from Russia.

If an opinion, which, indeed, is little more than a conjecture, may be hazarded in relation with this visit, it is this: that if at any time the missing archives of Maximilian's court should come to light it will be found that not until after the busy week for organists and chapelmusicians ending with Easter was leave of absence granted to Beethoven; and that, too, with no farther pecuniary aid from the Elector than possibly a quarter or two of his salary in advance. In 1787, Easter Monday fell upon the 9th of April, the day after the date of Neefe's letter. Making due allowance of time for the necessary preparations for so important a journey, as in those days it was from Bonn to Vienna, it may be reasonably conjectured that some time in May the youth reached the latter city.

Let another conjecture find place here: it is that Johann van Beethoven had not yet abandoned the hope of deriving pecuniary profit from the precocity of his son's genius; that he still expected the boy, after replacing his hard organ-style of playing by one more suited to the character of the pianoforte, to make his dream of a wonder-child in some degree a reality. Hence—at what fearful cost to the father in his poverty we know not—Ludwig is sent to the most admirable pianist, the best teacher then living, Mozart.

But enough of conjecture. The oft-repeated anecdote of Beethoven's introduction to Mozart is stripped by Prof. Jahn of Seyfried's superlatives and related in these terms:

Beethoven, who as a youth of great promise came to Vienna in 1786 (?)[1], but was obliged to return to Bonn after a brief sojourn, was taken to Mozart and at that musician's request played something for him which he, taking it for granted that it was a show-piece prepared for the occasion, praised in a rather cool manner. Beethoven observing this, begged Mozart to give him a theme for improvization. He always played admirably when excited and now he was inspired, too, by the presence of the master whom he reverenced greatly; he played in such a style that Mozart, whose attention and interest grew more and more, finally went silently to some friends who were sitting in an adjoining room, and said, vivaciously, "Keep your eyes on him; some day he will give the world something to talk about."

Ries ("Notizen," p. 86) merely says: "During his visit to Vienna he received some instruction from Mozart, but the latter, as Beethoven lamented, never played for him." Contrary to the conjecture above mentioned as to Johann van Beethoven's object in sending his son to Vienna, it seems, from the connection in which Ries introduces this remark, that the instruction given by Mozart to the youth was confined to composition. The lessons given were few—a fact which accounts for the circumstance that

[1]In the first edition of Jahn's "Mozart" the date is given as here. In later editions it was corrected in accordance with Thayer's suggestion to 1787.

no member of Mozart's family in after years, when Beethoven had become world-renowned, has spoken of them.

If it be considered that poor Mozart lost his beloved father on May 28, 1787, and that his mind was then fully occupied with his new operatic subject, "Don Giovanni," it will not be thought strange that he did not exhibit his powers as a pianist to a youth just beginning with him a course of study in composition, especially as the pupil, in his eyes, was a little, undersized boy of 14—as there is every reason to believe. That pupil's power of handling a theme, since Mozart probably knew nothing of his five years' practice at the organ and in the theatre, may well have surprised him; but in execution as a pianist he probably stood far, far below the master when at the same age, below the little Hummel (at that very time an inmate of Mozart's family), and certainly below Cesarius Scheidl (forgotten name!) aged ten, who had played a pianoforte concerto between the parts of an oratorio no longer ago than the preceding 22nd of December in the grand concert of the "Society of Musicians." Had not Beethoven's visit been so abruptly, unexpectedly and sorrowfully brought to an end, he would, doubtless, have had nothing to regret on the score of his master's playing.

In some written talks to Beethoven in the years of his deafness, still preserved, are found two allusions at least made by his nephew to this personal acquaintance with Mozart. In the first case the words are these: "You knew Mozart; where did you see him?" In the other, two or three years later: "Was Mozart a good pianoforte player? It was then still in its infancy." Of course Beethoven's replies are wanting; and herewith is exhausted all that, during the researches for this work, has been found relating to his first visit in Vienna. The Vienna newspapers of the time contained notices of the "wonder-children" Hummel and Scheidl, but none whatever of Beethoven.

That the youth in passing through Augsburg must have become acquainted with the pianoforte-maker Stein and his family is self-evident. There is something in a conversation-book which seems to prove this, and also to add evidence to the falsification of his age. It is this: in the spring of 1824 Andreas Streicher and his wife—the same Stein's "Mädl"—whose appearance at the pianoforte when a child of eight and a half years is so piquantly described by Mozart, called upon Beethoven on their way from Vienna into the country. A few sentences of the conversation, written in the hand of the composer's nephew, are preserved. The topic for a time is the packing of movables and Beethoven's removal into country lodgings for the summer; and at length they come upon the instruments manufactured by Streicher; after which Carl writes: "Frau von Streicher says that she is delighted that at 14 years of age you saw the instruments made by her father and now see those of her son." True, it may be said that this refers to Beethoven's knowledge of the Stein "Hammerclaviere" then in Bonn; but to any one thoroughly conversant with the subject these words are, like Iago's "trifles light as air," confirmation strong of the other view. His introduction to the family of the advocate Dr. Schaden in Augsburg, is certain. Reichardt was in that city in 1790 and wrote of Frau Nanette von Schaden as being of all the women he knew, those of Paris not excepted, far and away the greatest pianoforte player, not excelled perhaps, by any virtuoso in skill and certainty; also a singer with much expression and excellent declamation—"in every respect an amiable and interesting woman." The earliest discovered letter of Beethoven to Schaden, and dated Bonn, September 15, 1787, proves the friendship of the Schadens for him and fully explains the causes of his sudden departure from Vienna and the abrupt termination of his studies with Mozart.

I can easily imagine what you must think of me, and I can not deny that you have good grounds for an unfavorable opinion. I shall not, however, attempt to justify myself, until I have explained to you the reasons why I hope my apologies will be accepted. I must tell you that from the time I left Augsburg my cheerfulness as well as my health began to decline; the nearer I came to my native city the more frequent were the letters from my father urging me to travel with all possible speed, as my mother was not in a favorable state of health. I therefore hurried forward as fast as I could, although myself far from well. My longing once more to see my dying mother overcame every obstacle and assisted me in surmounting the greatest difficulties. I found my mother still alive but in the most deplorable state; her disease was consumption, and about seven weeks ago, after much pain and suffering, she died. She was such a kind, loving mother to me, and my best friend. Ah, who was happier than I when I could still utter the sweet name, mother, and it was heard? And to whom can I now speak it? Only to the silent image resembling her evoked by the power of the imagination. I have passed very few pleasant hours since my arrival here, having during the whole time been suffering from asthma, which may, I fear, eventually develop into consumption; to this is added melancholy—almost as great an evil as my malady itself. Imagine yourself in my place, and then I shall hope to receive your forgiveness for my long silence. You showed me extreme kindness and friendship by lending me three Carolins in Augsburg, but I must entreat your indulgence for a time. My journey cost me a great deal, and I have not the smallest hopes of earning anything here. Fate is not propitious to me in Bonn.

Pardon my detaining you so long with my chatter; it was necessary for my justification.

I do entreat you not to deprive me of your valuable friendship; nothing do I wish so much as in some degree to become worthy of your regard.

I am, with the highest respect
Your most obedient servant and friend,
L. v. Beethoven,
Court Organist to the Elector of Cologne.[1]

The Bonn "Intelligenzblatt" supplies a pendant to this sad letter:—"1787, July 17. Died, Maria Magdalena Koverich (*sic*), named van Beethoven, aged 49 years."[2] When Ferdinand Ries, some thirteen years later, presented his father's letter of introduction to Beethoven in Vienna, the latter "read the letter through" and said: "I cannot answer your father just now; but do you write to him that I have not forgotten how my mother died. He will be satisfied with that." "Later," adds Ries, "I learned that, the family being greatly in need, my father had been helpful to him on this occasion in every way."

A petition of Johann van Beethoven, offered before the death of his wife, describing his pitiable condition and asking aid from the Elector, has not been discovered; but the substance of it is found in a volume of "Geheime Staats-Protocolle" for 1787 in form following:

July 24, 1787

Your Elec. Highness has taken possession of this petition.

Court Musician makes obedient representation that he has got into a very unfortunate state because of the long-continued sickness of his wife and has already been compelled to sell a portion of his effects and pawn others and that he no longer knows what to do for his sick wife and many children. He prays for the benefaction of an advance of 100 rthlr. on his salary.

No record is found in the Düsseldorf archives of any grant of aid to the distressed family; hence, so far as now appears, the only successful appeal for assistance was made to Franz Ries, then a young man of 32 years, who generously aided in "every way" his unfortunate colleague. Where then was the Breuning family? Where Graf Waldstein? To these questions the reply is that Beethoven was still unknown to them—a reply which involves the

---

[1]Lady Wallace's translation, amended. The letter is preserved in the Beethoven-Haus Museum in Bonn.

[2]The age of Beethoven's mother at the time of her death is here incorrectly given. It should be 40.

utter rejection of the chronology adopted by Dr. Wegeler, in his "Notizen," of that part of the composer's life. This mistake, if indeed it prove to be such, is one which has been adopted without hesitation by all who have written upon the subject. The reader here, for the first time, finds Wegeler's account of Beethoven's higher intellectual development and his introduction into a more refined social circle placed after, instead of before, the visit to Vienna; and his introduction to the Breunings and Waldstein dated at the time when the youth was developing into the man, and not at a point upon the confines of childhood and youth.

This demands some explanation.

The history of Beethoven's Bonn life would be so sadly imperfect without the "Notizen" of Dr. Wegeler, which bear in every line such an impress of perfect candor and honesty, that they can be read only with feelings of gratefullest remembrance of their author and with fullest confidence in their authenticity. But no more in his case than in others can the reminiscences of an aged man be taken as conclusive evidence in regard to facts and occurrences of years long since past, when opposed to contemporary records, or involving confusion of dates. Some slight lapse of memory, misapprehension, or unlucky adoption of another's mistake, may lead astray and be the abundant source of error. Still, it is only with great diffidence and extreme caution that one can undertake to correct an original authority so trustworthy as Dr. Wegeler. Such corrections must be made, however; for only by this can many a difficulty be removed. An error in the Doctor's chronology might easily be occasioned by the long accepted false date of Beethoven's birth, insensibly influencing his recollections; and certainly when Dr. Wegeler, Madame von Breuning and Franz Ries, all alike venerable in years as in character, sit together discussing in 1837–8 occurrences of 1785–8, with nothing to aid their memories or control their reminiscences but an old Court Calendar or two, they may well to some extent have confounded times and seasons in the vague and misty distance of so many years; the more easily because the error is one of but two or three years at most. Bearing upon the point in question is the fact that Frau Karth—who distinctly remembers the death of Madame van Beethoven—has no recollections of the young Breunings and Waldstein until after that event.

Some words of Dr. Wegeler in an unprinted letter to Beethoven (1825): "inasmuch as the house of my mother-in-law was more your domicile than your own, especially after you lost your noble mother," seem to favor the usually accepted chronology: but if Beethoven was thus almost a member of the Breuning family as early as 1785 or 1786, how can the tone of the letter to Dr. Schaden be explained? Or how account for the fact, that, when he reached Bonn again and found his mother dying, and his father "in a very unfortunate state" and "compelled to sell a portion of his effects and pawn others and knew not what to do," it was to Franz Ries he turned for aid? The good Doctor is certainly mistaken as to the time when Beethoven found Mæcenases in the Elector and Waldstein; why not equally so in relation to the Breuning family?

If, now, his own account of his intimacy with the young musician—given in the preface to the "Notizen"—be examined, it will be found to strengthen what has just been said: "Born in Bonn in 1765, I became acquainted in 1782 with the twelve years old lad, who, however, was already known as an author, and lived in most intimate association with him uninterruptedly until September, 1787" (and still he could forget that friend's absence in Vienna only a few months before), "when, to finish my medical studies, I visited the Vienna schools and institutions. After my return in October, 1789, we continued to live together in an equally cordial association until Beethoven's later departure for Vienna towards the close of 1792, whither I also emigrated in October, 1794."

For more than two years, then, and just at this period, Dr. Wegeler was not in Bonn. Let still another circumstance be noted: Nothing has been discovered, either in the "Notizen" or, elsewhere, which necessarily implies that Wegeler himself intimately knew the Breunings until after his return from Vienna in 1789; moreover, in those days, when the distinctions of rank were so strongly marked, it is, to say the least, exceedingly improbable, that the son of an immigrant Alsatian shoemaker should have obtained entrée upon the supposed terms of intimacy in a household in which the oldest child was some six years younger than himself, and which belonged to the highest social, if not titled rank, until he by the force of his talents, culture, and high character, had risen to its level. That, after so rising, the obscurity of his birth was forgotten and the only daughter became his wife, is alike honorable to both parties. It is unnecessary to pursue the point farther; the reader, having his attention drawn to it, will observe for himself the many less prominent, but strongly corroborating circumstances of the narrative, which confirm the chronology adopted in it.   At all events it must stand until new and decisive facts against it be found.[1]

"My journey cost me a great deal, and I have not the smallest hope of earning anything here.   Fate is not propitious to me in Bonn."   In poverty, ill, melancholy, despondent, motherless, ashamed of and depressed by his father's ever increasing moral infirmity, the boy, prematurely old from the circumstances in which he had been placed since his eleventh year, had yet to bear another "sling and arrow of outrageous fortune."   The little

[1]Thayer's correction of Dr. Wegeler's account of Beethoven's first acquaintance with the family von Breuning was sharply criticized by a grandson of Wegeler in an article published in the *Coblenzer Zeitung* of May 20, 1890.   Thayer preserved Karl Wegeler's article in the library copy of his biography, and had he lived to revise his work he would undoubtedly either have corrected his assertions or confirmed them.   According to Dr. Wegeler (this is the younger Wegeler's argument, in brief), Beethoven had been introduced to the von Breuning family at least as early as 1785, and in that circle had already met Count Waldstein, who had aided him in securing his first salary as Court Organist.   The "Notizen" do not fix the dates, though they imply that the occurrences took place before 1785.   As to the statement of the Widow Karth, Wegeler urges that the testimony of a child five years old could have no weight as against that of persons of mature age, and that an acquaintance might well exist without intercourse in the Beethoven dwelling.   The letter to Dr. Schaden, the product of a melancholy mood, does not preclude the possibility that Beethoven had received help from another source, especially since great care had to be exercised in extending succor to him lest his sensibilities be hurt.   Certain it is that Wegeler, who did not go to Vienna till 1787, had been a faithful friend and helper in the period of Beethoven's destitution, as was proved by a thitherto unpublished letter of Beethoven to Wegeler, in which the former expressly stated that the latter had known him, Beethoven, almost since childhood.   If the von Breuning family were really not on hand at the time of Beethoven's trouble, the fact might be explained by their annual sojourn in the country, which was generally of considerable duration.   Thayer's assumption that Wegeler himself did not get intimately acquainted with the von Breunings until after his return from Vienna (in 1789) is at variance with the family recollections, which presented him as a young student (therefore before 1787) and with him Beethoven at the time when they became visitors at the house.   Weakness of memory on the part of a man so intellectually fresh and vigorous as Dr. Wegeler was in 1838 (he died ten years later) was not to be assumed; least of all can Dr. Wegeler have erred concerning the beginning of his acquaintance with the family from which he got his wife.   Finally, the intimate terms of friendship which existed between Beethoven and Eleonore von Breuning could be fully explained only on the theory of a childhood acquaintance.

In the first edition of Thayer's biography (1866) Dr. Deiters printed the text bearing on this question as it is given above without note or comment.   In the revised edition of Volume I (1901), he reproduced the original text in the body of the page but appended a footnote in which, while asserting that an authority like Thayer ought not to be opposed except "with great diffidence and extreme caution" (to use Thayer's words referring to Dr. Wegeler), he nevertheless upheld the contention of Dr. Wegeler's grandson.   He says: "The definite assertion of Wegeler that he made the acquaintance of Beethoven as early as 1782, which is supported by Beethoven's own words, 'you knew me almost since my childhood,' is not to be shaken.   As little can it be questioned that Wegeler had been introduced in the Breuning house as a student before his departure for Vienna (according to Gerhard von Breuning before his acquaintance with Beethoven began); here Dr. Wegeler could not have made an error.   Concerning his bringing Beethoven to the house he gives no date; the year 1785 is not mentioned in the "Notizen."   On page 45, however, it is stated that Stephan von Breuning "lived in closest affiliation with him (Beethoven) from his tenth year till his death."   Stephan was born August 17, 1774 (*Vide* "Aus dem Schwarzspanierhause," page 6); this would indicate the year 1784.   Wegeler's remark, "especially after you lost your noble mother," makes it clear as day that a close friendship existed before the death of Beethoven's mother.

sister, now a year and a half old—but here is the notice from the "Intelligenzblatt":—"Died, November 25, Margareth, daughter of the Court Musician Johann van Beethoven, aged one year." And so faded the last hope that the passionate tenderness of Beethoven's nature might find scope in the purest of all relations between the sexes—that of brother and sister.

Thus, in sadness and gloom, Beethoven's seventeenth year ended.

Chapter VII

The von Breuning Family—Beethoven Brought Under Re-
fining Influences — Count Waldstein, His Mæcenas—
The Young Musician is Forced to Become Head of the
Family.

IN 1527, the year in which the administration of the office of
Hochmeister of the Teutonic Order was united with that of the
Deutschmeister, whose residence had already been fixed at Mergentheim in 1525, this city became the principal seat of the order.
From 1732 to 1761 Clemens Augustus was *Hoch- und Deutschmeister*
of the order; according to the French edition of the Court Calendar
of 1761, Christoph von Breuning was *Conseiller d'État et Référen-
daire*, having succeeded his father-in-law von Mayerhofen in the
office.

Christoph von Breuning had five sons: Georg Joseph, Johann
Lorenz, Johann Philipp, Emanuel Joseph and Christoph. Lorenz
became chancellor of the Archdeanery of Bonn, and the *Freiadliges
Stift* at Neuss; after the death of his brother Emanuel he lived
in Bonn so that, as head of the family, he might care for the education of the latter's children. He died there in 1796. Johann
Philipp, born 1742 at Mergentheim, became canon and priest
at Kerpen, a place on the old highway from Cologne to Aix-la-
Chapelle, where he died June 12, 1831. Christoph was court
councillor at Dillingen.

Emanuel Joseph continued in the electoral service at Bonn;
at the early age of 20 years he was already court councillor (*Conseiller actuel*). He married Hélène von Kerich, born January 3, 1750,
daughter of Stephan von Kerich, physician to the elector. Her
brother, Abraham von Kerich, canon and scholaster of the
archdeanery of Bonn, died in Coblenz in 1821. A high opinion of
the intellect and character of Madame von Breuning is enforced
upon us by what we learn of her influence upon the youthful
Beethoven. Court Councillor von Breuning perished in a fire
in the electoral palace on January 15, 1777. The young widow

(she had barely attained her 28th year), continued to live in the house of her brother, Abraham von Kerich, with her three children, to whom was added a fourth in the summer of 1777. Immediately after the death of the father, his brother, the canon Lorenz von Breuning, changed his residence from Neuss to Bonn and remained in the same house as guardian and tutor of the orphaned children. These were:

1. Christoph, born May 13, 1771, a student of jurisprudence at Bonn, Göttingen and Jena, municipal councillor in Bonn, notary, president of the city council, professor at the law school in Coblenz, member of the Court of Review in Cologne, and, finally, *Geheimer Ober-Revisionsrath* in Berlin. He died in 1841.

2. Eleonore Brigitte, born April 23, 1772. On March 28, 1802, she was married to Franz Gerhard Wegeler of Beul-an-der-Ahr, and died on June 13, 1841, at Coblenz.

3. Stephan, born August 17, 1774. He studied law at Bonn and Göttingen, and shortly before the end of the electorship of Max Franz was appointed to an office in the Teutonic Order at Mergentheim. In the spring of 1801 he went to Vienna, where he renewed his acquaintance with Beethoven. They had simultaneously been pupils of Ries in violin playing. The Teutonic Order offering no chance of advancement to a young man, he was given employment with the War Council and became Court Councillor in 1818. He died on June 4, 1827. His first wife was Julie von Vering, daughter of Ritter von Vering, a military physician; she died in the eleventh month of her wedded life. He then married Constanze Ruschowitz, who became the mother of Dr. Gerhard von Breuning, born August 28, 1813, author of "Aus dem Schwarzspanierhause."

4. Lorenz (called Lenz, the posthumous child), born in the summer of 1777, studied medicine and was in Vienna in 1794–97 simultaneously with Wegeler and Beethoven. He died on April 10, 1798 in Bonn.[1]

---

[1]Dr. Deiters, differing with Thayer on the subject of the date of the beginning of the intimacy between Beethoven and the von Breuning family, omitted in the revised version of the Beethoven biography the author's comments on the brief biographical data concerning the sons, which were as follows: "These dates, communicated by Dr. Gerhard, son of Stephan von Breuning, prove a singular inaccuracy in Wegeler's remark ('Nachtrag zur Notizen,' page 26): 'Lenz, as the youngest of the three brothers, was nearest to Beethoven in age.'" Of Stephan he says: "Inasmuch as he had lived in intimate association with Beethoven from his tenth year up to his death." Many a proof of this general fact will hereafter appear; but whether this "intimate association" began quite so early is a question. The two were at the same time pupils of Franz Ries on the violin, and they may well have become acquainted in 1785 or 1786; but it was not favorable to extreme intimacy that four years' difference existed in their ages; and that the one was but a schoolboy while the other was already an organist, an author and accustomed to move among men.

Madame von Breuning, who died on December 9, 1838, after a widowhood of 61 years, lived in Bonn until 1815, then in Kerpen, Beul-an-der-Ahr, Cologne and finally with her son-in-law, Wegeler, in Coblenz.

The acquaintance between Beethoven and Stephan von Breuning may have had some influence in the selection of the young musician as pianoforte teacher for Eleonore and Lorenz,[1] an event (in consideration of circumstances already detailed and of the ages, real and reputed, of pupils and master) which may be dated at the close of the year 1787, and which was, perhaps, the greatest good that fate, now become propitious, could have conferred upon him; for he was now so situated in his domestic relations, and at such an age, that introduction into so highly refined and cultivated a circle was of the highest value to him both morally and intellectually. The recent loss of his mother had left a void in his heart which so excellent a woman as Madame von Breuning could alone in some measure fill. He was at an age when the evil example of his father needed a counterbalance; when the extraordinary honors so recently paid to science and letters at the inauguration of the university would make the strongest impression; when the sense of his deficiencies in everything but his art would begin to be oppressive; when his mental powers, so strong and healthy, would demand some change, some recreation, from that constant strain in the one direction of music to which almost from infancy they had been subjected; when not only the reaction upon his mind of the fresh and new intellectual life now pervading Bonn society, but his daily contact with so many of his own age, friends and companions now enjoying advantages for improvement denied to him, must have cost him many a pang; when a lofty and noble ambition might be aroused to lead him ever onward and upward; when, the victim of a despondent melancholy, he might sink into the mere routine musician, with no lofty aims, no higher object than to draw from his talents means to supply his necessities and gratify his appetites.

There must have been something very engaging in the character of the small, pockmarked youth, or he could not have so won his way into the affections of the Widow von Breuning and her children. In his "Notizen" Wegeler writes:

In this house reigned an unconstrained tone of culture in spite of youthful wilfulness. Christoph von Breuning made early essays in

[1]Gerhard von Breuning would have it appear from a statement on page 6 of his book "Aus dem Schwarzspanierhause," that Beethoven was recommended to the von Breunings by Wegeler.

poetry, as was the case (and not without success) with Stephan von Breuning much later. The friends of the family were distinguished by indulgence in social entertainments which combined the useful and the agreeable. When we add that the family possessed considerable wealth, especially before the war, it will be easy to understand that the first joyous emotions of Beethoven found vent here. Soon he was treated as one of the children of the family, spending in the house not only the greater part of his days, but also many nights. Here he felt that he was free, here he moved about without constraint, everything conspired to make him cheerful and develop his mind. Being five years older than Beethoven I was able to observe and form a judgment on these things.

It must not be forgotten that besides Madame von Breuning and her children the scholastic Abraham von Kerich and the canon Lorenz von Breuning were members of the household. The latter especially seems to have been a fine specimen of the enlightened clergy of Bonn who, according to Risbeck, formed so striking a contrast to the priests and monks of Cologne; and it is easy to trace Beethoven's life-long love for the ancient classics —Homer and Plutarch at the head—to the time when the young Breunings would be occupied with them in the original under the guidance of their accomplished tutor and guardian. The uncle, Philipp von Breuning, may also have been influential in the intellectual progress of the young musician, for to him at Kerpen "the family von Breuning and their friends went annually for a vacation of five or six weeks. There, too, Beethoven several times spent a few weeks right merrily, and was frequently urged to play the organ," as Wegeler tells us in the "Notizen." There let him be left enjoying and profiting by his intimacy with that family, and returning their kindness in some measure by instructing Eleonore and Lenz in music, while a new friend and benefactor is introduced.

Emanuel Philipp, Count Waldstein and Wartemberg von Dux, and his wife, a daughter of Emanuel Prince Lichtenstein, were parents of eleven children. The fourth son was Ferdinand Ernst Gabriel, born March 24, 1762. Uniting in his veins the blood of many of the houses of the Austrian Empire, there was no career, no line of preferment open to younger sons of titled families, which was not open to him, or to which he might not aspire. It was determined that he should seek activity in the Teutonic Order, of which Max Franz was Grand Master. According to the rules and regulations of the order, the young nobleman came to Bonn to pass his examinations and spend his year of novitiate. Could the time of his arrival there be determined with certainty, the

date would have a most important bearing either to confirm or
disprove the chronological argument of some of our earlier pages;
but one may well despair of finding so unimportant an event as
the journey of a young man of 25 from Vienna to the Rhine anywhere upon record. One thing bearing directly upon this point
may be read in the "Wiener Zeitung" of July 2, 1788. A correspondent in Bonn says that on "the day before yesterday," i.e.,
June 17, 1788, "our gracious sovereign, as Hoch- und Deutschmeister, gave the accolade with the customary ceremonies to
the Count von Waldstein, who had been accepted in the Teutonic
Order." Allowing for the regular year of novitiate, the Count
was certainly in Bonn before the 17th of June, 1787.

The misfortune of two unlucky Bohemian peasants, strange
as it may seem, gives us, after the lapse of a century, a satisfactory
solution of the difficulty. Some one reports in the "Wiener
Zeitung" of May, 19, 1787, that on the 4th of that month two
peasant houses were destroyed by fire in the village of Likwitz
belonging to Osegg, and adds: "Count Ferdinand von Waldstein,
moved by a noble spirit of humanity, hurried from Dux, took
charge of affairs and was to be found wherever the danger was
greatest." It was between May 4 and June 17, 1787, that Waldstein parted from his widowed mother and journeyed to the place
of his novitiate. His name may easily have become known to
Wegeler before the latter's departure from Bonn for Vienna.[1]
Here follows what the good doctor says of the Count—to what
degree correct or mistaken, the reader can determine for himself:

The first, and in every respect the most important, of the Mæcenases
of Beethoven was Count Waldstein, Knight of the Teutonic Order, and
(what is of greater moment here) the favorite and constant companion
of the young Elector, afterwards Commander of the Order at Virnsberg
and Chancellor of the Emperor of Austria. He was not only a connoisseur but also a practitioner of music. He it was who gave all manner
of support to our Beethoven, whose gifts he was the first to recognize
worthily. Through him the young genius developed the talent to improvise variations on a given theme. From him he received much
pecuniary assistance bestowed in such a way as to spare his sensibilities,
it being generally looked upon as a small gratuity from the Elector.

[1]Dr. Wegeler's grandson, in his criticism of Thayer's assertions concerning the
date of the beginning of the acquaintance between Beethoven and the von Breunings,
falls foul of even this ingenious demonstration, saying that the incident of the conflagration might have taken place when Count Waldstein was at home visiting his mother.
He could not believe that the Count had spent all of the first 24 years of his life at Dux
in "idyllic solitude," and argued that he might have visited Bonn *for the first time* at an
earlier date than 1787. Dr. Deiters held that the point was well taken; as if there was
no alternative for the young count between "idyllic solitude" at Dux and a sojourn
at Bonn!

Beethoven's appointment as organist, his being sent to Vienna by the Elector, were the doings of the Count. When Beethoven at a later date dedicated the great and important Sonata in C major, Op. 53, to him, it was only a proof of the gratitude which lived on in the mature man. It is to Count Waldstein that Beethoven owed the circumstance that the first sproutings of his genius were not nipped; therefore we owe this Mæcenas Beethoven's later fame.

Frau Karth remembered distinctly the 17th of June upon which Waldstein entered the order, the fact being impressed upon her mind by a not very gentle reminder from the stock of a sentinel's musket that the palace chapel was no place for children on such an occasion. She remembered Waldstein's visits to Beethoven in the years following in his room in the Wenzelgasse and was confident that he made the young musician a present of a pianoforte.

To save his line from extinction the Count obtained a dispensation from his vows and married (May 9, 1812) Maria Isabella, daughter of Count Rzewski. A daughter, Ludmilla, was born to him; but no son. He died on August 29, 1823, and the family of Waldsteins of Dux disappears. While all that Wegeler says of this man's kindness in obtaining the place of organist for Beethoven and of his influence upon his musical education is one grand mistake,[1] there is no reason whatever to doubt that those qualities which made the youth a favorite with the Breunings, added to his manifest genius, made their way to the young count's heart and gained for Beethoven a zealous, influential and active friend. Still, in June, 1778, Waldstein possessed no such influence as to render a petition for increase of salary, offered by his protégé, successful. That document has disappeared, but a paper remains, dated June 5, concerning the petition, which is endorsed "Beruhet." Whatever this word may here mean it is certain that Ludwig's salary as organist remained at the old point of 100 thalers, which, with the 200 received by his father, the three measures of grain and the small sum that he might earn by teaching, was all that Johann van Beethoven and three sons, now respectively in their eighteenth, fifteenth and twelfth years, had to live upon; and therefore so much the more necessity for the exercise of Waldstein's generosity.

After the death of the mother, says Frau Karth, a housekeeper was employed and the father and sons remained together in the lodgings in the Wenzelgasse. Carl was intended for the

[1] Thus in Mr. Thayer's original manuscript. Dr. Deiters omitted the remark in his revision, but it is here permitted to stand along with other controverted matters.

musical profession; Johann was put apprentice to the court apothecary, Johann Peter Hittorf. Two years, however, had hardly elapsed when the father's infirmity compelled the eldest son, not yet nineteen years of age, to take the extraordinary step of placing himself at the head of the family. One of Stephan von Breuning's reminiscences shows how low Johann van Beethoven had sunk: viz., that of having seen Ludwig furiously interposing to rescue his intoxicated father from an officer of police.

Here again the petition has disappeared, but its contents are sufficiently made known by the terms of the decree dated November 20, 1789:

His Electoral Highness having graciously granted the prayer of the petitioner and dispensed henceforth wholly with the services of his father, who is to withdraw to a village in the electorate, it is graciously commanded that he be paid in accordance with his wish only 100 rthr. of the annual salary which he has had heretofore, beginning with the approaching new year, and that the other 100 thlr. be paid to the suppliant's son besides the salary which he now draws and the three measures of grain for the support of his brothers.

It is probable that there was no intention to enforce this decree in respect of the withdrawal of the father from Bonn, and that this clause was inserted *in terrorem* in case he misbehaved himself; for he continued, according to Frau Karth, to dwell with his children, and his first receipt, still preserved, for the reduced salary is dated at Bonn—a circumstance, however, which alone would prove little or nothing.

Chapter VIII

The National Theatre of Max Franz—Beethoven's Artistic
Associates—Practical Experience in the Orchestra—The
"Ritterballet"—The Operatic Repertory of Five Years.

ARLY in the year 1788, the mind of the Elector, Max Franz,
was occupied with the project for forming a company of
Hofschauspieler; in short, with the founding of a National
Theatre upon the plan adopted by his predecessor in Bonn and by
his brother Joseph in Vienna. His finances were now in order, the
administration of public affairs in able hands and working smoothly,
and there was nothing to hinder him from placing both music and
theatre upon a better and permanent footing; which he now proceeded to do. The Klos troupe, which had left Cologne in March,
played for a space in Bonn, and on its dispersal in the summer
several of its better actors were engaged and added to others who
had already settled in Bonn. The only names which it is necessary to mention here are those of significance in the history of
Beethoven. Joseph Reicha was director; Neefe, pianist and stage-
manager for opera; in the orchestra were Franz Ries and Andreas
Romberg (violin), Ludwig van Beethoven (viola), Bernard
Romberg (violoncello), Nicolaus Simrock (horn) and Anton
Reicha (flute). A comparison of the lists of the theatrical establishment with that of the court chapel as printed in the Court
Calendars for 1778 and the following years, shows that the two
institutions were kept distinct, though the names for the greater
part appear in both. Some of the singers in the chapel played
in the theatrical orchestra, while certain of the players in the
chapel sang upon the stage. Other names appear in but one of
the lists.

As organist the name of Beethoven appears still in the Court
Calendar, but as viola player he had a place in both the orchestras.
Thus, for a period of full four years, he had the opportunity of
studying practically orchestral compositions in the best of all
schools—the orchestra itself. This body of thirty-one members,

under the energetic leadership of Reicha, many of them young
and ambitious, some already known as virtuosos and still keeping
their places in musical history as such, was a school for instrumental music such as Handel, Bach, Mozart and Haydn had not
enjoyed in their youth; that its advantages were improved both
by Beethoven and others of the younger men, all the world knows.

One fact worthy of note in relation to this company is the
youth of most of the new members engaged. Maximilian seems
to have sought out young talent, and when it proved to be of
true metal, gave it a permanent place in his service, adopted wise
measures for its cultivation, and thus laid a foundation upon
which, but for the outbreak of the French Revolution, and the
consequent dispersion of his court, would in time have risen a
musical establishment, one of the very first in Germany.

This is equally true of the new members of his orchestra.
Reicha himself was still rather a young man, born in 1757. He
was a virtuoso on the violoncello and a composer of some note;
but his usefulness was sadly impaired by his sufferings from gout.
The cousins Andreas and Bernhard Romberg, Maximilian had
found at Münster and brought to Bonn. They had in their boyhood, as virtuosos upon their instruments — Andreas violin,
Bernhard 'cello—made a tour as far as Paris, and their concerts
were crowned with success. Andreas was born near Münster in
1767, and Ledebur ("Tonkünstler Berlins") adopts the same year
as the date also of Bernhard's birth. They were, therefore, three
years older than Beethoven and now just past 21. Both were
already industrious and well-known composers and must have
been a valuable addition to the circle of young men in which
Beethoven moved. The decree appointing them respectively
Court Violinist and Court Violoncellist is dated November 19, 1790.

Anton Reicha, a fatherless nephew of the concertmaster,
born at Prague, February 27, 1770, was brought by his uncle to
Bonn. He had been already for some years in that uncle's care
and under his instruction had become a good player of the flute,
violin and pianoforte. In Bonn, Reicha became acquainted with
Beethoven, who was then organist at court. "We spent fourteen
years together," says Reicha, "united in a bond like that of Orestes
and Pylades, and were continually side by side in our youth.
After a separation of eight years we saw each other again in Vienna,
and exchanged confidences concerning our experiences." At the
age of 17 composing orchestral and vocal music for the Electoral
Chapel, a year later flautist in the theatre, at nineteen both flautist
and violinist in the chapel and so intimate a friend of Beethoven,

who was less than a year his junior—were Reicha's laurels no spur to the ambition of the other?

The names of several of the performers upon wind-instruments were new names in Bonn, and the thought suggests itself that the Elector brought with him from Vienna some members of the *Harmoniemusik* which had won high praise from Reichardt, and it will hereafter appear that such a band formed part of the musical establishment in Bonn—a fact of importance in its bearing upon the questions of the origin and date of various known works both of Beethoven and of Reicha, and of no less weight in deciding where and how these men obtained their marvellous knowledge of the powers and effects of this class of instruments.

The arrangements were all made in 1788, but not early enough to admit of the opening of the theatre until after the Christmas holidays, namely, on the evening of January 3, 1789. The theatre had been altered and improved. An incendiary fire threatened its destruction the day before, but did not postpone the opening. The opening piece was "Der Baum der Diana" by Vincenzo Martin. It may be thought not very complimentary to the taste of Maximilian that the first season of his National Theatre was opened thus, instead of with one of Gluck's or Mozart's masterpieces. It suffices to say that he, in his capacity of Grand Master of the Teutonic Order, had spent a good part of the autumn at Mergentheim and only reached Bonn on his return on the last day of January. Hence he was not responsible for that selection.

The season which opened on January 3, 1789, closed on May 23. Within this period the following operas were performed, Beethoven taking part in the performances as a member of the orchestra: "Der Baum der Diana" (*L'Arbore di Diana*), Martin; "Romeo und Julie," Georg Benda; "Ariadne" (duo-drama by Georg Benda); "Das Mädchen von Frascati" (*La Frascatana*), Paisiello; "Julie," Desaides; "Die drei Pächter" (*Les trois Fermiers*), Desaides; "Die Entführung aus dem Serail," Mozart; "Nina," Dalayrac; "Trofonio's Zauberhöhle" (*La grotta di Trofonio*), Salieri; "Der eifersüchtige Liebhaber" (*L'Amant jaloux*), Grétry; "Der Schmaus" (*Il Convivo*), Cimarosa; "Der Alchymist," Schuster; "Das Blendwerk" (*La fausse Magie*), Grétry.

The second season began October 13, 1789, and continued until February 23, 1790. On the 24th of February news reached Bonn of the death of Maximilian's brother, the Emperor Joseph II, and the theatre was closed. The repertory for the season comprised "Don Giovanni," Mozart (which was given three times);

"Die Colonie" (*L'Isola d'Amore*), Sacchini; "Der Barbier von Sevilla" (*Il Barbiere di Siviglia*), Paisiello; "Romeo und Julie," Georg Benda; "Die Hochzeit des Figaro" (*Le Nozze di Figaro*), Mozart (given four times); "Nina," Dalayrac; "Die schöne Schusterin," Umlauf; "Ariadne," Georg Benda; "Die Pilgrimme von Mecca," Gluck; "Der König von Venedig" (*Il Re Teodoro*), Paisiello; "Der Alchymist," Schuster; "Das listige Bauernmäd- chen" (*La finta Giardiniera*), Paisiello; "Der Doktor und Apothe- ker," Dittersdorf. A letter to the "Berliner Annalen des Theaters" mentions three operas which are not in the list of the theatrical calendar and indicates that the theatre was opened soon after receipt of the intelligence of the death of Joseph, and several pieces performed, among them *Il Marchese Tulipano* by Paisiello. The writer also mentions performances of Anfossi's (or Sarti's) *Avaro inamorato*, Pergolese's *Serva padrona* and *La Villanella di spirito*, composer unmentioned, by an Italian company headed by Madame Bianchi.

The third season began October 23, 1790, and closed on March 8, 1791. Between the opening and November 27, perform- ances of the following musical-dramatic works are recorded: "König Theodor in Venedig" (*Il Re Teodoro*), Paisiello; "Die Wilden" (*Azemia*), Dalayrac; "Der Alchymist," Schuster; "Kein Dienst bleibt unbelohnt," (?); "Der Barbier von Sevilla," Paisiello; "Die schöne Schusterin," Umlauf; "Lilla," Martini; "Die Geitzigen in der Falle," Schuster; "Nina," Dalayrac; "Dr. Murner," Schuster. On March 8, the season closed with a ballet by Horschelt, "Pyramus und Thisbe." The reporter in the "Theaterkalender" says:

On Quinquagesima Sunday (March 6) the local nobility performed in the Ridotto Room a characteristic ballet in old German costume. The author, His Excellency Count Waldstein, to whom the composition and music do honor, had shown in it consideration for the chief proclivities of our ancestors for war, the chase, love and drinking. On March 8, all the nobility attended the theatre in their old German dress and the parade made a great, splendid and respectable picture. It was also noticeable that the ladies would lose none of their charms were they to return to the costumes of antiquity.

Before proceeding with this history a correction must be made in this report: the music to the "Ritterballet," which was the characteristic ballet referred to, was not composed by Count Waldstein but by Ludwig van Beethoven. We shall recur to it presently. Owing to a long-continued absence of the Elector, the principal singers and the greater part of the orchestra, the fourth season did not begin till the 28th of December, 1791. Between that date and February 20, 1792, the following musical works were performed: "Doktor und Apotheker," Dittersdorf; "Robert und Caliste," Guglielmi; "Félix," Monsigny; "Die Dorf-deputirten," Schubauer; "Im Trüben ist gut Fischen" (*Fra due Litiganti, il Terzo gode*), Sarti; "Das rothe Käppchen," Dittersdorf; "Lilla," Martini; "Der Barbier von Sevilla," Paisiello; "Ende gut, Alles gut," music by the Electoral Captain d'Antoin; "Die Entführung aus dem Serail," Mozart; "Die beiden Savoyarden" (*Les deux petits Savoyards*), Dalayrac.

The fifth season began in October, 1792. Of the nine operas given before the departure of Maximilian and the company to Münster in December, "Die Müllerin" by De la Borde, "König Axur in Ormus" by Salieri, and "Hieronymus Knicker" by Ditters-dorf, were the only ones new to Bonn; and in only the first two of these could Beethoven have taken part, unless at rehearsals; for at the beginning of November he left Bonn—and, as it proved, forever. Probably Salieri's masterpiece was his last opera within the familiar walls of the Court Theatre of the Elector of Cologne.

Beethoven's eighteenth birthday came around during the rehearsals for the first season, of this theatre; his twenty-second just after the beginning of the fifth. During four years (1788–1792) he was adding to his musical knowledge and experience in a direction wherein he has usually been represented as deficient—as active member of an operatic orchestra; and the catalogue of works performed shows that the best schools of the day, save that of Berlin, must have been thoroughly mastered by him in all their strength and weakness. Beethoven's titanic power and grandeur would have marked his compositions under any circum-stances; but it is very doubtful if, without the training of those years in the Electoral "Toxal, Kammer und Theater" as member of the orchestra, his works would have so abounded in melodies of such profound depths of expression, of such heavenly serenity and repose and of such divine beauty as they do, and which give him rank with the two greatest of melodists, Handel and Mozart.

Chapter IX

Gleanings of Musical Fact and Anecdote—Haydn in Bonn—
A Rhine Journey—Abbé Sterkel—Beethoven Extem-
porises—Social and Artistic Life in Bonn—Eleonore von
Breuning—The Circle of Friends—Beethoven Leaves
Bonn Forever—The Journey to Vienna.

A S a pendant to the preceding sketches of Bonn's musical
history a variety of notices belonging to the last three years
of Beethoven's life in his native place are here brought together in chronological order. Most of them relate to him personally, and some of them, through errors of date, have been looked
upon hitherto as adding proofs of the precocity of his genius.

Prof. Dr. Wurzer communicated to the "Kölnische Zeitung"
of August 30, 1838, the following pleasant anecdote:

In the summer of the year 1790 or 1791 I was one day on business
in Godesberger Brunnen. After dinner Beethoven and another young
man came up. I related to him that the church at Marienforst (a cloister
in the woods behind Godesberg) had been repaired and renovated, and
that this was also true of the organ, which was either wholly new or at
least greatly improved. The company begged him to give them the
pleasure of letting them hear him play on the instrument. His great
good nature led him to grant our wish. The church was locked, but
the prior was very obliging and had it unlocked for us. B. now began
to play variations on themes given him by the party in a manner that
moved us profoundly; but what was much more significant, poor laboring
folk who were cleaning out the débris left by the work of repair, were so
greatly affected by the music that they put down their implements and
listened with obvious pleasure. *Sit ei terra levis!*

The greatest musical event of the year (1790) in Bonn
occurred just at its close—the visit of Joseph Haydn, on his way
to London with Johann Peter Salomon, whose name so often
occurs in the preliminary chapters of this work. Of this visit,
Dies has recorded Haydn's own account:

In the capital, Bonn, he was surprised in more ways than one. He
reached the city on Saturday [Christmas, December 25] and set apart

the next day for rest. On Sunday, Salomon accompanied Haydn to the court chapel to listen to mass. Scarcely had the two entered the church and found suitable seats when high mass began. The first chords announced a product of Haydn's muse. Our Haydn looked upon it as an accidental occurrence which had happened only to flatter him; nevertheless it was decidedly agreeable to him to listen to his own composition. Toward the close of the mass a person approached and asked him to repair to the oratory, where he was expected. Haydn obeyed and was not a little surprised when he found that the Elector, Maximilian, had had him summoned, took him at once by the hand and presented him to the virtuosi with the words: "Here I make you acquainted with the Haydn whom you all revere so highly." The Elector gave both parties time to become acquainted with each other, and, to give Haydn a convincing proof of his respect, invited him to dinner. This unexpected invitation put Haydn into an embarrassing position, for he and Salomon had ordered a modest little dinner in their lodgings, and it was too late to make a change. Haydn was therefore fain to take refuge in excuses which the Elector accepted as genuine and sufficient. Haydn took his leave and returned to his lodgings, where he was made aware in a special manner of the good will of the Elector, at whose secret command the little dinner had been metamorphosed into a banquet for twelve persons to which the most capable musicians had been invited.

Was the young musician one of these "most capable musicians"? Sunday evening, March 6th, came the performance of Beethoven's music to the "Ritterballet" before noticed; but without his name being known. Bossler's "Musikalische Correspondenz" of July 13, 1791, contains a list of the "Cabinet, Chapel and Court Musicians of the Elector of Cologne." Names designated by an asterisk were "solo players who may justly be ranked with virtuosi"; two asterisks indicated composers. Four names only—those of Joseph Reicha, Perner and the two Rombergs—have the two stars; Beethoven has none. "Hr. Ludwig van Beethoven plays pianoforte concertos; Hr. Neefe plays accompaniments at court and in the theatre and at concerts. . . . Concertante violas are played by virtuoso violinists"—that is all, except that we learn that the Elector is losing interest in the instrument on which Beethoven played in the orchestra: "His Electoral Highness of Cologne seldom plays the viola nowadays, but finds amusement at the pianoforte with operas, etc., etc."

At Mergentheim, the capital of the Teutonic Order, a grand meeting of commanders and knights took place in the autumn of 1791, the Grand Master Maximilian Francis presiding, and the sessions continuing from September 18 to October 20, as appears from the records at Vienna. The Elector's stay there seems to have been protracted to a period of at least three months. During his visit there of equal length two years before, time probably dragged heavily, so this time ample provision was made for theatrical and musical amusement. Among the visiting theatrical troupes was one called the "Häusslersche Gesellschaft," which played in summer at Nuremberg, in winter in Münster and Eichstädt. The entrepreneur was Baron von Bailaux, the chapelmaster Weber, the elder; and among the personnel were Herr Weber, the younger, and Madame Weber. From Max Weber's biography of his father it appears that these Webers were the brother and sister-in-law of Carl Maria von Weber, then a child of some five years. "The troupe," says the reporter of the "Theater-Kalender," "performs the choicest pieces and the grandest operas." So the father, Franz Anton von Weber, must have found himself at length in his own proper element, and still more so a year later, when he himself became the manager.

This company for a time migrated to Mergentheim and resumed the title of "Kurfürstliches Hoftheater." Beethoven soon came thither also. Did he, when in after years he met Carl Maria von Weber, remember him as a feeble child at Mergentheim? Had his intercourse there with Fridolin von Weber, pupil of Joseph Haydn, any influence upon his determination soon after to become also that great master's pupil?

Simonetti, Maximilian's favorite and very fine tenor concert-singer, and some twenty-five members of the electoral orchestra, with Franz Ries as conductor—Reicha was too ill—including Beethoven, the two Rombergs and the fine octet of wind-instruments, formed an equally ample provision for the strictly musical entertainments. Actors, singers, musicians—Simonetti and the women-singers excepted—most of them still young, all in their best years and at the age for its full enjoyment, made the journey in two large boats up the Rhine and Main. Before leaving Bonn the company assembled and elected Lux king of the expedition, who in distributing the high offices of his court conferred upon Bernhard Romberg and Ludwig van Beethoven the dignity of, and placed them in his service as, kitchen-boys—scullions. It was the pleasantest season of the year for such a journey, the summer heats being tempered by the coolness of the Rhine and the currents of air passing up and down the deep gorge of the river. Vegetation was at its best and brightest, and the romantic beauty of its old towns and villages had not yet suffered either by the desolations of the wars soon to break upon them or by the resistless and romance-destroying march of "modern improvement." Coblenz and Mayence were still capitals of states, and the huge fortress Rheinfels was not yet a ruin. When Risbeck passed down the Rhine ten years before, his boat "had a mast and sail, a flat deck with a railing, comfortable cabins with windows and some furniture, and in a general way in style was built like a Dutch yacht." In boats like this, no doubt, the jolly company made the slow and, under the circumstances, perhaps, tedious journey against the current of the "arrowy Rhine." But a glorious time and a merry they had of it. Want of speed was no misfortune to them, and in Beethoven's memory the little voyage lived bright and beautiful and was to him "a fruitful source of loveliest visions."

The Bingerloch was then held to be a dangerous, as it certainly was a difficult pass for boats ascending; for here the river, suddenly contracted to half its previous width, plunged amid long lines of rugged rocks into the gorge. So, leaving the boats to their conductors, the party ascended to the Niederwald; and there King Lux raised Beethoven to a higher dignity in his court— Wegeler does not state what it was—and confirmed his appointment by a diploma, or letters patent, dated on the heights above Rüdesheim. To this important document was attached by thread ravelled from a sail, a huge seal of pitch, pressed into the cover of a small box, which gave to the instrument a right imposing look—like the Golden Bull at Frankfort. This diploma from the hand of his comic majesty was among the articles taken by the possessor to Vienna where Wegeler saw it, still carefully preserved, in 1796.

At Aschaffenburg on the Main was the large summer palace of the Electors of Mainz; and here dwelt Abbé Sterkel, now a man of 40 years; a musician from his infancy, one of the first pianists of all Germany and without a rival in this part of it, except perhaps Vogler of Mannheim. His style both as composer and pianist had been refined and cultivated to the utmost, both in Germany and Italy, and his playing was in the highest degree light, graceful, pleasing—as Ries described it to Wegeler, "somewhat ladylike." Ries and Simrock took the young Romberg and Beethoven to pay their respects to the master, "who, complying with the general request, sat himself down to play. Beethoven, who up to this time," says Wegeler, "had not heard a great or celebrated pianoforte player, knew nothing of the finer nuances in the handling of the instrument; his playing was rude and hard. Now he stood with attention all on a strain by the side of Sterkel"; for this grace and delicacy, if not power of execution, which he now heard were a new revelation to him. After Sterkel had finished, the young Bonn concertplayer was invited to take his place at the instrument; but he naturally hesitated to exhibit himself after such a display. The shrewd Abbé, however, brought him to it by a pretence of doubting his ability.

A year or two before, Chapelmaster Vincenzo Righini, a colleague of Sterkel in the service of the Elector of Mayence, had published "Dodeci Ariette," one of which, "Vieni (Venni) Amore," was a melody with five vocal variations, to the same accompaniment. Beethoven, taking this melody as his theme, had composed, dedicated to the Countess of Hatzfeld and published twenty-four variations for the pianoforte upon it. Some of these were very difficult, and Sterkel now expressed his doubts if their author could himself play them. His honor thus touched, "Beethoven played not only these variations so far as he could remember them (Sterkel could not find them), but went on with a number of others no less difficult, all to the great surprise of the listeners, perfectly, and in the ingratiating manner that had struck him in Sterkel's playing."[1]

Once in Mergentheim the merry monarch and his jolly subjects had other things to think of and seem to have made a noise in the world in more senses than one. At all events Carl Ludwig Junker, Chaplain at Kirchberg, the residence of Prince Hohenlohe, heard of them and then went over to hear them. Junker was a dilettante composer and the author of some half-dozen small works upon music—musical almanacs published anonymously, and the like, all now forgotten save by collectors, as are his pianoforte concertos—but at that time he was a man of no small mark in the musical world of Western Germany. He came over to Mergentheim, was treated with great attention by the Elector's musicians, and showed his gratitude in a long letter to Bossler's "Correspondenz" (November 23, 1791), in which superlatives somewhat abound, but which is an exquisite piece of gossip and gives the liveliest picture that exists of the "Kapelle." We have room for only a portion of it:

Here I was also an eye-witness to the esteem and respect in which this chapel stands with the Elector. Just as the rehearsal was to begin Ries was sent for by the Prince, and upon his return brought a bag of gold. "Gentlemen," said he, "this being the Elector's name-day he sends you a present of a thousand thalers." And again, I was eye-witness of this orchestra's surpassing excellence. Herr Winneberger, Kapellmeister at Wallenstein, laid before it a symphony of his own composition,

---

[1] Wegeler's story of the meeting between Beethoven and Sterkel is confirmed in every detail by a letter from N. Simrock to Schindler, a copy of which was found among the posthumous papers of Thayer.

which was by no means easy of execution, especially for the wind-instruments, which had several solos *concertante*. It went finely, however, at the first trial, to the great surprise of the composer. An hour after the dinner-music the concert began. It was opened with a symphony of Mozart; then followed a recitative and air sung by Simonetti; next, a violoncello concerto played by Herr Romberger [Bernhard Romberg]; fourthly, a symphony by Pleyel; fifthly, an air by Righini, sung by Simonetti; sixthly, a double concerto for violin and violoncello played by the two Rombergs; and the closing piece was the symphony of Winneberger, which had very many brilliant passages. The opinion already expressed as to the performance of this orchestra was confirmed. It was not possible to attain a higher degree of exactness. Such perfection in the *pianos, fortes, rinforzandos*—such a swelling and gradual increase of tone and then such an almost imperceptible dying away, from the most powerful to the lightest accents—all this was formerly to be heard only in Mannheim. It would be difficult to find another orchestra in which the violins and basses are throughout in such excellent hands. . . . The members of the chapel, almost without exception, are in their best years, glowing with health, men of culture and fine personal appearance. They form truly a fine sight, when one adds the splendid uniform in which the Elector has clothed them—red, and richly trimmed with gold.

I heard also one of the greatest of pianists—the dear, good Bethofen, some compositions by whom appeared in the Spires "Blumenlese" in 1783, written in his eleventh year. True, he did not perform in public, probably the instrument here was not to his mind. It is one of Spath's make, and at Bonn he plays upon one by Steiner. But, what was infinitely preferable to me, I heard him extemporize in private; yes, I was even invited to propose a theme for him to vary. The greatness of this amiable, light-hearted man, as a virtuoso, may in my opinion be safely estimated from his almost inexhaustible wealth of ideas, the altogether characteristic style of expression in his playing, and the great execution which he displays. I know, therefore, no one thing which he lacks, that conduces to the greatness of an artist. I have heard Vogler upon the pianoforte—of his organ playing I say nothing, not having heard him upon that instrument—have often heard him, heard him by the the hour together, and never failed to wonder at his astonishing execution; but Bethofen, in addition to the execution, has greater clearness and weight of idea, and more expression—in short, he is more for the heart—equally great, therefore, as an *adagio* or *allegro* player. Even the members of this remarkable orchestra are, without exception, his admirers, and all ears when he plays. Yet he is exceedingly modest and free from all pretension. He, however, acknowledged to me, that, upon the journeys which the Elector had enabled him to make, he had seldom found in the playing of the most distinguished virtuosos that excellence which he supposed he had a right to expect. His style of treating his instrument is so different from that usually adopted, that it impresses one with the idea, that by a path of his own discovery he has attained that height of excellence whereon he now stands.

Had I acceded to the pressing entreaties of my friend Bethofen, to which Herr Winterberger added his own, and remained another day in Mergentheim, I have no doubt he would have played to me hours; and the day, thus spent in the society of these two great artists, would have been transformed into a day of the highest bliss.

There is one passage in this exceedingly valuable and interesting letter which, in the present state of knowledge of Beethoven's youth, is utterly inexplicable. It is this: "Yet he is exceedingly modest and free from all pretension. He, however, acknowledged to me that upon the journeys which the Elector had enabled him to make, he had seldom found in the playing of the most distinguished virtuosos that excellence which he supposed he had a right to expect." What were the journeys? Who can tell?

There is but one more to add to these musical reminiscences of that period—another visit of Joseph Haydn, who, having changed the plan of his route, returned in July *via* Bonn from London to Vienna. The electoral orchestra gave him a breakfast at Godesberg and there Beethoven laid before him a cantata "which received the particular attention of Haydn, who encouraged its author to continue study." It is not improbable that the arrangements were in part now made under which the young composer became a few months later the pupil of the veteran.

Many a eulogy has been written upon Max Franz for his supposed protection of, and favors granted to, the young Beethoven. It has, however, already been made clear that except the gracious reprimand at the time when the singer Heller was made the subject of the boy's joke, all the facts and anecdotes upon which those eulogies are based belong to a much later than the supposed period. The appointment of Beethoven as Chamber Musician (1789) was no distinguishing mark of favor. Half a dozen other youths of his age shared it with him. His being made Court Pianist was a matter of course; for whom had he as a rival? Had he been in any great degree a favorite of the Elector, what need had there been of his receiving from Waldstein, as Wegeler states, "much pecuniary assistance bestowed in such a way as to spare his sensibilities, it being generally looked upon as a small gratuity from the Elector?" One general remark may be made here which has a bearing upon this point, namely: that Beethoven's dedications of important works throughout his life were, as a rule, made to persons from whom he had received, or from whom he had hopes of receiving, pecuniary benefits. Indeed, in one notable case where such a dedication produced him nothing, he never forgot nor forgave the omission. Had he felt that Maximilian was in any single instance really generous toward him, why did he never dedicate any work to him? Why in all the correspondence, private memoranda and recorded conversations, which have been examined for this work, has Beethoven never mentioned him either in terms of gratitude, or in any manner whatever? All idea that his relations to the Elector were different from those of Bernhard Romberg, Franz Ries or Anton Reicha, must be given up. He was organist, pianist, member of the orchestra; and for these services received his pay like others. There is no proof of more, no indication of less.

But with Waldstein, the case was otherwise. The young count, eight years older than Beethoven, coming direct from Vienna, where his family connections gave him access to the salons of the very highest rank of the nobility, was thoroughly acquainted with the noblest and best that the imperial capital could show in the art of music. Himself more than an ordinary dilettante, he could judge of the youth's powers and became his friend. We have seen that he used occasionally to go to the modest room in the Wenzelgasse, that he even employed Beethoven to compose his "Ritterballet" music, and we shall see, that he foretold the future eminence of the composer and that the name, Beethoven, would stand next those of Mozart and Haydn on the roll of fame. Waldstein's name, too, is in Beethoven's roll of fame; it stands in the list of those to whom important works are dedicated. The dedication of the twenty-four variations on "Venni Amore" to the Countess Hatzfeld indicates, if it does not prove, that Beethoven's deserts were neither unknown nor unacknowledged at her house.

At that time the favorite places of resort for the professors of the new university and for young men whose education and position at court or in society were such as to make them welcome guests, was the house on the Market-place now known as the Zehrgarten; and there, says Frau Karth, Beethoven was in the habit of going. A large portion of this house was let in lodgings, and it is said that Eugène Beauharnais, with his wife and children, at one time occupied the first floor. Its mistress was the Widow Koch who spread also a table for a select company of boarders. Her name, too, often appears in the "Intelligenzblatt" of Bonn in advertisements of books and music. Of her three children, a son and two daughters, the beautiful Barbara—the Babette Koch mentioned in a letter of Beethoven's—was the belle of Bonn. Wegeler's eulogy of her ("Notizen," p. 58) contains the names of several members of that circle whom, doubtless, the young composer so often met at the house.

She was a confidential friend of Eleonore von Breuning, a lady who of all the representatives of the female sex that I met in a rather active and long life came nearest the ideal of a perfect woman—an opinion which is confirmed by all who had the good fortune to know her well. She was surrounded not only by young artists like Beethoven, the two Rombergs, Reicha, the twin brothers Kügelchen and others, but also by the intellectual men of all classes and ages, such as D. Crevelt, Prof. Velten, who died early, Fischenich, who afterward became Municipal Councillor, Prof. Thaddäus Dereser, afterward capitular of the cathedral, Wrede, who became a bishop, Heckel and Floret, secretaries of the Elector, Malchus, private secretary of the Austrian minister von Keverberg, later Government Councillor of Holland, Court Councillor von Bourscheidt, Christian von Breuning and many others.

About the time Beethoven left Bonn for Vienna, the wife of Count Anton von Belderbusch, nephew of the deceased minister of that name, had deserted her husband for the embraces of a certain Baron von Lichtenstein, and Babette Koch was engaged as governess and instructress of the motherless children. In process of time Belderbusch obtained a divorce (under the French law) from his adulterous wife and married the governess, August 9, 1802.

But it was in the Breuning house that Beethoven enjoyed and profited most. The mother's kindness towards him gave her both the right and the power to urge and compel him to the performance of his duties; and this power over him in his obstinate and passionate moods she possessed in a higher degree than any other person. Wegeler gives an anecdote in point: Baron Westphal von Fürstenberg, until now in the service of the Elector, was appointed minister to the Dutch and Westphalian Circuit and to the courts of Cologne and Trèves, his headquarters being at Bonn. He resided in the large house which is now occupied by the post-office, directly behind the statue of him who was engaged as music teacher in the count's family. The Breuning house was but a few steps distant diagonally across a corner of the square. Here Madame von Breuning was sometimes compelled to use her authority and force the young man to go to his lessons. Knowing that she was watching him he would go, *ut iniquæ mentis asellus*, but sometimes at the very door would turn back and excuse himself on the plea that to-day it was impossible to give a lesson—to-morrow he would give two; to which, as upon other occasions when reasoning with him was of no avail, the good lady would shrug her shoulders with the remark: "He has his *raptus* again," an expression which the rapt Beethoven never forgot. Most happy was it for him that in Madame von Breuning he had a friend who understood his character thoroughly, who cherished affection for him, who could and did so effectually act as peace-maker when the harmony between him and her children was disturbed. Schindler is a witness that just for this phase of her motherly care Beethoven, down to the close of life, was duly grateful.

In his later days he still called the members of this family his guardian angels of that time and remembered with pleasure the many reprimands which he had received from the lady of the house. "She understood," said he, "how to keep insects off the flowers." By insects he meant certain friendships which had already begun to threaten danger to the natural development of his talent and a proper measure of artistic consciousness by awakening vanity in him by their flatteries. He was already near to considering himself a famous artist, and therefore more inclined to give heed to those who encouraged him in his illusions than such as set before him the fact that he had still to learn everything that makes a master out of a disciple.

This is well said, is very probable in itself, and belongs in the category of facts as to which Schindler is a trustworthy witness.

Stephan von Breuning became so good a violinist as to play occasionally in the electoral orchestra. As he grew older, and the comparative difference in age between him and Beethoven lessened, the acquaintance between them became one of great intimacy. Frau Karth says he was a frequent visitor in the Wenzelgasse, and she had a lively recollection of "the noise they used to make with their music" in the room overhead. Lenz, the youngest of the Breunings, was but fifteen when his teacher left Bonn, but a few years after he became a pupil of Beethoven again in Vienna and became a good pianist. For him the composer seems to have cherished a warm affection, one to which the seven years' difference in their ages gave a peculiar tenderness. It has been supposed that Beethoven at one time indulged a warmer feeling than mere friendship for Eleonore von Breuning; but this idea is utterly unsupported by anything which has been discovered during the inquiries made for this work.

Beethoven's remarkable powers of improvising were often exhibited at the Breuning house. Wegeler has an anecdote here:

Once when Beethoven was improvising at the house of the Breunings (on which occasions he used frequently to be asked to characterize in the music some well-known person) Father Ries was urged to accompany him upon the violin. After some hesitation he consented, and this may have been the first time that two artists improvised a duo.

Beethoven had in common with all men of original and creative genius a strong repugnance to the drudgery of forcing the elements of his art into dull brains and awkward fingers; but that this repugnance was "extraordinary," as Wegeler says, does not appear. A Frau von Bevervörde, one of his Bonn pupils, assured Schindler that she never had any complaint to make of her teacher in respect to either the regularity of his lessons or his general course of instruction. Nor is there anything now to be gathered from the traditions at Vienna which justifies the epithet. Ries's experience is not here in point, for his relations to Beethoven were like those of little Hummel to Mozart. He received such instruction gratis as the master in leisure moments felt disposed to give. There was no pretence of systematic teaching at stated hours. The occasional neglect of a lesson at Baron Westphal's, as detailed in the anecdote above given, may be explained on other ground than that of extraordinary repugnance to teaching. Beethoven was, in 1791–'92, just at the age when the desire for distinction was fresh and strong; he was conscious of powers still not fully developed; his path was diverse from that of the other young men with whom he associated and who, from all that can be gathered now on the subject, had little faith in that which he had chosen. He must have felt the necessity of other instruction, or, at all events, of better opportunities to compare his powers with those of others, to measure himself by a higher standard, to try the effect of his compositions in another sphere, to satisfy himself that his instincts as a composer were true and that his deviations from the beaten track were not wild and capricious. Waldstein, we know from Wegeler (and this is confirmed by his own words), had faith in him and his works, and it will be seen that another, Fischenich, had also. But what would be said of him and his compositions in the city of Mozart, Haydn, Gluck? To this add the restlessness of an ambitious youth to whom the routine of duties, which must long since in great measure have lost the charm of novelty, had become tedious, and the natural longing of young men for the great world, for a wider field of action, had grown almost insupportable.

Or Beethoven's *raptus* may just then have had a very different origin; Jeannette d'Honrath, or Fräulein Westerhold, was perhaps the innocent cause—two young ladies whose names are preserved by Wegeler of the many for whom he says his friend at various times indulged transient, but not the less ardent, passions. The former was from Cologne, whence she occasionally came to Bonn to pass a few weeks with Eleonore von Breuning.

"She was a beautiful, vivacious blond, of good education," says Wegeler, "and amiable disposition, who enjoyed music greatly and possessed an agreeable voice; wherefore she several times teased our friend by singing a song, familiar at the time, beginning:

> 'Mich heute noch von dir zu trennen
> Und dieses nicht verhindern können,
> Ist zu empfindlich für mein Herz!'

for the favored rival was the Austrian recruiting officer in Cologne, Carl Greth, who married the young lady and died on October 15, 1827, as Field Marshal General, Commander of the 23rd Regiment of Infantry and Commandant at Temesvar."[1]

The passion for Miss d'Honrath was eclipsed by a subsequent fancy for a Fräulein von Westerhold. The Court Calendars of these years name "Hochfürstlich Münsterischer Obrist-Stallmeister, Sr. Excellenz der Hochwohlgeborne Herr Friedrich Rudolph Anton, Freyherr von Westerhold-Giesenberg, kurkölnischer und Hochstift-Münsterischer Geheimrath." This much betitled man, according to Neefe (Spazier's "Berlin. Mus. Zeitung"),

played the bassoon himself and maintained a fair band among his servants, particularly players of wind-instruments. He had two sons, one of whom was a master of the flute, and two daughters. The elder daughter—the younger was still a child—Maria Anna Wilhelmine, was born on July 24, 1774, married Baron Friedrich Clemens von Elverfeldt, called von Beverföde-Werries, on April 24, 1792, and died on November 3, 1852. She was an excellent pianist. In Münster, Neefe heard "the fiery Mad. von Elverfeldt play a difficult sonata by Sardi (not Sarti) with a rapidity and accuracy that were marvellous."

It is not surprising that Beethoven's talent should have met with recognition and appreciation in this musical family. He became the young woman's teacher, and as the chief equerry Count Westerhold had to accompany the Elector on his visits to Münster, where, moreover, he owned a house, there is a tradition in the family that young Beethoven went with them before the young lady's marriage in 1790. She it was with whom Beethoven was now in love. He had the disease violently, nor did he "let concealment, like a worm i' th' bud," feed upon his cheek. Forty years afterward Bernhard Romberg had anecdotes to relate of this "Werther love."

The strong doubt that any such feeling for Eleonore von Breuning was ever cherished by Beethoven has already been expressed. The letters to her from Vienna printed by Wegeler,

---

[1] In one of the Beethoven conversation books, *anno* 1823, may be read in Schindler's handwriting: "Captain V. Greth's address, Commandant in Temesvar."

and other correspondence still in manuscript, confirm this doubt by their general tone; but that a really warm friendship existed between them and continued down to the close of his life, with a single interruption just before he left Bonn, of the cause of which nothing is known, so much is certain. Among the few souvenirs of youthful friendship which he preserved was the following compliment to him on his twentieth birthday, surrounded by a wreath of flowers:

ZU B'S GEBURTSTAG VON SEINER SCHÜLERIN.

> Glück und langes Leben
> Wünsch ich heute dir;
> Aber auch daneben
> Wünsch ich etwas mir!
>
> Mir in Rücksicht deiner
> Wünsch ich deine Huld,
> Dir in Rücksicht meiner
> Nachsicht und Geduld.

1790   Von Ihrer Freundin u. Schülerin
                             Lorchen von Breuning.[1]

Another was a silhouette of Fräulein von Breuning. Referring to Beethoven's allusion to this in a letter to Wegeler (1825) the latter says: "In two evenings the silhouettes of all the members of the von Breuning family and more intimate friends of the house, were made by the painter Neesen of Bonn. In this way I came into the possession of that of Beethoven which is here printed. Beethoven was probably in his sixteenth year at the time";—far more probably in his nineteenth, the reader will say.

To the point of Beethoven's susceptibility to the tender passion let Wegeler again be cited:

> The truth as I learned to know it, and also my brother-in-law Stephan von Breuning, Ferdinand Ries, and Bernhard Romberg, is that there was never a time when Beethoven was not in love, and that in the highest degree. These passions, for the Misses d'Honrath and Westerhold, fell in his transition period from youth to manhood, and left impressions as little deep as were those made upon the beauties who had caused them. In Vienna, at all events so long as I lived there, Beethoven was always in love and occasionally made a conquest which would have been very difficult if not impossible for many an Adonis.

---

[1]From the Fischoff Manuscript. The verbal play can scarcely be given in English rhymed couplets. The sentiment is: "Happiness and long life I wish you to-day, but something do I crave for myself from you—your regard, your forbearance and your patience."

A review of some of the last pages shows that for the most part after 1789 the life of Beethoven was a busy one, but that the frequent absences of the Elector, as recorded in the newspapers of the day, left many a period of considerable duration during which, except for the meetings of the orchestra for rehearsal and study, he had full command of his time.   Thus he had plenty of leisure hours and weeks to devote to composition, to instruction in music, for social intercourse, for visits to Kerpen and other neighboring places, for the indulgence of his strong propensity to ramble in the fields and among the mountains, for the cultivation in that beautiful Rhine region of his warm passion for nature.

The new relations to his father and brothers, as virtual head of the family, were such as to relieve his mind from anxiety on their account.   His position in society, too, had become one of which he might justly be proud, owing, as it was, to no adventitious circumstances, but simply to his genius and high personal character.   Of illness in those years we hear nothing, except Wegeler's remark ("Notizen," 11): "When the famous organist Abbé Vogler played in Bonn (1790 or 1791) I sat beside Beethoven's sickbed"; a mere passing attack, or Wegeler would have vouchsafed it a more extended notice in his subsequent remarks upon his friend's health.   Thus these were evidently happy years, in spite of certain characteristic and gloomy expressions of Beethoven in letters hereafter to be given, and years of active intellectual, artistic and moral development.

The probability that in July, 1792, it had been proposed to Haydn to take Beethoven as a pupil has been mentioned; but it is pretty certain that the suggestion did not come from the Elector, who, there is little doubt, was in Frankfort at the coronation of his nephew Emperor Franz (July 14) at the time of Haydn's visit.   The indefatigable Karajan[1] is unable to determine precisely when the composer left London or reached Vienna; but it is known he was in the former city after July 1st and in the latter before August 4th.   Whatever arrangements may have been made between the pupil and master, they were subject to the will of the Elector, and here Waldstein may well have exerted himself to his protégé's advantage.   At all events, the result was favorable and the journey determined upon.   Perhaps, had Haydn found Maximilian in Bonn, he might have taken the young man with him; as it was, some months elapsed before his pupil could follow.

---

[1]"J. Haydn in London," page 53.

Some little space must be devoted to the question, whence the pecuniary resources for so expensive a journey to and sojourn in Vienna were derived. The good-hearted Neefe did not forget to record the event in very flattering terms when he wrote next year in Spazier's "Berliner Musik-Zeitung":

In November of last year Ludwig van Beethoven, assistant court organist and unquestionably now one of the foremost pianoforte players, went to Vienna *at the expense of our Elector* to Haydn in order to perfect himself under his direction more fully in the art of composition.

In a note he adds:

Inasmuch as this L. v. B. according to several reports is said to be making great progress in art and owes a part of his education to Herr Neefe in Bonn, to whom he has expressed his gratitude in writing, it may be well (Herr N's modesty interposing no objection) to append a few words here, since, moreover, they redound to the credit of Herr B.: "I thank you for your counsel very often given me in the course of my progress in my divine art. If ever I become a great man, yours will be some of the credit. This will give you the greater pleasure, since you can remain convinced, etc."

"At the expense of our Elector"—so says Neefe; so, too, Fischenich says of Beethoven "whom the Elector has sent to Haydn in Vienna." Maximilian, then, had determined to show favor to the young musician. This idea is confirmed by Beethoven's noting, in the small memorandum book previously referred to, the reception soon after reaching Vienna of 25 ducats and his disappointment that the sum had not been a hundred. (A receipt for his salary, 25 th. for the last quarter of this year, still in the Düsseldorf archives, is dated October 22, and seems at first sight to prove an advance per favor; but many others in the same collection show that payments were usually made about the beginning of the second month of each quarter.) There is also a paper in the Düsseldorf collection, undated, but clearly only a year or two after Beethoven's departure, by which important changes are made in the salaries of the Elector's musicians. In this list Beethoven does not appear among those paid from the *Landrentmeisterei* (i.e., the revenues of the state), but is to receive from the *Chatouille* (privy purse) 600 florins—a sum equivalent to the hundred ducats which he had expected in vain. It is true these changes were never carried out, but the paper shows the Elector's intentions.

With such facts before us, how is Beethoven to be relieved of the odium of ingratitude to his benefactor? By the circumstance that, for anything that appears, the good intentions of the Elector—excepting in an increase of salary hereafter to be noted, and the transmission of the 25 ducats—were never carried out; and the young musician, after receiving his quarterly payment two or three times, was left entirely dependent upon his own resources. Maximilian's justification lies in the sea of troubles by which he was so soon to be overwhelmed.

That the 100 ducats were not advanced to Beethoven before leaving Bonn is easily accounted for. In October, 1792, the French revolutionary armies were approaching the Rhine. On the 22nd they entered Mayence; on the 24th and 25th the archives and funds of the court at Bonn were packed up and conveyed down the Rhine. On the 31st the Elector, accompanied by the Prince of Neuwied, reached Cleve on his first flight from his capital. It was a time of terror. All the principal towns of the Rhine region, Trèves, Coblenz, etc., even Cologne, were deserted by the higher classes of the inhabitants. Perhaps it was owing to this that Beethoven obtained permission to leave Bonn for Vienna just then instead of waiting until the approaching theatrical and musical season had passed. But with the treasury removed to Düsseldorf, he had to content himself with just sufficient funds to pay his way to Vienna and the promise of more to be forwarded thither.

Beethoven's departure from Bonn called forth lively interest on the part of his friends. The plan did not contemplate a long sojourn in the Austrian capital; it was his purpose, after completing his studies there, to return to Bonn and thence to go forth on artistic tours.[1] This is proved by an autograph album dating from his last days in Bonn, which some of his intimate friends, obviously those with whom he was wont to associate at the Zehrgarten, sent with him on his way, now preserved in the Imperial Library at Vienna. The majority of the names are familiar to us, but many which one might have expected to find, notably those of the musicians of Bonn, are missing. Eleonore von Breuning's contribution was a quotation from Herder:

>Freundschaft, mit dem Guten,
>Wächset wie der Abendschatten,
>Bis des Lebens Sonne sinkt.[2]

Bonn, den 1. November   Ihre wahre Freundin Eleonore
      1792   Breuning.

[1] Neefe relates that on his second visit to England, Haydn had contemplated taking Beethoven with him.

[2] "Friendship, with that which is good, grows like the evening shadow till the setting of the sun of life."

Most interesting of all the inscriptions in the album, however, is that of Count Waldstein, which was first published by Schindler (Vol. I, p. 18) from a copy procured for him by Aloys Fuchs. It proves how great were the writer's hopes, how strong his faith in Beethoven:

Dear Beethoven! You are going to Vienna in fulfillment of your long-frustrated wishes. The Genius of Mozart is mourning and weeping over the death of her pupil. She found a refuge but no occupation with the inexhaustible Haydn; through him she wishes to form a union with another. With the help of assiduous labor you shall receive *Mozart's spirit from Haydn's hands.*

Your true friend

Bonn, October 29, 1792.   Waldstein.

The dates in the album prove that Beethoven was still in Bonn on November 1, 1792, and indicate that it was the last day of his sojourn there. In Duten's "Journal of Travels," as translated and augmented by John Highmore, Gent. (London, 1782) —a Baedeker's or Murray's handbook of that time—the post-road from Bonn to Frankfort-on-the-Main is laid down as passing along the Rhine *via* Andernach to Coblenz, and thence, crossing the river at Ehrenbreitstein, *via* Montabaur, Limburg, Würges and Königstein;—corresponding to the route advertised in the "Intelligenzblatt" a few years later—time 25 hours, 43 minutes.

This was the route taken by Beethoven and some unknown companion. Starting from Bonn at 6 a.m. they would, according to Dutens and Highmore, dine at Coblenz about 3 p.m. and be in Frankfort about 7 next morning.

The first three pages of the memorandum book above cited contain a record of the expenses of this journey as far as Würges. One of the items is this: "Trinkgeld (*pourboire*) at Coblenz because the fellow drove like the devil right through the Hessian army at the risk of a cudgelling, one small thaler." This army marched from Coblenz on November 5; but on the same day a French corps, having advanced from Mayence beyond Limburg, took possession of Weilburg. The travellers could not, therefore, have journeyed through Limburg later than the night of the 3rd. We conclude, then, that it was between November 1st and 3rd that Beethoven bade farewell to Bonn, and at Ehrenbreitstein saw Father Rhine for the last time.

The temptation is too strong to be resisted to add here the contents of the three pages of the memorandum book devoted to this journey, and the reasonings—fancies, if the reader prefers the term—drawn from them, upon which is founded the assertion that Beethoven had a travelling companion. This is probable in itself, and is confirmed by, first, two handwritings; second, the price paid for post-horses (thus, the first entry is for a station and a quarter at 50 *Stüber*, the regular price being one florin, or 40 *Stüber* per horse for a single passenger; there were, therefore, two horses and 10 *Stüber* extra per post for the second passenger); third, the word "us" in the record of the *Trinkgeld* at Coblenz; fourth, the accounts cease at Würges, but they would naturally have been continued to Vienna had they been noted down by Beethoven from motives of economy; fifth, the payment of 2 fl. for dinner and supper is certainly more than a young man, not overburdened with money, would in those days have spent at the post-house.

We may suppose, then, that the companions have reached the end of their journey in common, and sit down to compute and divide the expenses. Beethoven hands his blank-book to his friend, who writes thus:

(Page 1) From Bonn to Remagen, 1 1-4 Stat. at 50 Stbr. . 3 fl.
    From Remag. to Andernach, 1 1-2 St. 3.45
     Tip 45
     Tolls. 45
    From Andernach to Coblenz, 1 St. . . . . 3.
     Tips to Andernach 50
     " to Coblenz. . . . .
     Tolls to Andernach. 42
     Tolls to Coblenz. . . . .

These last three items are not carried out, and Beethoven now takes the book and adds the items of the "Tolls to Andernach" thus:

   Sinzig. . . . 7 St(über) Reinicke . . . . 5 St.
   Preissig. . . 10 St.   Norich . . . . 4 1-2 St.

These 26 Stüber, changed into Kreutzers, make up the 42 in the column above. On the next page he continues:

(Page 2) Coblenz, tolls. . . . . 30 x
    Rothehahnen (Red Cocks). 24 x
    Coblenz to Montebaur. . . . . 2 rthlr. and 1-2 d
    Tolls for Coblenz. . . . . 48 x
    Tip because the fellow drove like the devil right
     through the Hessian army at the risk of a
     cudgelling. . . . . .one small thaler
     Ate dinner. . . . . 2 fl.
    Post from Montebaur to Limburg. . . . . 3 fl. 57 x
    10 x road money
    15 x " "

(Page 3)   Supper.................................. 2 fl.
             in Limburg............................. 12 Batzen
             Tips................................... 14 x
             Grease money........................... 14 x
             Tip for postillion...................... 1 fl.

The other hand now writes:

> The same money for meals and tips, besides 12 x
> road money to Wirges.

The entries of the second and third pages are now changed into florin currency and brought together, making 22 fl. and 14 x; add the expenses on the first page to this sum and we have a total of about 35 fl. from Bonn to Würges for two young men travelling day and night, and no doubt as economically as was possible.

The next entries are by Beethoven's hand in Vienna, and we are left to imagine his arrival in Frankfort and his departure thence *via* Nuremberg, Regensburg, Passau and Linz in the public post-coach for Vienna. Proof will be found hereafter that he was in that city on or before November 10th, and that Schindler (Vol. I, p. 19) therefore confounds this journey with that of 1787, and is all wrong when he says "they travelled very slowly and the money which they had taken along was exhausted before they had traversed half the journey."

Chapter X

Beethoven's Creative Activity in Bonn—An Inquiry into
the Genesis of Many Compositions—The Cantatas on
the Death of Joseph II and the Elevation of Leopold
II — Songs, the "Ritterballet," the Octet and Other
Chamber Pieces.

BUT for the outbreak of the French Revolution, Bonn seems
to have been destined to become a brilliant centre of learning
and art. Owing to the Elector's taste and love for music, that
art became—what under the influence of Goethe poetry and drama
were in Weimar—the artistic expression and embodiment of the
intellectual character of the time. In this art, among musicians
and composers, Beethoven, endowed with a genius whose originality has rarely if ever been surpassed, "lived, moved and had
his being." His official superiors, Lucchesi, Reicha, Neefe, were
indefatigable in their labors for the church, the stage and the
concert-room; his companions, Andreas Perner, Anton Reicha,
the Rombergs, were prolific in all the forms of composition from
the set of variations to even the opera and oratorios; and in the
performance of their productions, as organist, pianist and viola
player, he, of course, assisted. The trophies of Miltiades allowed
no rest to Themistocles. Did the applause bestowed upon the
scenes, duos, trios, quartets, symphonies, operas of his friends
awaken no spirit of emulation in him? Was he contented to be
the mere performer, leaving composition to others? And yet
what a "beggarly account" is the list of compositions known to
belong to this period of his life![1] Calling to mind the activity of
others, particularly Mozart, developed in their boyhood, and

[1]The discoveries made after Thayer completed and printed his first volume in
German (1866), largely inspired by his labors, have made a thorough revision of this
chapter imperative. In all that follows the editor has accepted the statement of facts
made by Dr. Deiters in his revised version of the first volume published in 1901, but, in
pursuance of his plan as set forth in the introduction, has omitted that which seemed to
him more or less inconsequential, as well as that which belongs in the field of analysis
and criticism.

reflecting on the incentives which were offered to Beethoven
in Bonn, one may well marvel at the small number and the small
significance of the compositions which preceded the Trios Op. 1,
with which, at the age of 24 years, he first presented himself to
the world as a finished artist. But a change has come over the
picture in the progress of time. Not only are the beginnings of
many works which he presented to the world at a late day as the
ripe products of his genius to be traced back to the Bonn period;
fate has also made known to us compositions of his youth which,
for a long time, were lost in whole or in part, and which, in connection with the three great pianoforte quartets of 1785, not only
disclose a steady progress, but also discover the self-developed
individual artist at a much earlier date than has heretofore been
accepted. Now that we are again in possession of the cantatas
and other fruits of the Bonn period, or have learned to know them
better as such, we are able to free ourselves from the old notion
which presented Beethoven as a slowly and tardily developed
master.

The most interesting of Beethoven's compositions in the Bonn
period are unquestionably the cantatas on the death of Joseph II
and the elevation of Leopold II. Beethoven did not bring them
either to performance or publication; they were dead to the world.
Nottebohm called attention to the fact that manuscript copies
of their scores were announced in the auction catalogue of the
library of Baron de Beine in April, 1813. It seems probable that
Hummel purchased them at that time; at any rate, after his death
they found their way from his estate into the second-hand book-
shop of List and Francke in Leipsic, where they were bought in 1884
by Armin Fridmann of Vienna. Dr. Eduard Hanslick acquainted
the world with the rediscovered treasures in a feuilleton published
in the "Neue Freie Presse" newspaper of Vienna on May 13, 1884,
and the funeral cantata was performed for the first time at Vienna
in November, 1884, and at Bonn on June 29, 1885.[1] Both cantatas
were then included in the Complete Works of Beethoven published
by Breitkopf and Härtel. The "Cantata on the Death of Joseph
the Second, composed by L. van Beethoven," was written between
March and June, 1790. The Emperor died on February 20th,
and the news of his death reached Bonn on February 24th. The

[1]There have been a few performances of this cantata in Austria and Germany
since its publication. It was given at a concert of the Beethoven Association in New
York on March 16, 1920, under the direction of Mr. Sam Franko, with an English para-
phrase of the text by the Editor of this biography, designed to rid it of its local application and some of its bombast and make its sentiment applicable to any heroic emanci-
pator.

Lesegesellschaft at once planned a memorial celebration, which took place on March 19th. At a meeting held to make preparations for the function on February 28, Prof. Eulogius Schneider (who delivered the memorial address) expressed the wish that a musical feature be incorporated in the programme and said that a young poet had that day placed a poem in his hands which only needed a setting from one of the excellent musicians who were members of the society or a composer from elsewhere. Beethoven's most influential friends, at the head of them Count Waldstein, were members of the society. Here, therefore, we have beyond doubt the story of how Beethoven's composition originated. The minutes of the last meeting for preparation, held on March 17, state that "for various reasons the proposed cantata cannot be performed." Among the various reasons may have been the excessive difficulty of the parts for the wind-instruments which, according to Wegeler, frustrated a projected performance at Mergentheim; though it is also possible that Beethoven, who was notoriously a slow worker, was unable to complete the music in the short time which was at his disposal. The text of the cantata was written by Severin Anton Averdonk, son of an employee of the electoral Bureau of Accounts, and brother of the court singer Johanna Helene Averdonk, who, in her youth, was for a space a pupil of Johann van Beethoven. Beethoven set the young poet's ode for solo voice, chorus and orchestra without trumpets and drums. Brahms, on playing through the score, remarked: "It is Beethoven through and through. Even if there were no name on the title-page none other than that of Beethoven could be conjectured." The same thing may be said of the "Cantata on the Elevation of Leopold II to the Imperial Dignity, composed by L. v. Beethoven." Leopold's election as Roman Emperor took place on September 30, 1790, his coronation on October 9, when Elector Max Franz was present at Frankfort. This gives us a hint as to the date of the composition. Whether or not the Elector commissioned it cannot be said. Averdonk was again the poet. The two cantatas mark the culmination of Beethoven's creative labors in Bonn; they show his artistic individuality ripened and a sovereign command of all the elements which Bonn was able to teach him from a technical point of view.

Two airs for bass voice with orchestral accompaniment are, to judge by the handwriting, also to be ascribed to about 1790. The first is entitled "'Prüfung des Küssens' ('The Test of Kissing'), v. L. v. Beethowen." The use of the "w" instead of the "v" in the spelling of the name points to an early period for the composition.

The text of the second bears the title, "Mit Mädeln sich vertragen," and was taken by Beethoven from the original version of Goethe's "Claudine von Villa Bella." Paper, handwriting and the spelling of the name of the composer indicate the same period as the first air. The two compositions remained unknown a long time, but are now to be had in the Supplement to the Complete Works published by Breitkopf and Härtel.

To these airs must be added a considerable number of songs as fruits of Beethoven's creative labors in Bonn. The first of these, "Ich, der mit flatterndem Sinn," was made known by publication in the Complete Works. A sketch found among sketches for the variations on "Se vuol ballare," led Nottebohm to set down 1792 as the year of its origin. Of the songs grouped and published as Op. 52 the second, "Feuerfarbe," belongs to the period of transition from Bonn to Vienna. On January 26, 1793, Fischenich wrote to Charlotte von Schiller: "I am enclosing with this a setting of the 'Feuerfarbe' on which I should like to have your opinion. It is by a young man of this place whose musical talents are universally praised and whom the Elector has sent to Haydn in Vienna. He proposes also to compose Schiller's 'Freude,' and indeed strophe by strophe. Ordinarily he does not trouble himself with such trifles as the enclosed, which he wrote at the request of a lady." From this it is fair to conclude that the song was finished before Beethoven's departure from Bonn. Later he wrote a new postlude, which is found among *motivi* for the Octet and the Trio in C minor. Of the other songs in Op. 52 the origin of several may be set down as falling in the Bonn period. That of the first, "Urian's Reise um die Welt," we have already seen. Whether or not these songs, which met with severe criticism in comparison with other greater works of Beethoven, were published without Beethoven's knowledge, is doubtful.[1] Probability places the following songs in the period of transition, or just before it: "An Minna," sketched on a page with "Feuerfarbe," and other works written out in the early days of the Vienna period; a drinking-song, "to be sung at parting," "Erhebt das Glas mit froher Hand," to judge by the handwriting, an early work, presumably *circa* 1787; "Elegie auf den Tod eines Pudels"; "Die Klage," to be placed in 1790, inasmuch as the original manuscript form appears simultaneously

[1]See Vol. II, p. 210, of the first German edition of this work. Ries says, on page 124 of the "Notizen," apropos of the posthumous manuscripts: "All such trifles and things which he never meant to publish, as not considering them worthy of his name, were secretly brought into the world by his brothers. Such were the songs published when he had attained the highest degree of fame, composed years before at Bonn, previous to his departure for Vienna; and in like manner other trifles, written for albums, etc., were secretly taken from him and published."

with sketches of the funeral cantata; "Wer ist ein freier Mann?",
whose original autograph in the British Museum bears the inscription "ipse fecit L. v. Beethoven," and must be placed not later
than 1790, while a revised form is probably a product of 1795, and
to a third Wegeler appended a different text, "Was ist des Maurer's
Ziel?" published in 1806; the "Punschlied" may be a trifle older;
the autograph of "Man strebt die Flamme zu verhehlen," in the
possession of the Gesellschaft der Musikfreunde, which has been
placed in the year 1792, bears in Beethoven's handwriting the
words "pour Madame Weissenthurn par Louis van Beethoven."
Madame Weissenthurn was a writer and actress, and from 1789
a member of the company of the Burgtheater in Vienna, and it is
more than likely that Beethoven did not get acquainted with her
till he went to Vienna, although she was born on the Rhine.

Turn we now to the instrumental works which date back to
the Bonn period. The beginning is made with the work which,
in a manner, first brought Beethoven into close relationship with
the stage—the "Ritterballet," produced by the nobility on Carnival Sunday, March 6, 1791, and which, consequently, cannot have
been composed long before, say in 1790 or 1791. The ballet was
designed by Count Waldstein in connection with Habich, a
dancing-master from Aix-la-Chapelle. Of the contents of the piece
we know nothing more than is contained in the report from Bonn
printed three chapters back, namely, that it illustrated the predilection of the ancient Germans for war, the chase, love and
drinking; the music, being without words, can give us no further
help. It consists of eight short numbers, designed to accompany
the pantomime: 1, March; 2, German Song;[1] 3, Hunting Song;
4, Romance; 5, War Song; 6, Drinking Song; 7, German Dance;
8, Coda. It was intended that the music should be accepted as
Waldstein's and, therefore, Beethoven never published it.

It seems as if the last year of Beethoven's sojourn in Bonn
was especially influential in the development of his artistic character and ability. Of the works of 1792, besides trifles, there
were two of larger dimensions which, if we were not better advised,
would unhesitatingly be placed in the riper Vienna period. The
autograph of the Octet for wind-instruments, published after the
composer's death and designated at a later date as Op. 103, bears
the inscription "Parthia in Es" (above this, "dans un Concert"),
"Due Oboe, Due Clarinetti, Due Corni, Due Fagotti di L. v.
Beethoven." From a sketch which precedes suggestions for the

---

[1]The subject of the German Song was used by Beethoven later in a sonata.

song "Feuerfarbe," Nottebohm concludes that the Octet was composed in 1792, or, at the latest in 1793.   In the latter case it would be a Viennese product.   It is improbable, however, that Beethoven found either incentive or occasion soon after reaching Vienna to write a piece of this character, and it is significant that in his later years he never returned to a combination of eight in-struments.   But there was an incentive in Bonn in the form of the excellent dinner-music of the Elector described by Chaplain Junker, which was performed by two oboes, two clarinets, two horns and two bassoons.   It may be set down as a fruit of 1792, his last year in Bonn.   For the same combination of instruments, Beethoven also composed a Rondino in E-flat, published in 1829 by Diabelli, probably from the posthumous manuscript.   From the autograph Nottebohm argued that it was written in Bonn, and what has been said of the origin of the Octet applies also to the Rondino.   The autograph of a little duet in G for two flutes bears the inscription: "For Friend Degenharth by L..v. Beethoven. August 23rd, 1792, midnight."

We are lifted to a higher plane again by a work which in invention and construction surpasses the compositions already mentioned and still to be mentioned in the present category, and discloses the fully developed Beethoven as we know him—the Trio in E-flat, for violin, viola and violoncello, Op. 3.   Its publi-cation was announced by Artaria in February, 1797.   According to Wegeler, Beethoven was commissioned by Count Appony in 1795 to write a quartet.   He made two efforts, but produced first a Trio (Op. 3), and then a Quintet (Op. 4).   We know better the origin of the latter work now; but Wegeler is also mistaken about the origin of the Trio; it was a Bonn product.   Here the proof:

At the general flight from Bonn, whether the one at the end of October or that of December 15, 1793, the Elector ordered his chaplain, Abbé Clemens Dobbeler, to accompany an English lady, the Honourable Mrs. Bowater, to Hamburg.   "While there," says William Gardiner in his "Music and Friends," III, 142, "he was declared an emigrant and his property was seized.   Luckily he placed some money in our (English) government funds, and his only alternative was to proceed to England."   Dobbeler accom-panied Mrs. Bowater to Leicester.   She,

having lived much in Germany, had acquired a fine taste in music; and as the Abbé was a very fine performer on the violin, music was essential to fill up this irksome period (while Mrs. Bowater lived in lodgings before moving into old Dolby Hall). My company was sought with that of two of my friends to make up occasionally an instrumental quartett.

. . . Our music consisted of the Quartetts of Haydn, Boccherini, and Wranizky. The Abbé, who never travelled without his violin, had luckily put into his fiddle-case a Trio composed by Beethoven, just before he set off, which thus, in the year 1793, found its way to Leicester. This composition, so different from anything I had ever heard, awakened in me a new sense, a new delight in the science of sounds. . . . . When I went to town (London) I enquired for the works of this author, but could learn nothing more than that he was considered a madman and that his music was like himself. However, I had a friend in Hamburg through whom, although the war was raging at the time, I occasionally obtained some of these inestimable treasures.

What trio was this so praised by the enthusiastic Englishman? On the last page but one of Gardiner's "Italy, her Music, Arts and People" he writes, speaking of his return down the Rhine:

Recently we arrived at Bonn, the birthplace of Beethoven. About the year 1786, my friend the Abbé Dobler, chaplain to the Elector of Cologne, first noticed this curly, blackheaded boy, the son of a tenor singer in the cathedral. Through the Abbé I became acquainted with the first production of this wonderful composer. How great was my surprise in playing the viola part to his Trio in E-flat, so unlike anything I had ever heard. It was a new sense to me, an intellectual pleasure which I had never received from sounds.

Again, in a letter to Beethoven, Gardiner says, "Your Trio in E-flat (for violin, viola and bass"). To all but the blind this narrative pours a flood of light upon the whole question.[1]

There come up now for consideration the compositions in which Beethoven's principal instrument, the pianoforte, is employed. They carry us back a space, and to the earliest examples we add a related composition for violin.

It was a part of Beethoven's official duty to play pianoforte before the Elector, and it may therefore easily be imagined that after his first boyish attempt in 1784, he would continue to compose concertos and parts of concertos for the pianoforte and

---

[1]The Trio in E-flat was not published until 1797. It is therefore obvious that the music which Abbé Dobbeler carried with him to England must have been a manuscript copy. Dr. Deiters, accepting without attempt at contradiction Thayer's proof of its origin at a period not later than 1792, nevertheless puts forth the conjecture that the work may have been revised and reconstructed at a later date in Vienna, as was the case with other compositions. It is not to be supposed, he urges, that Beethoven, enjoying the celebrity that he did in 1797, would have published then with an opus number a production of his youth without first subjecting it to a thorough revision. Moreover, his earlier chamber compositions were in three movements, the minuet having been added for the first time in the Octet. It was scarcely conceivable that he should have simultaneously conceived a work in six movements unless he had had a Mozart model in his mind. But why not? We have seen from the story of the music admired at the court of Vienna from which the Elector came that the serenade form was in favor there. The Sonata for Pianoforte and Violoncello which Artaria announced in May, 1807, is an arrangement of this Trio, but it was not made by Beethoven.

orchestra, and not wait until 1795, when he publicly performed the "entirely new" concerto in B-flat. Quite recently the world has learned of a first movement for a pianoforte concerto in D, concerning which the first report was made by Guido Adler in 1888, and which was performed in Vienna on April 7, 1889, and then incorporated, as edited by Adler, in the supplement to the Complete Works. It was discovered in copy, solo and orchestra parts, in the possession of Joseph Bezeczny, the head of an educational institution for the blind in Prague, and the handwriting is his. Immediately after its first performance its authenticity was questioned by Dr. Paumgartner, who called attention to its Mozartian characteristics, but failed to advance any reason for doubting the testimony of so thorough a musical scholar as Adler. The latter had emphasized the resemblances to Mozart's works, which, indeed, are too obvious to escape attention; but for a long time after 1785, especially after Beethoven met Mozart personally in Vienna, the former was completely in the latter's thrall, and that his music should occasionally be reminiscent of his model is not at all singular. Such reminiscences are to be found in the quartets of 1785 and the trio for pianoforte and wind-instruments. It is safe to assume that the movement was written, as Adler suggests, in the period 1788-1793, perhaps before rather than after 1790, and that Beethoven attached little value to it and laid it permanently aside.

A companion-piece to this movement is the fragment of a Concerto for Violin in C major, of which the autograph is in the archives of the Gesellschaft der Musikfreunde in Vienna, the handwriting of which indicates that it belongs to the early Vienna if not the Bonn period. That it is a first transcription is indicated by the fact that there are many erasures and corrections. The fragment contains 259 measures, embracing the orchestral introduction, the first solo passage, the second *tutti* and the beginning of the free fantasia for the solo instrument; it ends with the introduction of a new transition *motif* which leads to the conjecture that the movement was finished and that the missing portion has been lost.[1]

A Trio in E-flat for Pianoforte, Violin and Violoncello, found among Beethoven's posthumous papers, was published in 1836 by Dunst in Frankfort-on-the-Main. On the original publication its authenticity was certified to by Diabelli, Czerny and Ferdinand Ries, and it was stated that the original manuscript

---

[1]Josef Hellmesberger, of Vienna, completed the movement, utilizing the existing *motivi*, and the piece was published by Friedrich Schreiber.

was in the possession of Schindler; Wegeler verified the hand-writing as that of Beethoven. Schindler cites Beethoven's utter-ance that he had written the work at the age of 15 years and de-scribed it as one of his "highest strivings in the free style of compo-sition," which was either a misunderstanding of Schindler's or a bit of irony on the part of Beethoven. Nearer the truth, at any rate, is a remark in Gräffer's written catalogue of Beethoven's works: "Composed *anno* 1791, and originally intended for the three trios, Op. 1, but omitted as too weak by Beethoven." Whether or not this observation rests on an authentic source is not stated.[1]

Whether or not the Pianoforte Trios, Op. 1, were composed in Bonn may be left without discussion here, since we shall be obliged to recur to the subject later. The facts about them that have been determined beyond controversy are, that they were published in 1795; were not ready in their final shape in 1794; and were already played in the presence of Haydn in 1793.

The Variations in E-flat for Pianoforte, Violin and Violoncello, which were published in 1804 by Hofmeister in Leipsic as Op. 44, apparently belong to the last year of Beethoven's life in Bonn. Nottebohm found a sketch of the work alongside one of the song "Feuerfarbe," which fact points to the year 1792; Beethoven in a letter to the publisher appears not to have laid particular store by it, a circumstance easily understood in view of the great works which had followed the youthful effort.

Besides these compositions, a Trio for Pianoforte, Flute and Bassoon,[2] concerning which all the information which we have came from the catalogue of Beethoven's effects sold at auction, has recently been published. It is No. 179 in the catalogue, where it is described as a composition of the Bonn period. On the auto-graph, preserved in Berlin, the title, placed at the end, is "Trio concertante a clavicembalo, flauto, fagotto, composto da Ludovico van Beethoven organista di S. S. (illegible word), cologne." The designation of the composer as organist, etc., fixes the place of its origin, and the handwriting indicates an early date.

---

[1]Dr. Deiters points out as characteristics of this Trio which indicate that it was not written by Beethoven at the age of 15, but long after the pianoforte quartets, the freedom in invention and development, the large dimensions of the free fantasia portion, its almost imperceptible return to the principal theme, and the introduction of a coda in the first movement. *Motivi* from this movement recur in later works, for instance, the Sonata in F minor, Op. 2, and the Pianoforte Concerto in C major. Beethoven seems to have used the designation "Scherzo" in it for the first time.

[2]The combination of instruments in this piece led Dr. Deiters to conjecture that it may have been composed for the family von Westerhold. Count von Westerhold played the bassoon, his son the flute, and his daughter the pianoforte.

Among the papers found in Beethoven's apartments after his death, was the manuscript of a Sonata in B-flat for Pianoforte and Flute, which passed into the hands of Artaria. It is not in Beethoven's handwriting, and the little evidence of its authenticity is not convincing.[1]

It is more than likely that the Variations for Pianoforte and Violin on Mozart's "Se vuol ballare" ought to be assigned to the latter part of the Bonn period. They were published in July, 1793, with a dedication to Eleonore von Breuning, to whom Beethoven sent the composition with a letter dated November 2, 1793.[2] The dedication leads to the presumption that the work was carried to Vienna in a finished state and there subjected to only the final polish. The postscript to the letter to Fräulein von Breuning betrays the reason for the hurried publication: Beethoven wanted to checkmate certain Viennese pianists whom he had detected copying peculiarities of his playing in improvisation which he suspected they would publish as their own devices.

Besides the pieces already mentioned, Beethoven wrote the following works for pianofore in Bonn:

1. A Prelude in F minor.[3] According to a remark on a printed copy shown to be authentic, Beethoven wrote it when he was 15 year old, that is, in 1786 or, the question of his age not being determined at the time, 1787. The prelude is, as a matter of fact, a fruit of his studies in the art of imitation; and the initiative, probably, came from Bach's Preludes.

2. Two Preludes through the Twelve Major Keys for Pianoforte or Organ; published by Hoffmeister in 1803 as Op. 39. Obviously exercises written for Neefe while he was Beethoven's teacher in composition.

3. Variations on the arietta "Venni Amore," by Righini, in D major—"Venni Amore," not "Vieni"; the arietta begins: "Venni Amore nel tuo regno, ma compagno del Timor." Righini gave his melody a number of vocal variations. Beethoven

---

[1]Dr. Deiters points out that Thayer, in transcribing the themes of this Trio, overlooked a *Largo*, which made the movements number four instead of three as given in the Chronological Catalogue. The existence of four movements added to the doubtful authenticity in the eyes of the German editor.

[2]This letter will appear later. The Variations are published in Series 12, No. 103, of the Complete Edition. In a catalogue of Breitkopf and Härtel of 1793, they are designated Op. 1; also in a catalogue in 1794 of Geyl and Hedler's. It is plain from a passage in the letter to Eleonore von Breuning ("I never would have written it in this way," etc.) that the Coda did not receive its definitive form until just before publication. Thayer was of the opinion when he wrote Vol. I of this work, that it had been appended in Vienna.

[3]It was published in 1805 by the Kunst- und Industriecomptoir of Vienna. Complete Works, Series 18, No. 195; *cf.* Nottebohm's "Beethoven's Studien," p. 6.

republished his in Vienna in 1801 through Traeg (Complete Works, Series 17, No. 178); composed about 1790 and published in Mannheim in 1791. They were inscribed to Countess Hatzfeld (née Countess de Girodin), who has been praised in this book as an eminent pianist. The story of the encounter between Beethoven and Sterkel in which these variations figure has also been told. Beethoven had a good opinion of them; Czerny told Otto Jahn that he had brought them with him to Vienna and used them to "introduce" himself.

Two books of variations are to be adjudged to the Bonn period because of their place of publication and other biographical considerations. They are the Variations in A major on a theme from Dittersdorf's opera "Das rothe Käppchen" ("Es war einmal ein alter Mann") and the Variations for four hands on a theme by Count Waldstein. Both sets were published by Simrock in Bonn, the first of Beethoven's compositions published in his native town. They were not published until 1794, but according to a letter to Simrock, dated August 2, 1794, the latter had received the first set a considerable time before, and Beethoven had held back the corrections while the other was already printed. Beethoven's intimate association with Waldstein in Bonn is a familiar story, but we hear nothing of it in the early Viennese days. The variations on a theme of his own seem likely to have been the product of a wish expressed by the Count. That Beethoven seldom wrote for four hands, and certainly not without a special reason, is an accepted fact.[1]

Another presumably Bonnian product which has come down to us only as a fragment is the Sonata in C major for Pianoforte,

[1]In the Fall of 1919, announcement was made by the newspapers that French investigators had discovered in the British Museum four thitherto unknown Beethoven autographs amongst manuscripts purchased from Julian Marshall. The editor of the second edition of Köchel's "Thematic Catalogue of Mozart's Works" had seen the manuscripts and included two of them as authentic Mozart compositions and two as probably such in the supplement to that work. They were a Trio in D, for pianoforte, Violin and Violoncello (two pages of the first *Allegro* missing, listed as K. No. 52a); three pieces for pianoforte, four hands, a *Gavotte* in F, an *Allegro* in B-flat, and a *Marcia lugubre* in C minor (six measures), No. 71a; a *Rondo* in B-flat, to which the editor assigned the year 1786, No. 511a; and a *Menuet* in C, for orchestra, the first of a set composed by Beethoven in 1795, which M. Chantavoine published in 1903 under the title "Douze Menuets inédits pour Orchestre. L. van Beethoven. (Œuvres posthumes. Au Ménestrel." Theodore Wyzewa and Georges de St. Foix made a study of the manuscripts and discussed them in "Le Guide Musical" of December, 1919, January and February, 1920. They were then set down as "pseudo-Mozarts." M. Charles Malherbe declared that none of the compositions was in Mozart's hand, and M. de St. Foix, after further consideration of the internal evidence, declared them all to be indubitably by Beethoven and gave his reasons in an essay published in "The Musical Quarterly" (New York and Boston, G. Schirmer) of April, 1920. He told the history of the manuscripts as follows: "They had been presented by the Emperor of Austria to the Sultan Abdul Aziz. The latter, who probably cared very little for these relics of the 18th century, presented them in

published in 1830 by Dunst in Frankfort, with a dedication to Eleonore von Breuning. It is probably the sonata which Beethoven, according to the letter to be given presently, had promised to his friend and which was fully sketched at the time. There would be no doubt of the fact that the sonata was written in Bonn if the presumption that the letter was written in Bonn were true; but even as it is, the fact that the letter says that it had been promised "long ago" indicates a pre-Viennese origin. All that is certain is that Eleonore von Breuning received it from Beethoven in 1796. In the copy sent to the publisher eleven measures at the end of the *Adagio* were lacking. These were supplied by Ferdinand Ries in the manner of Beethoven. There can scarcely be a doubt that Beethoven finished the *Adagio*, and it can be assumed that he also composed a last movement, which has been lost.

Concerning the Rondo in C major published in Bossler's "Blumenlese" of 1783, we have already spoken.[1]

It is a striking fact to any one who has had occasion to examine carefully the chronology of publication of Beethoven's works, that up to nearly the close of 1802 whatever appeared under his name was worthy of that name; but that then, in the period of the second, third and fourth symphonies, of the sonatas, Op. 47, 53, 57 and of "Leonore," to the wonder of the critics of that time serial advertisements of the "Kunst- und Industrie-Comptoir" in Vienna announce the Trios, Op. 30 and the seven Bagatelles, Op. 33; in another the "Grand Sinfonie," Op. 36, and the Variations on "God save the King"; on May 15, 1805, the Waldstein Sonata and the Romance, Op. 50; and on June 16 the songs, Op. 52, which the "Allgemeine Mus. Zeitung" describes as "commonplace, poor, weak, in part ridiculous stuff." Ries solves the enigma when he writes ("Notizen," 124) that all trifles, many things which he

turn to his musical director, Guatelli Pasha. An English collector, Julian Marshall, purchased them from the Pasha's son, W. Guatelli Bey, and when, later on, the British Museum acquired the Marshall Collection these manuscripts went over into its possession."

The *Gavotte* was played at a concert of the Beethoven Association in New York in January, 1920, by Madame Samaroff and Harold Bauer, being inserted as a movement in the Sonata in A major for four hands, Op. 6. Mr. Bauer also made an arrangement for two hands which has been published by G. Schirmer.

[1]The discoveries which have been made since Thayer wrote his first volume have very effectually disproved the old belief touching the sterility of the Bonn period. The inquiry which might still be pursued now is whether or not other compositions which have been attributed to a later period may not also have been composed, or at least projected and sketched, in Bonn. The point of view has changed, but what Thayer wrote over half a century ago is still so largely pertinent that it is here given in the body of the text with only such modifications as were necessary to bring it into harmony with the rest of the chapter.

never intended to publish because he deemed them unworthy of his name, were given to the world through the agency of his brother. In this manner the world was made acquainted with songs which he had written long before he went to Vienna from Bonn. Even little compositions which he had written in albums were filched and published.

But even if the widest latitude be given to the judgment in selecting from the publications of these years works belonging to the Bonn period, still what an exceedingly meagre list is the aggregate of Beethoven's compositions from his twelfth to the end of his twenty-second year! Mozart's, according to Köchel, reach at that age 293; Handel completed his twentieth year, February 23, 1705; on the twenty-fifth his second opera "Nero" was performed. And what had he not previously written!

This apparent lack of productiveness on the part of Beethoven has been noticed by other writers. One has disputed the fact and is of opinion that the composer in later years destroyed the manuscripts of his youth to prevent the possibility of injury to his fame by their posthumous publication. But this explanation is nonsense, as every one knows who has had an opportunity to examine the autograph collections in Vienna and there to remark with what scrupulous care even his most valueless productions were preserved by their author in all his migrations from house to house and from city to country throughout his Vienna life.

Beethoven attached absolutely no value to his autographs; after they had once been engraved they generally were piled on the floor in his living room or an anteroom among other pieces of music. I often brought order into his music, but when Beethoven hunted for anything, everything was sent flying in disorder. At that time I might have carried away the autograph manuscripts of all the pieces which had been printed, or had I asked him for them he would unquestionably have given them to me without a thought.

These words of Ries are confirmed by the small number of autographs of printed works in the auction catalogue of Beethoven's posthumous papers—most of them having remained in the hands of the publishers or having been lost, destroyed or stolen.

Another author has endeavored to supply the vacuum by deducing the chronology of Beethoven's works from their form, matter or general character as viewed by his eyes, referring all which seem to him below the standard of the composer at any particular period to an earlier one; and a very comical chronology he makes of it. His success certainly has not been such as to induce any attempt of the kind here; and yet that he is right in the general fact is the hypothesis which the following remarks are conceived to establish as truth. Schindler—who is often very positive on the ground that what he does not know cannot be true—in introducing his chronological table of Beethoven's works, published from 1796 to 1800, remarks: "It may be asserted with positiveness that none of the works catalogued below were composed before 1794"; upon which point the assertion is ventured that Schindler is thoroughly mistaken and that many of the works published by Beethoven during the first dozen years of his Vienna life were taken thither from Bonn. They doubtless were more or less altered, amended, improved, corrected, but nevertheless belong as compositions to those years when "Beethoven played pianoforte concertos, and Herr Neefe accompanied at Court in the theatre and in concerts." While the other young men were trying their strength upon works for the orchestra and stage, the performance of which would necessarily give them notoriety, the Court Pianist would naturally confine himself mostly to his own instrument and to chamber music—to works whose production before a small circle in the salons of the Elector, Countess Hatzfeld and others would excite little if any public notice. But here he struck out so new, and at that time so strange a path that no small degree of praise is due to the sagacity of Count Waldstein, who comprehended his aims, felt his greatness and encouraged him to trust to and be guided by his own instincts and genius.

That Beethoven also tried his powers in a wider field we know from the two cantatas, the airs in "Die schöne Schusterin" and the "Ritterballet." Carl Haslinger in Vienna also possessed an orchestral introduction to the second act of an unnamed opera which may as well be referred to the Bonn period as to any other; and it is not by any means a wild suggestion that he had tried his strength in other concertos for pianoforte and full orchestra than that of 1784. As to the compositions for two, six or eight windinstruments there was little if any danger of mistake in supposing them to have been written for the Elector's "Harmonie-Musik." But this is wandering from the point; to establish which the following remarks are in all humility submitted:

I. If a list be drawn up of Beethoven's compositions published between 1795 and December, 1802, with the addition of other works known to have been composed in those years, the result will be nearly as follows (omitting single songs and other minor pieces): symphonies, 2; ballet ("Prometheus"), 1; sonatas (solo and duo), 32; romances (violin and orchestra), 2; serenade, 1; duos (clarinet and bassoon), 3; sets of variations, 15; sets of dances, 5; "Ah! perfido" and "Adelaide," 2; pianoforte concertos, 3; trios (pianoforte and other instruments), 9; quartets, 6; quintets, 3; septet, 1; pianoforte rondos, 3; marches (for four hands), 3; oratorio ("Christus"), 1; an aggregate of 92 compositions in eight years or ninety-six months. And most of them *such* compositions! That Beethoven was a remarkable man all the world knows; but that he could produce at this rate, study operatic composition with Salieri, sustain, nay, increase his reputation as a pianoforte virtuoso, journey to Prague, Berlin and other places, correct proof-sheets for his publishers, give lessons and yet find time to write long letters to friends, to sleep, to eat, drink and be merry with companions of his own age—this is, to say the least, "a morsel difficult of digestion." The more so from the fact that at the very time when he began to devote himself more exclusively to composition such marvellous fertility suddenly ceased. The inference is obvious.

II. When Neefe, in 1793, calls Beethoven "beyond controversy one of the foremost pianoforte players," it excites no surprise. Ten years before he had played the most of Bach's "Well-Tempered Clavichord" and had now long held the offices of Second Court Organist and Concerto Player; but what sufficient reason could Waldstein have had for his faith that this pianist, by study and perseverance, would yet be able to seize and hold the sceptre of Mozart? And upon what grounds, too, could Fischenich, on January 26, 1793, write as he did to Charlotte von Schiller from Bonn (see *ante*) and add, "I expect something perfect from him, for so far as I know him he is wholly devoted to the great and sublime. . . . Haydn has written here that he would soon put him at grand operas and soon be obliged to quit composing."

Note the date of this—January 26, 1793. Haydn must have written some time before this, when Beethoven could not have been with him more than six or eight weeks. Did the master found his remark upon what he had seen in his pupil or upon the compositions which his pupil had placed before him? Wegeler has printed an undated and incomplete letter of Beethoven to Eleonore von Breuning, certainly, however, not later than the spring of 1794, which was accompanied by a set of variations and a rondo for pianoforte and violin. Do the following passages in this letter indicate anything?

I have a great deal to do or I would before this have transcribed the sonata *which I promised you long ago.* It is a mere sketch in my manuscript and it would be a difficult task even for the clever and practised Paraquin to copy it. You can have the rondo copied and return the score to me. It is the only one of my things which is, in a manner, suitable to you.

May these words not be paraphrased thus: "As to the sonata which I played at your house and of which I promised you a copy —it is in my manuscript hardly more than a sketch, so that I could not trust it to a copyist, not even to Paraquin, and I have not had leisure to transcribe it myself." And, finally, the closing lines of a short article in the "Jahrbuch der Tonkunst für Wien und Prag," 1776—which notice was not written later than the spring of 1795, nine or ten months before the publication of the Sonatas Op. 2—are pregnantly suggestive: "We have a number of beautiful sonatas by him, amongst which the last ones particularly distinguish themselves." These works were, therefore, well-known in manuscript even at the time when he was busy with his studies under Haydn and Albrechtsberger.

III.   If in spite of the above it still be objected that the *opera* 1 to 15, or 20, as you please, are of a character beyond the powers of Beethoven during his Bonn life, who *knows* this to be a fact? Has such an objection any other basis than a mere prejudice?

A fanciful theory has exhibited Beethoven to us as a rude, undeveloped genius, who, being transferred to Vienna and schooled two years by Haydn and Albrechtsberger, then began with the Trios Op. 1, wrought his way upward in eight years through the twenty-three compositions of *opera* 2 to 14 in a geometrical progression to the first pianoforte concertos, the ballet "Prometheus" and the Symphony in C! It is, however, known that in March, 1795, Beethoven played his Pianoforte Concerto in B-flat in Vienna, shortly afterward published the Trios, Op. 1, and in 1796 composed the two sonatas for pianoforte and violoncello in Berlin. A young man who at the age of 24 or 25 could give the public two such concertos could hardly have been such a rough diamond only three or four years before.

IV.   However convincing the preceding propositions may seem to the ordinary reader, the critical student of musical history justly demands something more. It is not enough for him to know that Op. 19 was composed before the publication of Op. 1; that Op. 2 is in part made up from the Pianoforte Quartets of 1785; that the Quintet Op. 4 is an arrangement of the "Parthia" in E-flat for wind-instruments afterwards published as Op. 103, and is now proved to belong to the Bonn period, and that a whole movement of the funeral cantata found its way into "Fidelio"—the argument is to him like an arch without its keystone until one or more of the important works be named specifically as Bonn compositions and proved to be such.[1]

[1]Thayer proceeds from this point to give the reasons for his belief that the Trios Op. 1 and 3 were written in Bonn. The origin of Op. 1 will be discussed hereafter; that of the latter has just been made clear by the story of Mrs. Bowater and Abbé Dobbeler.

Chapter XI

Beethoven in Vienna — Personal Details — Death of His
Father — Minor Expenditures and Receipts — Studies
with Albrechtsberger and Salieri.

IT would be pleasant to announce the arrival of Ludwig van
Beethoven in Vienna with, so to speak, a grand flourish of
trumpets, and to indulge the fancy in a highly-colored and
poetic account of his advent there; but, unluckily, there is none
of that lack of data which is favorable to that kind of composition; none of that obscurity which exalts one to write history as he
would have it and not as it really was. The facts are too patent.
Like the multitude of studious youths and young men who came
thither annually to find schools and teachers, this small, thin,
dark-complexioned, pockmarked, dark-eyed, bewigged young
musician of 22 years had quietly journeyed to the capital to
pursue the study of his art with a small, thin, dark-complexioned,
pockmarked, black-eyed and bewigged veteran composer. In
the well-known anecdote related by Carpani of Haydn's introduction to him, Anton Esterhazy, the prince, is made to call the
composer "a Moor." Beethoven had even more of the Moor in
his looks than his master. His front teeth, owing to the singular
flatness of the roof of his mouth, protruded, and, of course,
thrust out his lips; the nose, too, was rather broad and decidedly
flattened, while the forehead was remarkably full and round—
in the words of the late Court Secretary, Mähler, who twice
painted his portrait, a "bullet."

"Beethoven," wrote Junker, "confessed that in his journeys
he had seldom found in the playing of the most distinguished
virtuosos that excellence which he supposed he had a right to
expect." He now had an opportunity to make his observations
upon the pianists and composers at the very headquarters, then, of
German music, to improve himself by study under the best of them
and, by and by, to measure his strength with theirs. He found
very soon that the words of the poet were here also applicable:

"'Tis distance lends enchantment to the view," and did not find—now Mozart was gone—"what he supposed he had a right to expect." For the present, however, we have to do but with the young stranger in a large city, seeking lodgings, and making such arrangements for the future as shall not be out of due proportion to the limited pecuniary means at his command. If the minute details which here follow should seem to be too insignificant in themselves, the bearing they have upon some other future questions must justify their introduction.

Turning again to the memorandum book, the first entries which follow the notes of the journey from Bonn to Würges are merely of necessities to be supplied—"wood, wig-maker, coffee, overcoat, boots, shoes, pianoforte-desk, seal, writing-desk, pianoforte-money" and something illegible followed by the remark: "All beginning with next month." The next page gives a hint as to the day of his arrival. It contains the substance of two advertisements in the "Wiener Zeitung" of pianofortes for sale, one near the Hohen Markt and two "im Kramerschen Breihaus No. 257 im Schlossergassel, am Graben." The latter appears *for the last time* on the 10th of November; Beethoven was, therefore, then in Vienna.

But he intends to cultivate the Graces as well as the Muses. The next page begins with this: "Andreas Lindner, dancing-master, lives in the Stoss am Himmel, No. 415," to which succeeds a note, evidently of money received from the Elector, possibly in Bonn but more likely in Vienna: "25 ducats received of which, expended on November (?) half a sovereign for the pianoforte, or 6 florins, 40 kreutzer—2 florins were of my own money." The same page also shows him in the matter of his toilet preparing even then for entrance into society: "Black silk stockings, 1 ducat; 1 pair of winter silk stockings, 1 florin, 40 kreutzers; boots, 6 florins; shoes, 1 florin, 30 kreutzers." But these expenses in addition to his daily necessities are making a large inroad upon his "25 ducats received"; and on page 7 we read: "On Wednesday the 12th of December, I had 15 ducats." (The 12th of December fell upon Wednesday in the year 1792.) Omitting for the present what else stands upon page 7, here are the interesting contents of page 8—and how suggestive and pregnant they are: "In Bonn I counted on receiving 100 ducats here; but in vain. I have got to equip myself completely anew."

Several pages which follow contain what, upon inspection, proves evidently to be his monthly payments from the time when "all was to begin next month," of which the first may be given as a specimen: "House-rent, 14 florins; pianoforte, 6 florins, 49 kreutzers; eating, each time 12 kreutzers; meals with wine 6 and one-half florins; 3 kreutzers for B. and H.; it is not necessary to give the housekeeper more than 7 florins, the rooms are so close to the ground."[1]

Beethoven was hardly well settled in his lodgings, the novelty of his position had scarcely begun to wear off under the effect of habit, when startling tidings reached him from Bonn of an event to cloud his Christmas holidays, to weaken his ties to his native place, to increase his cares for his brothers and make an important change in his pecuniary condition. His father had suddenly died —"1792, Dec. 18, *obiit* Johannes Beethoff," says the death-roll of St. Remigius parish. The Elector-Archbishop, still in Münster, heard this news also and consecrated a joke to the dead man's memory. On the 1st of January, 1793, he wrote a letter to Court Marshal von Schall in which these words occur:

The revenues from the liquor excise have suffered a loss in the deaths of Beethoven and Eichhoff. For the widow of the latter, provision will be made if circumstances allow in view of his 40 years of service— in the electoral kitchen.

Franz Ries was again to befriend Beethoven and act for him in his absence, and the receipt for his first quarter's salary (25 th.) is signed "F. Ries, in the name of Ludwig Beethoven," at the usual time, namely the beginning of the second month of the quarter, February 4. But the lapse of Johann van Beethoven's pension of 200 thalers, was a serious misfortune to his son, particularly since the 100 ducats were not forthcoming. The correspondence between Beethoven and Ries not being preserved it can only be conjectured that the latter took the proper steps to obtain that portion of the pension set apart by the electoral decree for the support of the two younger sons; but in vain, owing to the disappearance of the original document; and that, receiving information of this fact, Beethoven immediately sent from Vienna the petition which follows, but which, as is mostly the case with that class of papers in the Bonn archives, is without date:

[1]Beethoven's first lodgings were in an attic-room which he soon exchanged for a room on the ground floor of a house No. 45 Alsterstrasse occupied by one Strauss, a printer. The house now on the site is No. 30. Another occupant of the house was Prince Lichnowsky, who soon after took him into his lodgings. He remained in this house until May, 1795.

Several years ago Your Serene Electoral Highness was graciously pleased to retire my father, the tenor singer van Beethoven, from service, and to set aside 100 thalers of his salary to me that I might clothe, nourish and educate my two younger brothers and also pay the debts of my father.

I was about to present this decree to Your Highness's Revenue Exchequer when my father urgently begged me not to do so inasmuch as it would have the appearance in the eyes of the public as if he were incapable of caring for his family, adding that he would himself pay me the 25 thalers quarterly, which he always did.

When, however, on the death of my father (in December of last year) I wished to make use of Your Highness's grace by presenting the above-mentioned gracious decree I learned to my terror, that my father had misapplied (*unterschlagen* = to embezzle) the same.

In most obedient veneration I therefore pray Your Electoral Highness for the gracious renewal of this decree and that Your Highness's Revenue Exchequer be directed to pay over to me the sum graciously allowed to me due for the last quarter at the beginning of last February.

Your Electoral and Serene Highness's
Most obedient and faithful
Lud. v. Beethoven; Court Organist.

The petition was duly considered by the Privy Council and with the result indicated by the endorsement:

ad sup. of the Court Organist L. van Beethoven	.... "The 100 reichsthaler which he is now receiving annually is increased by a further 100 reichsthaler in quarterly payments beginning with January 1st, from the 200 rth. salary vacated by the death of his father; he is further to receive the three measures of grain graciously bestowed upon him for the education of his brothers." The Electoral Court Chancellory will make the necessary provisions. Attest p.

The order to the exchequer followed on May 24th, and on June 15th, Franz Ries had the satisfaction of signing receipts— one for 25 thalers for January, February and March, and one for 50 thalers for the second quarter of the year; but from this time onward no hint has yet been discovered that Beethoven ever received anything from the Elector or had any resources but his own earnings and the generosity of newly-found friends in Vienna. These resources were soon needed. The remark that two florins of the payment towards the pianoforte were out of his own money proves that he possessed a small sum saved up by degrees from lesson-giving, from presents received and the like; but it could not have been a large amount, while the 25 ducats and the above recorded receipts of salary were all too small to have carried him through the summer of 1793. Here is the second of his monthly records of necessary and regular expenses in farther proof of this: "14 florins house-rent; 6 fl. 40 x, pianoforte; meals with wine, 15 fl. and a half; —(?), 3 florins; maid, 1," the sum total being as added by himself "11 ducats and one-half florin." And yet at the end of the year there are entries that show that he was not distressed for money. For instance: "the 24th October, i.e., reckoning from November 1st, 112 florins and 30 kreutzer"; "2 ducats for a seal; 1 florin, 25 kreutzers, copyist"; "Tuesday and Saturday from 7 to 8. Sunday from 11 to 12, 3 florins"; and the final entry not later in date than 1794 is: "3 carolins in gold, 4 carolins in crown thalers and 4 ducats make 7 carolins and 4 ducats and a lot of small change."

In what manner Beethoven was already in 1794 able to remain "in Vienna without salary until recalled," to quote the Elector's words, will hereafter appear with some degree of certainty; but just now he claims attention as pupil of Haydn and Albrechtsberger. The citations made in a previous chapter from the letters of Neefe and Fischenich prove how strong an impression Beethoven's powers, both as virtuoso and composer, had made upon Joseph Haydn immediately after his reaching Vienna; and no man then living was better able to judge on such points. But whether the famous chapelmaster, just returned from his English triumphs, himself a daring and successful innovator and now very busy with compositions in preparation for his second visit to London, was the man to guide the studies of a headstrong, self-willed and still more daring musical revolutionist was, *a priori*, a very doubtful question. The result proved that he was not.

The memorandum book has a few entries which relate to Haydn. On page 7, that which contains the 15 ducats on the 12th of October, 1792, there is a column of numerals, the first of which reads, "Haidn 8 groschen"; the other twelve, except a single "1," all "2"; and on the two pages which happen to have the dates of October 24 and 29, 1793, are these two entries: "22 x, chocolate for Haidn and me"; "Coffee, 6 x for Haidn and me." These notes simply confirm what was known from other sources, namely, that Beethoven began to study with Haydn very soon after reaching Vienna and continued to be his pupil until the end of the year 1793.[1] They indicate, also, that the scholar, whatever feelings he may have indulged towards the master in secret, kept on good terms with him, and that their private intercourse was not confined to the hours devoted to lessons in Haydn's room in

---

[1] Or the beginning of 1794, since Haydn left Vienna on January 19, of that year.

the Hamberger house, No. 992 on the (no longer existing) Wasserkunstbastei.

Concerning the course of study during that year, nothing can be added to the words of Nottebohm ("Allg. Mus. Zeitung," 1863–1864), founded upon a most thorough examination of all the known manuscripts and authorities which bear upon this question. Of the manuscripts Nottebohm says: "They are exercises in simple counterpoint on six plain chants in the old modes. . . . He must have written more." But what? On this point there are no indications to be found. It may be accepted with considerable certainty that the contrapuntal exercises were preceded by an introductory, though probably brief, study of the nature of consonances and dissonances. For this the last chapter of the first book of Fux's "Gradus ad Parnassum" might have served.

But this (adds Nottebohm) would not have sufficed to fill the entire period. In view of Haydn's predilection for Fux's system it is not conceivable that there were preliminary exercises, say in the free style or in the modern keys; there remains, therefore, no alternative but to go back further and opine that the study with Haydn began with the theory of harmony and exercises in which the system of Philipp Emanuel Bach might have been used.

"It is certain," says Schindler, "that Beethoven's knowledge of the science of harmony at the time when he began his study with Haydn did not go beyond thoroughbass." The correctness of this opinion of Schindler may be safely left to the judgment of the reader. The fact seems to be that Beethoven, conscious of the disadvantages attending the want of thorough systematic instruction, distrustful of himself and desirous of bringing to the test many of his novel and cherished ideas, had determined to accomplish a complete course of contrapuntal study, and thus renew, revise and reduce to order and system the great mass of his previous scientific acquirements. He would, at all events, thoroughly know and understand the *regular* that he might with confidence judge for himself how far to indulge in the *irregular*. To this view, long since adopted, the results of Nottebohm's researches add credibility. It explains, also, how a young man, too confident in the soundness of his views to be willing to alter his productions because they contained passages and effects censured by those about him for being other than those of Mozart and Haydn, was yet willing, with the modesty of true genius, to shut them up in his writing-desk until, through study and observation, he could feel himself standing upon the firm basis of sound

knowledge and then retain or exclude, according to the dictates
of an enlightened judgment.

Beethoven, however, very soon discovered that also in Haydn,
as a teacher, he had "not found that excellence which he supposed
he had a right to expect." Ries remembered a remark made by
him on this point: "Haydn had wished that Beethoven might
put the word, 'Pupil of Haydn,' on the title of his first works.
Beethoven was unwilling to do so because, as he said, though he
had had some instruction from Haydn he had never learned anything from him." Still more in point is the oft-repeated story
of Johann Schenk's kindness to Beethoven, related by Seyfried in
Gräfer's and Schilling's lexica and confirmed by Schindler, which,
when divested of its errors in dates, may be related thus: Among
Beethoven's earliest acquaintances in Vienna was the Abbé Joseph
Gelinek, one of the first virtuosos then in that city and an amazingly fruitful and popular composer of variations. It was upon
him that Carl Maria von Weber, some years afterwards, wrote
the epigram:

Kein Thema auf der Welt verschonte dein Genie,
Das simpelste allein—Dich selbst—variirst du nie!

"No theme on earth escaped your genius airy,—
The simplest one of all—yourself—you never vary."

Czerny told Otto Jahn that his father once met Gelinek
tricked out in all his finery. "Whither?" he inquired. "I am asked
to measure myself with a young pianist who is just arrived; I'll
use him up." A few days later he met him again. "Well, how
was it?" "Ah, he is no man; he's a devil. He will play me and
all of us to death. And how he improvises!" According to
Czerny, Gelinek remained a sworn enemy to Beethoven.

It was in Gelinek's lodgings that Schenk heard Beethoven
improvise for the first time,

a treat which recalled lively recollections of Mozart. With many mani-
festations of displeasure, Beethoven, always eager to learn, complained
to Gelinek that he was never able to make any progress in his contrapuntal studies under Haydn, since the master, too variously occupied,
was unable to pay the amount of attention which he wanted to the
exercises he had given him to work out. Gelinek spoke on the subject
with Schenk and asked him if he did not feel disposed to give Beethoven
a course in composition. Schenk declared himself willing, with ready
courtesy, but only under two conditions: that it should be without
compensation of any kind and under the strict seal of secrecy. The
mutual agreement was made and kept with conscientious fidelity.

Thus far Seyfried; we shall now permit Schenk to tell his own story:[1]

In 1792, His Royal Highness Archduke Maximilian, Elector of Cologne, was pleased to send his charge Louis van Beethoven to Vienna to study musical composition with Haydn. Towards the end of July, Abbé Gelinek informed me that he had made the acquaintance of a young man who displayed extraordinary virtuosity on the pianoforte, such, indeed, as he had not observed since Mozart. In passing he said that Beethoven had been studying counterpoint with Haydn for more than six months and was still at work on the first exercise; also that His Excellency Baron van Swieten had earnestly recommended the study of counterpoint and frequently inquired of him how far he had advanced in his studies. As a result of these frequent incitations and the fact that he was still in the first stages of his instruction, Beethoven, eager to learn, became discontented and often gave expression to his dissatisfaction to his friend. Gelinek took the matter much to heart and came to me with the question whether I felt disposed to assist his friend in the study of counterpoint. I now desired to become better acquainted with Beethoven as soon as possible, and a day was fixed for me to meet him in Gelinek's lodgings and hear him play on the pianoforte.

Thus I saw the composer, now so famous, for the first time and heard him play. After the customary courtesies he offered to improvise on the pianoforte. He asked me to sit beside him. Having struck a few chords and tossed off a few figures as if they were of no significance, the creative genius gradually unveiled his profound psychological pictures. My ear was continually charmed by the beauty of the many and varied motives which he wove with wonderful clarity and loveliness into each other, and I surrendered my heart to the impressions made upon it while he gave himself wholly up to his creative imagination, and anon, leaving the field of mere tonal charm, boldly stormed the most distant keys in order to give expression to violent passions. . . .

The first thing that I did the next day was to visit the still unknown artist who had so brilliantly disclosed his mastership. On his writing desk I found a few passages from his first lesson in counterpoint. A cursory glance disclosed the fact that, brief as it was, there were mistakes in every key. Gelinek's utterances were thus verified. Feeling sure that my pupil was unfamiliar with the preliminary rules of counterpoint, I gave him the familiar textbook of Joseph Fux, "Gradus ad Parnassum," and asked him to look at the exercises that followed. Joseph Haydn, who had returned to Vienna towards the end of the preceding year,[2] was intent on utilizing his muse in the composition of large masterworks, and thus laudably occupied could not well devote himself to the rules of grammar. I was now eagerly desirous to become the helper of the zealous student. But before beginning the instruction I made him understand that our coöperation would have to be kept secret. In

[1] The excerpt from Schenk's autobiography which follows was communicated to Thayer by Otto Jahn and included in the appendix to Vol. II of the original edition of this biography. The present editor has followed Dr. Deiters in his presentation of the case in Vol. I of the revised edition.

[2] Haydn, according to Wurzbach, returned to Vienna on July 24, 1792.

view of this I recommended that he copy every exercise which I corrected
in order that Haydn should not recognize the handwriting of a stranger
when the exercise was submitted to him.   After a year, Beethoven and
Gelinek had a falling out for a reason that has escaped me; both, it
seemed to me, were at fault.   As a result Gelinek got angry and be-
trayed my secret.   Beethoven and his brothers made no secret of it longer.

I began my honorable office with my good Louis in the beginning
of August, 1792,[1] and filled it uninterruptedly until May, 1793,[1] by which
time he finished double counterpoint in the octave and went to Eisenstadt.   If His Royal Highness had sent his charge at once to Albrechtsberger his studies would never have been interrupted and he would
have completed them.

Here follows a passage, afterward stricken out by Schenk,
in which he resents the statement that Beethoven had finished
his studies with Albrechtsberger.   This would have been advisable, but if it were true, Gelinek as well as Beethoven would have
told him of the fact.   "On the contrary, he admitted to me that
he had gone to Herr Salieri, Royal Imperial Chapelmaster, for
lessons in the free style of composition."   Then Schenk continues:

About the middle of May he told me that he would soon go with
Haydn to Eisenstadt and stay there till the beginning of winter; he did
not yet know the date of his departure.   I went to him at the usual hour
in the beginning of June but my good Louis was no longer to be seen.   He
left for me the following little billet which I copy word for word:

"Dear Schenk!

It was not my desire to set off to-day for Eisenstadt.   I should
like to have spoken with you again.   Meanwhile rest assured of my
gratitude for the favors shown me.   I shall endeavor with all my might
to requite them.   I hope soon to see you again, and once more to enjoy
the pleasure of your society.   Farewell and
do not entirely forget
your
Beethoven."

It was my intention only briefly to touch upon my relations with
Beethoven; but the circumstances under which, and the manner in
which I became his guide in musical composition constrained me to
be somewhat more explicit.   For my efforts (if they can be called efforts)
I was rewarded by my good Louis with a precious gift, viz.: a firm bond
of friendship which lasted without fading till the day of his death.
Written in the summer of 1830.

A chronological difficulty is presented by Schenk's story of
the cessation of the instruction.   There can be no doubt that it
began towards the beginning of August, 1793, as confirmed by the

[1]Schenk is in error as to both dates.   He means, of course, 1793 and 1794.

distinct utterance of Schenk (who errs in the year, however), particularly by the statement that the study with Haydn had already endured six months.   Schenk's instruction is said to have lasted till the end of May, 1794, and the definitive mention of the month makes an error improbable.   But at this time Haydn was already long in England, while Schenk's narrative represents Beethoven as saying that he intended going to Eisenstadt with Haydn; moreover, Beethoven was already Albrechtsberger's pupil and as such was no longer in need of secret help.   Nevertheless, the continuance of the relations with Schenk is easily possible and they were not likely to be interrupted so long as Beethoven remained in Vienna; this is indicated by the reference to double counterpoint, which Beethoven did not study under Haydn but with Albrechtsberger; also Schenk's intimation that if the Elector had sent his charge "at once" to Albrechtsberger shows that instruction with the latter had already begun.   The letter to Schenk, though cast in friendly terms, can nevertheless be interpreted as a declination of further services, a breaking off of the relationship between teacher and pupil, for which the journey to Eisenstadt was a welcome excuse.   But we learn only from Schenk that Beethoven was to make the journey with Haydn, and he may have been mistaken in this as he was in the year.   It is very conceivable that Beethoven had received an invitation to visit him from Prince Esterhazy, who must surely have got acquainted with him in Vienna.   He who is unwilling to accept this, must place the letter and the journey in the last months of 1793, which is in every respect improbable.

The relations between Haydn and his pupil did not long continue truly cordial; yet Beethoven concealed his dissatisfaction and no break occurred.   Thoughtless and reckless of consequences, as he often in later years unfortunately exhibited himself when indulging his wilfulness, he was at this time responsible to the Elector for his conduct, and Haydn, moreover, was too valuable and influential a friend to be wantonly alienated.   So, whatever feelings he cherished in secret, he kept them to himself, went regularly to his lessons and, as noted above, occasionally treated his master to chocolate or coffee.   It was, of course, Haydn who took the young man to Eisenstadt, and, as Neefe tells us, he wished to take him to England.   Why was that plan not carried out?   Did Maximilian forbid it?   Would Beethoven's pride not allow him to go thither as Haydn's pupil?   Did zeal for his contrapuntal studies prevent it?   Or had his relations to the Austrian nobility already become such as offered him higher hopes of success in

Vienna than Haydn could propose in London? Or, finally, was it his ambition rather to make himself known as Beethoven the composer than as Beethoven the pianoforte virtuoso? Pecuniary reasons are insufficient to account for the failure of the plan; for Haydn, who now knew the London public, could easily have removed all difficulty on that score. Neefe's letter was written near the end of September, 1793, when already "a number of reports" had reached Bonn "that Beethoven had made great progress in his art." These "reports," we know from Fischenich, came in part from Haydn himself. Add to that the wish to take his pupil with him to England—which was certainly the highest compliment he could possibly have paid him—and the utter groundlessness of Beethoven's suspicions that Haydn "was not well-minded towards him," as Ries says in his "Notizen" (page 85), is apparent. Yet these suspicions, added to the reasons above suggested, sufficiently explain the departure of the master for London without the company of his pupil, who now (January, 1794) was transferred to Albrechtsberger.

In the pretty extensive notes copied from the memorandum book already so much cited, there are but two which can with any degree of certainty be referred to a date later than 1793. One of them is this:

> Schuppanzigh, 3 times a W. (Week?)
> Albrechtsberger, 3 times a W. (Week?)

The necessary inference from this is that Beethoven began the year 1794 with three lessons a week in violin-playing from Schuppanzigh (unless the youth of the latter should forbid such an inference) and three in counterpoint from the most famous teacher of that science. Seyfried affirms that the studies with the latter continued "two complete years with tireless persistency." The coming narrative will show that other things took up much of Beethoven's attention in 1795, and that before the close of that year, if not already at its beginning, his course with Albrechtsberger ended.[1]

The instruction which Beethoven received from Albrechtsberger (and which was based chiefly on the master's "Anweisung zur Komposition") began again with simple counterpoint, in which Beethoven now received more detailed directions than had been given by Haydn. Albrechtsberger wrote down rules for him,

---

[1]The investigations of Nottebohm, in "Beethoven's Studien" and "Beethoveniana," have been relied on in the compilation of the story of the study under Albrechtsberger, which takes the place of the original narrative by Thayer.

Beethoven did the same and worked out a large number of exercises on two plain-song melodies which Albrechtsberger then corrected according to the rules of strict writing. There followed contrapuntal exercises in free writing, in imitation, in two-, three- and four-part fugue, choral fugue, double counterpoint in the different intervals, double fugue, triple counterpoint and canon. The last was short, as here the instruction ceased. Beethoven worked frequently in the immediate presence and with the direct coöperation of Albrechtsberger. The latter labored with obvious conscientiousness and care, and was ever ready to aid his pupil. If he appears at times to have been given over to minute detail and conventional method, it must be borne in mind that rigid schooling in fixed rules is essential to the development of an independent artist, even if he makes no use of them, and that it is only in this manner that freedom in workmanship can be achieved. Of this the youthful Beethoven was aware and every line of his exercises bears witness that he entered into his studies with complete interest and undivided zeal.[1] This was particularly the case in his exercises in counterpoint and imitation, where he strove to avoid errors, and their beneficial results are plainly noticeable in his compositions. Several of the compositions written after the lessons, disclose how "he was led from a predominantly figurative to a more contrapuntal manner of writing." There is less of this observable in the case of fugue, in which the instruction itself was not free from deficiencies; and the pupil worked more carelessly. The restrictive rules occasionally put him out of conceit with his work; "he was at the age in which, as a rule, suggestion and incitation are preferred to instruction," and his stubborn nature played an important rôle in the premises. However, it ought to be added that he was also at an age when his genial aptness in invention and construction had already found exercise in other directions. Even though he did not receive thorough education in fugue from Albrechtsberger, he nevertheless learned the constituent elements of the form and how to apply them. Moreover, in his later years he made all these things the subjects of earnest and devoted study independent of others; and in the compositions of his later years he returned with special and manifest predilection to the fugued style. Nothing could be more incorrect than to emphasize Beethoven's lack of theoretical education. If, while studying with Albrechtsberger, but more particularly in his independent compositions, Beethoven ignored many

---

[1] Once Beethoven writes an unprepared seventh-chord with a suspension on the margin of an exercise and adds the query: "Is it allowed?"

of the strict rules, it was not because he was not able to apply
them, but because he purposely set them aside.   Places can be
found in his exercises in which the rules are violated; but the testimony of the ear acquits the pupil.   Rules are not the objects of
themselves, they do not exist for their own sake, and in despite of
all artistic systems; it is the reserved privilege of the evolution of
art-means and prescient, forward genius to point out what in
them is of permanent value, and what must be looked upon as
antiquated.   Nature designed that Beethoven should employ
music in the depiction of soul-states, to emancipate melody and
express his impulses in the free forms developed by Ph. Em. Bach,
Mozart, Haydn and their contemporaries.   In this direction he
had already disclosed himself as a doughty warrior before the instruction in Vienna had its beginning, and it is very explicable
that to be hemmed in by rigid rules was frequently disagreeable
to him.   He gradually wearied of "creating musical skeletons."
But all the more worthy of recognition, yea, of admiration, is the
fact that the young composer who had already mounted so high,
should by abnegation of his creative powers surrender himself to
the tyranny of the rules and find satisfaction in conscientious
practice of them.

Nottebohm summed up his conclusions from the investigations which he made of Beethoven's posthumous papers thus:
prefacing that, after 1785, Beethoven more and more made the
manner of Mozart his own, he continues:

The instruction which he received from Haydn and Albrechtsberger enriched him with new forms and media of expression and these
effected a change in his mode of writing.   The voices acquired greater
melodic flow and independence.   A certain opacity took the place of
the former transparency in the musical fabric.   Out of a homophonic
polyphony of two or more voices, there grew a polyphony that was real.
The earlier obbligato accompaniment gave way to an obbligato style
of writing which rested to a greater extent on counterpoint.   Beethoven
has accepted the principle of polyphony; his part-writing has become
purer and it is noteworthy that the compositions written immediately
after the lessons are among the purest that Beethoven ever composed.
True, the Mozart model still shines through the fabric, but we seek it
less in the art of figuration than in the form and other things which are
only indirectly associated with the obbligato style.   Similarly, we can
speak of other influences—that of Joseph Haydn, for instance.   This
influence is not contrapuntal.   Beethoven built upon his acquired and
inherited possessions.   He assimilated the traditional forms and means
of expression, gradually eliminated foreign influences and, following
the pressure of his subjective nature with its inclination towards the
ideal, he created his own individual style.

As is known, Seyfried in his book entitled "Ludwig van Beethoven's Studien im Generalbasse," which appeared in 1832, gathered together all that was to be found in the way of exercises, excerpts from textbooks, etc., in Beethoven's posthumous papers and presented them in so confused and arbitrary a manner that only the keenness and patience of a Nottebohm could point the way through the maze; Seyfried would have us believe that the entire contents of his book belonged to the studies under Albrechtsberger.

It will require no waste of words, says Nottebohm (p. 198), to prove the incompatibility of such a claim with the results of our investigations. As a matter of fact, only the smallest portion of the "Studies" can be traced back to the instruction which Beethoven received from Albrechtsberger. The greater part had nothing to do with this instruction and, aside from the changes made, belongs to the other labors. In the smaller portion Seyfried made things as easy for himself as possible. Of Beethoven's exercises he took only such as he found cleanly copied or legibly written, and omitted those which were difficult to decipher because of many corrections. This is the explanation of the fact that Seyfried did not include a single exercise in strict simple counterpoint. If all the passages bearing on the course followed under Albrechtsberger were brought together and all the errors made in the presentation overlooked, we should still have but a fragmentary and faulty reflection of that study. Neither need we enter upon a discussion of the marginal notes attributed to Beethoven which so plentifully besprinkle Seyfried's book. The fact is that in all the manuscripts which belong to the studies under Albrechtsberger not one of the "sarcastically thrown out" marginal notes is to be found. The glosses which do appear as Beethoven's . . . . are of a wholly different character from those printed by Seyfried. They show that Beethoven was deeply immersed and interested in the matter. It would, indeed, be inexplicable what could have persuaded Beethoven to continue study with a teacher with whom, as Seyfried would have us believe, he was in conflict already at the beginning of simple counterpoint. He had it in his power to discontinue his studies at any moment.

A doubt has been hinted above whether Beethoven's studies under Albrechtsberger were continued beyond the beginning of the year 1795. If all these exercises in counterpoint, fugue and canon, and all those excerpts from Fux, C. P. E. Bach, Türk, Albrechtsberger, and Kirnberger, which Seyfried made the basis of his "Studien"—and mingled in a confusion inextricable by any one possessing less learning, patience, sagacity and perseverance than Nottebohm—had already belonged to the period of his pupilage, their quantity alone, taken in connection with the writer's other occupations, would indeed preclude such a doubt; but knowing that perhaps the greater portion of those manuscripts belongs to a period many years later, and considering the great facility in writing which Beethoven had already acquired before coming to Vienna, there seems to be no indication of any course of study which might not easily be completed during the one year with Haydn (and Schenk) and one year with Albrechtsberger. Schönfeld, in the "Jahrbuch der Tonkunst für Wien und Prag," supposes that Beethoven was still the pupil of the latter at the time when he wrote, which was in the spring of 1795. His words are: "An eloquent proof of his [Beethoven's] real love of art is the circumstance that he has placed himself in the hands of our immortal Haydn, in order to be initiated into the sacred mysteries of composition. This great master has, in his absence, turned him over to our great Albrechtsberger." There is nothing decisive in this; and yet it is all that appears to confirm the "two years" of Seyfried; while on the other hand Wegeler, who, during all the year 1795, was much with Beethoven, has nowhere in his "Notizen" any allusion whatever to his friend as being still a student under a master.

Referring to the number of pages (160) of exercises and the three lessons a week, Nottebohm calculates the period of instruction to have been about fifteen months. Inasmuch as among the exercises in double counterpoint in the tenth there is found a sketch belonging to the second movement of the Trio, Op. 1, No. 2, which Trio was advertised as finished on May 9th, 1795, it follows that the study was at or near its end at that date. The conclusion of his instruction from Albrechtsberger may therefore be set down at between March and May, 1795.

The third of Beethoven's teachers in Vienna was the Imperial Chapelmaster Anton Salieri; but this instruction was neither systematic nor confined to regular hours. Beethoven took advantage of Salieri's willingness "to give gratuitous instruction to musicians of small means." He wanted advice in vocal composition, and submitted to Salieri some settings of Italian songs which the latter corrected in respect of verbal accent and expression, rhythm, metrical articulation, subdivision of thought, mood, singableness, and the conduct of the melody which comprehended all these things. Having himself taken the initiative in this, Beethoven devoted himself earnestly and industriously to these exercises, and they were notably profitable in his creative work. "Thereafter [also in his German songs] he treated the text with much greater care than before in respect of its prosodic structure, as also of its contents and the prescribed situation," and acquired a good method of declamation. That Salieri's influence extended beyond the period in which Beethoven's style developed itself independently cannot be asserted, since many other and varied influences made themselves felt later.

This instruction began soon after Beethoven's arrival in Vienna and lasted in an unconstrained manner at least until 1802; at even a later date he asked counsel of Salieri in the composition of songs, particularly Italian songs. According to an anecdote related by Czerny, at one of these meetings for instruction Salieri found fault with a melody as not being appropriate to the air. The next day he said to Beethoven: "I can't get your melody out of my head." "Then, Herr von Salieri," replied Beethoven, "it cannot have been so utterly bad." The story may be placed in the early period; but it appears from a statement by Moscheles that Beethoven still maintained an association with Salieri in 1809. Moscheles, who was in Vienna at this time, found a note on Salieri's table which read: "The pupil Beethoven was here!"

Ries, speaking of the relations between Haydn, Albrechtsberger and Salieri as teachers and Beethoven as pupil, says: "I knew them all well; all three valued Beethoven highly, but were also of one mind touching his habits of study. All of them said Beethoven was so headstrong and self-sufficient (*selbstwollend*) that he had to learn much through harsh experience which he had refused to accept when it was presented to him as a subject of study." Particularly Albrechtsberger and Salieri were of this opinion; "the dry rules of the former and the comparatively unimportant ones of the latter concerning dramatic composition (according to the Italian school of the period) could not appeal to Beethoven." It is now known that the "dry rules" of Albrechtsberger could make a strong appeal to Beethoven as appertaining to theoretical study, and that the old method of composition to which he remained true all his life always had a singular charm for him as a subject of study and investigation.

Here, as in many other cases, the simple statement of the difficulties suggests their explanation. Beethoven the pupil may have honestly and conscientiously followed the precepts of his instructors in whatever he wrote in that character; but Beethoven the composer stood upon his own territory, followed his own tastes and impulses, wrote and wrought subject to no other control. He paid Albrechtsberger to teach him counterpoint—not to be the censor and critic of his compositions. And Ries's memory may well have deceived him as to the actual scope of the strictures made by the old master, and have transferred to the pupil what, fully thirty years before, had been spoken of the composer.

As has been mentioned, Beethoven's relations with Salieri at a later date were still pleasant; the composer dedicated to the chapelmaster the three violin sonatas, Op. 12, which appeared in 1799. Nothing is known of a dedication to Albrechtsberger. According to an anecdote related by Albrechtsberger's grandson Hirsch, Beethoven called him a "musical pedant"; yet we may see a remnant of gratitude toward his old teacher in Beethoven's readiness to take an interest in his young grandson.

We have now to turn our attention to Beethoven's relations to Viennese society outside of his study.

Chapter XII

Music in Vienna in 1793—Theatre, Church and Concert-
Room—A Music-Loving Nobility—The Esterhazys,
Kinsky, Lichnowsky, von Kees and van Swieten—
Composers: Haydn, Kozeluch, Förster and Eberl.

THE musical drama naturally took the first place in the musical
life of Vienna at this period. The enthusiasm of Joseph II for
a national German opera, to which the world owed Mozart's
exquisite "Entführung," proved to be but short-lived, and the
Italian *opera buffa* resumed its old place in his affections. The new
company engaged was, however, equal to the performance of
"Don Giovanni" and "Figaro" and Salieri's magnificent "Axur."
Leopold II reached Vienna on the evening of March 13, 1790, to
assume the crown of his deceased brother, but no change was, for
the present, made in the court theatre. Indeed, as late as July
5 he had not entered a theatre, and his first appearance at the opera
was at the performance of "Axur," September 21, in the company
of his visitor King Ferdinand of Naples; but once firmly settled
on the imperial throne, Joseph's numerous reforms successfully
annulled, the Turkish war brought to a close and his diverse coro-
nations happily ended, the Emperor gave his thoughts to the
theatre. Salieri, though now but forty-one years of age, and rich
with the observation and experience of more than twenty years
in the direction of the opera, was, according to Mosel, graciously
allowed, but according to other and better authorities, compelled,
to withdraw from the operatic orchestra and confine himself to
his duties as director of the sacred music in the court chapel and
to the composition of one operatic work annually, if required.
The "Wiener Zeitung" of January 28, 1792, records the appointment of Joseph Weigl, Salieri's pupil and assistant, now twenty-
five years old, "as Chapelmaster and Composer to the Royal
Imperial National Court Theatre with a salary of 1,000 florins."
The title Composer was rather an empty one. Though already
favorably known to the public, he was forbidden to compose new

operas for the court stage.   To this end famous masters were to
be invited to Vienna.   A first fruit of this new order of things was
the production of Cimarosa's "Il Matrimonio segreto," February
7, 1792, which with good reason so delighted Leopold that he
gave the performers a supper and ordered them back into the theatre
and heard the opera again *da capo*.   It was among the last of the
Emperor's theatrical pleasures; he died March 1st, and his wife
on the 15th of May following.   Thus for the greater part of the
time from March 1 to May 24, the court theatres were shut; and
yet during the thirteen months ending December 15, 1792, Italian
opera had been given 180 times—134 times in the Burg and 46
times in the Kärnthnerthor-Theater—and ballet 163 times; so
that, as no change for the present was made, there was abundance
, in these branches of the art for a young composer, like Beethoven,
to hear and see.   All accounts agree that the company then performing was one of uncommon excellence and its performances,
with those of the superb orchestra, proved the value of the long
experience, exquisite taste, unflagging zeal and profound knowledge of their recent head, Salieri.   Such as Beethoven found the
opera in the first week of November, 1792, such it continued for
the next two years—exclusively Italian, but of the first order.

A single stroke of extraordinary good fortune—a happy
accident is perhaps a better term—had just now given such prosperity to a minor theatrical enterprise that in ten years it was to
erect and occupy the best playhouse in Vienna and, for a time,
to surpass the Court Theatre in the excellence and splendor of its
operatic performances.   We mean Schikaneder's Theater auf der
Wieden; but in 1793 its company was mean, its house small, its
performances bad enough.

Schikaneder's chapelmaster and composer was John Baptist
Henneberg; the chapelmaster of Marinelli, head of another German company in the Leopoldstadt, was Wenzel Müller, who
had already begun his long list of 227 light and popular compositions to texts magical or farcical.   Some two weeks after Beethoven's arrival in Vienna, on November 23rd, Schikaneder announced, falsely, the one-hundredth performance of "Die Zauberflöte," an opera the success of which placed his theatre a few years
later upon a totally different footing, and brought Beethoven into
other relations to it than those of an ordinary visitor indulging
his comical taste, *teste* Seyfried, for listening to and heartily
enjoying very bad music.

The leading dramatic composers of Vienna, not yet named,
must receive a passing notice.   Besides Cimarosa, who left Vienna

a few months later, Beethoven found Peter Dutillieu, a Frenchman by birth but an Italian musician by education and profession, engaged as composer for the Court Theatre. His "Il Trionfo d'Amore" had been produced there November 14, 1791, and his "Nanerina e Padolfino" had lately come upon the stage. Ignaz Umlauf, composer of "Die schöne Schusterin" and other not unpopular works, had the title of Chapelmaster and Composer to the German Court Opera, and was Salieri's substitute as chapelmaster in the sacred music of the Court Chapel. Franz Xavier Süssmayr, so well known from his connection with Mozart, was just now writing for Schikaneder's stage; Schenk for Marinelli's and for the private stages of the nobility; and Paul Wranitzky, first violinist and so-called Musikdirektor in the Court Theatre, author of the then popular "Oberon" composed for the Wieden stage, was employing his very respectable talents for both Marinelli and Schikaneder.

The church music of Vienna seems to have been at a very low point in 1792 and 1793. Two composers, however, whose names are still of importance in musical history, were then in that city devoting themselves almost exclusively to this branch of the art; Albrechtsberger, Court Organist, but in a few months (through the death of Leopold Hoffmann, March 17, 1793) to become musical director at St. Stephen's; and Joseph Eybler (some five years older than Beethoven), who had just become *Regens chori* in the Carmelite church, whence he was called to a similar and better position in the Schottische Kirche two years later.

Public concerts, as the term is now understood, may be said not to have existed, and regular subscription concerts were few. Mozart gave a few series of them, but after his death there appears to have been no one of sufficient note in the musical world to make such a speculation remunerative. Single subscription concerts given by virtuosos, and annual ones by some of the leading resident musicians, of course, took place then as before and since. The only real and regular concerts were the four annual performances in the Burgtheater, two at Christmas and two at Easter, for the benefit of the musicians' widows and orphans. These concerts, established mainly by Gassmann and Salieri, were never exclusive in their programmes—oratorio, symphony, cantata, concerto, whatever would add to their attraction, found place. The stage was covered with the best musicians and vocalists of the capital and the superb orchestra was equally ready to accompany the playing of a Mozart or of an ephemeral *Wunderkind*. Risbeck was told ten years before that the number taking part in orchestra

and chorus had even then on some occasions reached 400—a statement, however, which looks much like exaggeration.

Very uncommon semi-private concerts were still kept up in
1793. The reader of Mozart's biography will remember that in
1782 this great composer joined a certain Martin in giving a series
of concerts during the morning hours in the Augarten Hall, most
of the performers being dilettanti and the music being furnished
from the library of von Kees. These concerts found such favor
that they were renewed for several years and generally were twelve
in number.

Ladies of even the highest nobility permitted themselves to be heard.
The auditorium was extremely brilliant and everything was conducted in
so orderly and decent a fashion that everybody was glad to support the
institute to the best of his energies. The receipts from the chief subscription were expended entirely on the cost of the concerts. Later
Herr Rudolph assumed the direction. ("Allg. Mus. Zeitung," III, 45.)

This man, still young, and a fine violin-player, was the director
when Beethoven came to Vienna, and the extraordinary spectacle
was still to be seen of princes and nobles following his lead in the
performance of orchestral music to an audience of their own class
at the strange hours of from 6 to 8 in the morning!

From the above it appears that Vienna presented to the
young musician no preëminent advantages either in opera, church-
music or its public concerts. Other cities equalled the Austrian
capital in the first two, and London was then far in advance of all
in the number, variety and magnificence of the last. It was in
another field that Vienna surpassed every competitor. As Gluck
twenty years before had begun the great revolution in operatic
music completed by Mozart, so Haydn, building on the foundation of the Bachs and aided by Mozart, was effecting a new development of purely instrumental music which was yet to reach
its highest stage through the genius and daring of the youth now
his pupil. The example set by the Austrian family through so
many generations had produced its natural effect, and a knowledge of and taste for music were universal among the princes and
nobles of the empire. Some of the more wealthy princes, like
Esterhazy, maintained musical establishments complete even to
the Italian opera; others were contented with hearing the mass
sung in their house-chapel to an orchestral accompaniment; where
this was impossible, a small orchestra only was kept up, often composed of the officials and servants, who were selected with regard
to their musical abilities; and so down to the band of wind-instruments, the string quartet, and even to a single organ-player,

pianist or violinist. What has been said in a former chapter of music as a quasi-necessity at the courts of the ecclesiastical princes, applies in great measure to the secular nobility. At their castles and country-seats in the summer, amusement was to be provided for many an otherwise tedious hour; and in their city residences during the winter they and their guests could not always feast, dance or play at cards; and here, too, music became a common and favored recreation. At all events, it was the fashion. Outside the ranks of the noble-born, such as by talents, high culture or wealth occupied high social positions, followed the example and opened their salons to musicians and lovers of music, moved thereto for the most part by a real, rarely by a pretended, taste for the art—in either case aiding and encouraging its progress. Hence, an enormous demand for chamber music, both vocal and instrumental, especially the latter. The demand created the supply by encouraging genius and talent to labor in that direction; and thus the Austrian school of instrumental music soon led the world, as in the previous generation the demand for oratorios in England gave that country the supremacy in that branch of art.

During certain months of the year, Vienna was filled with the greatest nobles, not only of the Austrian states, but of other portions of the German Empire. Those who spent their time mostly in their own small courts came up to the capital but for a short season; others reversed this, making the city their usual residence and visiting their estates only in summer. By the former class many a once (if not still) famous composer in their service was thus occasionally for short periods brought to the metropolis—as Mozart by the brutal Archbishop of Salzburg, and Haydn by Prince Esterhazy. By the latter class many of the distinguished composers and virtuosos resident in the city were taken into the country during the summer to be treated as equals, to live like gentlemen among gentlemen. Another mode of encouraging the art was the ordering or purchasing of compositions; and this not only from composers of established reputation, as Haydn, Mozart, C. P. E. Bach, but also from young and as yet unknown men; thus affording a twofold benefit—pecuniary aid and an opportunity of exhibiting their powers.

The instrumental virtuosos, when not permanently engaged in the service of some prince or theatre, looked in the main for the reward of their studies and labors to the private concerts of the nobility. If at the same time they were composers, it was in such concerts that they brought their productions to a hearing. The reader of Jahn's biography of Mozart will remember how much

even he depended upon this resource to gain the means of support
for himself and family. Out of London, even so late as 1793, there
can hardly be said to have existed a "musical public," as the term
is now understood, and in Vienna at least, with its 200,000 inhabitants, a virtuoso rarely ventured to announce a concert to which
he had not already a subscription, sufficient to ensure him against
loss, from those at whose residences he had successfully exhibited
his skill. Beethoven, remaining "in Vienna without salary until
recalled" by Max, found in these resources and his pupils an ample
income.

But this topic requires something more than the above general remarks. Some twelve years previous to Beethoven's coming
to Vienna, Risbeck, speaking of the art in that capital, had written:

Musicians are the only ones (artists) concerning whom the nobility
exhibit taste. Many houses maintain private bands for their own delectation, and all the public concerts prove that this field of art stands in
high respect. It is possible to enlist four or five large orchestras here,
all of them incomparable. The number of real virtuosos is small, but
as regards the orchestral musicians scarcely anything more beautiful
is to be heard in the world.

How many such orchestras were still kept up in 1792–'93 it
is, probably, now impossible to determine. Those of Princes Lobkowitz, Schwarzenberg and Auersperg may safely be named.
Count Heinrich von Haugwitz and doubtless Count Batthyany
brought their musicians with them when they came to the capital
for "the season." The Esterhazy band, dismissed after the death
of Haydn's old master, seems not yet to have been renewed. Prince
Grassalkowitz (or Kracsalkowitz) had reduced his to a band of
eight wind-instruments—oboes, clarinets, bassoons, horns—a kind
of organization then much in vogue. Baron Braun had one to
play at dinner as at the supper in "Don Giovanni"—an accessory
to the scene which Mozart introduced out of his own frequent
experience. Prince Karl Lichnowsky and others retained their
own players of string quartets.

The grandees of the Bohemian and Moravian capitals—
Kinsky, Clamm, Nostiz, Thun, Buquoi, Hartig, Salm-Pachta,
Sporck, Fünfkirchen, etc.—emulated the Austrian and Hungarian
nobles. As many of them had palaces also in Vienna, and most,
if not all, spent part of the year there, bringing with them a few
of the more skilful members of their orchestras to execute chamber
music and for the nucleus of a band when symphonies, concertos
and grand vocal works were to be executed, they also added
their contingent to the musical as well as to the political and

fashionable life of the metropolis. The astonishingly fruitful last eight years of Mozart's life falling within the period now under contemplation, contributed to musical literature compositions wonderfully manifold in character and setting an example that forced other composers to leave the beaten track. Haydn had just returned from his first stay in London, enriched with the pregnant experience acquired during that visit. Van Swieten had gained during his residence in Berlin appreciation of and love for the works of Handel, Bach and their schools, and since his return to Vienna, about 1778, had exerted, and was still exerting, a very powerful and marked influence upon Vienna's musical taste.

Thus all the conditions precedent for the elevation of the art were just at this time fulfilled at Vienna, and in one department— that of instrumental music—they existed in a degree unknown in any other city. The extraordinary results as to the quantity produced in those years may be judged from the sale-catalogue (1779) of a single music-dealer, Johann Traeg, which gives of symphonies, symphonies-concertantes and overtures (the last being in a small minority) the extraordinary number of 512. The music produced at private concerts given by the nobility ranged from the grand oratorios, operas, symphonies, down to variations for the pianoforte and to simple songs. Leading musicians and composers, whose circumstances admitted of it, also gave private concerts at which they made themselves and their works known, and to which their colleagues were invited. Prince Lobkowitz, at the time Beethoven reached Vienna, was a young man of twenty years. He was born on December 7, 1772, and had just married, on August 2, a daughter of Prince Schwarzenberg. He was a violinist of considerable powers and so devoted a lover of music and the drama, so profuse a squanderer of his income upon them, as in twenty years to reduce himself to bankruptcy. Precisely Beethoven's supposed age, the aristocrat of wealth and power and the aristocrat of talent and genius became exceedingly intimate, occasionally quarrelling and making up their differences as if belonging by birth to the same sphere.

The reigning Prince Esterhazy was that Paul Anton who, after the death of his father on February 25, 1790, broke up the musical establishment at Esterhaz and gave Haydn relief from his thirty years of service. He died on January 22, 1794, and was succeeded by his son Nicholas, a young man just five years older than Beethoven. Prince Nicholas inherited his grandfather's taste for music, reëngaged an orchestra, and soon became known as one of the most zealous promoters of Roman Catholic church-music. The best composers of Vienna, including Beethoven, wrote masses for the chapel at Esterhaz, where they were performed with great splendor.

Count Johann Nepomuk Esterhazy, "of the middle line zu Frakno," was a man of forty-five years, a good performer upon the oboe, and (which is much to his credit) had been a firm friend and patron of Mozart.

Of Count Franz Esterhazy, a man of thirty-five years, Schönfeld, in his "Jahrbuch der Tonkunst," thus speaks: "This great friend of music at certain times of the year gives large and splendid concerts at which, for the greater part, large and elevated compositions are performed—particularly the choruses of Handel, the 'Sanctus' of Emanuel Bach, the 'Stabat Mater' of Pergolese, and the like. At these concerts there are always a number of the best virtuosos."

It was not the present Prince Joseph Kinsky (who died in 1798 in his forty-eighth year) who at a later period became a distinguished patron of Beethoven, but his son Ferdinand Johann Nepomuk, then a bright boy of eleven years, born on December 4, 1781, upon whose youthful taste the strength, beauty and novelty of that composer's works made a deep impression. Prince Carl Lichnowsky, the pupil and friend of Mozart, had a quartet concert at his dwelling every Friday morning. The regularly engaged musicians were Ignaz Schuppanzigh, son of a professor in the Real-Schule, and a youth at this time of sixteen years (if the musical lexica are to be trusted), first violin; Louis Sina, pupil of Förster, also a very young man, second violin; Franz Weiss, who completed his fifteenth year on January 18, 1793, viola; and Anton Kraft, or his son Nicholas, a boy of fourteen years (born December 18, 1778), violoncello. It was, in fact, a quartet of boy virtuosos, of whom Beethoven, several years older, could make what he would.

The Prince's wife was Marie Christine, twenty years of age, one of those "Three Graces," as Georg Förster called them, daughters of that Countess Thun in whose house Mozart had found such warm friendship and appreciation, and whose noble qualities are so celebrated by Burney, Reichardt and Förster. The Princess, as well as her husband, belonged to the better class of amateur performers upon the pianoforte.

Court Councillor von Kees, Vice-President of the Court of Appeals of Lower Austria, was still living. He was, says Gyrowetz, speaking of a period a few years earlier, "recognized as the foremost music-lover and dilettante in Vienna; and twice a week he

gave in his house society concerts at which were gathered together
the foremost virtuosos of Vienna, and the first composers, such as
Joseph Haydn, Mozart, Dittersdorf, Hoffmeister, Albrechtsberger,
Giarnovichi and so on. Haydn's symphonies were played there."
In Haydn's letters to Madame Genzinger the name of von Kees
often occurs—the last time in a note of August 4, 1792, which
mentions that the writer is that day to dine with the Court Councillor. This distinguished man left on his death (January 5, 1795)
a very extensive collection of music.

   Gottfried, Freiherr van Swieten, son of Maria Theresia's
famous Dutch physician, says Schönfeld, is,

as it were, looked upon as a patriarch of music. He has taste only for
the great and exalted. He himself many years ago composed twelve
beautiful symphonies ("stiff as himself," said Haydn). When he attends
a concert our semi-connoisseurs never take their eyes off him, seeking to
read in his features, not always intelligible to every one, what ought to be
their opinion of the music. Every year he gives a few large and brilliant
concerts at which only music by the old masters is performed. His prefer-
ence is for the Handelian manner, and he generally has some of Handel's
great choruses performed. As late as last Christmas (1794) he gave such
a concert at Prince von Paar's, at which an oratorio by this master was
performed.

   Neukomm told Prof. Jahn that in concerts, "if it chanced that
a whispered conversation began, His Excellency, who was in the
habit of sitting in the first row of seats, would rise solemnly, draw
himself up to his full height, turn to the culprits, fix a long and
solemn gaze upon them, and slowly resume his chair. It was
effective, always." He had some peculiar notions of composition;
he was, for instance, fond of imitations of natural sounds in music
and forced upon Haydn the imitation of frogs in "The Seasons."
Haydn himself says:

   This entire passage in imitation of a frog did not flow from my
pen. I was constrained to write down the French croak. At an orchestral performance this wretched conceit soon disappears, but it cannot
be justified in a pianoforte score. Let the critics be not too severe on
me. I am an old man and cannot revise all this again.

   But to van Swieten, surely, is due the credit of having founded
in Vienna a taste for Handel's oratorios and Bach's organ and
pianoforte music, thus adding a new element to the music there.
The costs of the oratorio performances were not, however, defrayed
by him, as Schönfeld seems to intimate. They were met by the
association called by him into being, and of which he was perpet-
ual secretary, whose members were the Princes Liechtenstein,

Esterhazy, Schwarzenberg, Auersperg, Kinsky, Trautmannsdorf, Sinsendorf, and the Counts Czernin, Harrach, Erdödy and Fries; at whose palaces as well as in van Swieten's house and sometimes in the great hall of the Imperial Royal Library the performances were given at midday to an audience of invited guests. Fräulein Martinez, who holds so distinguished a place in Burney's account of his visit to Vienna—that pupil of Porpora at whose music-lessons the young Joseph Haydn forty years before had been employed as accompanist—still flourished in the Michael's House and gave a musical party every Saturday evening during the season.

Court Councillor and Chamber Paymaster von Meyer (says Schönfeld) is so excellent a lover of music that his entire personnel in the chancellary is musical, among them being such artists as a Raphael and a Hauschka. It will readily be understood, therefore, that here in the city as well as at his country-seat there are many concerts. His Majesty the Emperor himself has attended some of these concerts.

These details are sufficient to illustrate and confirm the remarks made above upon Vienna as the central point of instrumental music. Of the great number of composers in that branch of the art whom Beethoven found there, a few of the more eminent must be named.

Of course, Haydn stood at the head. The next in rank—*longo intervallo*—was Mozart's successor in the office of Imperial Chamber Composer, Leopold Kozeluch, a Bohemian, now just forty years of age. Though now forgotten and, according to Beethoven, "miserabilis," he was renowned throughout Europe for his quartets and other chamber music. A man of less popular repute but of a solid genius and acquirements far beyond those of Kozeluch, whom Beethoven greatly respected and twenty-five years later called his "old master," was Emanuel Aloys Förster, a Silesian, now forty-five years of age. His quintets, quartets and the like ranked very high, but at that time were known for the most part only in manuscript. Anton Eberl, five years the senior of Beethoven, a Viennese by birth, had composed two operettas in the sixteenth year of his age which were produced at the Kärnthnerthor-Theater, one of which gained the young author the favor of Gluck. He seems to have been a favorite of Mozart and caught so much of the spirit and style of that master as to produce compositions which were printed by dishonest publishers under Mozart's name, and as his were sold throughout Europe. In 1776 he accompanied the Widow Mozart and her sister, Madame Lange, the vocalist, in the tour through Germany, gaining that reputation in other cities which he enjoyed at home, both as pianist and composer. His force was in instrumental composition, and we shall hereafter see him for a moment as a symphonist bearing away the palm from Beethoven!

Johann Vanhall, whose name was so well known in Paris and London that Burney, twenty years before, sought him out in his garret in a suburb of Vienna, was as indefatigable as ever in production. Gerber says in his first Lexicon (1792) that Breitkopf and Härtel had then fifty of his symphonies in manuscript. His fecundity was equal to that of Haydn; his genius such that all his works are now forgotten. It is needless to continue this list.

One other fact illustrating the musical tastes and accomplishments of the higher classes of the capital may be added. There were, during the winter 1792–93, ten private theatres with amateur companies in activity, of which the more important were in the residences of the nobles Stockhammer, Kinsky, Sinsendorf and Strassaldo, and of the bookseller Schrambl. Most of these companies produced operas and operettas.

Chapter XIII

Beethoven in Society—Concerts—Wegeler's Recollections—
Compositions—The First Trios—Sonatas Dedicated to
Haydn—Variations—Dances for the Ridotto Rooms—
Plays at Haydn's Concert.

HOWEVER quiet and "without observation" Beethoven's
advent in Vienna may have been at that time when men's
minds were occupied by movements of armies and ideas of
revolution, he could hardly have gone thither under better auspices.
He was Court Organist and Pianist to the Emperor's uncle; his
talents in that field were well known to the many Austrians of rank
who had heard him in Bonn when visiting there or when paying
their respects to the Elector in passing to and from the Austrian
Netherlands; he was a pupil of Joseph Haydn—a circumstance in
itself sufficient to secure him a hearing; and he was protected by
Count Waldstein, whose family connections were such that he could
introduce his favorite into the highest circles, the imperial house
only excepted. Waldstein's mother was a Liechtenstein; his grandmother a Trautmannsdorf; three of his sisters had married respectively into the families Dietrichstein, Crugenburg and Wallis;
and by the marriages of uncles and aunts he was connected
with the great houses Oettingen-Spielberg, Khevenhüller-Melisch,
Kinsky, Palfy von Erdöd and Ulfeld—not to mention others less
known. If the circle be extended by a degree or two it embraces
the names Kaunitz, Lobkowitz, Kohary, Fünfkirchen, Keglevics
and Colloredo-Mansfeld.

Dr. Burney, in closing his "Present State of Music in Germany," notes the distinction in the styles of composition and performance in some of the principal cities of that country, "Vienna
being most remarkable for fire and animation; Mannheim for
neat and brilliant execution; Berlin for counterpoint and Brunswick for taste." Since Burney's tour (1772) Vienna had the
highest example of all these qualities united in Mozart. But he
had passed away, and no great pianist of the first rank remained;

there were extraordinary dilettanti and professional pianists "of very neat and brilliant execution," but none who possessed great "fire, animation and invention," qualities still most valued in Vienna and in which the young Beethoven, with all the hardness and heaviness of manipulation caused by his devotion to the organ, was wholly unrivalled. With all the salons in the metropolis open to him, his success as a virtuoso was, therefore, certain. All the contemporary authorities, and all the traditions of those years, agree in the fact of that success, and that his playing of Bach's preludes and fugues especially, his reading of the most difficult scores at sight and his extemporaneous performances excited ever new wonder and delight. Schindler records that van Swieten, after musical performances at his house, "detained Beethoven and persuaded him to add a few fugues by Sebastian Bach as an evening blessing," and he preserves a note without date, though evidently belonging to Beethoven's first years in Vienna, which proves how high a place the young man had then won in the old gentleman's favor:

To Mr. Beethoven in Alstergasse, No. 45, with the Prince Lichnowsky: If there is nothing to hinder next Wednesday I should be glad to see you at my home at half past 8 with your nightcap in your bag. Give me an immediate answer.

Swieten.

There is also an entry in the oft-cited memorandum book belonging in date to October or November, 1793, which may be given in this connection: "Supped in the evening at Swieten's, 17 pourboire. To the janitor 4 x for opening the door."

But the instant and striking success of Beethoven as virtuoso by no means filled up the measure of his ambition. He aspired to the higher position of composer, and to obtain this more was needed than the performance of variations, however excellent. To this end he selected the three Trios afterwards published as Op. 1, and brought them to performance at the house of Prince Lichnowsky. Happily for us, Beethoven related some particulars concerning this first performance of these compositions in Vienna to his pupil Ries, who gives the substance of the story thus:

It was planned to introduce the first three Trios of Beethoven, which were about to be published as Op. 1, to the artistic world at a soirée at prince Lichnowsky's. Most of the artists and music-lovers were invited, especially Haydn, for whose opinion all were eager. The Trios were played and at once commanded extraordinary attention. Haydn also said many pretty things about them, but advised Beethoven not to publish the third, in C minor. This astonished Beethoven, inasmuch as he considered the third the best of the Trios, as it is still the one which gives the greatest pleasure and makes the greatest effect. Consequently, Haydn's remark left a bad impression on Beethoven and led him to think that Haydn was envious, jealous and ill-disposed toward him. I confess that when Beethoven told me of this I gave it little credence. I therefore took occasion to ask Haydn himself about it. His answer, however, confirmed Beethoven's statement; he said he had not believed that this Trio would so quickly and easily be understood and so favorably received by the public.

The Fischoff manuscript says:

The three Trios for pianoforte, violin and violoncello, Op. 1 (the pearls of all sonatas), which are in fact his sixth work, justly excited admiration, though they were performed in only a few circles. Wherever this was done, however, connoisseurs and music-lovers bestowed upon them undivided applause, which grew with the succeeding works as the hearers not only accustomed themselves to the striking and original qualities of the master but grasped his spirit and strove for the high privilege of understanding him.

More than two years passed by, however, before the composer thought fit to send these Trios to the press; perhaps restrained by a feeling of modesty, since he was still a student, perhaps by a doubt as to the success of compositions so new in style, or by prudence, choosing to delay their publication until they had been so often performed from the manuscript as to secure their comprehension and appreciation, and thus an adequate number of subscribers. In the meantime he prepared the way for them by publishing a few sets of variations. "Beethoven had composed variations on themes from Mozart's 'Zauberflöte,' which he had already sketched in Bonn, and Zmeskall took it upon himself to submit them to a publisher; but they had only a small sale." (The Fischoff MS.) This refers doubtless to the Variations "Se vuol ballare" from "Le Nozze di Figaro," which, having been revised and improved by a new coda, came out in July, 1793, with a dedication to Eleonore von Breuning. It was not until the next year that the thirteen variations upon the theme "Es war einmal ein alter Mann," from Dittersdorf's "Rothkäppchen," appeared, and these were followed by those for four hands on the Waldstein theme, first advertised in January, 1795.

In fact, Beethoven evidently was in no haste to publish his compositions. It will presently be seen that he sent the "Se vuol ballare" variations to press partly at the request of others and partly to entrap the rival pianists of Vienna. A few years later we shall find him dashing off and immediately publishing variations on popular theatrical melodies; but works of greater scope, and especially his pianoforte concertos, were for the most part long retained in his exclusive possession. Thus the Pianoforte Concerto in B-flat major, Op. 18, though supposed by Tomaschek to have been composed at Prague in 1798, certainly (if Beethoven's own words in a letter to Breitkopf and Härtel are to be believed) preceded in composition that in C major, Op. 15, and must, therefore, have been finished at the latest in March, 1795, and was doubtless often played by him at private concerts during the period now before us. It was not published until 1801.

Let the reader now recall to mind some of the points previously dwelt upon: the Fischenich letter of January and Neefe's letter of October, 1793, which record the favorable reports sent to Bonn of Beethoven's musical progress; his studies with Haydn and Schenk; the cares and perplexities caused him temporarily by the death of his father, and the unpleasant circumstances attending that event; his steady success as a virtuoso; his visit in the summer to Prince Esterhazy; and it is obvious with what industry and energy he engaged in his new career, with what zeal and unfaltering activity he labored to make the most of his opportunities. In one year after leaving Bonn he felt his success secure, and no longer feared Hamlet's "slings and arrows of outrageous fortune." This is indicated in a passage ("O, how we shall then rejoice together,"etc.) of the earliest of his Vienna letters which has been preserved—that letter in which, as Wegeler remarks, "he asked pardon for much more error than he had committed," and which, though often reprinted from the "Notizen," is too important and characteristic to be here omitted.

Vienna, November 2, 93.

Most estimable Leonore!
My most precious friend!
Not until I have lived almost a year in the capital do you receive a letter from me, and yet you were most assuredly perpetually in my liveliest memory. Often in thought I have conversed with you and your dear family, though not with that peace of mind which I could have desired. It was then that the wretched misunderstanding hovered before me and my conduct presented itself as most despicable. But it was too late. O, what would I not give could I obliterate from my life those actions so degrading to myself and so contrary to my character. True, there were many circumstances which tended to estrange us, and I suspect that tales whispered in our ears of remarks made one about the other were chiefly that which prevented us from coming to an understanding. We both believed that we were speaking from conviction; whereas it was only in anger, and we were both deceived. Your good and noble character, my dear friend, is sufficient assurance to me that you forgave me long ago. But we are told that the sincerest contrition

consists in acknowledgment of our faults; and to do this has been my desire. And now let us drop the curtain on the affair, only drawing from it this lesson—that when friends quarrel it is much better to have it out face to face than to turn to a go-between.

With this you will receive a dedication from me to you concerning which I only wish that the work were a larger one and more worthy of you. I was plagued here to publish the little work, and I took advantage of the opportunity, my estimable E., to show my respect and friendship for you and my enduring memory of your family. Take this trifle and remember that it comes from a friend who respects you greatly. Oh, if it but gives you pleasure, my wishes will be completely fulfilled. Let it be a reminder of the time when I spent so many and such blessed hours at your home. Perhaps it will keep me in your recollection until I eventually return to you, which, it is true, is not likely to be soon. But how we shall rejoice then, my dear friend—you will then find in your friend a happier man, from whose visage time and a kindlier fate shall have smoothed out all the furrows of a hateful past.

If you should chance to see B. Koch, please say to her that it is not nice of her never once to have written to me. I wrote to her twice and three times to Malchus, but no answer. Say to her that if she doesn't want to write she might at least urge Malchus to do so. In conclusion I venture a request; it is this: I should like once again to be so happy as to own a waistcoat knit of hare's wool by your hands, my dear friend. Pardon the immodest request, my dear friend, but it proceeds from a great predilection for everything that comes from your hands. Privately I may also acknowledge that a little vanity is also involved in the request; I want to be able to say that I have something that was given me by the best and most estimable girl in Bonn. I still have the waistcoat which you were good enough to give me in Bonn, but it has grown so out of fashion that I can only treasure it in my wardrobe as something very precious because it came from you. You would give me much pleasure if you were soon to rejoice me with a dear letter from yourself. If my letters should in any way please you I promise in this to be at your command so far as lies in my power, as everything is welcome to me which enables me to show how truly I am

Your admiring,
true friend
L. v. Beethoven.

P.S. The V. [variations] you will find a little difficult to play, especially the trills in the *coda;* but don't let that alarm you. It is so contrived that you need play only the trill, leaving out the other notes because they are also in the violin part. I never would have composed a thing of the kind had I not often observed that here and there in Vienna there was somebody who, after I had improvised of an evening, noted down many of my peculiarities, and made parade of them next day as his own. Foreseeing that some of these things would soon appear in print, I resolved to anticipate them. Another reason that I had was to embarrass the local pianoforte masters. Many of them are my deadly enemies, and I wanted to revenge myself on them, knowing that once in a while somebody would ask them to play the variations and they would make a sorry show with them.

Except Beethoven's memorandum, "Schuppanzigh 3 times each W.; Albrechtsberger 3 times each W.", which indicates his change of instructors, there is nothing to be recorded until, probably in May or June (1794), we come to the fragment of another letter to Eleonore von Breuning also contained in Wegeler's "Notizen" (p. 60), which has particular interest both as showing how bitterly his conscience reproached him for acts inconsistent with the forbearance and command of temper due to friendship, but in which he ever remained too apt to indulge, and as adding some implied confirmation of the argument previously made in relation to the compositions of the Bonn period. In this letter he acknowledges receipt of a cravat embroidered by Eleonore and protests that thoughts of her generosity and his unworthiness had brought him to tears. He continues: "Do pray believe me that little as I have deserved it, *my friend* (let me always call you such), I have suffered much and still suffer from the loss of your friendship. . . . As a slight return for your kind recollection of me I take the liberty of sending these Variations and the Rondo with violin (accompaniment). I have a great deal to do or I should have transcribed the Sonata I promised you long ago. It is a mere sketch in manuscript, and to copy it would be a difficult, etc." The letter is signed: "The friend who still reveres you, Beethowen" (*sic*).[1]

In January, 1794, Elector Max had paid a short visit to Vienna, where, perhaps, it was determined that Beethoven should remain "without salary until recalled." After the declaration of war by the Empire against France, the electorate, as a German state, could no longer remain neutral; and thus it came to pass that in October the victorious French army marched into Bonn. The Elector fled to Frankfort-on-the-Main, November 6th, thence to Münster, while his court and all such as were obnoxious to the republican authorities dispersed in all directions for safety.

One of these fugitives, a young man of twenty-nine years but already the Rector of the University, to "save his head" hastened away to Vienna—Dr. Wegeler. He reached that capital

---

[1] Though Thayer fixed the date of this letter in May or June, 1794, Dr. Deiters believed that it was of a much earlier date and may, indeed, have been written before Beethoven went to Vienna. For his theory Dr. Deiters found a plausible argument in the spelling of the name with a "w" instead of a "v," and the reiterated references to a misunderstanding which had long been right. The letter has no date or superscription and Wegeler assumed that it was the continuation of one whose first page had been lost. If the letter was written in Bonn it would prove that the Rondo (probably that in G for Pianoforte and Violin, B. and H. Series XII, No. 102) was composed before the beginning of the Viennese period; which might well be. The Sonata is probably the unfinished one in C, dedicated to Eleonore von Breuning.

in October and found Beethoven not in the "room on the ground floor" where "it was not necessary to pay the housekeeper more than 7 florins," but living as a guest in the family of Prince Karl Lichnowsky; and this explains sufficiently the cessation of those records of monthly payments before noticed.

The reminiscences of Wegeler for the period of his stay in Vienna, excepting those which may be better introduced chronologically in other connections, may well find place here. They are interesting and characteristic in themselves and indicate, also, the great change for the better in Beethoven's pecuniary condition; for a man who keeps a servant and a horse cannot, if honest, be a sufferer from poverty:

Carl, Prince of Lichnowsky, Count Werdenberg, Dynast Granson, was a very great patron, yes, a friend of Beethoven's, who took him into his house as a guest, where he remained at least a few years. I found him there toward the end of the year 1794, and left him there in the middle of 1796. Meanwhile, however, Beethoven had almost always a home in the country.

The Prince was a great lover and connoisseur of music. He played the pianoforte, and by studying Beethoven's pieces and playing them more or less well, sought to convince him that there was no need of changing anything in his style of composition, though the composer's attention was often called to the difficulties of his works. There were performances at his house every Friday morning, participated in by four hired musicians—Schuppanzigh, Weiss, Kraft and another (Link?), besides our friend; generally also an amateur, Zmeskall. Beethoven always listened with pleasure to the observations of these gentlemen. Thus, to cite a single instance, the famous violoncellist Kraft in my presence called his attention to a passage in the finale of the Trio, Op. 1, No. 3, to the fact that it ought to be marked "sulla corda G," and the indication 4-4 time which Beethoven had marked in the finale of the second Trio, changed to 2-4. Here the new compositions of Beethoven, so far as was feasible, were first performed. Here there were generally present several great musicians and music-lovers. I, too, as long as I lived in Vienna, was present, if not every time, at least most of the time.

Here a Hungarian count once placed a difficult composition by Bach in manuscript before him which he played *a vista* exactly as Bach would have played it, according to the testimony of the owner. Here the Viennese author Förster once brought him a quartet of which he had made a clean copy only that morning. In the second portion of the first movement the violoncello got out. Beethoven stood up, and still playing his own part sang the bass accompaniment. When I spoke about it to him as a proof of extraordinary acquirements, he replied with a smile: "The bass part *had* to be so, else the author would have known nothing about composition." To the remark that he had played a *presto* which he had never seen before so rapidly that it must have been impossible to see the individual notes, he answered: "Nor is that necessary; if you read rapidly there may be a multitude of typographical errors, but you neither see nor give heed to them, so long as the language is a familiar one."

After the concert the musicians generally stayed to dine. Here there gathered, in addition, artists and savants without regard to social position. The Princess Christiane was the highly cultivated daughter of Count Franz Joseph von Thun, who, a very philanthropic and respectable gentleman, was disposed to extravagant enthusiasm by his intercourse with Lavater, and believed himself capable of healing diseases through the power of his right hand.

The following undated letter also belongs to the years of Beethoven's intimate association with Wegeler in Vienna (1794–96). It is significant of Beethoven's character. Though easily offended and prone to anger, no sooner was the first ebullition of temper past than he was so reconciliatory and open to explanation that usually his contrition was out of all proportion to his fault. For this reason, and because it presents the friend in a light which provoked a protest from his modesty, Wegeler was unwilling to make public the entire letter.[1]

Dearest! Best! In what an odious light you have exhibited me to myself! I acknowledge it, I do not deserve your friendship. You are so noble, so considerate, and the first time that I ranged myself alongside of you I fell so far below you! Ah, for weeks I have displeased my best and noblest friend! You think that I have lost some of my goodness of heart, but, thank Heaven! it was no intentional or deliberate malice which induced me to act as I did towards you; it was my inexcusable thoughtlessness which did not permit me to see the matter in its true light. O, how ashamed I am, not only for your sake but also my own. I can scarcely trust myself to ask for your friendship again. Oh, Wegeler, my only comfort lies in this, that you have known me almost from my childhood, and yet, O let me say for myself, I was always good, and always strove to be upright and true in my actions—otherwise how could you have loved me? Could I have changed so fearfully for the worse in such a short time? Impossible; these feelings of goodness and love of righteousness cannot have died forever in me in a moment. No, Wegeler, dearest, best, O, venture again to throw yourself entirely into the arms of your B.; trust in the good qualities you used to find in him; I will guarantee that the pure temple of sacred friendship which you erect shall remain firm forever; no accident, no storm shall ever shake its foundations—firm—forever—our friendship—pardon—oblivion—a new upflaming of the dying, sinking friendship—O, Wegeler, do not reject this hand of reconciliation. Place yours in mine—O, God!—but no more; I am coming to throw myself in your arms, to entreat you to restore to me my lost friend. And you will give yourself to me, your penitent, loving, never-forgetting   Beethoven again.

It was only now that I received your letter, because I have just returned home.

[1]This was done by Wegeler's grandson, Carl Wegeler, in an essay published in the "Coblenz Zeitung" on May 20, 1890.

In this connection Wegeler comes to speak of the outward
conditions of Beethoven: "Beethoven," he says on page 33,

brought up under extremely restricted circumstances, and as it were,
under guardianship, though that of his friends, did not know the
value of money and was anything but economical. Thus, to cite a
single instance, the Prince's dinner hour was fixed at 4 o'clock. "Now,"
said Beethoven, "it is desired that every day I shall be at home at half-
past 3, put on better clothes, care for my beard, etc.—I can't stand that!"
So it happened that he frequently went to the taverns, since, as has been
said, in this as in all other matters of economy, he knew nothing about
the value of things or of money. The Prince, Wegeler continues, who
had a loud, metallic voice, once directed his serving-man that if ever
he and Beethoven should ring at the same time the latter was to be first
served. Beethoven heard this, and the same day engaged a servant for
himself. In the same manner, once when he took a whim to learn to
ride, which speedily left him, the stable of the Prince being offered him,
he bought a horse.

Concerning his friend's affairs of the heart, Wegeler had opportunity to make observations in Vienna. He relates on page 43
that while he was in the capital Beethoven "was always in love
and made many conquests which would have been difficult if not
impossible for many an Adonis." Beethoven's antipathy to
teaching before he left Bonn has already been noticed. In Vienna
he developed a still stronger repugnance to playing in society when
requested to do so. He often complained to Wegeler how griev-
ously this put him out of sorts, whereupon the latter sought to
entertain him and quiet him by conversation. "When this purpose was reached," he continues,

I dropped the conversation, seated myself at the writing table, and
Beethoven, if he wanted to continue the discourse, had to sit down on
the chair before the pianoforte. Soon, still turned away from the instrument, he aimlessly struck a few chords out of which gradually grew
the most beautiful melodies. Oh, why did I not understand more of
music! Several times I put ruled paper upon the desk as if without
intention, in order to get a manuscript of his; he wrote upon it but then
folded it up and put it in his pocket! Concerning his playing I was
permitted to say but little, and that only in passing. He would then
go away entirely changed in mood and always come back again gladly.
The antipathy remained, however, and was frequently the cause of
differences between Beethoven and his friends and well-wishers.

There is still one other reminiscence of Wegeler in the appendix
to the "Notizen" (page 9) worthy of citation. "At one time private lectures were given in Vienna on Kant, which had been
arranged by Adam Schmidt, Wilhelm Schmidt, Hunczovsky, Göp-
fert and others. In spite of my urgings Beethoven refused to

attend a single one of them." There is no reference in Wegeler's "Notizen" to instruction received by Beethoven from Albrechtsberger. With his old colleague in the Court Orchestra in Bonn, Nicolaus Simrock, though he was a much older·man, Beethoven remained in touch after his removal to Vienna. Simrock, who was highly esteemed both as man and musician, had embarked in business as a music publisher in Bonn. The Variations on a theme from Dittersdorf's "Rothkäppchen," were published by him (at the latest in the early part of 1794), as well as those for pianoforte four hands on a theme by Count Waldstein (some time in the same year). It is to the latter composition that the following letter refers:

Vienna, August 2, 1794.

Dear Simrock:

I deserve a little scolding from you for holding back your Variations so long, but, indeed, I do not lie when I say that I was hindered from correcting them sooner by an overwhelming amount of business. You will note the shortcomings for yourself, but I must wish you joy on the appearance of your engraving, which is beautiful, clear and legible. Verily, if you keep on thus you will become chief among cutters, that is, note cutters[1]. In my former letter I promised to send you something of mine and you interpreted the remark as being in the language of the cavaliers. How have I deserved such a title? Faugh! who would indulge in such language in these democratic days of ours? To free myself from the imputation as soon as I have finished the grand revision of my compositions, which will be soon, you shall have something which you will surely engrave. I have also been looking about me for a commissioner and have found a right capable young fellow for the place. His name is Traeg. You have naught to do but to write to him or me about the conditions which you want to make. He asks of you one-third *rabate*. The devil take all such bargaining! It is very hot here. The Viennese fear that they will soon be unable to eat ice-cream, there having been little cold last winter and ice being scarce. Many persons of importance have come here and it was said that a revolution was imminent; but it is my belief that so long as the Austrian has his dark beer and sausage he will not revolt. It is said that the suburban gates are to be closed at ten o'clock at night. The soldiers' guns are loaded with bullets. No one dares speak aloud for fear of arrest by the police. Are your daughters grown? Bring one up to be my wife, for if I am to remain single in Bonn I shall not stay long, of a surety. You also must be living in fear. How is good Ries? I shall write to him soon for he can have only an unfavorable opinion of me—but this damned writing! I cannot get over my antipathy towards it. Have you performed my piece yet? Write to me occasionally.

Please send also a few copies of the first Variations.

Your
Beethoven.

---

[1]An early example of Beethoven's fondness for punning. *Stechen* means many things in German—among them to sting, stab, tilt in a tournament, take a trick at cards—as well as to engrave, or cut in metal.

These "first Variations" obviously are those on the theme from "Rothkäppchen"; those referred to in the early part of the letter the ones on Count Waldstein's theme. The "piece" whose performance he inquires about is the Octet, and the allusion to it justifies the belief that it was composed for the wind-instrument players of Bonn who found no opportunity to play it while Beethoven was still in his native city. The letter, like that written to Eleonore von Breuning, shows that Beethoven was still thinking of the possibility or probability of a return to Bonn. Its cheerful tone discloses a comfortable, satisfied frame of mind— the mood from which the first Trios proceeded.

We return to the chronological record of events. The first of these in the year 1795, was Beethoven's first appearance in public as virtuoso and composer. The annual concerts in the Burgtheater established by Gassmann for the benefit of the widows of the Tonkünstlergesellschaft were announced for the evenings of March 29 and 30. The vocal work selected for performance was an oratorio in two parts, "Gioas, Re di Giuda," by Antonio Cartellieri; the instrumental, a Concerto for Pianoforte and Orchestra, composed and played by Ludwig van Beethoven. Cartellieri was a young man of twenty-three years (born in Danzig, September 27, 1772) who, a year or two since, had come from Berlin to study operatic composition with the then greatest living composer in that field, Salieri. As the direction of these Widow and Orphan concerts was almost exclusively in the hands of Salieri, one is almost tempted to think that he may on this occasion have indulged a pardonable vanity in bringing forward two of his pupils, if we did not know how strong an attraction the name of Beethoven must have been for the public which, as yet, had had no opportunity to learn his great powers except by report. The day of the performance drew near but the Concerto was not yet written out. "Not until the afternoon of the second day before the concert did he write the rondo, and then while suffering from a pretty severe colic which frequently afflicted him. I [Wegeler] relieved him with simple remedies so far as I could. In the anteroom sat four copyists to whom he handed sheet after sheet as soon as it was finished. . . . At the first rehearsal, which took place the next day in Beethoven's room, the pianoforte was found to be half a tone lower than the wind-instruments. Without a moment's delay Beethoven had the wind-instruments and the others tune to B-flat instead of A and played his part in C-sharp." Thus Wegeler in his "Notizen" (pg. 36). But he has confounded two compositions. The concerto which Beethoven played on March

29, 1795, was not that in C (Op. 15) which was not yet finished, but, in all probability, that in B-flat (Op. 19). For the fact that the Concerto in B-flat was composed before that in C we have the testimony of Beethoven himself, who wrote to Breitkopf and Härtel on April 22, 1801: "I simply want to call your attention to the fact that one of my first Concertos will be published by Hoffmeister, which is not among my best works, and one also by Mollo which, though composed later, etc." The Concerto in B-flat was published in 1801 by Hoffmeister and that in C in the same year by Mollo and Co. in Vienna, the latter a little in advance of the former, wherefore there need be no surprise at the earlier *opus* number.

Beethoven also took part in the second concert on March 30, the minutes of the Tonkünstlerschaft recording that he "improvised on the pianoforte"; and though busily engaged he also embraced an opportunity to testify to his devotion to the manes of Mozart. On March 31, 1795, Mozart's widow arranged a performance of "La Clemenza di Tito" in the Burgtheater. "After the first part," says the advertisement, "Mr. Ludwig van Beethoven will play a Concerto of Mozart's composition on the Pianoforte." We opine that this concerto was Mozart's in D minor, which Beethoven loved especially and for which he wrote cadenzas.

The Trios, Op. 1, had now become so well known and appreciated in musical circles as to justify their publication, and accordingly, an advertisement inviting subscriptions for Ludwig van Beethoven's "three Grand Trios" appeared in the "Wiener Zeitung" on May 16, 1795. Three days later a contract was signed by the author and Artaria and Company. The printed list of subscribers gives 123 names, mostly belonging to the higher circles, with subscriptions amounting to 241 copies. As Beethoven paid the publisher but one florin per copy, and the subscription price was one ducat, he made a handsome profit out of the transaction.[1]

We must tarry a moment longer with these Trios. That the author is disposed to place their origin in the Bonn period has already appeared. Argument in favor of this view can be found in the fact of their early performance in Vienna, for there can be no reasonable question of the correctness of Ries's story, for which Beethoven himself was authority, that they were played at the house of Prince Lichnowsky, in the presence of Haydn. This performance must have taken place before January 19, 1794, because on that day Haydn started again for England. Now, Beethoven's sketches show that he was still working on at least the second and

[1]The son of Artaria told Nohl that his father had told him that he got the money to pay Beethoven without the composer's knowledge from Prince Lichnowsky.

third of the Trios after 1794, and that they were not ready for the printer before the end of that year. Further explanation is offered by the following little circumstances: since Haydn was present, the performance at Prince Lichnowsky's must have been from manuscript. In the morning meeting which probably took place only a short time before the soirée, Beethoven's attention was called to the desirability of changing in the last movement of the second Trio, the time-signature from 4-4 to 2-4. Beethoven made the change. From these facts it may be concluded that after a first there was a final revision of these Trios and that the former version disappeared or was destroyed after the latter was made. It has repeatedly been intimated that the author believes that the rewriting of compositions completed in Beethoven's early period is farther-reaching than is generally assumed. The case therefore seems to present itself as follows: Haydn heard the Trios at Lichnowsky's in their first state; Beethoven then took them up for revision and in the course of 1794 and the beginning of 1795 brought them to the state in which we know them. It is not possible to say positively whether or not the first form, particularly of the first Trio, dates back to the Bonn period.

An interesting anecdote connected with these Trios may well find place here; it is contributed by Madame Mary de Fouche, daughter of Tomkison, who, in the seventh decade of the nineteenth century, was one of the more famous pianoforte manufacturers of London: In the early days of the century, a little society of musicians—J. B. Cramer, the pianist; F. Cramer, violinist, half-brother of the preceding; J. P. Salomon, whose name has so often come .up in previous chapters of this work; Bridgetower, a mulatto and celebrated violinist, whose name we shall meet again; Watts, tenor; Morant, also tenor, who married the great Dussek's widow; Dahmen, Lindley and Crossdale, violoncellists—was in the habit of meeting regularly at Mr. Tomkison's to try over and criticise such new music of the German school as came to the London dealers. At one of these meetings the new Trios of Beethoven, Op. 1, were played through, J. B. Cramer at the pianoforte. "This is the man," he cried, "who is to console us for the loss of Mozart!" According to the recollection of Cipriani Potter, this was after Cramer had made the personal acquaintance of Beethoven in Vienna, and had heard him play there.

Some other incidents recorded by Wegeler belong to this year. Haydn reached Vienna upon his return from his second visit to England on August 20. Beethoven had now ready the three Sonatas, Op. 2, and at one of the Friday morning concerts at

Prince Lichnowsky's he played them to Haydn, to whom they were dedicated.

Here (says Wegeler on page 29 of the 'Notizen'), Count Appony asked Beethoven to compose a quartet for him for a given compensation, Beethoven not yet having written a piece in this genre. The Count declared that contrary to custom he did not want to have exclusive possession of the quartet for half a year before publication, nor did he ask that it be dedicated to him, etc. In response to repeated urgings by me, Beethoven twice set about the task, but the first effort resulted in a grand violin Trio (Op. 3), the second in a violin Quintet (Op. 4).

How much mistaken Wegeler was in these concluding statements has already been indicated.

The three Pianoforte Sonatas dedicated to Haydn were, therefore, the second group of compositions which Beethoven considered illustrative of his artistic ideals and worthy of publication. Nothing can be said with positiveness touching the time of their origin. Schönfeld's words in his "Jahrbuch der Tonkunst von Wien und Prag": "We already have several of his Sonatas, among which his last are particularly noteworthy," which were written at least eight months before the Sonatas appeared in print, lead to the conclusion that the Sonatas were known in Vienna in manuscript in the spring of 1795. Their appearance in print was announced in the "Wiener Zeitung" of March 9, 1796.

Still another anecdote recorded by Wegeler refers to another composition of this period: "Beethoven was seated in a box at the opera with a lady of whom he thought much at a performance of 'La Molinara.' When the familiar *Nel cor più non mi sento* was reached the lady remarked that she had possessed some variations on the theme but had lost them. In the same night Beethoven wrote the six variations on the melody and the next morning sent them to the lady with the inscription: *Variazioni, etc., Perdute par la—ritrovate par Luigi van Beethoven.* They are so easy that it is likely Beethoven wished that she should be able to play them at sight." Paisiello's "La Molinara," composed in 1788 for Naples, was performed on March 8, 1794 in the Court Opera, and again on June 24 and 27, 1795, in the Kärnthnerthor-Theater in Vienna. Considering the time of the publication of these unpretentious but genial little variations, their composition may be set down after the latter performances. At the same period Beethoven wrote variations on another theme (*Quant' è più bello*) from the same opera, which were published before the former and dedicated to Prince Carl Lichnowsky. It is likely that a few more sets of variations, a form of composition for which Beethoven had a strong predilection at the time, had their origin in these early years of Beethoven's life in Vienna. The Variations in C on the "Menuet à la Vigano" from the ballet "Le Nozze disturbate," may confidently be assigned to the year 1795. The ballet was performed for the first time on May 18, 1795, at Schikaneder's theatre; the Variations are advertised as published on February 27, 1796.

The Gesellschaft der bildenden Künstler had, in the year 1792, established an annual ball in the Redoutensaal in the month of November; and Haydn, just then returned covered with glory from England, composed a set of twelve minuets and twelve German dances for the occasion. In 1793, the Royal Imperial Composer Kozeluch followed Haydn's example. In 1794, Dittersdorf wrote the same number of like dances for the large hall, and Eybler for the small. In view of this array of great names, and considering that as yet the Trios, Op. 1, were the only works of a higher order than the Variations which Beethoven had sent to press, the advertisements for the annual ball to be given upon the 22nd of November, 1795, give a vivid proof of the high reputation which the young man had gained as a composer now at the end of his third year in Vienna. These advertisements conclude thus: "The music for the Minuets and German dances for this ball is an entirely new arrangement. For the larger room they were written by the Royal Imperial Chapelmaster Süssmayr; for the smaller room by the master hand of Mr. Ludwig van Beethoven out of love for the artistic fraternity." These dances, arranged for pianoforte by Beethoven himself, came from the press of Artaria a few weeks later, as did also Süssmayr's; Beethoven's name in the advertisement being in large and conspicuous type.

As the year began with the first, so it closed with Beethoven's second appearance in public as composer and virtuoso; and here is the advertisement of the performance from the "Wiener Zeitung" of December 16:

Next Friday, the 18th instant, Mr. the Chapelmaster Haydn will give a grand musical concert in the small Redoutensaal, at which Mad. Tomeoni and Mr. Mombelli will sing. Mr. van Beethoven will play a Concerto of his composing on the Pianoforte, and three grand symphonies, not yet heard here, which the Chapelmaster composed during his last sojourn in London, will be performed.

One would gladly know what concerto was played.[1] But there was little public criticism then outside of London and very

[1] I was probably that in B-flat. See Nottebohm's "Zweite Beethoveniana," page 72t

rarely any in Vienna. The mere fact of the appearance of Beethoven at his old master's concert is, however, another proof that too much stress has been laid upon a hasty word spoken by him to Ries. Haydn wanted that Beethoven should put "Pupil of Haydn" on the title-page of his first works. Beethoven was unwilling to do so because, as he said, "though he had taken some lessons from Haydn he had never learned anything from him." Nothing could be more natural than for Haydn, knowing nothing of the studies of his pupil with Schenk, to express such a wish in relation to the Sonatas dedicated to him, and equally natural that the author should refuse; but to add to the attractions of the concert was a very different matter—a graceful and delicate compliment which he could with pleasure make.

This chapter may appropriately close with the one important family event of this year. The father, the mother, two infant brothers and two infant sisters slept in the churchyard at Bonn; but Ludwig, Caspar and Johann were never more to look upon their graves. The three brothers were now reunited. Vienna had become their new home and not one of them beheld the rushing Rhine again.

Chapter XIV

The Years 1796 and 1797—Beethoven in Prague and Berlin
—King Frederick William II and Prince Louis Ferdinand
—Himmel, Fasch and Zelter—Compositions and Publications.

THE narrative resumes its course with the year 1796, the twenty-sixth of Beethoven's life and his fourth in Vienna. If not yet officially, he was *de facto* discharged from his obligations to the Elector Maximilian and all his relations with Bonn and its people were broken off. Vienna had become his home, and there is no reason to suppose that he ever afterwards cherished any real and settled purpose to exchange it for another—not even in 1809 when, for the moment, he had some thought of accepting Jerome Bonaparte's invitation to Cassel.

He had now entered his course of contrapuntal study with Albrechtsberger; he was first of the pianoforte players of the capital and his name added attraction even to the concert which Haydn, returning again from his London triumphs, had given to introduce some of his new works to the Viennese; his "masterhand" was already publicly recognized in the field of musical composition; he counted many nobles of the higher ranks in his list of personal friends and had been, perhaps even now was, a member of Prince Carl Lichnowsky's family. The change in his pecuniary condition might have thrown a more equitable temperament than his off its balance. Three years ago he anxiously noted down the few kreutzers occasionally spent for coffee or chocolate "für Haidn und mich"; now he keeps his own servant and a horse. His brothers, if at all a burden, were no longer a heavy one. Carl Caspar, according to the best information now obtainable, soon gained moderate success in the musical profession and, with probably some occasional aid from Ludwig both pecuniary and in obtaining pupils, earned sufficient for his comfortable support; while Johann had secured a situation in that apothecary shop "Zum Heiligen Geist" which, in 1860, was still to be seen in tbe Kärnthnerstrasse near the former site of the gate of that name.[1] His wages were, of course, small and we shall soon see that Ludwig offers him assistance if needed, though not to Karl; but Johann's position gradually improved and he was able in a few years to save enough to enable him, unaided by his brother, to purchase and establish himself in a business of his own.[2]

"Fate had become propitious to Beethoven"; and a final citation from the memorandum book will show in what spirit he was determined to merit the continuance of Fortune's favor. If we make allowance for the old error as to his real age, this citation may belong to a period a year or two later; but may it not be one of those extracts from books and periodical publications which all his life long he was so fond of making? This seems to be the more probable supposition. The words are these: "Courage! In spite of all bodily weaknesses my spirit shall rule. You have lived 25 years. This year must determine the complete man. Nothing must remain undone."

And now let the chronological narrative of events be resumed. As the year 1795 had ended with a public appearance of Beethoven as pianoforte player and composer, so also began the year 1796; and, as on a former occasion in a concert by Haydn, so this time he played at a concert given by a singer, Signora Bolla, who afterward became famous, in the Redoutensaal. Again he played a pianoforte concerto.

"In 1796," says Wegeler ("Nachträge," p. 18), "the two older Breuning brothers, Christoph and Stephan, find him (Beethoven) at Nuremberg on a return journey to Vienna. Which journey is not specified. None of the three having a passport from Vienna they were all detained at Linz, but soon liberated through my intervention at Vienna." And from a letter written by Stephan von Breuning to his mother, dated January, 1796, Wegeler quotes: "From Nuremberg, Beethoven travelled all the way in company with us. The three Bonnians thus attracted the attention of the police, who thought they had made a wonderful discovery. I do not believe that there could be a less dangerous man than Beethoven." Wegeler's suggestion that Beethoven was returning "perhaps from Berlin" is of course out of the question. But between the date of Haydn's concert (December 18th) and Stephan von Breuning's letter, if written towards the end of January, there was ample time, even in those days of post-coaches, for a journey to Prague and

---

[1] It is now No. 16 of the extended Operngasse.

[2] Czerny described Beethoven's brothers to Otto Jahn as follows: "Carl: small of stature, red-haired, ugly; Johann: large, dark, a handsome man and complete dandy."

thence across the country to Mergentheim or Ellingen, at that time the temporary residences of Elector Maximilian.   The necessity of Beethoven's knowing precisely in what relation he was to stand with the Elector in the future, accounts sufficiently for his being in Nuremberg at that time, especially if he had had occasion to visit Prague during the Christmas holidays, which is not improbable.   Dlabacz, in his "Künstler-Lexikon," has a paragraph of which this is a part: "v. Beethoven, a Concertmaster on the pianoforte.   In the year 1795, he gave an academy in Prague at which he played with universal approval."   It is true that Dlabacz may here record a concert given during Beethoven's stay in the Bohemian capital some weeks later; but, on the one hand, no other notice of such a concert has been discovered; and, on the other, the "universal approval" on this occasion may have been an inducement for him to return thither so soon.

At all events, his delay in Vienna after coming from Nuremberg was short and was doubtless occupied with the last corrections of the Sonatas, Op. 2, dedicated to Haydn, the six Menuets (second part), the Variations on the theme from "Le Nozze disturbate" and those on "Nel cor più non mi sento," all of which works are advertised in the "Wiener Zeitung" in the course of the next two months, while their author was again in Prague or cities farther North.   For the following letter we are indebted to Madame van Beethoven, widow of the composer's nephew, Carl:

To my brother Nicholaus Beethoven

to be delivered at the apothecary shop at the Kärnthner Thor Mr. von Z.[1] will please hand this letter to the wig-maker who will care for its delivery.

Prague, February 19th (1796).

Dear Brother!

So that you may at least know where I am and what I am doing I must needs write you.   In the first place I am getting on well—very well.   My art wins for me friends and respect; what more do I want?   This time, too, I shall earn considerable money.   I shall remain here a few weeks more and then go to Dresden, Leipsic and Berlin.   It will probably be six weeks before I shall return.   I hope that you will be more and more pleased with your sojourn in Vienna; but beware of the whole guild of wicked women.   Have you yet called on Cousin Elss?   You might write to me at this place if you have inclination and time.

[1]"Mr. von Z." is doubtless Zmeskall, who is thus shown to have been a trusted friend of Beethoven's in 1796.   "This time" indicates plainly that Beethoven had been in Prague before.   Through the words: "Greetings to Brother Caspar" the pen has been heavily drawn, and, if the color of the ink can be trusted after so many years, it was done at the time of writing.   "F. Linowsky" is Fürst (Prince) Lichnowsky.

F. Linowsky will probably soon return to Vienna; he has already gone from here. If you need money you may go to him boldly, for he still owes me some.

For the rest I hope that your life will grow continually in happiness and to that end I hope to contribute something. Farewell, dear brother, and think occasionally of

Your true, faithful brother
L. Beethoven.

Greetings to Brother Caspar.
My address is The Golden Unicorn
on the Kleinseite.

A debt of gratitude is certainly due Johann van Beethoven for having carefully preserved this letter for full half a century and leaving it to his heirs, notwithstanding all the troubles which afterwards arose between the brothers, since it is hardly more valnable and interesting for the facts which it states directly than for what it indicates and suggests more or less clearly.

It, with other considerations, render it well nigh certain that Beethoven had now come to Prague with Prince Lichnowsky as Mozart had done, seven years before, and that upon leaving Vienna he had had no intention of pursuing his journey farther; but encouraged by the success thus reported to his brother, he suddenly determined to seek instruction and experience, pleasure, profit and fame in an extended tour. Had he projected this journey already in Vienna, how could all recollection of it have been lost by Wegeler? How could von Breuning in the letter cited above have omitted all mention of it? Nor is it possible to think that Beethoven, still so young and still so unknown outside the Austrian and Bohemian capitals, having so many powerful and influential friends there, and there only, could at this time have gone forth to seek elsewhere some permanent position with a fixed salary. The remarks which have been preserved, made by him in writing or conversation, expressing a desire for such an appointment, all belong to a later period, and cannot by any torture of language be made to refer to this, when he was looking into the future with well-grounded hopes and serene confidence of advancement in his new home. Vienna seemed to offer him all his ambition could crave; why should he seek his fortune beyond her walls?

It is pleasant to note his care for the welfare of his brother Johann, which care, doubtless, the other brother did not need. But how could Prince Lichnowsky have been indebted to Ludwig?

The musical public of Prague was the same that had so recently honored itself by its instant and noble appreciation of Mozart, and had given so glorious a welcome to "Figaro," "Don

Giovanni" and "Titus." There being no royal or imperial court there, and the public amusements being less numerous than in Vienna, the nobility were thrown more on their own resources for recreation; and hence, besides the traditional taste of the Bohemians for instrumental music, their capital was, perhaps, a better field for the virtuoso than Vienna. No notice of any public concert given by Beethoven on this visit has been discovered, either in the newspapers of the time or in the reminiscences of Thomaschek and others; and "the considerable money" earned "this time" must have been the presents of the nobility for his performances in their salons, and, perhaps, for compositions.

The conception of the aria "Ah, perfido! spergiuro" is generally associated with Beethoven's sojourn in Prague. The belief rests upon the fact that upon the cover of a copy which he revised Beethoven wrote the words "Une grande Scène mise en musique par L. v. Beethoven à Prague, 1796." On the first page is written: *Recitativo e Aria composta e dedicata alla Signora Contessa di Clari da L. v. Beethoven.* The opus number, 46, in this title is in the handwriting of Al. Fuchs, who owned a copy. Now, on November 21st, 1796, Madame Duschek, the well known friend of Mozart, at a concert in Leipsic sang "An Italian Scena composed for Madame Duschek by Beethoven," and it was easy to conclude that the aria was really written by Beethoven for Madame Duschek. On a page of sketches preserved in Berlin among others there are sketches belonging to "Ah, perfido!" which do not agree with the printed page. On the lower margin of the first page is the remark: *pour Mademoiselle la Comtesse de Clari.* Nottebohm is led by these things to surmise that the aria was written in Vienna in 1795, before the visit to Prague. In any case, we are permitted to associate the date 1796 only with the completion of the work in Prague; and the purpose may well have been to have it sung by Madame Duschek, who is thus proved to have belonged to the circle of Beethoven's friends in Prague. Nevertheless, the aria was originally intended for the Countess Josephine Clari, a well known amateur singer who married Count Christian Clam-Gallas in 1797. The scena first appeared in print in the fall of 1805, when it was published in a collection made by Hoffmeister and Kühnel. Beethoven placed it upon the programme of his concert in 1808.

Another family in which Beethoven was received on the footing of a friend was that of Appellate Councillor Kanka. Both father and son were dilettante composers and instrumental players—the father on the violoncello, the son on the pianoforte.

Gerber gives them a place in his Lexicon. "Miss Jeanette" (the daughter), says the eulogistic Schönfeld, "played the pianoforte with great expression and skill." The son adopted his father's profession, became a distinguished writer on Bohemian law, and in later years did Beethoven good service as legal adviser.

There is in the Artaria collection, a thick fascicle of sketches and musical fragments from Beethoven's hand in which papers from the Bonn period down to the close of the century are stitched together in such disorder as to show that they were thus joined merely for preservation. One sheet of mere sketches bears, if correctly deciphered, this inscription: "Written and dedicated to Gr. C. G. as a souvenir of his stay in P." On the fourth page of the sheet stands "these 4 Bagtalles by B." with something more illegible. May not some yet unknown composition of Beethoven be still in the possession of the family Clam-Gallas? Count Christian and his two daughters are numbered by Schönfeld among the fine pianoforte players of Prague, and these few notices exhaust the information obtained upon this visit of Beethoven there. His next appearance is in Berlin. No record has been found of the proposed visit to either Dresden or Leipsic, although his journey, it would seem, must have taken him through the Saxon capital.

In after years he was fond of talking about his sojourn in Berlin, and some particulars have thus been preserved. "He played," says Ries,

several times at court (that of King Frederick William II), where he played the two grand sonatas with *obbligato* violoncello, Op. 5, written for Duport, first violoncellist of the King, and himself. On his departure he received a gold snuff-box filled with Louis d'ors. Beethoven declared with pride that it was not an ordinary snuff-box, but such an one as it might have been customary to give to an ambassador.

This king shared his uncle Frederick II's love for music, while his taste was better and more cultivated. His instrument was the violoncello, and he often took part in quartets and sometimes in the rehearsals of Italian operas. He exerted a powerful and enduring influence for good upon the musical taste of Berlin. It was he who caused the operas of Gluck and Mozart to be performed there and introduced oratorios of Handel into the court concerts. His appreciation of Mozart's genius, and his wish to attach that great master to his court, are well known; and these facts render credible a statement with which Carl Czerny closes a description of Beethoven's extemporaneous playing contributed to Cock's "London Musical Miscellany" (August 2nd, 1852):

His improvisation was most brilliant and striking. (In whatever company he might chance to be, he knew how to produce such an effect upon every hearer that frequently not an eye remained dry, while many would break out into loud sobs; for there was something wonderful in his expression in addition to the beauty and originality of his ideas and his spirited style of rendering them.   After ending an improvisation of this kind he would burst into loud laughter and banter his hearers on the emotion he had caused in them.   "You are fools!" he would say.) Sometimes he would feel himself insulted by these indications of sympathy.   "Who can live among such spoiled children?" he would cry, and only on that account (as he told me) he declined to accept an invitation which the King of Prussia gave him after one of the extemporary performances above described.

Chapelmaster Reichardt had withdrawn himself from Berlin two years before, having fallen into disfavor because of his sympathy with the French Revolution.   Neither Himmel nor Righini, his successors, ever showed a genius for chamber music of a high order, and, indeed, there was no composer of reputation in this sphere then living in that quarter.   The young Beethoven by his two sonatas had proved his powers and the King saw in him precisely the right man to fill the vacancy—no small proof of superior taste and judgment.   What the German expression was which the translator of Czerny's letter has rendered "accept an invitation which the King gave him" there is no means of knowing; but as it stands it can only mean an invitation to enter permanently into his service.   The death of the King the next year, of course, prevented its being ever renewed.

Friedrich Heinrich Himmel, five years older than Beethoven, whom the King had withdrawn from the study of theology and caused to be thoroughly educated as a musician, first under Naumann in Dresden and afterwards in Italy, had returned the year before and had assumed his duties as Royal Pianist and Composer. As a virtuoso on his instrument his only rival in Berlin was Prince Louis Ferdinand, son of Prince August and nephew of Frederick II, two years younger than Beethoven and endowed by nature with talents and genius which would have made him conspicuous had fortune not given him royal descent.   He and Beethoven became well known to each other and each felt and did full justice to the other's musical genius and attainments.   Now let Ries speak again:

In Berlin he (Beethoven) associated much with Himmel, of whom he said that he had a pretty talent, but no more; his pianoforte playing, he said, was elegant and pleasing, but he was not to be compared with Prince Louis Ferdinand.   In his opinion he paid the latter a high compliment when once he said to him that his playing was not that of a king or prince but more like that of a thoroughly good pianoforte player. He fell out with Himmel in the following manner: One day when they were together Himmel begged Beethoven to improvise; which Beethoven did. Afterwards Beethoven insisted that Himmel do the same. The latter was weak enough to agree; but after he had played for quite a time Beethoven remarked: "Well, when are you going fairly to begin?" Himmel had flattered himself that he had already performed wonders; he jumped up and the men behaved ill towards each other. Beethoven said to me: "I thought that Himmel had been only preluding a bit." Afterwards they were reconciled, indeed, but Himmel could never forgive or forget[1]. They also exchanged letters until Himmel played Beethoven a shabby trick. The latter always wanted to know the news from Berlin. This bored Himmel, who at last wrote that the greatest news from Berlin was that a lamp for the blind had been invented. Beethoven ran about with the news and all the world wanted to know how this was possible. Thereupon he wrote to Himmel that he had blundered in not giving more explicit information. The answer which he received, but which does not permit of communication, not only put an end to the correspondence but brought ridicule upon Beethoven, who was so inconsiderate as to show it then and there.

With Carl Friedrich Christian Fasch and Carl Friedrich Zelter he also made a friendly acquaintance, and twice at least attended meetings of the Singakademie, which then numbered about 90 voices. The first time, June 21st, says the "Geschichte der Singakademie":

A chorale, the first three numbers of the mass and the first six of the 119th Psalm were sung for him. Hereupon he seated himself at the pianoforte and played an improvisation on the theme of the final fugue: "Meine Zunge rühmt im Wettgesang dein Lob." The last numbers of "Davidiana" (a collection of versets by Fasch) formed the conclusion. No biographer has mentioned this visit or even his sojourn in Berlin. Nor does Fasch pay special attention to it; but the performance must have pleased, for it was repeated at the meeting on the 28th.

The performance of the Society must also have pleased Beethoven, and with good reason; for Fasch's mass was in sixteen parts and the psalm and "Davidiana," in part, in eight; and no such music was then to be heard elsewhere north of the Alps.

In 1810, Beethoven, speaking of his playing on that occasion, told Mme. von Arnim (then Elizabeth Brentano) that at the close his hearers did not applaud but came crowding around him weeping; and added, ironically, "that is not what we artists wish—we want applause!" Fasch's simple record of Beethoven's visit is this:

June 21, 1796. Mr. van Beethoven extemporized on the "Davidiana," taking the fugue theme from Ps. 119, No. 16. . . . Mr. Beethoven,

---

[1] Beethoven told the story to Mme. von Arnim with the additional particular that they were walking in Unter den Linden and went thence into a private room of the principal coffee-house where there was a pianoforte, for the exhibition of their skill.

pianist from Vienna, was so accommodating as to permit us to hear an
improvisation. . . . June 28, Mr. van Beethoven was again so obliging
as to play an improvisation for us.

Early in July, the King left Berlin for the baths of Pyrmont,
the nobility dispersed to their estates or to watering-places, and
the city "was empty and silent." Beethoven, therefore, could
have had no inducement to prolong his stay; but the precise time
of his departure is unknown. Schindler names Leipsic as one of
the cities in which, during this tour, Beethoven "awakened interest
and created a sensation by his pianoforte playing, and, particularly, by his brilliant improvisation"; but no allusion in any public
journal of that or any subsequent period, not even the faintest
tradition, has been discovered to confirm the evidently erroneous
statements. Moreover, Rochlitz in his account of a visit to the
composer in 1822 remarks, "I had not yet seen Beethoven"; and
again, "It was only as a youth that he . . . . . passed through
(Leipsic)." So, until some new discovery be made, this must also
find its place in the long list of Schindler's mistakes.

Notwithstanding Wegeler's statement ("Notizen," 28) that he
left Beethoven a member of the family of Prince Lichnowsky "in
the middle of 1796," it is as certain as circumstantial evidence
can well make it that the Doctor and Christoph von Breuning had
returned to Bonn before Beethoven reached Vienna again; but
Stephan and Lenz were still there. The former obtained at this
time an appointment in the Teutonic Order, which so many of his
ancestors had served, and his name appears in the published "Calendars of the Order" from 1797 to 1803, both inclusive, as "Hofrathsassessor." He then soon departed from Vienna to Mergentheim, whence he wrote (November 23rd) with other matters the
following upon Beethoven to Wegeler and Christoph:

I do not know whether or not Lenz has written you anything
about Beethoven; but take notice that I saw him in Vienna and that
according to my mind, which Lenz has confirmed, he has become somewhat staider, or, perhaps I should say, has acquired more knowledge
of humanity through travels (or was it because of the new ebullition
of friendship on his arrival?) and a greater conviction of the scarceness
and value of good friends. A hundred times, dear Wegeler, he wishes
you here again, and regrets nothing so much as that he did not follow
much of your advice. ("Notizen," page 19.)

Except this notice of his bearing and demeanor, there is a
complete hiatus in Beethoven's history from his appearance in the
Singakademie until the following November. The so-called
Fischoff Manuscript has, it is true, a story of a "dangerous illness"

which was caused by his own imprudence this summer; but as it is in date utterly irreconcilable with other known facts, it will receive its due consideration hereafter. The most plausible suggestion is that coming back, flushed with victory, with the success of his tour and delighted with the novelty of travelling at his ease, he made that excursion to Pressburg and Pesth of which afterwards Ries was informed and made record ("Notizen," page 109), but of which no other account is known.

And thus we come to November. This was the year of that astounding series of victories ending at Arcole, gained by the young French general Napoleon Bonaparte. The Austrian government and people alike saw and feared the danger of invasion, a general uprising took place and volunteer corps were formed in all quarters. For the Vienna corps, Friedelberg wrote his "Abschiedsgesang an Wiens Bürger beim Auszug der Fahnen-Division der Wiener Freiwilliger," and Beethoven set it to music. The original printed edition bears date "November 15, 1795." It does not appear to have gained any great popularity, and a drinking-song ("Lasst das Herz uns froh erheben") was afterwards substituted for Friedelberg's text, and published by Schott in Mayence.

The rapid progress of the French army had caused the Germans in Italy to become distrustful of the future and to hasten homeward. Among them were Beethoven's old companions in the Bonn orchestra, the cousins Andreas and Bernhard Romberg, who in the spring of this year (May 26th), had kissed the hand of the Queen of Naples, daughter of the Empress Maria Theresia, and then departed to Rome to join another friend of the Bonn period, Karl Kügelgen. The three coming north arrived at Vienna in the autumn; the Rombergs remained there for a space with Beethoven, while Kügelgen proceeded to Berlin. Baron von Braun—not to be mistaken for Beethoven's "first Mæcenas" the Russian Count Browne—had heard the cousins the year before in Munich and invited them "to give Vienna an opportunity to hear them." There is no notice of their concert in the Vienna newspapers of the period, and the date is unknown. From Lenz von Breuning is gleaned an additional fact which alone gives interest to the concert for us. He writes to Wegeler in January, 1797—not 1796, as erroneously printed in the appendix to the "Notizen," page 20—and after the meeting with the von Breunings at Nuremberg:

Beethoven is here again;[1] he played in the Romberg concert. He is the same as of old and I am glad that he and the Rombergs still get along with each other. Once he was near a break with them; I interceded

[1]After the journey to Pesth?

and achieved my end to a fair extent. Moreover, he thinks a great deal of me just now.

It it clear that the Rombergs, under the circumstances, must have largely owed their limited success to Beethoven's name and influence. In February, 1797, they were again in their old positions in Schroeder's orchestra in Hamburg.

Beethoven during this winter must be imagined busily engaged with pupils and private concerts, perhaps also with his operatic studies with Salieri, certainly with composition and with preparation for and the oversight of various works then passing through the press; for in February and April, Artaria advertises the two Violoncello Sonatas, Op. 5, the Pianoforte Sonata for four hands, Op. 6, the Trio, Op. 3, the Quintet, Op. 4, and the Twelve Variations on a Danse Russe; these last are the variations which he dedicated to the Countess Browne and which gave occasion for the anecdote related by Ries illustrating Beethoven's forgetfulness; for this dedication he had·

received a handsome riding-horse from Count Browne as a gift. He rode the animal a few times, soon after forgot all about it and, worse than that, its food also. His servant, who soon noticed this, began to hire out the horse for his own benefit and, in order not to attract the attention of Beethoven to the fact, for a long time withheld from him all bills for fodder. At length, however, to Beethoven's great amazement he handed in a very large one, which recalled to him at once his horse and his neglectfulness. ("Notizen," page 120.)

On Thursday, April 6, 1797, Schuppanzigh gave a concert, on the programme of which Beethoven's name figured twice. Number 2 was an "Aria by Mr. van Beethoven, sung by Madame Tribolet (-Willmann);" No. 3 was "a Quintet for Pianoforte and 4 wind-instruments, played and composed by Mr. L. v. Beethoven." This was the beautiful Quintet, Op. 16, the time of whose origin is thus more definitely indicated than in the "Chronologisches Verzeichniss," a fact for which we are indebted to Nottebohm.

But the war was renewed and the thoughts of the Viennese were occupied with matters more serious than the indulgence of their musical taste. On the 16th of March, Bonaparte forced the passage of the Tagliamento and Isonzo. During the two weeks following he had conquered the greater part of Carniola, Carinthia and the Tyrol, and was now rapidly approaching Vienna. On the 11th of February, Lorenz Leopold Hauschka's "Gott erhalte unsern Kaiser" with Haydn's music had been sung for the first time in the theatre and now, when, on April 7th, the Landsturm was called out, Friedelberg produced his war-song "Ein grosses, deutsches Volk sind wir," to which Beethoven also gave music. The printed copy bears date April 14th, suggesting the probability that it was sung on the occasion of the grand consecration of the banners which took place on the Glacis on the 17th. Beethoven's music was, however, far from being so fortunate as Haydn's, and seems to have gained as little popularity as his previous attempt; but as the preliminaries to a treaty of peace were signed at Leoben on the 18th, and the armies, so hastily improvised, were dismissed three weeks afterwards, the taste for war-songs vanished.

The little that is known of Beethoven's position as a teacher at this period is very vague and unsatisfactory; enough, however, to render it sufficiently certain that he had plenty of pupils, many of them young ladies of high rank who paid him generously. In the triple capacity of teacher, composer and pianist his gains were large and he was able to write in May to Wegeler that he was doing well and steadily better.

It is very possible that the illness mentioned by the Fischoff Manuscript may have occurred during this summer. There can be little doubt that the original authority for the statement is Zmeskall, and therefore the fact of such an attack may be accepted as certain, but the date—being, as there given, clearly wrong, as well as the inference that in it lay the original cause of the composer's subsequent loss of hearing—must be left mainly to conjecture. From May to November, 1797, Beethoven's history is still a blank and nothing but the utter silence of Lenz von Breuning in his correspondence with his family at Bonn on a topic so likely to engage his sympathies as the dangerous illness of his friend, appears to prevent the filling of this blank in part by throwing him upon a bed of sickness. True, Lenz may have written and the letter have been lost or destroyed; or he may have neglected to write because of his approaching departure from Vienna, which took place in the autumn. His album, still preserved, has among its contributors Ludwig and Johann van Beethoven and Zmeskall. Ludwig wrote as follows:

> Truth exists for the wise,
> Beauty for a feeling heart:
> They belong to each other.

Dear, good Breuning;

Never shall I forget the time which I spent with you in Bonn as well as here. Hold fast your friendship for me; you will always find me the same.

Vienna 1797   Your true friend
the 1st of October.   L. v. Beethoven.

They never met again.   Lenz died on April 10th of the following year.   In November, Beethoven enjoyed a singular compliment paid him by the association of the Bildende Künstler—a repetition of his minuets and trios composed two years before for the artists' ball; and on the 23rd of December, he again contributed to the attractions of the Widows' and Orphans' Concert by producing the Variations for two Oboes and English Horn on "Là ci darem la mano," played by Czerwenka, Reuter and Teimer.   His publications in 1797, besides those mentioned at the beginning of the year, were the Twelve Variations for Pianoforte and Violoncello on the theme from Handel's "Judas Maccabæus," precise date unknown; the Pianoforte Sonata, Op. 7; and the Serenade, Op. 8, both advertised by Artaria and Co., October 7th.   Finally, the Rondo in C, Op. 51, No. 1, published by Artaria with the catalogue number 711.

We come to a consideration of the facts touching the compositions of the years 1796 and 1797.

Among the most widely known of these is "Adelaide."   The composition of this song must have been begun in the first half of 1795, if not earlier, for sketches of it are found among the exercises in double counterpoint written for Albrechtsberger. Other sheets containing sketches for "Adelaide" and the setting of Bürger's "Seufzer eines Ungeliebten" are preserved in the library of the Gesellschaft der Musikfreunde in Vienna and the British Museum in London.   The song was published by Artaria in 1797, under the title "Adelaide von Matthisson.   Eine Kantate für eine Singstimme mit Begleitung des Klaviers.   In Musik gesetzt und dem Verfasser gewidmet von Ludwig van Beethoven."   The opus number 46 was given to it later.   In 1800 Beethoven sent a copy of the song to the poet and accompanied it with the following letter:

Most honored Sir!
     You are herewith receiving from me a composition which has been in print for several years, but concerning which you probably, to my shame, know nothing.   Perhaps I can excuse myself and explain how it came about that I dedicated something to you which came so warmly from my heart yet did not inform you of the fact, by saying that at first I was unaware of your place of residence, and partly also I was diffident, not knowing but that I had been over-hasty in dedicating a work to you without knowing whether or not it met with your approval.
     Even now I send you "Adelaide" with some timidity.   You know what changes are wrought by a few years in an artist who is continually going forward; the greater the progress one makes in art the less

one is satisfied with one's older works. My most ardent wish will be fulfilled if my musical setting of your heavenly "Adelaide" does not wholly displease you, and if it should move you soon to write another poem of its kind, and you, not finding my request too immodest, should send it to me at once, I will put forth all my powers to do your beautiful poetry justice. Look upon the dedication as partly a token of the delight which the composition of your A. gave me, partly as an evidence of my gratitude and respect for the blessed pleasure which your poetry has always given, *and always will* give me.

Vienna, August 4th, 1800.

When playing "Adelaide" sometimes recall
        your sincere admirer
                                Beethoven.

Whether or not Matthisson answered this letter is not known; but when he republished "Adelaide" in the first volume of his collected poems in 1815, he appended to it a note to this effect: "Several composers have vitalized this little lyric fantasy with music; but according to my strong conviction none of them so threw the text into the shade with his melody as the highly gifted Ludwig van Beethoven in Vienna." The "Opferlied," the words of which were also written by Matthisson, is one of the poems to which Beethoven repeatedly recurred. "It seems always to have presented itself to him as a prayer," says Nottebohm. Its last words, "The beautiful to the good," were written in autograph albums even in his later years. The origin of the composition is to be ascribed to 1795, as Nottebohm enters it in his catalogue. It was thus possible for Wegeler to know it in 1797, when he put a Masonic text under the music. It had not yet been published at that time, however, which fact accounts for the discovery of sketches for it in a sketchbook of 1798-1799 described by Nottebohm.

It was not published until later, probably in 1808, when it came with two other songs from the press of Simrock. Beethoven composed the poem a second time, utilizing the beginning of his first melody, for solo, chorus and orchestra (Op. 121b). To this setting we shall recur hereafter. There is still another song which must be brought into the story of this period. It is the "Seufzer eines Ungeliebten," with its two parts based on two independent but related poems by Bürger. Particular interest attaches to the second part, "Gegenliebe," from the fact that its melody was used afterward by Beethoven for the variations in the "Choral Fantasia," Op. 80. Sketches for this melody are found associated with sketches for "Adelaide" on a sheet in the archives of the Gesellschaft der Musikfreunde. Nottebohm fixes the year of the

song's origin as 1795. It was first published as late as 1837 by
Diabelli along with the song, "Turteltaube, du klagest," which was
composed much later. The Italian song, "O care selve, o cara
felice libertà" (from Metastasio's "Olimpiade"), entered under
number 264 in Thayer's "Chronologisches Verzeichniss," appears
as a chorus for three voices at the end of the Albrechtsberger
exercises, and hence may be placed in the year 1795, as is done by
Nottebohm, who adds that it originated simultaneously with the
setting of "Wer ist ein freier Mann?" Here mention must also
be made of two arias which Beethoven wrote for introduction in
Umlauf's comic opera "Die schöne Schusterin." These songs were
assigned to the Bonn period in the first edition of this biography
because the opera was performed in Bonn in the years 1789 and
1790. The two songs composed by Beethoven are an arietta, or
rather strophic song, "O welch' ein Leben," for tenor, and an aria,
"Soll ein Schuh nicht drücken?" for soprano. The words of the
latter are in the original libretto. The words of the tenor song,
though not part of the original text, were obviously written for
the opera. The melody was afterward used by Beethoven as a
setting for Goethe's "Mailied," published in 1805, as Op. 52. Both
songs, as written for the opera, were published for the first time
in the Complete Edition of Beethoven's works from the copies
preserved in the Berlin Library.

Most important of the instrumental compositions of this
period is the Quintet for Strings, Op. 4, which is frequently set
down as an arrangement (or revised transcription) of the Octet,
Op. 103. The Quintet, however, though it employs the same
motivi as the Octet, is an entirely new work, made so by the radical
changes of structure—changes of register to adapt the themes to
the stringed instruments and changes in the themes themselves.
The origin of the Quintet can be placed anywhere in the period
from 1792 (when the Octet was probably begun) to the beginning
of 1797, when the Quintet was advertised as "wholly new." There
is a clue in the Wegeler anecdote already related in connection
with the String Trio, Op. 3, in the chapter of this work devoted to
the works composed in Bonn. In 1795, Count Appony commissioned Beethoven to compose a quartet, the honorarium being
fixed. Wegeler's recollection was that Beethoven twice undertook
the task; but the first effort resulted in the String Trio and the
second in "a quintet (Op. 4)." There is not sufficient internal
evidence to reject the story so far as it affects the Quintet (the
Trio has already been subjected to study), and from its structure
it might well be argued that the composition was undertaken as a

quartet and expanded into a quintet in the hands of the composer. If Count Appony's commission was given in 1795, the date of the completion of the Quintet may be set down as 1796. Artaria, who published the work, advertised it in the "Wiener Zeitung" of February 8th, 1797.

The two Sonatas for Pianoforte and Violoncello, Op. 5, belong to the year 1796, and are the fruits of the visit to Berlin. There is no reason to question Ries's story that Beethoven composed them for Pierre Duport and played them with him. The dedication to Friedrich Wilhelm II and the character of the works lend credibility to Ries's account of their origin. Beethoven played them with Bernhard Romberg in Vienna at the close of 1796 or beginning of 1797, and they were published soon afterward, being advertised by Artaria in the "Wiener Zeitung" of February 8th, 1797. The Twelve Variations on a theme from Handel's "Judas Maccabæus," were published by Artaria in 1797, dedicated to the Princess Lichnowsky, *née* Countess Thun. There were no performances of Handel's oratorios in Vienna at this time, but it is not improbable that the suggestion for the Variations came from Baron van Swieten.

Here seems to be the place to refer to the Allegro movement in sonata-form for viola and violoncello which Beethoven gave the title, "Duett mit zwei Augengläsern obbligato von L. v. Beethoven" (Duet with two Eyeglasses obbligato, by L. v. Beethoven), to be found in the volume of sketches from this period (1784-1800) which the British Museum bought from J. N. Kafka in 1875.[1] There ought to be a hint as to the identity of the two players "with two eyeglasses obbligato." Here is also the place for the three Duos for Clarinet and Bassoon first published by André in Offenbach. The Sextet for Wind-Instruments published by Breitkopf and Härtel in 1810 (it received the opus number 71 later), belongs to this period. Sketches for the last movement, which differ from the ultimate form, however, are found amongst the sketches for the Pianoforte Sonata, Op. 10, No. 3. The inception of the Sonata must fall sometime between the middle of 1796 and the middle of 1798, since the subscription for it was opened in the beginning of July, 1798, and other works of a similar character were already completed in 1797. It is, therefore, possible to place the origin of the earlier movements of the Sextet in an earlier period, say 1796–97, a proceeding which is confirmed by the circumstance that the beginning is found before sketches for "Ah,

---

[1] See the articles by J. S. Shedlock in "The Musical Times," June to December, 1892. Mr. Shedlock made a copy of the duet for Dr. Deiters.

perfido!" (which was composed in 1796 at the latest), on a sheet of sketches in the Artaria collection.   The Kafka volume of sketches in the British Museum contains sketches for the minuet and trio of the Sextet, "Ah, perfido!" and the Pianoforte Sonata, Op. 49, No. 2.   This fact also indicates the year 1796.   Beethoven let the work lie a long time.   It had its first hearing at a chamber concert for the benefit of Schuppanzigh in April, 1805; but it was not until 1809 that he gave it out for publication.   On August 3rd of that year he wrote to Breitkopf and Härtel: "By the next mail-coach you will receive a song, *or perhaps two*, and a sextet for wind-instruments," and on August 8th: "The sextet is one of my earlier things and, moreover, was written in a single night—nothing can really be said of it beyond that it was written by an author who at least has produced a few better works; yet for many people such works are the best."   The statement that the work was written in a single night must be taken in a Pickwickian sense, for sketches of it have been found.

It is plain that at this time Beethoven had a particular predilection for wind-instruments.   Erich Prieger owned a fragment of a Quintet in E-flat for Oboe, three Horns and Bassoon, formerly in the possession of Artaria.   The beginning of the first movement is lacking, but can be supplied from the repetition in the second part.   The Adagio is intact, but there are only a few measures of the Minuet.   Influenced, no doubt, by the performances of such compositions, Beethoven composed at this time two works for two oboes and English horn.   Nottebohm surmises that they were instigated by a terzetto for two oboes and English horn composed by a musician named Wendt and performed at a concert of the Tonkünstler-Gesellschaft by three brothers, Johann, Franz and Philipp Teimer, on December 23rd, 1793.   One of the two works, the Trio which was published as Op. 87, is pretty well known, since it was made accessible to wider circles by arrangements published in Beethoven's day and with his approval.   Artaria published it in April, 1806, without opus number.   He also published it for two violins and viola as Op. 29, and finally as a Sonata for Pianoforte and Violin.   The last transcription was published first, as stated in Thayer's Catalogue.   Nothing of a historical nature is known of the Variations on "Là ci darem" for the same instruments beyond the fact that they were performed on December 23rd, 1797, at the concert for the benefit of the Widows and Orphans in the National Court Theatre.   On a free page of the autograph (after the sixth variation) there are some miscellaneous sketches, among them a motive for the Adagio of Op. 3, another which was used in the Serenade, Op. 25, and, more remarkable still, a few measures of "Adelaide," on which he was at work in 1793, and which appeared in print in 1797. Obviously, the Variations were finished, and we may set down at the latest the year 1795 for their beginning.

The Sextet for four stringed instruments and two horns, Op. 81b, also belongs to this early period and in all likelihood was conceived before the Sextet for wind-instruments. Sketches for the first two movements are upon a sheet in the Berlin library by the side of sketches for the song, "Seufzer eines Ungeliebten." Sketches for this song keep company with some for "Adelaide." The Sextet is therefore to be credited to the year 1795, or perhaps 1794. It was published in 1819 by Simrock in Bonn. In a letter which Beethoven sent to Simrock with the MS. (but which has been lost) he had written to the publisher, who was an admirable horn player, that "the pupil had given his master many a hard nut to crack." As to whether or not, and if so when and where, the Sextet had been played before being sent to Simrock there is, as yet, no conclusive evidence.

The beautiful Quintet in E flat, Op. 16, for Pianoforte and Wind-Instruments, was played at a concert given by Schuppanzigh on April 6th, 1797, being number 5 on the programme which described it as "A Quintet for the Fortepiano accompanied by four Wind-Instruments, played and composed by Mr. Ludwig van Beethoven." It had probably been completed not long before. Sketches are found in connection with a remark concerning the Sonata in C minor, Op. 10, No. 1.

It was in all probability composed between 1794 and the beginning of 1797. In the minutes of a meeting of the Tonkünstler-Gesellschaft under date May 10th, 1797, occurs this entry: "On the second day Mr. van Beethoven produced a Quintet and distinguished himself in the Quintet and incidentally by an improvisation." The word "dabey" (incidentally) seems to indicate that he introduced an improvisation in the Quintet as he did on a later occasion to the embarrassment of the other players, but to the delight of the listeners. Ries tells the story in his "Notizen," p. 79. It was at a concert at which the famous oboist Friedrich Ramm, of Munich, took part.

In the final Allegro there occur several holds before a resumption of the theme. At one of these Beethoven suddenly began to improvise, took the Rondo as a theme and entertained himself and the others for a considerable space; but not his associates. They were displeased, and Ramm even enraged (aufgebracht). It really was comical to see these gentlemen waiting expectantly every moment to go on, continually lifting their instruments to their lips, then quietly putting them down again. At last Beethoven was satisfied and dropped again into the Rondo. The entire audience was delighted.

Wasielewski doubts the correctness of the story, since there is but one hold in the Finale. Dr. Deiters thought that Ries confounded the last with the first movement, in which the clarinet enters after a *fermata*. The Quintet was published by Mollo in Vienna in 1801, and was dedicated to Prince Schwarzenberg. It appeared simultaneously in one arrangement made by Beethoven himself as a Quartet for Pianoforte and Strings, as Ries expressly declares. Beethoven had nothing to do with the arrangement as a String Quartet published by Artaria as Op. 75.

Touching the history of the Serenade for Violin, Viola and Violoncello, Op. 8, little else is known beyond the fact that its publication was announced in the "Wiener Zeitung" on October 7th, 1797, by Artaria. Mr. Shedlock called attention in the "Musical Times" of 1892 (p. 525) to sketches which appeared along with others of the Pianoforte Concerto in B-flat, and the Trio, Op. 1, No. 2. That Beethoven valued the work highly is a fair deduction from the fact that he published it soon after its composition and authorized the publication of an arrangement for Pianoforte and Viola which he had revised. This arrangement received the opus number 42, though probably not from Beethoven. Hoffmeister in Leipzig, who published it in 1804, under the title "Notturno pour Fortepiano et Alto arrangé d'un Notturno pour Violon, Alto et Violoncello et revu par l'auteur—Œuvre 42," advertised it in the "Intelligenzblatt der Zeitschrift für die elegante Welt" on December 17, 1803. It is this arrangement, no doubt, to which Beethoven referred in a letter to Hoffmeister, dated September 22nd, 1803, in which he said: "These transcriptions are not mine, though they were much improved by me in places. Therefore, I am not willing to have you state that I made them, for that would be a lie and I could find neither time nor patience for such work." According to the view of Dr. Deiters, which was shared also by Nottebohm, the Serenade, Op. 25, also belongs here. It was probably composed before Op. 8. Beethoven entrusted its publication in the beginning of 1802 to Cappi, who had just begun business. Then, like Op. 8, it was published by Hoffmeister as Op. 41, in an arrangement for Pianoforte and Flute (or Violin), which, no doubt, was included in Beethoven's protest against being set down as the transcriber.

Prominent among the compositions of this time is the Sonata in E-flat for Pianoforte, Op. 7. The only evidence of the date of its composition is the announcement of its publication by Artaria in the "Wiener Zeitung" of October 7th, 1797. There are sketches for the third movement in the Kafka volume, but they afford no help in fixing a date. The Sonata is inscribed to the Countess Babette Keglevich, one of Beethoven's pupils, who afterwards married Prince Innocenz Odescalchi in Pressburg. Nottebohm quotes the following from a letter written by a nephew of the Countess: "The Sonata was composed for her when she was still a maiden. It was one of the hobbies, of which he (Beethoven) had many, that, living as he did vis-à-vis, he came in morning gown, slippers and tasseled cap (Zipfelmütze) to give her lessons." Inasmuch as the sketches mentioned belong only to the third movement and the sheet contains the remark: "diverse 4 bagatelles de inglese Ländler, etc.," Nottebohm supposes that the movement was originally intended for one of the Bagatelles and was later incorporated in the Sonata. It is very probable that the two little Sonatas, Op. 49, belong to this period. Everybody knows that the second movement of the second Sonata (the minuet) is based on the same motive as the third movement of the Septet. That the motive is older in the Sonata than in the Septet is proved by the fact that sketches for it are found along with some to "Ah, perfido!" (1795–96) and the Sextet for Wind-Instruments, Op. 71. This circumstance establishes its early origin, say in 1795 or, at latest, 1796. Nottebohm considers it likely that the first Sonata was finished at the latest in 1798, certainly before the Sonata "Pathétique" and the Trio for strings, Op. 9, No. 3. The Sonatas were ready for publication as early as 1802, in which year brother Carl offered them to André in Offenbach. They were not published until 1805, when they appeared with the imprint of the Bureau d'Arts et d'Industrie, as appears from an advertisement in the "Wiener Zeitung" of January 19th, 1805. Here, too, belongs the little Sonata in D for four hands, Op. 6, published by Artaria in October, 1797, as Nottebohm surmises. It was probably composed for purposes of instruction. Except a few trifles (marches, and two sets of variations) Beethoven wrote nothing more for four hands, though Diabelli offered him 40 ducats for a four-hand sonata in 1824.

In the pianoforte compositions of these two years are to be included the Variations in A on a Russian dance from the ballet "Das Waldmädchen," published in April, 1797, and dedicated to the Countess Browne, née Bietinghoff. "Das Waldmädchen," by

Traffieri, music by Paul Wranitzky, was first performed at the Kärnthnerthor-Theater on September 28, 1796, and was repeated sixteen times the same year. This fixes the time of the composition of the Variations approximately. They were probably written before the end of 1796.

There are a few other compositions brought to light by Nottebohm and Mandyczewski, which call for notice. No. 299, Series XXV (Supplement), B. and H. Complete Works, is an Allegretto in C minor, ¾ time; No. 295 a Bagatelle, also in C minor ¾, Presto, sketches for which are associated with those for the C minor Sonata, Op. 10, No. 1. From the remark: "Very short minuets to the new sonatas. The Presto remains for that in C minor," written about this time Nottebohm concludes that this Bagatelle was conceived as an intermezzo in the C minor Sonata, and that, possibly, the Allegretto had a similar origin.[1]

A unique place among Beethoven's early works is occupied by the two pieces for mandolin with pianoforte accompaniment first published in the Complete Edition. Thayer, who knew of the sketches at Artaria's, but seems not to have seen the composition recovered by Nottebohm, which is called Sonatine, associated Beethoven's purpose with Krumpholz, who was a virtuoso on the mandolin; but Mylich, Amenda's student companion, may have been in the composer's mind.

The fact that no compositions for orchestra save the dances for the Redoutensaal, to be referred to presently, have been preserved, is not to be taken as conclusive evidence that Beethoven did not venture into the field of orchestral music in the Bonn and early Vienna days. Such an assertion is less likely to be made now than before the discovery of the two Imperial cantatas of 1790. Moreover, Mr. Shedlock's extracts from the Kafka sketchbook in the British Museum show that Beethoven tried his youthful hand at a symphony. Among the earliest of the sketches there is one in C minor marked "Sinfonia," which begins as follows:

Nottebohm notes the theme also in his "Zweite Beethoveniana" (P. 577). Shedlock's contention that out of this theme grew the second movement of the first Pianoforte Quartet (composed in

[1]"Beethoveniana," p. 31. Later Beethoven wanted to give the Sonata an Intermezzo in C major (*Ibid.*, p. 479), but did not carry out the intention.

1785) is incontestable. The symphonic sketch is therefore of earlier date than 1785. In 1909, Prof. Fritz Stein, Musical Director of the University of Jena, announced that in the collection of music of the Academic Concerts, founded in 1780, he had discovered the complete parts of a symphony in four movements in C "par Louis van Beethoven." These words are in the handwriting of the copy-ist on the second violin part; on the 'cello part is written: "Sym-phonie von Beethoven." Dr. Hugo Riemann,[1] after a glance through the score prepared by Prof. Stein and put at his disposal, gave it as his opinion that the symphony might well be a com-position by Beethoven. Thematically, he says it suggests partly the Mannheim school, partly Haydn; the instrumentation is nearer Mozart than Stamitz or Cannabich.

Mention of Beethoven's orchestral dances has already been made. Schindler's remark that the musicians of Vienna "refused citizenship" to Beethoven's efforts to write Austrian dance music is discredited, at least so far as Viennese society is concerned, by the success of his dances composed for the Redoutensaal and the very considerable number of his waltzes, ländlers, minuets, écos-saises, allemandes and contra-dances which have been preserved. Only the smaller portion of these dances have been included in the Complete Edition of Breitkopf and Härtel. Thus in Series II there are 12 minuets and 12 German dances; in Series XXV (Supplement), 6 "Ländrische Tänze" for two violins and bass, 6 German dances for pianoforte and violin, and, for pianoforte alone, 6 German dances, 6 écossaises and a few miscellaneous dances; in Series XVIII (Small Pieces for Pianoforte) there are 6 minuets and 13 "Ländrische" (1-6 identical with those numbered 7-13 in Series II, but transcribed). There are many dances as yet unpub-lished. For instance, among the Artaria MSS. purchased by Erich Prieger, there are 12 écossaises, of which 6 are as yet un-known, also 12 "Deutsche" for pianoforte and 6 minuets for two violins and bass, which have never been printed. The three orchestral dances noted by Thayer in the Thematic Catalogue as No. 290, of the Artaria collection, are Nos. 3, 9 and 11 of the 12 minuets which A. von Perger discovered in the archives of the Künstler-Pensions-Institut in 1872, and which were published by Heugel in Paris in pianoforte transcription in 1903 and in score and parts in 1906, edited by Chantavoine. They were composed for the Künstlersocietät and are now in the Court Library at Vienna. (MS. 16,925.)

[1]See Vol. II, p. 60, of the revised edition of "Ludwig van Beethoven's Leben" by Thayer, 1910.

Chapter XV

General Bernadotte—His Connection with the "Heroic" Symphony—Rival Pianists—J. Wölffl—Dragonetti and Cramer—Compositions of the Years 1798 and 1799.

E ARLY in the year 1798, a political event occurred which demands notice here from its connection with one of Beethoven's noblest and most original works—the "Sinfonia Eroica." The singular tissue of error which, owing to carelessness in observing dates, has been woven in relation to its origin may be best destroyed by a simple statement of fact.

The extraordinary demands made by the French Directory upon the Austrian government as preliminary to the renewal of diplomatic intercourse, after the peace of Campo Formio—such as a national palace and French theatre for the minister and the right of jurisdiction over all Frenchmen in the Austrian dominions —all of which were rejected by the Imperial government, had aroused to a high pitch the public curiosity both as to the man who might be selected for the appointment and as to the course he might adopt. This curiosity was by no means diminished by the intelligence that the new minister was Jean Baptiste Bernadotte, the young general who had borne so important a part in the recent invasion of Istria. He arrived in Vienna on February 5th, 1798. The state of the Empress's health, who was delivered of the Archduchess Maria Clementine on the 1st of March, delayed the private audience of Bernadotte for the presentation of his credentials to the Emperor until the second of that month, and his public audience until the 8th of April. During the festivities of the court, which then took place, Bernadotte was always present, and a reporter of that day says both the Emperor and Empress held more conversation with him than with any other of the "cercle." This familiar intercourse, however, came speedily to an end; for on the 13th Bernadotte had the rashness to display the hated tricolor from his balcony and to threaten to defend it by force. A riot occurred, and it was thought that in the extreme excitement of popular feeling nothing but the strong detachments of cavalry and infantry detailed for his protection saved his life—saved it to ascend the throne of Sweden on the twentieth anniversary of his arrival in Vienna!

Since etiquette allowed a foreign minister neither to make nor receive visits in his public capacity until after his formal reception at court, the General, during the two months of his stay, except the last five days, "lived very quietly." Those who saw him praised him as "well behaved, sedate and modest." In his train was Rudolph Kreutzer, the great violinist.

Bernadotte had now just entered his 34th year; Kreutzer was in his 32nd; both of them, therefore, in age, as in tastes and acquirements, fitted to appreciate the splendor of Beethoven's genius and to enjoy his society. Moreover, as the Ambassador was the son of a provincial advocate, there was no difference of rank by birth, which could prevent them from meeting upon equal terms. Under such circumstances, and remembering that just at that epoch the young General Bonaparte was the topic of universal wonder and admiration, one is fully prepared for the statement of Schindler upon the origin of the "Heroic" Symphony:

> The first idea for the symphony is said to have gone out from General Bernadotte, then French Ambassador in Vienna, who esteemed Beethoven very highly. This I heard from several of Beethoven's friends. I was also told so by Count Moritz Lichnowsky (brother of Prince Lichnowsky), who was often in the society of Bernadotte with Beethoven. . . .

Again in 1823:

> Beethoven had a lively recollection that Bernadotte had really first inspired him with the idea of the "Eroica" Symphony.

This is from Schindler's work in its first form. His unfortunate propensity sometimes to accept the illusions of his fancy for matters of fact is exhibited in the corresponding passage in his third edition:

> In Bernadotte's salon, which was open to notabilities of all ranks of life, Beethoven also appeared. He had already made it known that he was a great admirer of the First Consul of the Republic. From the General emanated the suggestion that Beethoven celebrate the greatest hero of his age in a musical composition, It was not long (!) before the thought had become a deed. (Vol. I, page 101.)

In proceeding with the history of the Symphony, Schindler extracts largely from Beethoven's own copy of Schleiermacher's translation of Plato. That the idea of Bonaparte as First Consul may have influenced the form and matter of the Symphony, when he came to the labor of its composition, and that Beethoven may have based for himself a sort of system of political ethics upon Schleiermacher's Plato—all this is very possible; but Bernadotte was far away from Vienna before the consular form of government was adopted at Paris, and the "Sinfonia Eroica" had been publicly performed at Vienna before the Plato came from the Berlin press!

It is certainly to be regretted that so much fine writing by Schindler and his copyists on this point should be exploded by a date—like a ship by a single shell; but how could anyone believe that the much-employed Beethoven, at the age of 27, he who had refused two years before, even despite Wegeler's urging, to listen to a single private lecture on Kant, had become in so short a time a Platonic philosopher?

Let us return to a field where Beethoven was even now more at home than he ever became in Plato's political philosophy. Salieri had again engaged him for the "Widows and Orphans" concerts of April 1st and 2nd at which Haydn's "Seven Last Words" was sung and Beethoven's Pianoforte Quintet played. Kaiser Franz and the imperial family were present.

It was now no longer the case that Beethoven was without a rival as pianoforte virtuoso. He had a competitor fully worthy of his powers; one who divided about equally with him the suffrages of the leaders in the Vienna musical circles. In fact the excellencies peculiar to the two were such and so different, that it depended upon the taste of the auditor to which he accorded the praise of superiority. Joseph Wölffl of Salzburg, two years younger than Beethoven, a "wonder-child," who had played a violin concerto in public at the age of seven years, was a pupil of Leopold Mozart and Michael Haydn. Being in Vienna, when but eighteen years old, he was engaged, on the recommendation of Mozart, by the Polish count Oginsky, who took him to Warsaw. His success there, as pianoforte virtuoso, teacher and composer, was almost unexampled. But it is only in his character as pianist that we have to do with him; and a reference may be made to the general principle, that a worthy competition is the best spur to genius. When we read in one of his letters Beethoven's words "I have also greatly perfected my pianoforte playing," they will cause no surprise; for only by severe industry and consequent improvement could he retain his high position, in the presence of such rivals as Wölffl and, a year or two later, J. B. Cramer. A lively picture of Wölffl by Tomaschek, who heard him in 1799, in his autobiography

sufficiently proves that his party in Vienna was composed of those
to whom extraordinary execution was the main thing; while Beethoven's admirers were of those who had hearts to be touched.   A
parallel between Beethoven and Wölffl in a letter to the "Allgemeine
Musikalische Zeitung" (Vol. I, pp. 24, 25) dated April 22, 1799, just
at the time when the performances of both were topics of general
conversation in musical circles, and still fresh in the memory of
all who had heard them, is in the highest degree apposite to the
subject of this chapter.   The writer says:

> Opinion is divided here touching the merits of the two; yet it
> would seem as if the majority were on the side of the latter (Wölffl).
> I shall try to set forth the peculiarities of each without taking part in
> the controversy.   Beethoven's playing is extremely brilliant but has
> less delicacy and occasionally he is guilty of indistinctness.   He shows
> himself to the greatest advantage in improvisation, and here, indeed,
> it is most extraordinary with what lightness and yet firmness in the
> succession of ideas Beethoven not only varies a theme given him on
> the spur of the moment by figuration (with which many a virtuoso makes
> his fortune and—wind) but really develops it.   Since the death of
> Mozart, who in this respect is for me still the *non plus ultra*, I have
> never enjoyed this kind of pleasure in the degree in which it is provided
> by Beethoven.   In this Wölffl fails to reach him.   But W. has advan-
> tages in this that, sound in musical learning and dignified in his compo-
> sitions, he plays passages which seem impossible with an ease, precision
> and clearness which cause amazement (of course he is helped here by
> the large structure of his hands) and that his interpretation is always,
> especially in Adagios, so pleasing and insinuating that one can not
> only admire it but also enjoy. . . . .   That Wölffl likewise enjoys an
> advantage because of his amiable bearing, contrasted with the some-
> what haughty pose of Beethoven, is very natural.

No biography of Beethoven which makes any pretence to
completeness, can omit the somewhat inflated and bombastic
account which Seyfried gives of the emulation between Beethoven
and Wölffl.   Ignatz von Seyfried at the period in question was one
of Schikaneder's conductors, to which position he had been called
when not quite twenty-one years of age, and had assumed its
duties March 1, 1797.   He was among the most promising of the
young composers of the capital, belonged to a highly respectable
family, had been educated at the University, and his personal character was unblemished.   He would, therefore, naturally have access
to the musical salons and his reminiscences of music and musicians
in those years may be accepted as the records of observation.   The
unfavorable light which the researches of Nottebohm have thrown
upon him as editor of the so-called "Beethoven Studien" does not
extend to such statements of fact as might easily have come under

his own cognizance; and the passage now cited from the appendix of the "Studien," though written thirty years after the events it describes, bears all the marks of being a faithful transcript of the writer's own memories:

Beethoven had already attracted attention to himself by several compositions and was rated a first-class pianist in Vienna when he was confronted by a rival in the closing years of the last century. Thereupon there was, in a way, a revival of the old Parisian feud of the Gluckists and Piccinists, and the many friends of art in the Imperial City arrayed themselves in two parties. At the head of Beethoven's admirers stood the amiable Prince Lichnowsky; among the most zealous patrons of Wölffl was the broadly cultured Baron Raymond von Wetzlar, whose delightful villa (on the Grünberg near the Emperor's recreation-castle) offered to all artists, native and foreign, an asylum in the summer months, as pleasing as it was desirable, with true British loyalty. There the interesting combats of the two athletes not infrequently offered an indescribable artistic treat to the numerous and thoroughly select gathering. Each brought forward the latest product of his mind. Now one and anon the other gave free rein to his glowing fancy; sometimes they would seat themselves at two pianofortes and improvise alternately on themes which they gave each other, and thus created many a four-hand Capriccio which if it could have been put upon paper at the moment would surely have bidden defiance to time. It would have been difficult, perhaps impossible, to award the palm of victory to either one of the gladiators in respect of technical skill. Nature had been a particularly kind mother to Wölffl in bestowing upon him a gigantic hand which could span a tenth as easily as other hands compass an octave, and permitted him to play passages of double notes in these intervals with the rapidity of lightning. In his improvisations even then Beethoven did not deny his tendency toward the mysterious and gloomy. When once he began to revel in the infinite world of tones, he was transported also above all earthly things;—his spirit had burst all restricting bonds, shaken off the yoke of servitude, and soared triumphantly and jubilantly into the luminous spaces of the higher æther. Now his playing tore along like a wildly foaming cataract, and the conjurer constrained his instrument to an utterance so forceful that the stoutest structure was scarcely able to withstand it; and anon he sank down, exhausted, exhaling gentle plaints, dissolving in melancholy. Again the spirit would soar aloft, triumphing over transitory terrestrial sufferings, turn its glance upward in reverent sounds and find rest and comfort on the innocent bosom of holy nature. But who shall sound the depths of the sea? It was the mystical Sanscrit language whose hieroglyphs can be read only by the initiated. Wölffl, on the contrary, trained in the school of Mozart, was always equable; never superficial but always clear and thus more accessible to the multitude. He used art only as a means to an end, never to exhibit his acquirements. He always enlisted the interest of his hearers and inevitably compelled them to follow the progression of his well-ordered ideas. Whoever has heard Hummel will know what is meant by this. . . .

But for this (the attitude of their patrons) the *protégés* cared very little.   They respected each other because they knew best how to appreciate each other, and as straightforward honest Germans followed the principle that the roadway of art is broad enough for many, and that it is not necessary to lose one's self in envy in pushing forward for the goal of fame!

Wölffl proved his respect for his rival by dedicating to "M. L. van Beethoven" the pianoforte sonatas, Op. 7, which were highly commended in the "Allg. Mus. Zeit." of Leipsic of January, 1799. Another interesting and valuable discussion of Beethoven's powers and characteristics as a pianoforte virtuoso at this period is contained in the autobiography of Tomaschek, who heard him both in public and in private during a visit which Beethoven made again this year to Prague.   Tomaschek was then both in age (he was born on April 17, 1774) and in musical culture competent to form an independent judgment on such a subject.

In the year 1798, says Tomaschek (unfortunately without giving any clue to the time of the year), in which I continued my juridical studies, Beethoven, the giant among pianoforte players, came to Prague.   He gave a largely attended concert in the Konviktssaal, at which he played his Concerto in C major, Op. 15, and the Adagio and graceful Rondo in A major from Op. 2, and concluded with an improvisation on a theme given him by Countess Sch... (Schick?), "Ah tu fosti il primo oggetto," from Mozart's "Titus" (duet No. 7).   Beethoven's magnificent playing and particularly the daring flights in his improvisation stirred me strangely to the depths of my soul; indeed I found myself so profoundly bowed down that I did not touch my pianoforte for several days. . . . I heard Beethoven at his second concert, which neither in performance nor in composition renewed again the first powerful impression. This time he played the Concerto in B-flat which he had just composed in Prague.[1]   Then I heard him a third time at the home of Count C., where he played, besides the graceful Rondo from the A major Sonata, an improvisation on the theme: "Ah! vous dirai-je, Maman."   This time I listened to Beethoven's artistic work with more composure.   I admired his powerful and brilliant playing, but his frequent daring deviations from one motive to another, whereby the organic connection, the gradual development of idea was put aside, did not escape me.   Evils of this nature frequently weaken his greatest compositions, those which sprang from a too exuberant conception.   It is not seldom that the unbiassed listener is rudely awakened from his transport.   The singular and original seemed to be his chief aim in composition, as is confirmed by the answer which he made to a lady who asked him if he often attended Mozart's operas.   "I do not know them," he replied, "and do not care to hear the music of others lest I forfeit some of my originality."

---

[1] It will be seen in a letter of Beethoven's that this concerto was in fact composed before that in C major; but it is not improbable that the last movement was written in Prague.

The veteran Tomaschek when he wrote thus had heard all the greatest virtuosos of the pianoforte, who, from the days of Mozart to 1840, had made themselves famous; and yet Beethoven remained for him still "the lord of pianoforte players" and "the giant among pianoforte players." Still, great as he was now when Tomaschek heard him, Beethoven could write three years later that he had greatly perfected his playing.

It is only to be added to the history of the year 1798, that it is the time in which Beethoven fixes the beginning of his deafness. Like it, the year 1799 offers, upon the whole, but scanty materials to the biographers of Beethoven—standing in broad contrast to the next and, indeed all succeeding years, in which their quantity and variety become a source of embarrassment.

Two new and valuable, though but passing acquaintances, were made by Beethoven this year, however—with Domenico Dragonetti, the greatest contrabassist known to history, and John Baptist Cramer, one of the greatest pianists. Dragonetti was not more remarkable for his astounding execution than for the deep, genuine musical feeling which elevated and ennobled it. He was now—the spring of 1799, so far as the means are at hand of determining the time—returning to London from a visit to his native province, and his route taking him to Vienna he remained there for several weeks. Beethoven and he soon met and they were mutually pleased with each other. Many years afterwards Dragonetti related the following anecdote to Samuel Appleby, Esq., of Brighton, England: "Beethoven had been told that his new friend could execute violoncello music upon his huge instrument, and one morning, when Dragonetti called at his room, he expressed his desire to hear a sonata. The contrabass was sent for, and the Sonata, No. 2, of Op. 5, was selected. Beethoven played his part, with his eyes immovably fixed upon his companion, and, in the finale, where the arpeggios occur, was so delighted and excited that at the close he sprang up and threw his arms around both player and instrument." The unlucky contrabassists of orchestras had frequent occasion during the next few years to know that this new revelation of the powers and possibilities of their instrument to Beethoven, was not forgotten.

Cramer, born at Mannheim, 1771, but from early infancy reared and educated in England, was successively the pupil of the noted Bensor, Schroeter and Clementi; but, like Beethoven, was in no small degree self-taught. He was so rarely and at such long intervals on the Continent that his extraordinary merits have never been fully understood and appreciated there. Yet for a period of many years in the first part of the nineteenth century he was undoubtedly, upon the whole, the first pianist of Europe. The object of his tour in 1799 was not to display his own talents and acquirements, but to add to his general musical culture and to profit by his observations upon the styles and peculiar characteristics of the great pianists of the Continent. In Vienna he renewed his intercourse with Haydn, whose prime favorite he had been in England, and at once became extremely intimate with Beethoven.

Cramer surpassed Beethoven in the perfect neatness, correctness and finish of his execution; Beethoven assured him that he preferred his touch to that of any other player; his brilliancy was astonishing; but yet taste, feeling, expression, were the qualities which more eminently distinguished him. Beethoven stood far above Cramer in power and energy, especially when extemporizing. Each was supreme in his own sphere; each found much to learn in the perfections of the other; each, in later years, did full justice to the other's powers. Thus Ries says: "Amongst the pianoforte players he [Beethoven] had praise for but one as being distinguished—John Cramer. All others were but little to him." On the other hand, Mr. Appleby, who knew Cramer well, was long afterwards told by him, "No man in these days has heard extempore playing, unless he has heard Beethoven."

Making a visit one morning to him, Cramer, as he entered the anteroom, heard Beethoven extemporizing by himself, and remained there more than half an hour "completely entranced," never in his life having heard such exquisite effects, such beautiful combinations. Knowing Beethoven's extreme dislike to being listened to on such occasions, Cramer retired and never let him know that he had so heard him.

Cramer's widow communicates a pleasant anecdote. At an Augarten Concert the two pianists were walking together and hearing a performance of Mozart's pianoforte Concerto in C minor (Köchel, No. 491); Beethoven suddenly stood still and, directing his companion's attention to the exceedingly simple, but equally beautiful motive which is first introduced towards the end of the piece, exclaimed: "Cramer, Cramer! we shall never be able to do anything like that!" As the theme was repeated and wrought up to the climax, Beethoven, swaying his body to and fro, marked the time and in every possible manner manifested a delight rising to enthusiasm.

Schindler's record of his conversations upon Beethoven with Cramer and Cherubini in 1841 is interesting and valuable. He has, however, left one important consideration unnoticed, namely,

that the visits of those masters to Vienna were five years
apart—five years of great change in Beethoven—a period during
which his deafness, too slight to attract Cramer's attention, had
increased to a degree beyond concealment, and which, joined to his
increased devotion to composition and compulsory abandonment
of all ambition as a virtuoso, with consequent neglect of practice,
had affected his execution unfavorably.   Hence the difference in
the opinions of such competent judges as Cramer, describing him
as he was in 1799–1800, Cherubini in 1805–6, and two years later
Clementi, afford a doubtless just and fair indication of the decline
of Beethoven's powers as a mere pianist—not extending, however,
at least for some years yet, to his extemporaneous performances.
We shall find from Ries and others ample confirmation of the fact.
    And now let Schindler speak:

To the warm feeling of Cramer for Beethoven I owe the more
important matters. . . . Cherubini, disposed to be curt, characterized
Beethoven's pianoforte playing in a single word: "rough."   The gentleman Cramer, however, desired that less offence be taken at the rudeness
of his performance than at the unreliable reading of one and the same
composition—one day intellectually brilliant and full of characteristic
expression, the next freakish to the verge of unclearness; often confused.
(Which is confirmed by Ries, Czerny and others.)   Because of this a
few friends expressed a wish to hear Cramer play several works publicly
from the manuscript.   This touched a sensitive spot in Beethoven;
his jealousy was aroused and, according to Cramer, their relations became strained.

This strain, however, left no such sting behind it as to diminish
Cramer's good opinion of Beethoven both as man and artist, or
hinder his free expression of it.   To this fact the concurrent testimony of his widow and son, and those enthusiasts for Beethoven
Charles Neate, Cipriani Potter and others who knew Cramer well,
bear witness.   It was the conversation of Cramer about Beethoven
which induced Potter, after the fall of Napoleon, to journey to
Vienna, to make the acquaintance of the great master and, if
possible, become his pupil.
    Cramer's musical gods were Handel and Mozart, notwith-
standing his life-long love for Bach's clavier compositions; hence
the abrupt transitions, the strange modulations, and the, until
then, unheard passages, which Beethoven introduced ever more
freely into his works—many of which have not yet found universal
acceptance—were to him, as to Tomaschek and so many other of
his contemporaries, imperfections and distortions of compositions,
which but for them were models of beauty and harmonious proportion.   He once gave this feeling utterance with comic exaggeration,

when Potter, then a youth, was extolling some abstruse combinations, by saying: "If Beethoven emptied his inkstand upon a piece of music paper you would admire it!"

Upon Beethoven's demeanor in society, Schindler proceeds thus:

The communications of both (Cramer and Madame Cherubini) agreed in saying that in mixed society his conduct was reserved, stiff and marked by artist's pride; whereas among his intimates he was droll, lively, indeed, voluble at times, and fond of giving play to all the arts of wit and sarcasm, not always wisely especially in respect of political and social prejudices. To this the two were able to add much concerning his awkwardness in taking hold of such objects as glasses, coffee cups, etc., to which Master Cherubini added the comment: "Toujours brusque." These statements confirmed what I had heard from his older friends touching the social demeanor of Beethoven in general.

Cramer reached Vienna early in September, and remained there, according to Schindler, through the following winter; but he does not appear to have given any public concerts, although, during the first month of his stay, we learn from a newspaper, he "earned general and deserved applause by his playing." It is needless to dwell upon the advantages to Beethoven of constant intercourse for several months with a master like Cramer, whose noblest characteristics as pianist were the same as Mozart's, and precisely those in which Beethoven was deficient.

Let us pass in review the compositions which had their origin in the years 1798 and 1799. First of all come the three Trios for stringed instruments, Op. 9. The exact date of their conception has not yet been determined, all that is positive being that Beethoven sold them to Traeg on March 16, 1798, and that the publisher's announcement of them appeared on July 21st of the same year. The only sketches for the Trios quoted by Nottebohm show them in connection with a sketch for the last movement of the "Sonate pathétique," which was published in 1799; but this proves nothing. It may be easily imagined that Beethoven desired to make more extended use of the experience gained in writing the Trios, Op. 3, and that he therefore began sketching Op. 9 in 1796 or 1797. Beethoven dedicated the works to Count Browne in words such as could hardly have been called forth by the present of a horse. Perhaps some future investigator will be able to show upon what grounds Beethoven in the dedication called Count

Browne his "first Mæcenas," a title better deserved by Prince Lichnowsky.

The first two concertos for pianoforte call for consideration here, for it was not until 1798 that they acquired the form in which they are now known. That the Concerto in B-flat was the earlier of the two has been proved in a preceding chapter of this volume. It was this Concerto and not the one in C major (as Wegeler incorrectly reported) that was played in March, 1795. Wegeler's error was due to the circumstance that the Concerto in C was published first. Sketches for the Concerto in B-flat major are found among the exercises written for Albrechtsberger, sketches for the Sonata in E major (Op. 14, No. 1), and others for a little quartet movement which was owned by M. Malherbe of Paris; on this sheet occurs a short exercise with the remark "Contrapunto all' ottava" which points to the beginning of 1795 or even 1794. The sketch is an obviously early form of a passage in the free fantasia. This agrees with the statement that on March 29, 1795, Beethoven played a new concerto, the key of which is not indicated. It is most likely that it was this in B-flat, since the one in C did not exist at the time. Beethoven, it appears, played it a few times afterward in Vienna and then rewrote it. According to Tomaschek's account he played the B-flat Concerto (expressly distinguished from that in C) in 1798, again in Prague. Tomaschek added, "which he had composed in Prague." This is confounding the original version with the revision, concerning which Nottebohm gives information in his "Zweite Beethoveniana" on the basis of sketches which point to 1798. The fact of the revision is proved by Beethoven's memoranda, such as "To remain as it was," "From here on everything to remain as it was." The revision of the first movement was radical, and the entire work was apparently undertaken in view of an imminent performance, most likely that of Prague in 1798. It was published by Hoffmeister und Kühnel and dedicated to Carl Nikl Edlen von Nikelsberg.

That the Concerto in C was composed later than that in B-flat has been proved by Beethoven's testimony as well as other external evidences and is confirmed by the few remaining sketches analyzed by Nottebohm. They appear in connection with a sketch for the cadenza for the B-flat Concerto which, therefore, must have been finished when its companion was begun. A sketch for a cadenza for the C major Concerto comes after sketches for the Sonata in D, Op. 10, No. 3, which was published in 1798. This new concerto must, therefore, have been finished. According to the testimony of Tomaschek he played it in 1798 in the Konviktsaal in Prague.

Schindler says he played it for the first time "in the spring of 1800 in the Kärnthnerthor-Theater," but this concert is likely to have been that of April 2nd, 1800, described by Hanslick in his "Ge. schichte des Concertwesens in Wien" (p. 127). Schindler evidently knew nothing of the performance in Prague and a confusion must be at the bottom of Czerny's statement that the Concerto was played in the Kärnthnerthor-Theater in 1801. The Concerto in C, dedicated to the Countess Odescalchi, née Keglevich, was published by Mollo in Vienna in 1801. There are three cadenzas for the first movement of the Concerto, the last two of which call for an extended compass of the pianoforte and are thus shown to be of later date than the first.

To these concertos must be added the Rondo in B-flat for Pianoforte and Orchestra found unfinished among Beethoven's compositions and published by Diabelli and Co. in 1829. Sonnleithner, on the authority of Diabelli, says it was completed by Czerny, who also filled out the accompaniment. There is no authentic record of the time of its composition. O. Jahn surmised that it may have been designed for the Concerto in B-flat. Its contents indicate an earlier period. A sketch printed by Nottebohm associated with a Romanza for Pianoforte, Flute and Bassoon, judged by the handwriting, is not of later date than 1795. E. Mandyczewski compared the original manuscript, now in the library of the Gesellschaft der Musikfreunde, with the printed form and decided that the work was completed in plan and *motivi* by Beethoven, who, however, did not carry out the cadenzas and only indicated the passages. The share which Czerny had in it is thus indicated; he added the cadenzas and extended the pianoforte passages which Beethoven had only indicated, making them more effective and brilliant. The use of the high registers of the pianoforte, which Czerny employs somewhat too freely in view of the simple character of the piece, was not contemplated by Beethoven, who once remarked of Czerny: "He uses the piccolo too much for me." In Mandyczewski's opinion the handwriting points to a time before 1800, and the contents indicate the early Vienna if not the Bonn period. Mandyczewski also thinks that the romanza-like Andante is palpably a very early composition and that the correspondence in key and measure with the B-flat Concerto might indicate that it was originally designed as a part of that work, a supposition which is strengthened by the fact that the original manuscript is neither dated nor signed. This internal evidence has much in its favor, the more since it is not at all obvious what might have prompted Beethoven to write an independent rondo for concert use. There is no external evidence; if there were, the conception of the B-flat Concerto would have to be set at a much earlier date than has yet been done. The first Vienna sketches for the Concerto, as Nottebohm shows, prove that the present three movements belonged together from the beginning. They were, therefore, surely played at the first performance in 1795. Nottebohm, who repeated Jahn's surmise in his "Thematisches Verzeichniss," changed his mind after a study of the sketches and rejected the notion that the rondo had been designed for the Concerto. Only by assuming an earlier date for the rondo can the theory be upheld. Attention may here be called to Wegeler's statement ("Notizen," p. 56) that the rondo of the first Concerto (he says, of course, the Concerto in C) was not composed until the second afternoon before the performance. There may possibly have been another. This is not necessarily disproved by the fact that sketches for the present one were in existence. The question is not settled by the evidence now before us, but the probabilities are with Mandyczewski.

Now begins the glorious series of sonatas. The first were the three (Op. 10) which, though begun in part at an earlier date, were definitively finished and published in 1798. Eder, the publisher, opened a subscription for them by an advertisement in the "Wiener Zeitung," July 5th, 1798; therefore they were finished at that time. The sketching for them had begun in 1796, as appears from Nottebohm's statement,[1] and Beethoven worked on the three simultaneously. Sketches for the first movement of the first Sonata are mixed with sketches for the soprano air for Umlauf's "Schusterin" which have been attributed to 1796, and the Variations for three Wind-Instruments which were played in 1797. Sketches for the third sonata are found among notes for the Sextet for Wind-Instruments (composed about 1796) and also for the Concerto in C minor, which, therefore, was begun thus early, and for one of the seven country dances which appeared in 1799, or perhaps earlier. The sketches for the last movement of No. 3 are associated alone with sketches for a cadenza for the C major Concerto which Beethoven played in Prague in 1798, and may therefore be placed in this year. It follows that the three sonatas were developed gradually in 1796–98, and completed in 1798. From the sketches and the accompanying memoranda[2] we learn, furthermore, that for the first Sonata, which now has three movements, a fourth, an Intermezzo,

---

[1]"Zweite Beethoveniana," p. 29 et seq.

[2]Among sketches for the second movement of the Quintet, Op. 16, Beethoven wrote: "For the new sonatas very short minuets. The Scherzo remains for that in C minor." And in another sketch he writes: "Intermezzo for the sonata in C minor." —Nottebohm, "Zweite Beethoveniana," 32, 479.

was planned on which Beethoven several times made a beginning but permitted to fall. Two of these movements became known afterwards as "Bagatelles." We learn also that the last movement of the first Sonata, and the second movement of the second, were originally laid out on a larger scale.

The "Sonate pathétique," Op. 13, was published by Eder, in Vienna, in 1799, and afterwards by Hoffmeister, who announced them on December 18 of the same year. Sketches for the rondo are found among those for the Trio, Op. 9, and after the beginning of a fair copy of the Sonata, Op. 49, No. 1. From this there is no larger deduction than that the Sonata probably had its origin about 1798. One of the sketches, however, indicates that the last movement was originally conceived for more than one instrument, probably for a sonata for pianoforte and violin. Beethoven published the two Sonatas, Op. 14, which he dedicated to the Baroness Braun, immediately after the "Sonate pathétique." They came from the press of Mollo and were announced on December 21, 1799. The exact time of their composition cannot be determined definitely. Up to the present time no sketches for the second are known to exist; copious ones for the first, however, are published by Nottebohm in his "Zweite Beethoveniana" (p. 45 et seq.), some of which appear before sketches for the Sonata, Op. 12, No. 3, then approaching completion, and some after sketches for the Concerto in B-flat. Because of this juxtaposition, Nottebohm places the conception of the Sonata in 1795.

Touching the history of the Trio, Op. 11, for Pianoforte, Clarinet and Violoncello, little is known. It was advertised as wholly new by Mollo and Co. on October 3, 1798, and is inscribed to the Countess Thun. Sketches associated with works that are unknown or were never completed are in the British Museum and set forth by Nottebohm in his "Zweite Beethoveniana" (p. 515). The sketch for the Adagio resembles the beginning of the minuet in the Sonata, Op. 49, No. 2, and is changed later; this points approximately to 1798. The last movement consists of a series of variations on the theme of a trio from Weigl's opera "L'Amor marinaro," beginning "Pria ch'io l'impegno." Weigl's opera was performed for the first time on October 15, 1797. Czerny told Otto Jahn that Beethoven took the theme at the request of a clarinet player (Beer?) for whom he wrote the Trio. The elder Artaria told Cipriani Potter in 1797, that he had given the theme to Beethoven and requested him to introduce variations on it into a trio, and added that Beethoven did not know that the melody was Weigl's until after the Trio was finished, whereupon he grew very angry on finding it out.   Czerny says in the supplement to his "Pianoforte School":

> It was at the wish of the clarinet player for whom Beethoven wrote this Trio that he employed the above theme by Weigl (which was then very popular) as the finale.   At a later period he frequently contemplated writing another concluding movement for this Trio, and letting the variations stand as a separate work.

If Czerny is correct in his statement, obvious deductions from it are these, which are scarcely consistent with Artaria's story: if the theme was "very popular" at the time the opera must have had several performances, and it is not likely that the melody was unfamiliar to Beethoven, who also, it may be assumed, wrote the title of Weigl's trio, which is printed at the beginning of the last movement of Beethoven's composition.   Beethoven produced the Trio for the first time at the house of Count Fries on the occasion of his first meeting with Steibelt.   The three Sonatas for Pianoforte and Violin, Op. 12, were advertised in the "Wiener Zeitung" of January 12, 1799, as published by Artaria, which would seem to place their origin in 1798.   The program of a concert given by Madame Duschek on March 29, 1798, preserved in the archives of the Gesellschaft der Musikfreunde, announces a sonata with accompaniment to be played by Beethoven.   The accompanying (*obbligato*) instrument is not mentioned, but the work may well have been one of these Sonatas.   Nottebohm discusses the juxtaposition of sketches for the second Sonata with sketches for the Pianoforte Concerto in B-flat and the sonata in E, Op. 14, No. 1, and is inclined to fix 1795 as the year of the sonata's origin.   But we are in the dark as to whether the sketches for the Pianoforte Concerto were for its original or its revised form.

Among the instrumental compositions of this year belong the Variations for Pianoforte and Violoncello on "Ein Mädchen oder Weibchen" from Mozart's "Zauberflöte," of which nothing more is known than that Traeg announced their publication on September 12, 1798.   They were afterward taken over by Artaria. The Variation for Pianoforte on a theme from Grétry's "Richard, Cœur de Lion" ("Une fièvre brûlante") were announced as newly published on November 7, 1798, by Traeg; Cappi and Diabelli acquired them later.   Sketches for them are found by the side of sketches for the first movement of the Sonata in C minor, Op. 10, No. 1, which circumstance indicates that 1796 was the year of their origin.   According to Sonnleithner, "Richard, Cœur de Lion" was first performed at the Hoftheater, Vienna, on

January 7, 1788; then again on June 13, 1799 in the Theater auf den Wieden; but a ballet, "Richard Löwenherz," by Vigano, music by Weigl, in which Grétry's romance, "Une fièvre brûlante," was interpolated, was brought forward on July 2, 1795, in the Hof- und Nationaltheater and repeated often in that year, and it was thence, no doubt, that the suggestion for the variations came to Beethoven. The six little Variations on a Swiss air were published, according to Nottebohm, by Simrock in Bonn in 1798. The ten Variations on "La stessa, la stessissima" from Salieri's "Falstaff, ossia le tre Burle," were announced as just published in the "Wiener Zeitung" of March 2, 1799. Salieri's opera was performed on January 3 (Wlassak says January 6), 1799, in the Hoftheater; Beethoven's, therefore, was an occasional composition conceived and produced in a very short time. Sketches are found among some for the first Quartet, Op. 18, and others. The Variations are dedicated to the Countess Babette Keglevich. Twice more in the same year operatic productions induced similar works. The publication of the Variations on "Kind, willst du ruhig schlafen?" from Winter's "Unterbrochenes Opferfest," was announced in the "Wiener Zeitung" of December 21, 1799, by Mollo and Co.; the opera had its first performance in Vienna on June 15, 1796, and was repeated frequently within the years immediately following—six times in 1799. In this case also it may be assumed that publication followed hard on the heels of composition. Sketches are found in companionship with others belonging to the Quartet, Op. 18, No. 5, and the Septet. The Variations on "Tändeln und Scherzen," from Süssmayr's opera "Soliman II, oder die drei Sultaninnen," belong to the same time. The opera was performed on October 1, 1799, in the Hoftheater; the publication of the variations by Hoffmeister was announced in the "Wiener Zeitung" on December 18, 1799. They may have been printed previously by Eder. They were dedicated to Countess Browne, née von Bietinghoff. It is interesting to learn from Czerny that these Variations were the first of Beethoven's compositions which the master gave him to study when he became his pupil. Before them he had pieces by C. P. E. Bach and after them the "Sonate pathétique."

As evidence pointing to the period in which the first Symphony was written we have, first of all, the report of the first performance on April 2, 1800; but inasmuch as the copying of the parts and the rehearsals must have consumed a considerable time, the period would be much too short (especially in view of Beethoven's method of working) if we were also to assume that the Symphony originated in 1800. It is very likely that, with the Quartets, it was sketched at an earlier period and worked out in the main by 1799 at the latest. It was published toward the end of 1801 by Hoffmeister and Kühnel as Op. 21, dedicated to Baron van Swieten and advertised in the "Wiener Zeitung" of January 16, 1802. Beethoven had already planned a symphony while studying with Albrechtsberger. Nottebohm reports on his purposes after a study of some sketches and from him we learn that the theme of the present last movement was originally intended for a first movement. Beethoven must have worked on this composition in 1794–'95, perhaps at the suggestion of van Swieten—a conclusion suggested by the fact that the dedication of the first symphony went to him. Beethoven abandoned this early plan and turned to other ideas for the new symphony, but there is no clue as to the precise time when this was done. In 1802, Mollo published an arrangement of the symphony as a quintet at the same time that Hoffmeister and Kühnel published a like arrangement of the Septet. Beethoven published the following protest in the "Wiener Zeitung" of October 20, 1802:

I believe that I owe it to the public and myself publicly to announce that the two Quintets in C major and E-flat major, of which the first (taken from a symphony of mine) has been published by Mr. Mollo in Vienna, and the second (taken from my familiar Septet, Op. 20) by Mr. Hoffmeister in Leipzig, are not original quintets but transcriptions prepared by the publishers. The making of transcriptions at the best is a matter against which (in this prolific day of such things) an author must protest in vain; but it is possible at least to demand of the publishers that they indicate the fact on the title-page, so that the honor of the author may not be lessened and the public be not deceived. This much to hinder such things in the future. At the same time I announce that a new Quintet of mine in C major, Op. 29, will shortly be published by Breitkopf and Härtel in Leipzig.

Mention may here be made in conclusion of the two French songs, "Que le temps (jour) me dure" (Rousseau) and "Plaisir d'aimer," recovered from sketches and described by Jean Chantavoine in "Die Musik" (Vol. I, No. 12, 1902). The origin of the latter is fixed in 1799, by its association with a sketch for the Quartets, Op. 18.

Chapter XVI

Beethoven's Social Life in Vienna—His Friends: Vogl, Kiesewetter, Zmeskall, Amenda, Count Lichnowsky, Eppinger, Krumpholz—Schuppanzigh and His Quartet—Hummel—Friendships with Women—His Dedications.

THE chronological progress of the narrative must again be interrupted for a chapter or two, since no picture of a man's life can be complete without the lights or shades arising from his social relations—without some degree of knowledge respecting those with whom he is on terms of equality and intimacy and whose company he most affects. The attempt to draw such a picture in the case of Beethoven, that is, during his first years in Vienna, leaves much to be desired, for, although the search for materials has not been very unsuccessful, many of the data are but vague and scattered notices. In a Conversation Book, bearing Beethoven's own date "on the 20th of March, 1820," some person unknown writes:

> Do you want to know where I first had the honor and good fortune to see you? More than 25 years ago I lived with Frank of Prague in the Drachengassel in the old Fish Market. Several noblemen, for instance His Excellency van B. Cristen (?), Heinerle, Vogl (now a singer), Kösswetter, basso, now Court Councillor, Greyenstein (?), has long been living in France, etc. There we often
>
> musicicised, etc.
> supperized, etc.
> punchized, etc.
>
> and at the conclusion Your Excellency often rejoiced us at my P. F. I was then Court Councillor in the War Office (?). I have practised since then at least 15 thousand métiers—Did we meet in Prague? In what year?—1796—3 days—I was in Prague also in 1790-1-2.

There is nothing in the portions of this Conversation Book, copied for this work, to show who this man of "15 thousand métiers" was, now sitting with Beethoven in an eating-house, and recalling to his memory the frolics of his first year and a quarter in Vienna; nor are Heinerle, Cristen, Greyenstein and Frank of Prague sufficiently known to fame as to be now identified; but Johann Michael Vogl, less than two years older than Beethoven, was afterward a very celebrated tenor of the opera. In 1793-4 he was still pursuing the study of jurisprudence, which he abandoned in 1795 for the stage. May not this early friendship for Beethoven have been among the causes of the resuscitation of "Fidelio" in 1814, for the benefit performance of Vogl, Saal and Weinmüller?

There is a story, first put in circulation by a certain August Barth, to the effect that the singer of that name once finding Beethoven employed in burning a mass of musical and other papers, sang one vocal piece thus destined to destruction, was pleased with it, and saved the immortal "Adelaide!" The story is sufficiently refuted by the fact that when Barth first came to Vienna, in 1807, the "Adelaide" had been in print some ten years. If the name Vogl be substituted in the tale, there may, perhaps, be so much truth in it as this: that he was consulted upon the merits of the composition by Beethoven, approved it, and first sang it and made it known—as he was the first, years afterwards, to sing in public the "Erlkönig" and other fine productions of Franz Schubert. The "Kösswetter, basso," was Raphael George Kiesewetter, who lived to be renowned as a writer upon topics of musical history, and to play a part in the revival of ancient music in Vienna, not less noteworthy than that of Thibaut in Heidelberg. At the period of the "music-making, supping and punch drinking" by the "noblemen" in the apartments of Frank of Prague, Kiesewetter was a young man of twenty, engaged, like Vogl, in the study of the law. In the spring of 1794—and thus the date of these meetings is determined—he received an appointment in the military chancellary, and went at once to the headquarters at Schwetzingen on the Rhine. More important and valuable during these years, as subsequently, was the warm, sincere friendship of Nicolaus Zmeskall von Domanovecz, an official in the Royal Hungarian Court Chancellary. "You belong to my earliest friends in Vienna," writes Beethoven in 1816. Zmeskall, to quote the words of Sonnleithner,

was an expert violoncellist, a sound and tasteful composer. Too modest to publish his compositions, he willed them to the archives of the Gesellschaft der Musikfreunde. After personal examination I can only give assurance that his three string quartets would entitle him to an honorable place among masters of the second rank, and are more deserving to be heard than many new things which, for all manner of reasons, we are compelled to hear.

That Zmeskall was a very constant attendant at the musical parties of Prince Carl Lichnowsky and frequently took part in them, may be seen from Wegeler's record. He was ten years older than Beethoven, had been long enough in Vienna to know the best society there, into which he was admitted not more because of his musical attainments than because of the respectability of his position and character; and was, therefore, what the young student-pianist needed most, a friend, who at the same time could be to a certain degree an authoritative adviser, and at all times was a judicious one. On the part of Zmeskall there was an instant and hearty appreciation of the extraordinary powers of the young stranger from the Rhine and a clear anticipation of his splendid artistic future. A singular proof of this is the care with which he preserved the most insignificant scraps of paper, if Beethoven had written a few words upon them; for, certainly, no other motive could have induced him to save many notes of this kind and of no importance ten, fifteen, twenty years, as may be seen in the published letters of the composer. On the part of Beethoven, there was sincere respect for the dignity and gravity of Zmeskall's character, which usually restrained him within proper limits in their personal intercourse; but he delighted, especially in the earlier period, to give, in his notes and letters, full play to his queer fancies and sometimes extravagant humour.

Here are a few examples in point:

To His Well Well Highest and Bestborn, the Herr von Zmeskall, Imperial and Royal as also Royal and Imperial Court Secretary:
Will His High and Wellborn, His Herrn von Zmeskall's Zmeskallity have the kindness to say where we can speak to him to-morrow?
We are your most damnably
devoted
Beethoven.

My dearest Baron Muckcartdriver.
Je vous suis bien obligé pour votre faiblesse de vos yeux. Moreover I forbid you henceforth to rob me of the good humor into which I occasionally fall, for yesterday your Zmeskall-damanovitzian chatter made me melancholy. The devil take you; I want none of your moral (precepts) for Power is the morality of men who loom above the others, and it is also mine; and if you begin again to-day I'll torment you till you agree that everything that I do is good and praiseworthy (for I am going to the Swan—the Ox would be preferable, yet this rests with your Zmeskallian Domanovezian decision (*réponse*).
Adieu Baron Ba. . . .ron, r o n / n o r / o r n / r n o / o n r /
(*voilà quelque chose* from the old pawnshop.)

Mechanical skill was never so developed in Beethoven that he could make good pens from goose quills—and the days of other

pens were not yet. When, therefore, he had no one with him to
aid him in this, he usually sent to Zmeskall for a supply. Of
the large number of such applications preserved by his friend
and now scattered in all civilized lands as autographs, here are
two specimens.

Best of Music Counts! I beg of you to send me one or a few pens
of which I am really in great need. As soon as I learn where real good,
and admirable pens are to be found I will buy some of them. I hope to
see you at the Swan today.

Adieu, most precious
Music Count
yours etc.

His Highness von Z. is commanded to hasten a bit with the plucking
out of a few of his quills (among them, no doubt, some not his own). It
is hoped that they may not be too tightly grown. As soon as you have
done all that we shall ask we shall be, with excellent esteem your

F———
Beethoven.

Had Zmeskall not carefully treasured these notes, they would
never have met any eye but his own; it is evident, therefore, that
he entered fully into their humor, and that it was the same to
him, whether he found himself addressed as "Baron," "Count,"
"Cheapest Baron," "Music Count," "Baron Muckcartdriver,"
"His Zmeskallian Zmeskallity," or simply "Dear Z."—which last
is the more usual. He knew his man, and loved him; and these
"quips and quiddities" were received in the spirit which begat
them. The whole tenor of the correspondence between the two
shows that Zmeskall had more influence for good upon Beethoven
than any other of his friends; he could reprove him for faults,
and check him when in the wrong, without producing a quarrel
more serious than the one indicated in the protest, above given,
against interrupting his "good humor."

As a musician, as well as man and friend, Zmeskall stood high
in Beethoven's esteem. His apartments, No. 1166, in that huge
conglomeration of buildings known as the Bürgerspital, were for
a long series of years the scene of a private morning concert, to
which only the first performers of chamber music and a very
few guests were admitted. Here, after the rupture with Prince
Lichnowsky, Beethoven's productions of this class were usually
first tried over. Not until Beethoven's death did their correspondence cease.

Another young man who gained an extraordinary place in
Beethoven's esteem and affection, and who departed from Vienna

before anything occurred to cause a breach between them, was
a certain Karl Amenda, from the shore of the Baltic, who died some
forty years later as Provost in Courland.   He was a good violinist,
belonged to the circle of dilettanti which Beethoven so much affected,
and, on parting, received from the composer one of his first attempts
at quartet composition.   His name most naturally suggests itself
to fill the blank in a letter to Ries, July, 1804, wherein some living
person, not named, is mentioned as one with whom he (Beethoven) "never had a misunderstanding," but he adds "although
we have known nothing of each other for nearly six years," which
was not true of Amenda, since letters passed between them in
1801.   The small portion of their written correspondence which
has been made public shows that their friendship was of the romantic character once so much the fashion; and a letter of Amenda
is filled with incense which in our day would bear the name of
almost too gross flattery.   But times change and tastes with them.
His name appears once in the Zmeskall correspondence, namely, in
a mutilated note now in the Royal Imperial Court Library, beginning "My cheapest Baron! Tell the guitarist to come to me to-day.
Amenda is to make an *Amende* (part torn away) which he deserves
for his bad pauses (torn) provide the guitarist."

Karl Amenda was born on October 4, 1771, at Lippaiken in
Courland.   He studied music with his father and Chapelmaster
Beichtmer, was so good a violinist that he was able to give a concert at 14 years of age, and continued his musical studies after he
was matriculated as a student of theology at the University of
Jena.   After a three years' course there he set out on a tour, and
reached Vienna in the spring of 1798.   There he first became pre-
centor for Prince Lobkowitz and afterward music-teacher in the
family of Mozart's widow.   How, thereupon, he became acquainted
with Beethoven we are able to report from a document still in
the possession of the family, which bears the superscription "Brief
Account of the Friendly Relations between L. v. Beethoven and
Karl Friedrich Amenda, afterward Provost at Talsen in Courland,
written down from oral tradition":

> After the completion of his theological studies K. F. Amenda goes to
> Vienna, where he several times meets Beethoven at the table d'hôte,
> attempts to enter into conversation with him, but without success, since
> Beeth. remains very *réservé*. After some time Amenda, who mean-
> while had become music-teacher at the home of Mozart's widow, receives
> an invitation from a friendly family and there plays first violin in a
> quartet. While he was playing somebody turned the pages for him,
> and when he turned about at the finish he was frightened to see Beet-
> hoven, who had taken the trouble to do this and now withdrew with a

bow. The next day the extremely amiable host at the evening party appeared and cried out: "What have you done? You have captured Beethoven's heart! B. requests that you rejoice him with your company." A., much pleased, hurries to B., who at once asks him to play with him. This is done and when, after several hours, A. takes his leave, B. accompanies him to his quarters, where there was music again. As B. finally prepared to go he said to A.: "I suppose you can accompany me." This is done, and B. kept A. till evening and went with him to his home late at night. From that time the mutual visits became more and more numerous and the two took walks together, so that the people in the streets when they saw only one of them in the street at once called out: "Where is the other one?" A. also introduced Mylich, with whom he had come to Vienna, to B., and Mylich often played trios with B. and A. His instrument was the second violin or viola. Once when B. heard that Mylich had a sister in Courland who played the pianoforte prettily, he handed him a sonata in manuscript with the inscription: "To the sister of my good friend Mylich." The manuscript was rolled up and tied with a little silk ribbon. B. complained that he could not get along on the violin. Asked by A. to try it, nevertheless, he played so fearfully that A. had to call out: "Have mercy—quit!" B. quit playing and the two laughed till they had to hold their sides. One evening B. improvised marvellously on the pianoforte and at the close A. said: "It is a great pity that such glorious music is born and lost in a moment." Whereupon B.: "There you are mistaken; I can repeat every extemporization"; whereupon he sat himself down and played it again without a change. B. was frequently embarrassed for money. Once he complained to A.; he had to pay rent and had no idea how he could do it. "That's easily remedied," said A. and gave him a theme ("Freudvoll und Leidvoll") and locked him in his room with the remark that he must make a beginning on the variations within three hours. When A. returns he finds B. on the spot but ill-tempered. To the question whether or not he had begun B. handed over a paper with the remark: "There's your stuff!" (*Da ist der Wisch!*) A. takes the notes joyfully to B.'s landlord and tells him to take it to a publisher, who would pay him handsomely for it. The landlord hesitated at first but finally decided to do the errand and, returning joyfully, asks if other bits of paper like that were to be had. But in order definitely to relieve such financial needs A. advised B. to make a trip to Italy. B. says he is willing but only on condition that A. go with him. A. agrees gladly and the trip is practically planned. Unfortunately news of a death calls A. back to his home. His brother has been killed in an accident and the duty of caring for the family devolves on him. With doubly oppressed heart A. takes leave of B. to return to his home in Courland. There he receives a letter from B. saying: "Since you cannot go along, I shall not go to Italy." Later the friends frequently exchanged thoughts by correspondence.[1]

[1]Amenda returned to his home in Courland in the fall of 1799. The friends corresponded with each other for a time, but the majority of Beethoven's letters are lost. While a student at the University in Leipzig, Amenda's grandson placed some of them in the hands of a publisher at his request and did not get them back. Amenda was first a private teacher, became a preacher in Talsen in 1802, provost of the diocese of Kadau in 1820, consistorial councillor in 1830 and died on March 8, 1836. A portrait painted in 1808, is preserved in the Beethoven Museum in Bonn.

Though, as we have learned, it was music which brought Beethoven into contact with Amenda, it was the latter's amiability and nobility of character that endeared him to the composer, who cherished him as one of his dearest friends and confided things to him which he concealed from his other intimates—his deafness, for instance.   A striking proof of Beethoven's affection is offered by the fact that he gave Amenda a copy of his Quartet in F (Op. 18, No. 1), writing on the first violin part:

Dear Amenda: Take this quartet as a small memorial of our friendship, and whenever you play it recall the days which we passed together and the sincere affection felt for you then and which will always be felt by

Your true and warm friend

Ludwig van Beethoven.

Vienna, 1799, June 25.

In a letter written nearly a year later Beethoven asks his friend not to lend the quartet, as he had revised it.   A letter written, evidently, about the time of Amenda's departure from Vienna indicated that Beethoven was oppressed at this period with another grief than that caused by the loss of his friend's companionship.   Beethoven speaks of his "already lacerated heart," says that "the worst of the storm is over" and mentions an invitation to Poland—which he had accepted.   Nothing came of this Polish enterprise.   Dr. A. C. Kalischer suspected that the lacerated heart was due to the composer's unrequited love for Magdalena Willmann, a singer then in Vienna to whom he made a proposal of marriage which was never answered.

Count Moritz Lichnowsky, brother of Prince Carl, of whom we shall not lose sight entirely until the closing scene, was another of the friends of those years.   He had been a pupil of Mozart, played the pianoforte with much skill and was an influential member of the party which defended the novelty and felt the grandeur of his friend's compositions.   Schindler saw much of him during Beethoven's last years, and eulogizes the "noble Count" in very strong terms.

Another of that circle of young dilettanti, and one of the first players of Beethoven's compositions, was a young Jewish violinist, Heinrich Eppinger.   He played at a charity concert in Vienna, making his first appearance there in 1789.   "He became, in after years," says a correspondent of the time, "a dilettante of the most excellent reputation, lived modestly on a small fortune and devoted himself entirely to music."   At the period before us Eppinger was one of Beethoven's first violins at the private concerts of the

nobility. Häring, who became a distinguished merchant and
banker, belonged now to this circle of young amateur musicians,
and in 1795 had the reputation of being at the head of the amateur
violinists. The youthful friendship between him and the composer was not interrupted as they advanced into life, and twenty
years later was of great advantage to Beethoven.

But a more interesting person for us is the instructor under
whom Beethoven in Vienna resumed his study of the violin (a
fact happily preserved by Ries)—Wenzel Krumpholz. He was a
brother of the very celebrated Bohemian harp player who drowned
himself in the Seine in 1790. In his youth Krumpholz had been
for a period of three years a pupil of Haydn at Esterhaz and had
played first violin in the orchestra there. He left Esterhaz to enter
the service of Prince Kinsky, but came to Vienna in 1795 to join
the operatic orchestra, and at once became noted as a performer
in Haydn's quartets. He was (says Eugene Eiserle in Glöggl's
"Neue Wiener Musik-Zeitung" of August 13, 1857),

a highly sensitive art-enthusiast, and one of the first of those who foresaw
and recognized Beethoven's greatness. He attached himself to Beethoven with such pertinacity and self-sacrifice that the latter, though he always called him "his fool," accepted him as "a most intimate friend," made
him acquainted with all his plans for compositions and generally reposed
the utmost confidence in him. Krumpholz formed also an exceedingly
close friendship with his countryman Wenzel Czerny, a music-teacher
living in the Leopoldstadt, and from 1797 onward spent most of his
leisure evenings with the Czerny family, and thus the little son Karl,
in his eighth and ninth years, learned almost daily what works Beethoven
had in hand, and, like Krumpholz, became filled with enthusiasm for
the tone-hero.

Krumpholz was a virtuoso on the mandolin, and hence, probably, that page of sketches by Beethoven in the Artaria Collection
headed "Sonatine für Mandolin u. P. F." Among the Zmeskall
papers in the Royal Imperial Library in Vienna there is a half-
sheet of coarse foolscap paper upon which is written with lead-
pencil in huge letters by the hand of Beethoven,

The Music Count is dismissed with infamy to-day.—
The First Violin will be exiled to the misery of Siberia.
The *Baron* is forbidden for a whole month to ask questions and
never again to be overhasty, and he must concern himself with nothing
but his *ipse miserum.*

                                                  B.

"Music Count" and "Baron" are, of course, Zmeskall; but
these notices of Beethoven's various first violins show the folly

of attempting to decide whether one of them or Schuppanzigh was to be sent to Siberia, so long as there is no hint whatever as to the time and occasion of the note.

The very common mistake of forgetting that there is a time in the lives of distinguished men when they are but aspirants to fame, when they have their reputations still to make, often, in fact, attracting less notice and raising feebler hopes of future distinction in those who know them, than many a more precocious contemporary—this mistake has thrown the figures of Schuppanzigh and his associates in the quartet concerts at Prince Carl Lichnowsky's into a very false prominence in the picture of these first seven years of Beethoven's Vienna life. The composer himself was not the Beethoven whom *we* know. Had he died in 1800, his place in musical history would have been that of a great pianoforte player and of a very promising young composer, whose decease thus in his prime had disappointed well-founded hopes of great future eminence.

This is doubly true of the members of the quartet. Had they passed away in early manhood, not one of them, except perhaps young Kraft, the only one who ever distinguished himself as a virtuoso upon his instrument, would have been remembered in the annals of music. They were during these years but laying the foundation for future excellence and celebrity as performers of Mozart's, Haydn's, Förster's and Beethoven's quartets. Schuppanzigh, first violin, and Weiss, viola, alone appear to have been constantly associated in their quartet-playing. Kraft, violoncellist, was often absent, when his father, or Zmeskall, or some other, supplied his place; and as the second violin was often taken by the master of the house, when they were engaged for private concerts, Sina was, naturally, absent. Still, from 1794 to 1799, the four appear to have practised much and very regularly together. They enjoyed an advantage known to no other quartet that of playing the compositions of Haydn and Förster under the eyes of the composers, and being taught by them every effect that the music was intended to produce. Each of the performers, therefore, knowing precisely the intentions of the composer, acquired the difficult art of being independent and at the same time of being subordinate to the general effect. When Beethoven began to compose quartets he had, therefore, a set of performers schooled to perfection by his great predecessors, and who already had experience in his own music through his trios and quartets.

Ignatz Schuppanzigh, the leader, born 1776, died March 2, 1830 in Vienna, originally studied music as a dilettante and became a capital player of the viola; but, about the time when Beethoven came to Vienna, he exchanged that instrument for the violin and made music his profession. He was fond of directing orchestral performances and seems to have gained a considerable degree of local reputation and to have been somewhat of a favorite in that capacity before reaching his 21st year. In 1798–99, he took charge of those concerts in the Augarten established by Mozart and Martin, and afterwards led by Rudolph. Seyfried, writing after his death, calls Schuppanzigh a "natural born and really energetic leader of the orchestra." The difference in age, character and social position between him and Beethoven was such as not to admit between them that higher and nobler friendship which united the latter and Zmeskall; but they could be, and were, of great use to each other, and there was a strong personal liking, if not affection, which was mutual. Schuppanzigh's person early assumed very much of the form and proportions of Sterne's Dr. Slop, and after his return from Russia he is one of the "Milord Falstaffs" of Beethoven's correspondence and Conversation Books. His obesity was, however, already the subject of the composer's jests, and he must have been an exceedingly good-tempered young man, to bear with and forgive the coarse and even abusive text of the short vocal piece (1801) headed "Lob auf den Dicken" ("Praise of the Fat One"). But it is evidently a mere jest, and was taken as such. It is worthy of note that Beethoven and Schuppanzigh in addressing each other used neither the familiar "du" nor the respectful "Sie," but "er"—a fact which has been supposed to prove Beethoven's great contempt for the violinist; but as it would prove equal contempt on the other side, it proves too much. Of Sina and Weiss, both Silesians by birth, there is little that need be added here. Weiss became the first viola player of Vienna, and a not unsuccessful composer of ballet and other music.

Anton Kraft (the father) came from Bohemia to pursue his legal studies in Vienna, but abandoned them to enter the Imperial Court Orchestra as violoncellist. In 1778, he accepted an invitation from Haydn to join the orchestra in Esterhaz; where, on the 18th of December of the same year, his son Nicholas Anton was born. The child, endowed by nature with great musical talents, enjoyed the advantages of his father's instructions and example and of growing up under the eye of Haydn and in the constant study of that great musician's works. Upon the death of Esterhazy and the dispersion of his orchestra, Kraft came with his son, now in his fourteenth year, to Vienna. On April 15th,

1792, Nicholas played a concerto composed by his father at the "Widows and Orphans" concert, and on the 21st again appeared in a concert given by the father.   Notwithstanding a very remarkable success, the son was destined for another profession than music; and from this time until his eighteenth year, he played his instrument only as an amateur, and as such Beethoven first knew the youth.   But when the young Prince Lobkowitz formed his orchestra in 1796, both the Krafts were engaged, and Nicholas Anton thenceforth made music his profession.   In the maturity of his years and powers, his only rival among all the German violoncellists was Bernhard Romberg.

Schindler, with his characteristic inattention to dates, observes, speaking of Schuppanzigh, Weiss and the elder Kraft:

These three artists are intimately connected with the development of Beethoven and, indeed, with a large portion of his creations; wherefore they will frequently be remembered here.   Meanwhile it may suffice to say that it was to this company of practically-trained musicians that the rising young composer owed his knowledge of the efficient use of stringed instruments.   In addition are to be mentioned Joseph Friedlowsky, who taught our master the mechanism of the clarinet, and the famous hornist, Johann Wenzel Stich, who called himself Giovanni Punto in Italian, to whom Beethoven owed what he knew of the proper writing for horn, of which he already gave striking illustration in his Sonata for Horn, Op. 17.   In the mechanism of the flute and its construction, which underwent so many changes in the first decades of the century, Carl Scholl steadily remained Beethoven's instructor.

There is doubtless some degree of truth in this in so far as it relates to a later period.   Punto, of course, gave Beethoven a new revelation of the powers and possibilities of the horn, as Dragonetti did of the contrabass; but he first came to Vienna near the end of 1799, and died at Prague only three years after (February 16, 1803).   All the others here named by Schindler —with one exception, the elder Kraft—were youths of 16-18 years, when Beethoven composed his first and second concertos works which prove that he was not altogether ignorant of the use of orchestral instruments!   Had Schindler known something of the history of Max Franz's orchestra in Bonn, he would have avoided many a mistake.[1]

---

[1]Beethoven did not always follow the suggestions of these men.   According to an anecdote told by Doležalek to Otto Jahn, Kraft once complained that a passage was not playable.   "It's got to be," answered Beethoven   In a like vein K. Holz relates that "Beethoven asked an excellent artist whether or not certain things were possible"; the question of how difficult they were did not enter.   Thus Friedlowsky for clarinet, Czerwensky for oboe, Hradezky and Herbst for horn.   If others complained of impossibilities the answer was "They can do it and you must."   (From Thayer's papers.)

Johann Nepomuk Hummel, the pupil of Mozart, was another of the youths whom Beethoven drew into his circle. In 1795, the elder Hummel brought back his son to Vienna (from that very successful concert tour which had occupied the last six years and had made the boy known even to the cities of distant Scotland) and put him to the studies of counterpoint and composition with Albrechtsberger and Salieri. He seems to have been quietly at his studies, playing only in private, until April 28th, 1799, when he again appeared in public both as pianist and composer, in a concert in the Augartensaal, directed by Schuppanzigh. "He performed a symphony besides a melodrama composed for the occasion and between them played prettily *composed* improvisations on the pianoforte." That the talented and promising boy of seventeen years should, upon arriving home again, seek the acquaintance and favor of one who during his absence had made so profound an impression upon the Vienna public as Beethoven, and that the latter should have rejoiced to show kindness to Mozart's favorite pupil, hardly needs to be mentioned. A chapter of description would not illustrate the nature of their intercourse so vividly, as two short but exceedingly characteristic notes of Beethoven's which Hummel preserved and which found their way into print after his death:

I

He is not to come to me again. He is a treacherous dog and may the fiayer get all such treacherous dogs!

II

Herzens Natzerl:
      You are an honest fellow and I now see you were right. Come, then, to me this afternoon. You'll find Schuppanzigh here also and we two will bump, thump and pump you to your heart's delight. A kiss from

Your
Beethoven
also called Mehlschöberl.[1]

In a letter to Eleonore von Breuning, Beethoven described many of the Vienna pianists as his "deadly enemies." Schindler's observations upon the composer's relations with the Viennese

[1]The humor to which Beethoven resorts in this note in order to show his contrition necessarily evaporates in any attempt to translate its Viennese colloquialisms. "Herzens Natzerl" is to be understood as "Dear little Ignacius of my heart," Nazerl being an affectionate diminutive of Ignaz or Ignacius. Why it should have been applied to Hummel, whose Christian names were Johann Nepomuk, does not appear. "Mehlschoberl" is a term which has survived in the Austrian cuisine of to-day, the article itself being a sort of soup dumpling.

musicians, though written in his peculiar style, seem to be very judicious and correct.

Nobody is likely to expect, he says (Vol. I, 23-24), that an artist who made his way upwards as our Beethoven, although almost confining his activities exclusively to aristocratic circles that upheld him in extraordinary fashion, would remain free from the attacks of his colleagues; on the contrary, the reader will be prepared to see a host of enemies advance against him because of the shining qualities and evidences of genius of our hero, in contrast with the heavy burden of social idiosyncrasies and uncouthness. More than anything else, what seemed least tolerable to his opponents was the notion that his appearance, the excitability which he controlled too little in his intercourse with his colleagues and his lack of consideration in passing judgment were natural accompaniments of genius. His too small toleration of many bizarreries and weaknesses of high society, and on the other hand his severe demand on his colleagues for higher culture, even his Bonn dialect, afforded his enemies more than enough material to revenge themselves on him by evil gossip and slander. . . . The musicians in Vienna at that time, with a very few exceptions, were lacking, not only in artistic, but also in the most necessary degree of general, education and were as full of the envy of handicraftsmen as the members of the guilds themselves. There was a particular antipathy to all foreigners as soon as they manifested a purpose to make their homes in the imperial city.

Schindler might have added that the change had been in no small degree produced through the instructions and example of Beethoven as they acted upon the Czernys, Moscheles and other young admirers of his genius. In short, Beethoven's instant achievement of a position as artist only paralleled by Mozart and of a social rank which Gluck, Salieri, Haydn had gained only after making their names famous throughout Europe, together with the general impression that the mantle of Mozart had fallen upon him—all this begat bitter envy in those whom his talents and genius overshadowed; they revenged themselves by deriding him for his personal peculiarities and by condemning and ridiculing the novelties in his compositions; while he met their envy with disdain, their criticisms with contempt; and, when he did not treat their compositions with indifference, but too often only noticed them with sarcasm.

This picture, certainly, is not an agreeable one, but all the evidence proves it, unfortunately, faithful. Such men as Salieri, Gyrowetz, Weigl, are not to be understood as included in the term "pianist" as used by Beethoven in his letter to Eleonore von Breuning. For these men "stood high in Beethoven's respect," says Schindler, and his words are confirmed to the fullest extent by the Conversation Books and other authorities; which also show that Eybler's name might have been added to the list. They were all more or less older than Beethoven, and for their contrapuntal learning, particularly in the case of Weigl and Eybler, he esteemed them very highly.   No indications, however, have been found, that he was upon terms of close private friendship and intimacy with either.

Beethoven was no exception to the general rule, that men of genius delight in warm and lasting friendships with women of superior minds and culture—not meaning those "conquests" which, according to Wegeler, even during his first three years in Vienna, "he occasionally made, which if not impossible for many an Adonis would still have been difficult." Let such matters, even if details concerning them were now attainable, be forgotten.   His celibacy was by no means owing to a deliberate choice of a single life. What is necessary and proper of the little that is known on *this* point will, in due time, be imparted simply and free from gloss or superfluous comment.   As to his friendships with the other sex, it would be throwing the view of them into very false perspective to employ those of later years in giving piquancy to a chapter here.   Let them also come in due order and thus, while they lose nothing of interest, they may, perchance afford relief and give brightness to canvas which otherwise might sometimes become too sombre.   Happily during these prosperous years now before us, the picture has been for the most part bright and sunny and the paucity of the information upon the topic in question is of less consequence.

In the present connection one of our old Bonn friends again comes upon the scene.   The beautiful, talented and accomplished Magdalene Willmann was invited to sing at Venice during the carnival of 1794.   She left Bonn the preceding summer with her brother Max and his wife (Fräulein Tribolet) to fulfill the engagement.   After leaving Venice, they gave a concert in Gratz, and journeyed on to Vienna.   Here Max and his wife remained, having accepted engagements from Schikaneder, while Magdalene went on to Berlin.   Not suiting the operatic public there she returned to Vienna, and was soon engaged to sing both German and Italian parts in the Court Opera.   Beethoven renewed his intercourse with them and soon became so captivated with the charms of the beautiful Magdalene as to offer her his hand.   This fact was communicated to the author by a daughter of Max Willmann, still living in 1860, who had often heard her father speak of it. To the question, why her aunt did not accept the offer of Beethoven, Madame S. hesitated a moment, and then, laughing, replied: "Because he was so ugly, and half crazy!" In 1799, Magdalene married a certain Galvani, but her happiness was short; she died toward the end of 1801.

Two letters of Beethoven to be found in the printed collection have been preserved from the period before us, addressed to Christine Gerhardi, a young woman of high distinction in society at the time for the splendor of her talents and her high culture. Dr. Sonnleithner wrote of her:

> She was the daughter of an official at the court of the Emperor Leopold II . . . an excellent singer, but remained a dilettante and sang chiefly in concerts for charitable purposes (which she herself arranged), or for the benefit of eminent artists. Old Professor Peter Frank was director of the general hospital of Vienna in the neighborhood of which (No. 20 Alserstrasse) she lived. He was a great lover of music, but his son, Dr. Joseph Frank, was a greater; he made essays in composition and arranged musical soirées at the home of his father at which Beethoven and Fräulein Gerhardi took part, playing and singing. The son frequently composed cantatas, which Beethoven corrected, for the name-days and birthdays of his father, and in which Fräulein Gerhardi sang the soprano solos. . . . . She was at the time the most famous amateur singer in Vienna, and inasmuch as Haydn knew her well there is no doubt but that he had her in mind when he composed "The Creation"; indeed, she sang the soprano part with great applause not only at Schwarzenberg but also at the first performance in the Burgtheater. All reports agree that she met Beethoven often at Frank's and that he frequently accompanied her singing on the pianoforte. He did not give her lessons.

Dr. Joseph von Frank and Christine Gerhardi were married on August 20, 1798; they moved away from Vienna in 1804.

A few notes upon certain young women to whom Beethoven dedicated compositions at this period of his life may form no inappropriate close to this chapter. It was much the custom then for teachers of music to dedicate their works to pupils, especially to those who belonged to the higher social ranks—such dedications being at the same time compliments to the pupils and advertisements for the instructors, with the farther advantage often of being sources of pecuniary profit. When, therefore, we read the name of Baroness Albini on the title-page of certain sonatas by Sterkel, of Julia Countess Guicciardi on one by Kleinheinz, of Anna Countess Mailath on songs by Teyber, we assume at once the probability in these and like instances that the relation of master and pupil existed. Beethoven also followed the custom; and the young ladies, subjects of the following notices, are all known or supposed to have taken lessons of him.

Anna Louisa Barbara ("La Comtesse Babette") was the daughter of Karl Count Keglevics de Busin, of Hungarian

Croatian lineage, and Barbara Countess Zichy. She married Prince Innocenz d'Erba Odescalchi on the 10th of February, 1801 (another authority gives 1800). Beethoven's dedications to her are the Sonata, Op. 7 (published in 1797), the Variations "La stessa la stessissima" (1799), and the Pianoforte Concerto, Op. 15, 1801—the last to her as Princess Odescalchi. A note by the composer to Zmeskall—which, judging both from its contents and the handwriting, could not have been written later than 1801-2 —shows that the Odescalchi palace was one of those at which he took part in musical soirées.

"Countess Henriette Lichnowsky," writes Count Amade, "was the sister of the ruling Prince Carl, and was doubtless married to the Marquis of Carneville after the dedication to her of the Rondo (G major, Op. 51, No. 2, published in September, 1802); she lived in Paris after her marriage and died about 1830." The Rondo was first dedicated to Countess Giulietta Guicciardi, but Beethoven asked it back in exchange for the C-sharp minor Sonata; to which fact we shall recur presently. Countess Thun, to whom Beethoven dedicated the Clarinet Trio, Op. 11, in 1797, was the mother of Prince Carl Lichnowsky and Countess Henriette Lichnowsky. She died May 18, 1800. The Sonata in E-flat, Op. 27, No. 1, was dedicated to Josepha Sophia, wife of Prince Johann Joseph von Liechtenstein, daughter of Joachim Egon, Landgrave of Fürstenberg-Weitra. She was born on June 20, 1776, married on April 22, 1792 and died February 23, 1848. Whether her father was related at all, and if so, how, to the Fürstenberg in whose house Beethoven gave lessons in Bonn, is not known. Her husband, however, was first cousin to Count Ferdinand von Waldstein. The Baroness Braun to whom Beethoven dedicated the two Pianoforte Sonatas Op. 14 and the Sonata for Horn in 1801, was the wife of Baron Peter von Braun, lessee of the National-theater and afterwards of the Theater an der Wien. The dedications disclose an early association which eventually led to Beethoven's being asked to compose an opera. It is not known that Beethoven was a social visitor in the house of Baron Braun, but he was a highly respected guest in the house of Count Browne, to whose wife Beethoven dedicated the "Waldmädchen" Variations and the three Pianoforte Sonatas, Op. 10.

Chapter XVII

Beethoven's Character and Personality—His Disposition—
Love of Nature—Relations with the Opposite Sex—
Literary Tastes—His Letters—Manner of Composing
—The Sketchbooks—Origin of His Deafness.

THE year 1800 is an important era in Beethoven's history. It
is the year in which, cutting loose from the pianoforte, he
asserted his claims to a position with Mozart and the still
living and productive Haydn in the higher forms of chamber and
orchestral composition—the quartet and the symphony. It is
the year, too, in which the bitter consciousness of an increasing
derangement of his organs of hearing was forced upon him and the
terrible anticipation of its incurable nature and of its final result
in almost total deafness began to harass and distress him. The
course of his life was afterwards so modified, on the one hand,
by the prosperous issue of these new appeals to the taste and
judgment of the public, and, on the other, by the unhappy progress
of his malady, each acting and reacting upon a nature singularly
exceptional, that for this and other reasons some points in his
personal character and habits, and a few general remarks upon
and illustrations of another topic or two must be made before
resuming the narrative of events.

A true and exhaustive picture of Beethoven as a man would
present an almost ludicrous contrast to that which is generally
entertained as correct. As sculptors and painters have each in
turn idealized the work of his predecessor, until the composer
stands before us like a Homeric god—until those who knew him
personally, could they return to earth, would never suspect that
the grand form and noble features of the more pretentious portraits
are intended to represent the short muscular figure and pock-
pitted face of their old friend—so in literature evoked by the composer a similar process has gone on, with a corresponding suppression of whatever is deemed common and trivial, until he is made
a being living in his own peculiar realm of gigantic ideas, above

and apart from the rest of mankind—a sort of intellectual Thor, dwelling in "darkness and clouds of awful state," and making in his music mysterious revelations of things unutterable! But it is really some generations too soon for a conscientious investigator of his history to view him as a semi-mythological personage, or to discover that his notes to friends asking for pens, making appointments to dinner at taverns, or complaining of servants, are "cyclopean blocks of granite," which, like the "chops and tomato sauce" of Mr. Pickwick, contain depths unfathomable of profound meaning. The present age must be content to find in Beethoven, with all his greatness, a very human nature, one which, if it showed extraordinary strength, exhibited also extraordinary weaknesses.

It was the great misfortune of Beethoven's youth—his impulses good and bad being by nature exceedingly quick and violent —that he did not grow up under the influence of a wise and strict parental control, which would have given him those habits of self-restraint that, once fixed, are a second and better nature, and through which the passions, curbed and moderated, remain only as sources of noble energy and power. His very early admission into the orchestra of the theatre as cembalist, was more to the advantage of his musical than of his moral development. It was another misfortune that, in those years, when the strict regulations of a school would have compensated in some measure for the unwise, unsteady, often harsh discipline of his father, he was thus thrown into close connection with actors and actresses, who, in those days, were not very distinguished for the propriety of their manners and morals. Before his seventeenth or eighteenth year, when he became known to the Breuning family and Count Waldstein, he could hardly have learned the importance of cultivating those high principles of life and conduct on which in later years he laid so much stress. And, at that period of life, the character even under ordinary circumstances is so far developed, the habits have become so far formed and fixed, and the natural tendencies have acquired so much strength, that it is, as a rule, too late to conquer the power of a perfect self-command. At all events, the consequences of a deficient early moral education followed Beethoven through life and are visible in the frequent contests between his worse and his better nature and in his constant tendency to extremes. To-day, upon some perhaps trivial matter, he bursts into ungovernable wrath; to-morrow, his penitence exceeds the measure of his fault. To-day he is proud, unbending, offensively careless of those claims which society grants to people of high rank; to-morrow his humility is more than adequate to the occasion. The poverty in which he grew up was not without its effect upon his character. He never learned to estimate money at its real value; though often profuse and generous to a fault, even wasteful, yet at times he would fall into the other extreme. With all his sense of nobility of independence, he early formed the habit of leaning upon others; and this the more, as his malady increased, which certainly was a partial justification; but he thus became prone to follow unwise counsels, or, when his pride was touched, to assert an equally unwise independence. At other times, in the multitude of counsellors he became the victim of utter irresolution, when decision and firmness were indispensable and essential to his welfare. Thus, both by following the impulse of the moment, and by hesitation when a prompt determination was demanded, he took many a false step, which could no longer be retrieved when reflection brought with it bitter regret.

It would be doing great injustice both to Beethoven and to the present writer to understand the preceding remarks as being intended to represent the composer's lapses in these regards, as being more than unpleasant and unfortunate episodes in the general tenor of his life; but as they did occur to his great disadvantage, the fact cannot be silently passed over.

A romantically sentimental admiration of the heroes of ancient classic literature, having its origin in Paris, had become widely the fashion in Beethoven's youth. The democratic theories of the French sentimentalists had received a new impulse from the dignified simplicity of the foreign representatives of the young American Republic, Franklin, Adams, Jay—from the retirement to private life on their plantations and farms of the great military leaders in the contest, Washington, Greene, Schuyler, Knox and others, after the war with England was over; from the pride taken by the French officers, who had served in America, in their insignia of the order of the Cincinnati; and even from the letters and journals of German officers, who, in captivity, had formed friendships with many of the better class of the republican leaders, and seen with their own eyes in what simplicity they lived while guiding the destinies of the new-born nation. Thus through the greater part of Central Europe the idea became current of a pure and sublime humanity, above and beyond the influence of the passions, of which Cincinnatus, Scipio, Cato, Washington, Franklin, were the supposed representatives. Zschokke makes his Heuwen say: "Virtue and the heroes of antiquity had inspired me with enthusiasm for virtue and heroism"; and so, also, Beethoven. He exalted his imagination and fancy by the perusal of the German poets and translations of the ancient and English classics, especially Homer, Plutarch and Shakespeare; dwelt fondly upon the great characters as models for the conduct of life; but between the sentiment which one feels and the active principle on which he acts, there is often a wide cleft. That Beethoven proved to be no Stoic, that he never succeeded in governing his passions with absolute sway, was not because the spirit was unwilling; the flesh was weak. Adequate firmness of character had not been acquired in early years. But those who have most thoroughly studied his life, know best how pure and lofty were his aspirations, how wide and deep his sympathies with all that is good, how great his heart, how, on the whole, heroic his endurance of his great calamity. They can best feel the man's true greatness, admire the nobility of his nature, and drop the tear of sorrow and regret upon his vagaries and faults. He who is morbidly sensitive, and compelled to keep constant ward and watch over his passions, can best appreciate and sympathize with the man, Beethoven.

Truth and candor compel the confession, that in those days of prosperity he bore his honors with less of meekness than we could wish; that he had lost something of that modesty and ingenuousness eulogized by Junker ten years before, in his Mergentheim letter. His "somewhat lofty bearing" had even been reported by the correspondent of the "Allgemeine Musikalische Zeitung." Traces of self-sufficiency and even arrogance—faults almost universal among young and successful geniuses, often in a far higher degree than was true of Beethoven, and with not a tithe of his reason—are unquestionably visible. No one can read without regret his remarks upon certain persons not named, with whom at this very time he was upon terms of apparently intimate friendship. "I value them," he writes, "only by what they do for me. . . . I look upon them only as instruments upon which I play when I feel so disposed." His "somewhat lofty bearing" was matter for jest to the venerable Haydn, who, according to a trustworthy tradition, when Beethoven's visits to him had become few and far between would inquire of other visitors: "How goes it with our Great Mogul?" Nor would the young nobles, whose society he frequented, take offence; but it certainly made him enemies among those whom he "valued according to their service and looked upon as mere instruments" —and no wonder!

Pierson, in his edition of the so-called "Beethoven's Studien," has added to Seyfried's personal sketches a few reminiscences of that Griesinger, who was so long Saxon Minister in Vienna, and to whom we owe the valuable "Biographische Notizen über Joseph Haydn." One of his anecdotes is to the purpose here and may be taken as substantially historical.

When he was still only an attaché, and Beethoven was little known except as a celebrated pianoforte player, both being still young, they happened to meet at the house of Prince Lobkowitz. In conversation with a gentleman present, Beethoven said in substance, that he wished to be relieved from all bargain and sale of his works, and would gladly find some one willing to pay him a certain income for life, for which he should possess the exclusive right of publishing all he wrote; adding, "and I would not be idle in composition. I believe Goethe does this with Cotta, and, if I mistake not, Handel's London publisher held similar terms with him."

"My dear young man," returned the other, "You must not complain; for you are neither a Goethe nor a Handel, and it is not to be expected that you ever will be; for such masters will not be born again." Beethoven bit his lips, gave a most contemptuous glance at the speaker, and said no more. Lobkowitz endeavored to appease him, and in a subsequent conversation said:

"My dear Beethoven, the gentleman did not intend to wound you. It is an established maxim, to which most men adhere, that the present generation cannot possibly produce such mighty spirits as the dead, who have already earned their fame."

"So much the worse, Your Highness," retorted Beethoven; "but with men who will not believe and trust in me because I am as yet unknown to universal fame, I cannot hold intercourse!"

It is easy for this generation, which has the productions of the composer's whole life as the basis of its judgment of his powers, to speak disparagingly of his contemporaries for not being able to discover in his first twelve or fifteen works good reason for classing him with Goethe and Handel; but he who stands upon a mountain cannot justly ridicule him on the plain for the narrow extent of his view. It was as difficult then to conceive the possibility of instrumental music being elevated to heights greater than those reached by Haydn and Mozart. as it is for us to conceive of Beethoven being hereafter surpassed.

In the short personal sketches of Beethoven's friends which have been introduced, the dates of their births have been noted so far as known, that the reader may observe how very large a proportion of them were of the same age as the composer, or still younger—some indeed but boys—when he came to Vienna. And so it continued. As the years pass by in our narrative and names familiar to us disappear, the new ones which take their places, with rare exceptions, are still of men much younger than himself. The older generation of musical amateurs at Vienna, van Swieten and his class, had accepted the young Bonn organist and patronized him, as a pianist. But when Beethoven began to press his claims as a composer, and, somewhat later, as his deafness increased, to neglect his playing, some of the elder friends had passed away, others had withdrawn from society, and the number was few of those who, like Lichnowsky, could comprehend that departures from the forms and styles of Mozart and Haydn were not necessarily faults. With the greater number, as perfection necessarily admits of no improvement and both quartet and symphony in *form* had been carried to that point by Haydn and Mozart, it was a perfectly logical conclusion that farther progress was impossible. They could not perceive that there was still room for the invention or discovery of new elements of interest, beauty, power; for such perceptions are the offspring of genius. With Beethoven they were instinctive.

One more remark: Towards the decline of life, the masterpieces of literature and art, on which the taste was formed, are apt to become invested in the mind with a sort of nimbus of sanctity; hence, the productions of a young and daring innovator, even when the genius and talent displayed in them are felt and receive just acknowledgement, have the aspect, not only of an extravagant and erring waste of misapplied powers, but of a kind of profane audacity. For these and similar reasons Beethoven's novelties found little favor with the veterans of the concert-room.

The criticism of the day was naturally ruled and stimulated by the same spirit. Beethoven's own confession how it at first wounded him, will come in its order; but after he felt that his victory over it was sure—was in fact gained with a younger generation—he only laughed at the critics; to answer them, except by new works, was beneath him. Seyfried says of him (during the years of the "Eroica," "Fidelio," etc.): "When he came across criticisms in which he was accused of grammatical errors he rubbed his hands in glee and cried out with a loud laugh: 'Yes, yes! they marvel and put their heads together because they do not find it in any school of thoroughbass!'" But for the young of both sexes, Beethoven's music had an extraordinary charm. And this not upon technical grounds, nor solely for its novelties, always an attractive feature to the young, but because it appealed to the sensibilities, excited emotions and touched the heart as no other purely instrumental compositions had ever done. And so it was that Beethoven also in his quality of composer soon gathered about him a circle of young disciples, enthusiastic admirers. Their homage may well have been grateful to him— as such is to every artist and scholar of genius, who, striking out and steadfastly pursuing a new path, subjects himself to the sharp animadversions of critics who, in all honesty, really can see little or nothing of good in that which is not to be measured and judged by old standards. The voice of praise under such circumstances is doubly pleasing. It is known that, when Beethoven's works began to find a just appreciation from a new generation of critics, who had indeed been schooled by them, he collected and preserved a considerable number of laudatory articles, whose fate cannot now be traced. When, however, the natural and just satisfaction which is afforded by the homage of honest admirers and deservedly eulogistic criticism, degenerates into a love of indiscriminate praise and flattery, it becomes a weakness, a fault. Of this error in Beethoven there are traces easily discernible, and especially in his later years; there are pages of fulsome eulogy addressed to him in the Conversation Books, which would make the reader blush for him, did not the mere fact that such books existed remind him of the bitterness of the composer's lot. The failing was also sometimes his misfortune for those who were most profuse in their flatteries, and thus gained his ear, were by no means the best of his counsellors. But aside from the attractive force of his genius, Beethoven possessed a personal magnetism, which attached his young worshippers to him and, all things considered, to his solid and lasting benefit in his private affairs. Just at this time, and for some years to come, his brothers usually rendered him the aid he needed; but thenceforth to the close of his life, the names of a constant succession of young men will appear in and vanish from our narrative, who were ever necessary to him and ever ready at his call with their voluntary services.

Beethoven's love of nature was already a marked trait of his character. This was indulged and strengthened by long rambles upon the lofty hills and in the exquisitely beautiful valleys which render the environs of Vienna to the north and west so charming. Hence, when he left the city to spend the hot summer months in the country, with but an exception or two in a long series of years, his residence was selected with a view to the indulgence of this noble passion. Hence, too, his great delight in the once celebrated work of Christian Sturm: "Beobachtungen über die Werke Gottes," which, however absurd much of its natural philosophy (in the old editions) appears now in the light of advanced knowledge, was then by far the best manual of popular scientific truth, and was unsurpassed in fitness to awaken and foster a taste for, and the understanding of, the beauties of nature. Schindler has recorded the master's life-long study and admiration of this book. It was one which cherished his veneration for the Creator and Preserver of the universe, and yet left his contempt for procrustean religious systems and ecclesiastical dogmas its free course. "To him, who, in the love of Nature, holds communion with her visible forms, she speaks a various language," says Bryant. Her language was thoroughly well understood by Beethoven; and when, in sorrow and affliction, his art, his Plutarch, his "Odyssey," proved to be resources too feeble for his comfort, he went to Nature for solace, and rarely failed to find it.

Art has been so often disgraced by the bad morals and shameless lives of its votaries, that it is doubly gratifying to be able to affirm of Beethoven that, like Handel, Bach and Mozart, he did honor to his profession by his personal character and habits. Although irregular, still he was as simple and temperate in eating and drinking as was possible in the state of society in which he lived. That he was no inordinate lover of wine or strong drinks is certain. No allusion is remembered in any of his letters, notes, memoranda, nor in the Conversation Books, which indicates a liking for any game of chance or skill. He does not appear to have known one playing-card from another. Music, books, conversation with men and women of taste and intelligence, dancing, according to Ries (who adds that he could never learn to dance in time—but Beethoven's dancing days were soon over—), and, above all, his long walks, were his amusements and recreations. His whim for riding was of short duration—at all events, the last allusion to any horse owned by him is in the anecdote on a previous page.

One rather delicate point demands a word: and surely, what Franklin in his autobiography could confess of himself, and Lockhart mention without scruple of Walter Scott, his father-in-law, need not be here suppressed. Nor can it well be, since a false assumption on the point has been made the basis already of a considerable quantity of fine writing, and employed to explain certain facts relative to Beethoven's compositions. Spending his whole life in a state of society in which the vow of celibacy was by no means a vow of chastity; in which the parentage of a cardinal's or archbishop's children was neither a secret nor a disgrace; in which the illegitimate offspring of princes and magnates were proud of their descent and formed upon it well-grounded hopes of advancement and success in life; in which the moderate gratification of the sexual was no more discountenanced than the satisfying of any other natural appetite—it is nonsense to suppose, that, under such circumstances, Beethoven could have puritanic scruples on that point. Those who have had occasion and opportunity to ascertain the facts, know that he had not, and are also aware that he did not always escape the common penalties of transgressing the laws of strict purity. But he had too much dignity of character ever to take part in scenes of low debauchery, or even when still young to descend to the familiar jesting once so common between tavern girls and the guests. Thus, as the elder Simrock related, upon the journey to Mergentheim recorded in the earlier pages of this work, it happened at some place where the company dined, that some of the young men prompted the waiting-girl to play off her charms upon Beethoven. He received her advances and familiarities with repellent coldness; and as she, encouraged by the others, still persevered, he lost his patience, and put an end to her importunities by a smart box on the ear.

The practice, not uncommon in his time, of living with an unmarried woman as a wife, was always abhorrent to him—how much so, a sad story will hereafter illustrate; to a still greater degree an intrigue with the wife of another man. In his later years he so broke off his once familiar intercourse with a distinguished composer and conductor of Vienna, as hardly to return his greetings with common politeness. Schindler affirmed that the only reason for this was that the man in question had taken to his bed and board the wife of another.

The names of two married women might be here given, to whom at a later period Beethoven was warmly attached; names which happily have hitherto escaped the eyes of literary scavengers, and are therefore here suppressed. Certain of his friends used to joke him about these ladies, and it is certain that he rather enjoyed their jests even when the insinuations, that his affection was beyond the limit of the Platonic, were somewhat broad; but careful enquiry has failed to elicit any evidence that even in these

cases he proved unfaithful to his principles. A story related by
Jahn is also to the point, viz.: that Beethoven only by the urgent
solicitations of the Czerny family was after much refusal persuaded
to extemporize in the presence of a certain Madame Hofdemel.
She was the widow of a man who had attempted her life and then
committed suicide; and the refusal of Beethoven to play before
her arose from his having the general belief at the time, that a
too great intimacy had existed between her and Mozart. Jahn,
it may be observed, has recently had the great satisfaction of
being able to prove the innocence of Mozart in this matter and
of rescuing his memory from the only dark shadow which rested
upon it. This much on this topic it has been deemed necessary
to say here, not only for the reason above given, but to put an
end to long-prevailing misconceptions and misconstructions of
passages in Beethoven's letters and private memoranda and to
save farther comment when they shall be introduced hereafter.

Beethoven's fine sense for the lyric element in poetry was
already conspicuous in the fine tact with which the texts of his
songs, belonging in date to his last years in Bonn, were selected
from the annual publications in which most of them appeared.
Another fine proof of this is afforded by a glance through the older
editions of Matthisson's poems. In the fourth (1797), there are
but two which are really well adapted to composition in the song-
form—the "Adelaide" and "Das Opferlied." A third Beethoven
left unfinished. He had doubtless been led to attempt its composition through the force of its appeal to his personal feelings
and sympathies, but soon discovering its non-lyrical character
abandoned it. It is the "Wunsch."

Rochlitz in his letters from Vienna (1822) reports Beethoven's
humorous account of his enthusiasm for Klopstock in his early
life:

Since that summer in Carlsbad I read Goethe every day, that
is, when I read at all. He (Goethe) has killed Klopstock for me. You
are surprised? And now you laugh? Ah ha! It is because I have
read Klopstock. I carried him about with me for years while walking
and also at other times. Well, I did not always understand him, of
course. He leaps about so much and he begins at too lofty an elevation.
Always *Maestoso*, D-flat major! Isn't it so? But he is great and uplifts
the soul nevertheless. When I could not understand him I could sort
of guess. If only he did not always want to die! That will come quickly
enough. Well, it always sounds well, at any rate, etc.

Thus, whatever scattered hints bearing upon the point come
under our notice combine to impart a noble idea of Beethoven's
poetic taste and culture, and to show that the allusions to the

ancient classic authors in his letters and conversation were not made for display, but were the natural consequence of a love for and a hearty appreciation of them derived from their frequent perusal in translations.

Beethoven's correspondence forms so important a portion of his biography that something must be said here upon his character as a letter-writer. A few of his autograph letters bear marks of previous study and careful elaboration; but, in general, whatever he wrote in the way of private correspondence was dashed off on the spur of the moment, and with no thought that it would ever come under any eye but that for which it was intended. It is therefore easy to imagine how energetically he would have protested could he have known that his most insignificant notes were preserved in such numbers, and that the time would come when they would all be made public; or, still worse, that some which were but the offspring of momentary pique against those with whom he lived in closest relations would be used after his death to their injury; and that outbursts of sudden passion—when the wrong was perhaps as often on his side as on the other—after all the parties concerned had passed away, would have an almost judicial authority accorded to them.

In studying a collection of some eight hundred of his letters and notes,[1] originals and copies in print or manuscript, the most striking fact is the insignificance of by far the greater number —that so few bear marks of any care in their preparation, or contain matter of any intrinsic value. In fact, perhaps the greater part of the short notes to Zmeskall and others owe their origin to Beethoven's dislike of entrusting oral messages to his servants. For the most part it is in vain to seek in his correspondence anything bearing upon the theory or art of music; very seldom is any opinion expressed upon the productions of any contemporary composer; no vivid sketches of men and manners flow from his pen, like those which render the letters of Mozart and Mendelssohn so charming. The proportion of their correspondence which possesses more than a merely biographical value was large; of Beethoven's very small.

His letters, of course, exhibit the usual imperfections of a hasty and confidential correspondence; sometimes, indeed, of an aggravated character. Some of them contain loose statements

---

[1] The number of known letters and documents has grown greatly since Thayer wrote these words. Kalischer's Collection numbers over 1200 and Emerich Kastner gives the first lines of 1380 in Frimmel's second "Beethoven Jahrbuch" published in 1909.

of fact, such as all men are liable to make through haste or
imperfect knowledge; others contain passages of which the only
conceivable explanation is Schindler's statement that Beethoven
sometimes amused himself with the harmless mystification of
others; but, taken together, the more important letters—while
they usually evince his difficulty in finding the best expressions
of his thoughts and his constant struggle with the rules of his
mother tongue—place his truth and candor in a very favorable
light and sometimes rise into a rude eloquence. The reader feels
that when the writer is unjust he is under the influence of a mistake or passion—and, as a rule, it is not too late to detect such
injustice; that his errors of fact are simply mistakes, honestly
made and easily corrected; that if, in the mass, a few paragraphs
occur which can be neither fully justified nor excused, it is not
to be forgotten that they were not intended for our eyes and that
they were written under the constant pressure of a great calamity,
which made him doubly sensitive and irritable; and so it will
be easy, like Sterne's Recording Angel, to blot such passages with
a tear.

Another striking fact of Beethoven's correspondence, when
viewed as a whole, is the proof it affords that, except in his hours
of profound depression, he was far from being the melancholy
and gloomy character of popular belief. He shows himself here
—as he was by nature—of a gay and lively temperament, fond of
a jest, an inveterate though not always a very happy punster,
a great lover of wit and humor. It is a cause for profound
gratitude that it was so; since he thus preserved an elasticity
of spirits that enabled him to escape the consequences of brooding
in solitude over his great misfortune; to rise superior to his fate
and concentrate his great powers upon his self-imposed tasks; and
to meet with hope and courage the cruel fortune which put an
end to so many well-founded expectations and ambitious projects,
and confined him to a single road to fame and honor—that of
composition. It happens that several of the more valuable and
interesting of his letters belong to the period immediately following that now before us, and in them we are able to trace, with
reasonable accuracy, the effect which his incipient and increasing
deafness produced upon him—first, the anxiety caused by earliest
symptoms; then the profound grief bordering upon despair when
the final result had become certain; and at last his submission
to and acceptance of his fate. There is in truth something nobly
heroic in the manner in which Beethoven at length rose superior
to his great affliction. The magnificent series of works produced

in the ten years from 1798 to 1808 are no greater monuments to his genius than to the godlike resolution with which he wrought out the inspirations of that genius under circumstances most fitted to weaken its efforts and restrain its energies.

Beethoven was seldom without a folded sheet or two of music paper in his pocket upon which he wrote with pencil in two or three measures of music hints of any musical thought which might occur to him wherever he chanced to be. Towards the end of his life his Conversation Books often answered the same purpose; and there are traditions of bills-of-fare at dining-rooms having been honored with ideas afterwards made immortal. This habit gave Abbé Gelinek a foundation for the following amusing nonsense as related by Tomaschek: "He (Gelinek) declared," says Tomaschek,

as if it were an aphorism, that all of Beethoven's compositions were lacking in internal coherency and that not infrequently they were overloaded. These things he looked upon as grave faults of composition and sought to explain them from the manner in which Beethoven went about his work, saying that he had always been in the habit of noting every musical idea that occurred to him upon a bit of paper which he threw into a corner of his room, and that after a while there was a considerable pile of the memoranda which the maid was not permitted to touch when cleaning the room. Now when Beethoven got into a mood for work he would hunt a few musical *motivi* out of his treasure-heap which he thought might serve as principal and secondary themes for the composition in contemplation, and often his selection was not a lucky one. I (Tomaschek) did not interrupt the flow of his passionate, yet awkward speech, but briefly answered that I was unfamiliar with Beethoven's method of composing but was inclined to think that the aberrations occasionally to be found in his compositions were to be ascribed to his individuality, and that only an unprejudiced and keen psychologist, who had had an opportunity to observe Beethoven from the beginning of his artistic development to its maturity in order gradually to familiarize himself with his views on art, could fit himself to give the musical world an explanation of the intellectual cross-relationships in Beethoven's glorious works, a thing just as impossible to his blind enthusiasts as to his virulent opponents. Gelinek may have applied these last words to himself, and not incorrectly.

This conversation took place in 1814, the day after a rehearsal of Beethoven's Symphony in A—the Seventh! Gelinek's pile of little bits of paper in the corner of the room, when touched by the wand of truth, resolves itself into blank music books, to which his new ideas were transferred from the original slight pencil sketches, and frequently with two or three words to indicate the kind of composition to which they were suited. Divers anecdotes are current which pretend to give the origin of some

of the themes thus recorded and afterwards wrought out, but
few judicious readers will attach much weight to most of them.
For although conceptions can sometimes be traced directly to
their exciting causes, the musical composer can seldom say more
than that they occurred to him at such a time and place—and
often not even that. It is certainly not improbable that Beethoven's admirers may have questioned him upon this point, as
Schindler did upon the "Pastoral" Symphony, and that he was
able to satisfy them; but Handel's "Harmonious Blacksmith"
may be taken as the type of most of the current stories, which
only need truth to make them interesting.

To return to the sketchbooks—which performed a twofold
office; being not alone the registers of new conceptions, but containing the preliminary studies of the instrumental works into
which they were wrought out. The introduction to the excellent
pamphlet, "Ein Skizzenbuch von Beethoven, beschrieben und
in Auszügen dargestellt von Gustav Nottebohm," though properly
confined by him to the single book which he was describing, is
equally true of so many that have been examined with care as
to warrant its general application. The following extracts may
be taken as true of the greater part of the sketchbooks:

Before us (he says) lies a volume in oblong folio (*Teatro*) of 192
pages and bearing 16 staves on each page, and, save a few empty places,
containing throughout notes and sketches in Beethoven's handwriting for
compositions of various sorts. The volume is bound in craftsman's
style, trimmed, and has a stout pasteboard cover. It was bound thus
before it was used or received the notes. [Excepting the number of
pages this description applies to most of the true sketchbooks.] The
sketches are for the greater part one-part; that is, they occupy but a
single staff, only exceptionally are they on two or more staves. [In
some of the later books the proportion of sketches in two or more parts
is much greater than in this.] It is permissible to assume in advance that
they were written originally and in the order in which they follow each
other in the sketchbook. When a cursory glance over the whole does
not seem to contradict this assumption, a careful study nevertheless
compels a modification at times. It is to be observed that generally
Beethoven began a new page with a new composition; and, moreover,
that he worked alternately or simultaneously at different movements.
As a result, different groups of sketches are crowded so closely together
that in order to find room he was obliged to make use of spaces which
had been left open, and thus eventually sketches for the most different
compositions had to be mixed together and brought into companionship. [In some of the books "vi-" not infrequently meets the eye. It
was the one of Beethoven's modes of keeping the clue in the labyrinth
of sketches, being part of the word *vide*. The second syllable, "-de,"
can always be found on the same or a neighboring page. "N.B.,"

"No. 100," "No. 500," "No. 1000," etc., and in later sketches "meilleur," are common, all which signs are explained by Schindler as being a whimsical mode of estimating the comparative value of different musical ideas, or of forms of the same. Again Nottebohm continues: In spite of this confused working it is plain that Beethoven, as a rule, was conscious from the beginning of the goal for which he was striving, that he was true to his first concept and carried out the projected form to the end. The contrary is also true at times, and the sketchbook (like others) disclosed a few instances in which Beethoven in the course was led from the form originally conceived into another, so that eventually something different appeared from what was planned in the first instance. (Once more.) In general it may be observed that Beethoven in all his work begun in the sketchbook proceeded in the most varied manner, and at times reached his goal in a direction opposite to that upon which he first set out. [At times] the thematic style dominates; the first sketch breaks off abruptly with the principal subject and the work that follows is confined to transforming and reshaping the thematic kernel at first thrown on the paper until it appears to be fitted for development; then the same process is undertaken with intermediary sections; everywhere we find beginnings, never a whole; a whole comes before us only outside of the sketchbook, in the printed composition where sections which were scattered in the sketchbook are brought together. [In other cases] the thematic manner is excluded; every sketch is aimed at a unity and is complete in itself; the very first one gives the complete outline for a section of a movement; those that follow are then complete reshapings of the first, as other readings directed towards a change in the summary character, or a reformation of the whole, an extension of the middle sections, etc. Naturally, the majority of the sketches do not belong exclusively to either of the two tendencies, but hover between them, now leaning toward one, now toward the other.

One readily sees that, when the general plan of a work is clear and distinct before the mind, it is quite indifferent in what order the various parts are studied; and that Beethoven simply adopted the method of many a dramatic and other author, who sketches his scenes or chapters not in course but as mood, fancy or opportunity dictates. It is equally evident that the composer could have half a dozen works upon his hands at the same time, not merely without disadvantage to any one of them, but to the gain of all, since he could turn to one or another as the spirit of composition impelled; like the author of a profound literary work, who relieves and recreates his mind by varying his labors, and executes his grand task all the more satisfactorily, because he, from time to time, refreshes himself by turning his attention to other and lighter topics. When Beethoven writes to Wegeler: "As I am writing now I often compose three or four pieces at once," he could have referred only to the preliminary studies of the sketchbooks. Sometimes, it is true, works were laid aside incomplete after he had begun the task of writing them out in full, and finished when occasion demanded; but as a rule his practice was quite different, viz.: All the parts of a work having been thus studied until he had determined upon the form, character and style of every important division and subdivision, and recorded the results in his sketchbook by a few of the first measures, followed by "etc." or "and so on," the labor of composition may be said to have been finished, and there remained only the task of writing out the clean copy of what now existed full and complete in his mind, and of making such minor corrections and improvements as might occur to him on revision. The manuscripts show that these were sometimes very numerous, though they rarely extend to any change in the form or to any alteration in the grand effect except to heighten it, or render it more unexpected or exciting. When upon reflection he was dissatisfied with a movement as a whole he seems rarely to have attempted its improvement by mere correction, choosing rather to discard it at once and compose a new one based either upon the same themes or upon entirely new motives. The several overtures to "Fidelio" are illustrations of both procedures.

The sketches of the greater part of Beethoven's songs, after the Bonn period, are preserved, and prove with what extreme care he wrought out his melodies. The sketchbook analysed by Nottebohm affords a curious illustration in Matthison's "Opferlied," the melody being written out in full not less than six times, the theme in substance remaining unchanged. Absolute correctness of accent, emphasis, rhythm—of prosody, in short—was with him a leading object; and various papers, as well as the Conversation Books, attest his familiarity with metrical signs and his scrupulous obedience to metrical laws. Since the shameful mutilation and dispersion of Beethoven's manuscripts at the time of their sale, probably no one person has been able to trace and examine half of the sketchbooks; still, enough have come under observation during the researches for this work to establish with reasonable certainty these points:

I. That each sketchbook was filled in pretty regular course from beginning to end before a new one was taken.

II. That had the collection been kept entire it would have afforded the means of determining with a good degree of certainty the chronology of most of his instrumental works, after coming to Vienna, as to their first conception and studies—excluding, of course, those which, in one form or another, he brought with him from Bonn.

III. That the more important vocal compositions were studied separately.

IV. That only from the sketchbooks can an adequate idea of the vast fertility of Beethoven's genius be formed. They are in music, like Hawthorne's "Notebooks" in literature, the record of a never ceasing flow of new thoughts and ideas, until death sealed the fountain forever. There are themes and hints, never used, for all kinds of instrumental compositions, from the trifles, which he called "Bagatelles," to symphonies, evidently intended to be as different from those we know as they are from each other; and these hints are in such numbers, that those which can be traced in the published works are perhaps much the smaller proportion of the whole. Whoever has the will and opportunity to devote an hour or two to an examination of a few of these monuments of Beethoven's inventive genius, will easily comprehend the remark which he made near the close of his life: "It seems to me that I have just begun to compose!"[1]

One topic more demands brief notice before closing this chapter. In the "Merrymaking of the Countryfolk" of Beethoven's "Pastoral" Symphony, at the point where the fun grows most fast and furious and the excitement rises to its height, an ominous sound, as of distant thunder, gives the first faint warning of the coming storm. So in the life of the composer at the moment of that highest success and prosperity, which we have labored to place vividly before the mind of the reader, just when he could first look forward with well-grounded confidence to the noblest gratification of a musician's honorable ambition, a new and discordant element thrust itself into the harmony of his life. This was the symptoms of approaching deafness. His own account fixes their appearance in the year 1799; then they were still so feeble and intermittent, as to have caused him at first no serious anxiety; but in another year they had assumed so much the appearance of a chronic and increasing evil, as to compel him to abandon plans for travel which he had formed, and for which he was

---

[1]Opportunities for studying Beethoven's sketchbooks have greatly increased since Mr. Thayer wrote these words. Nottebohm, who rendered an incalculable service to all students of the great composer after the book from which our author quotes, published a volume entitled "Beethoveniana" in 1872, and a second entitled "Zweite Beethoveniana" in 1887. To these the revisors of this biography have repeatedly referred in tracing the history of Beethoven's compositions. A collection of sketches formerly owned by J. N. Kafka and now in the British Museum was described by Mr. J. S. Shedlock in "The Musical Times" (July to December, 1892). A volume containing sketches for the last quartets is at the present writing in the possession of Mr. Cecilio de Roda of Madrid and was described by the "Rivista Italiana" (Nos. XI-XIV, 1907) and also published in pamphlet form under the title "Un Quaderno di autografi di Beethoven del 1825."

preparing himself, with great industry and perseverance, to appear in
the twofold capacity of virtuoso and composer. Instead, therefore,
in 1801, of having "long since journeyed through half the world,"
he, for two years, had been confined to Vienna or its immediate
vicinity, vainly seeking relief from surgeons and physicians.

It is not difficult to imagine calamities greater than that
which now threatened Beethoven—as, the loss of sight to a Raphael
or Rubens in the height of their fame and powers; a partial
paralysis or other incurable disease of the brain cutting short the
career of a Shakespeare or Goethe, a Bacon or Kant, a Newton
or Humboldt. Better the untimely fate of a Buckle, than to
live long years of unavailing regret over the blasted hopes and
promise of early manhood. In such cases there remains no
resource; hope itself is dead. But to Beethoven, even if his
worst fears should prove prophetic and his infirmity at length
close all prospects of a career as virtuoso and conductor, the field
of composition still remained open. This he knew, and it saved
him from utter despair. Who can say that the world has not
been a gainer by a misfortune which stirred the profoundest
depths of his being and compelled the concentration of all his
powers into one direction?

As the disease made progress and the prospect of relief became
less, notwithstanding a grief and anxiety which caused him such
mental agony as even to induce the thought of suicide, he so well
succeeded in keeping it concealed from all but a few intimate
and faithful friends, that no notice whatever is to be found of
it until 1802 except in papers from his own hand. They form
a very touching contrast to his letters to other correspondents.
Neither the head nor the heart is to be envied of the man who
can read them without emotion. The two most important are
letters to Wegeler giving full details of his case; doubly valuable
because they are not merely letters to a friend, but an elaborate
account of the symptoms and medical treatment of his disease,
made to a physician of high standing who thoroughly understood the constitution of the patient. They are therefore alike
significant for what they contain and for what they omit. No
hypothesis as to the cause of the evil can be entertained, which
is discordant with them. Reserving them, however, for their
proper places in the order of time, a story or two inconsistent
with them may here be disposed of.

The so-called Fischoff Manuscript says

In the year 1796, Beethoven, on a hot summer day, came greatly
overheated to his home, threw open doors and windows, disrobed down

to his trousers and cooled himself in a draft at the open window. The
consequence was a dangerous sickness which, on his convalescence, settled
in his organs of hearing, and from this time his deafness steadily increased.

In this passage both the date and the averment are irreconcilable with the letters to Wegeler.

Dr. Weissenbach, in his "Reise zum Congress" (1814), gives
what appears to be the same story but in fewer words. "He
(Beethoven) once endured a fearful attack of typhus. From
this time dates the decay of his nervous system, and probably
also the, to him, great misfortune of the loss of hearing." Neither
a typhus nor a typhoid fever is a matter of a few days or weeks
if severe; and the chronology of our narrative is, to say the least,
so far fixed and certain as to exclude the possibility of his having
passed through any very serious illness of that nature since he
came to Vienna. But it is not at all improbable that, in 1784
or 1785, he may have been a victim to this frightful disorder,
and that it may have been the cause of his melancholy condition
of health at the time of his mother's death, and of the chronic
diarrhœa with which he was so long troubled. True, there is
no record of such an illness; but that proves nothing. There is
no record that he passed through an attack of small-pox, except
that which the disease left upon his face.

But the most extraordinary and inexplicable account of the
origin of his deafness is that given by Beethoven himself to the
English pianist, Charles Neate, in 1815. Mr. Neate was once
urging Beethoven to visit England and mentioned as a farther
inducement the great skill of certain English physicians in treating diseases of the ear, assuring him that he might cherish hopes
of relief. Beethoven replied in substance as follows: "No; I
have already had all sorts of medical advice. I shall never be
cured—I will tell you how it happened. I was once busy writing
an opera—

Neate: "Fidelio?"

Beethoven: "No. It was not 'Fidelio.' I had a very ill-
tempered, troublesome *primo tenore* to deal with. I had already
written two grand airs to the same text, with which he was dissatisfied, and now a third which, upon trial, he seemed to approve and
took away with him. I thanked the stars that I was at length
rid of him and sat down immediately to a work which I had
laid aside for those airs and which I was anxious to finish. I
had not been half an hour at work, when I heard a knock at my
door, which I at once recognized as that of my *primo tenore*. I
sprang up from my table under such an excitement of rage, that,

as the man entered the room, I threw myself upon the floor as they do upon the stage (here B. spread out his arms and made a gesture of illustration), coming down upon my hands. When I arose I found myself deaf and have been so ever since. The physicians say, the nerve is injured."

That Beethoven really related this strange story cannot be questioned; the word of the venerable Charles Neate to the author is sufficient on that point. What is to be thought of it, is a very different matter. Here at least it may stand without comment.

Chapter XVIII

Beethoven's Brothers—His First Concert on His Own Account—Punto and the Sonata for Horn—Steibelt Confounded—E. A. Förster and the First Quartets—The Septet and First Symphony—Beethoven's Homes—Hoffmeister—Compositions and Publications of 1800.

IT is not easy to conceive upon what ground the opinion became current, as it did, that Beethoven in the year 1800 and for several years to come was still burdened with the support of his brothers—young men now respectively in their 26th and 24th years. This mistake as to Johann has already been exposed. Leaving Ludwig for the first quarter of this year doubly busy—having, in addition to his usual occupations, his preparations to make for a grand concert in April—we turn, for a page, to his brother Carl.

In the "Hof- und Staats-Schematismus" for the year 1800, at the end of the list of persons employed in the "K. K. Universal-Staatschuldenkasse" are the names of two "Praktikanten"; the first is "Mr. Carl v. Beethoven lives in the Sterngasse, 484." In the same publication appears a new department or bureau of the above-named office called the "K. K. n. öst. Klassen-Steuer-Kasse" and the second of the three bureau officers is "Mr. Carl v. Beethoven lives unterm Tuchladen, 605."

It is not improbable that, while simply "Praktikant," he may have needed occasional pecuniary aid, but his preferment to the place of "Kassa-Officier" rendered him independent. This appointment is dated March 24th, 1800, and gave him a salary of 250 florins. Small as the sum now appears, it was amply sufficient, with what he could earn by teaching music (and the brother of the great Beethoven could have no lack of pupils), to enable him to live comfortably. In fact, he was better off than many a colleague in the public service, who still with care and economy managed to live respectably. It may therefore be confidently asserted that Beethoven was henceforth relieved of all care on account of Carl, as of Johann, until the bankruptcy of the government and Carl's broken health many years later, made fraternal assistance indispensable.

At the beginning of this year Carl had tried his fortune as a composer—but probably with slender profit, since no second venture has been discovered. Six minuets, six "Deutsche" and six contradances by him are advertised in the "Wiener Zeitung" of January 11, in double editions, one for clavier and one for two violins and violoncello. The concert for which Beethoven had been preparing during the winter took place on the 2d of April. It was his first public appearance for his own benefit in Vienna, and, so far as is known, anywhere except in Prague. All that is now to be ascertained in relation to it is contained in the advertisement, in the programme, and in a single notice, sent to the "Allgemeine Musikalische Zeitung." The programme, which was in the possession of Madame van Beethoven (widow of the composer's nephew) is as follows:

To-day, Wednesday, April 2nd, 1800, Herr *Ludwig van Beethoven* will have the honor to give a grand concert for his benefit in the Royal Imperial Court Theatre beside the Burg. The pieces which will be performed are the following:

1. A grand symphony by the late Chapelmaster Mozart.
2. An aria from "The Creation" by the Princely Chapelmaster Herr Haydn, sung by Mlle. Saal.
3. A grand Concerto for the Pianoforte, played and composed by Herr *Ludwig van Beethoven*.
4. A Septet, most humbly and obediently dedicated to Her Majesty the Empress, and composed by Herr *Ludwig van Beethoven* for four stringed and three wind-instruments, played by Messrs. Schuppanzigh, Schreiber, Schindlecker, Bär, Nickel, Matauschek and Dietzel.
5. A Duet from Haydn's "Creation," sung by Mr. and Mlle. Saal.
6. Herr *Ludwig van Beethoven* will improvise on the pianoforte.
7. A new grand symphony with complete orchestra, composed by Herr *Ludwig van Beethoven*.

Tickets for boxes and stalls are to be had of Herr van Beethoven at his lodgings in the Tiefen Graben, No. 241, third storey, and of the box-keeper.

Prices of admission are as usual.

The beginning is at half-past 6 o'clock.

The correspondent of the "Allgemeine Musikalische Zeitung" described the concert as the most interesting affair of its kind given for a long time, said the new concerto had "many beauties, especially in the first two movements," praised the "taste and feeling" exhibited in the Septet, and in the Symphony found "much art, novelty and wealth of ideas"; but, he continues: "unfortunately there was too much use of the wind-instruments, so that the music sounded more as if written for a military band than an orchestra." The rest of the notice is devoted to scolding the band for inattention to the conductor. Which of the piano-forte Concertos Beethoven played on this occasion is nowhere intimated. The Symphony in C soon became known throughout Germany; while the Septet achieved a sudden popularity so widely extended and enduring as at length to become an annoyance to the composer.[1]

Before the month was out Beethoven again played in public in a concert given by Johann Stich, known as Punto. This Bohemian virtuoso, after several years of wandering, had lately come to Vienna from Paris, *via* Munich. As a performer upon the horn he was unrivalled by any predecessor or contemporary; but as a composer he was beneath criticism. Beethoven's delight in any one whose skill afforded him new experience of the powers and possible effects of any orchestral instrument is known to the reader. Nothing more natural, therefore, than his readiness to compose a sonata for himself and Punto to be played at the latter's concert on April 18th. Ries informs us that "though the concert was announced with the Sonata the latter was not yet begun. Beethoven began the work the day before the performance and it was ready for the concert." His habit of merely sketching his own part and of trusting to his memory and the inspiration of the moment, even when producing his grand Concertos in public, probably rendered him good service on this occasion. The "Allgemeine Musikzeitung" (III, 704) preserves also the interesting fact that owing to the enthusiastic applause the Sonata was immediately repeated.

April 27th was the anniversary of the day on which Maximilian Franz entered Bonn to assume the duties of Elector and Archbishop. Sixteen years had passed and on this day he, with a small retinue, again entered Vienna. He took refuge "in an Esterhazy villa in a suburb," while the small château near

---

[1] "He could not endure his Septet and grew angry because of the universal applause with which it was received." (Czerny to Jahn.) "The theme of the Variations is said to be a Rhenish folksong." (*Ibid.*)

which now stands the railway station at Hetzendorf, behind
Schönbrunn Garden, was preparing for his residence; whither he
soon removed, and where for the present we leave him.

At the end of February or early in March, the charlatan
Daniel Steibelt gave a concert in Prague which brought him in
1800 florins, and in April or May, "having finished his speculation,
he went to Vienna, his purse filled with ducats, where he was
knocked in the head by the pianist Beethoven," says Tomaschek.
Ries relates how:

When Steibelt came to Vienna with his great name, some of Beethoven's friends grew alarmed lest he do injury to the latter's reputation.
Steibelt did not visit him; they met first time one evening at the house
of Count Fries, where Beethoven produced his new Trio in B-flat major
for Pianoforte, Clarinet and Violoncello (Op. 11), for the first time.[1]
There is no opportunity for particular display on the part of the pianist
in this Trio.   Steibelt listened to it with a sort of condescension, uttered
a few compliments to Beethoven and felt sure of his victory.   He played
a Quintet of his own composition, improvised, and made a good deal of
effect with his tremolos, which were then something entirely new.   Beethoven could not be induced to play again.   A week later there was
again a concert at Count Fries's; Steibelt again played a quintet which
had a good deal of success.   He also played an improvisation (which
had, obviously, been carefully prepared) and chose the same theme on
which Beethoven had written variations in his Trio.[2]   This incensed
the admirers of Beethoven and him; he had to go to the pianoforte and
improvise.   He went in his usual (I might say, ill-bred) manner to
the instrument as if half-pushed, picked up the violoncello part of
Steibelt's quintet in passing, placed it (intentionally?) upon the stand
upside down and with one finger drummed a theme out of the first few
measures.   Insulted and angered he improvised in such a manner that
Steibelt left the room before he finished, would never again meet him
and, indeed, made it a condition that Beethoven should not be invited
before accepting an offer.

It was, and still is, the custom at Vienna for all whose vocations and pecuniary circumstances render it possible, to spend
all or some portion of the summer months in the country.
The aristocracies of birth and wealth retire to their country-seats,
live in villas for the season or join the throngs at the great watering-places; other classes find refuge in the villages and hamlets
which abound in the lovely environs of the city, where many a
neat cottage is built for their use and where the peasants generally
have a spare room or two, cleanly kept and neatly furnished.
Beethoven's habit of escaping from town during the hot months

[1]This is, of course, an error, as the Trio had been before the public since October
3rd, 1798.
[2]From Weigl's "Corsair aus Liebe."

was, therefore, nothing peculiar to him. We have reached the point whence, with little if any interruption, Beethoven can be followed from house to house, in city and country, through the rest of his life; a matter of great value in fixing the true dates of important letters and determining the chronology of his life and works—but for the first seven years the record is very incomplete.

Carl Holz told Jahn: "He (Beethoven) lived at first in a little attic-room in the house of the book-binder Strauss in the Alservorstadt, where he had a miserable time." This is one of the facts which an inquisitive young man like Holz would naturally learn of the master during the short period when he was his factotum. This attic-room must have been soon changed for the room "on the ground-floor" mentioned in a previous chapter. An undated note of van Swieten is directed to Beethoven at "No. 45 Alsergasse, at Prince Lichnowsky's"; but in the Vienna directory for 1804 no street is so named, and the only number 45 in the "Alsergrund" is in the Lämmelgasse, property of Georg Musial; but Prince Josef Lichnowsky is named as owner of No. 125 in the Hauptstrasse of that suburb. This was the same house; it had merely changed numbers. The site is now occupied by the house No. 30 Alserstrasse. Thence Beethoven went as a guest to the house occupied by Prince Lichnowsky. In May, 1795, Beethoven, in advertising the Trios, Op. 1, gives the "residence of the author" as the "Ogylisches Haus in the Kreuzgasse behind the Minorite church, No. 35 in the first storey"; but that is no reason to think that Prince Lichnowsky then lived there. Where Beethoven was during the next few years has not been ascertained, but, as has been seen by the concert bill on a preceding page, he was during the winter of 1799–1800 in the Tiefen Graben "in a very high and narrow house," as Czerny wrote to F. Luib.[1] For the summer of 1800, he took quarters for himself and servant in one of those houses in Unter-Döbling, an hour's walk, perhaps, from town, to which the readiest access is by the bridge over the brook on the North side of the Döbling hospital for the insane. The wife of a distinguished Vienna advocate occupied with her children another part of the same

___

[1]According to Frimmel, "Beethoven's Wohnungen," Vienna "Neue Freie Presse," August 11, 1899, this house was that of Court Councillor Greiner, then No. 241, afterwards 235, now No. 10 in the Tiefen Graben which, slightly altered, still remains. On the strength of Czerny's statement that one had to look up to the fifth or sixth storey to see Beethoven, and the old report that Beethoven lived "in the Kleine Weintraube," Frimmel was led to think that possibly he lived in one of the houses on the higher ground behind the Greiner house to which there was access from the open place "Am Hof" as well as from the houses in the Tiefen Graben and the Greiner house. The houses which bore the sign "Zur Weintraube" were situated "am Hofe."

house.   One of these children was Grillparzer, afterward famous
as a poet.   The zeal with which Beethoven at this period labored
to perfect his pianoforte playing, and his dislike to being listened
to, have been already noted.   Madame Grillparzer was a lady of
fine taste and culture, fond of music and therefore able to appreciate the skill of her fellow-lodger, but ignorant of his aversion
to listeners.   Her son, in 1861, still remembered Beethoven's
incessant practice and his mother's habit of standing outside her
own door to enjoy his playing.   This continued for some time;
but one day Beethoven sprang from the instrument to the door,
opened it, looked out to see if any one was listening, and unfortunately discovered the lady.   From that moment he played no
more.   Madame Grillparzer, thus made aware of his sensitiveness
on this point, informed him through his servant that thenceforth her door into the common passageway should be kept
locked, and she and her family would solely use another.   It
was of no avail; Beethoven played no more.

Another authentic and characteristic anecdote can belong
only to this summer.   There lived in a house hard by a peasant
of no very good reputation, who had a daughter remarkably
beautiful, but also not of the best fame.   Beethoven was greatly
captivated by her and was in the habit of stopping to gaze at
her when he passed by where she was at work in farmyard or
field.   She, however, made no return of his evident liking and
only laughed at his admiration.   On one occasion the father was
arrested for engaging in a brawl and imprisoned.   Beethoven took
the man's part and went to the magistrates to obtain his release.
Not succeeding, he became angry and abusive, and in the end
would have been arrested for his impertinence but for the strong
representations made by some, who knew him, of his position in
society and of the high rank, influence and power of his friends.

Throughout this period of Beethoven's life, each summer is
distinguished by some noble composition, completed, or nearly
so, so that on his return to the city it was ready for revision and
his copyist.   Free from the demands of society, his time was his
own; his fancy was quickened, his inspiration strengthened, in
field and forest labor was a delight.   The most important work
of the master bears in his own hand the date, 1800, and may
reasonably be supposed to have been the labor of this summer.
It is the Concerto in C minor for Pianoforte and Orchestra, Op. 37.

At the approach of autumn Beethoven returned to his old
quarters in the Tiefen Graben.   In this year Krumpholz introduced
to him Johann Emanuel (possibly Johann Nepomuk Emanuel)

Doležalek, a young man of 20 years, born in Chotieborz in Bohemia, who had come to Vienna to take lessons from Albrechtsberger. He played the pianoforte and violoncello, was a capable musician, in his youth a rather popular composer of Bohemian songs and then, for half a century, one of the best teachers in the capital. Toward the close of his life he was frequently occupied with the arrangement of private concerts, chiefly quartet parties, for Prince Czartoryski and other prominent persons. As long as he lived he was an enthusiastic admirer of Beethoven, and enjoyed the friendship of the composer till his death. Among his observations are the statements concerning the hatred of Beethoven felt by the Vienna musicians already noted. Koželuch, he relates, threw the C minor Trio at his (Doležalek's) feet when the latter played it to him. Speaking of Beethoven, Koželuch said to Haydn: "We would have done that differently, wouldn't we, Papa?" and Haydn answered, smilingly, "Yes, we would have done that differently." Haydn, says Doležalek, could not quite reconcile himself with Beethoven's music. It was Doležalek who witnessed the oft-told scene in the Swan tavern when Beethoven insisted on paying without having eaten.

One of the most prolific and popular composers whom Beethoven found in Vienna was Franz Anton Hoffmeister, "Chapelmaster and R. I. licensed Music, Art and Book Seller." He was an immigrant from the Neckar valley and (born 1754) much older than Beethoven, to whom he had extended a warm sympathy and friendship, doubly valuable from his somewhat similar experience as a young student in Vienna. This is evident from the whole tone of their correspondence. In 1800, Hoffmeister left Vienna and in Leipzig formed a copartnership with Ambrosius Kühnel, organist of the Electoral Saxon Court Chapel, and established a publishing house there, still retaining his business in Vienna. As late as December 5, 1800, his signature is as above given; but on the 1st of January, 1801, the advertisements in the public press announce the firm of "Hoffmeister and Kühnel, *Bureau de Musique* in Leipzig." Since 1814 the firm name has been C. F. Peters. Knowing Beethoven personally and so intimately, it is alike creditable to the talents of the one and the taste and appreciation of the other that Hoffmeister, immediately upon organizing his new publishing house, should have asked him for manuscripts. To his letter he received an answer dated Dec. 15, 1800, in which Beethoven says:

. . . . *Per primo* you must know that I am very sorry that you, my dear brother in music, did not earlier let me know something (of your doings) so that I might have marketed my quartets with you, as well as many other pieces which I have sold, but if Mr. Brother is as conscientious as many other honest engravers who grave us poor composers to death, you will know how to derive profit from them when they appear. I will now set forth in brief what Mr. Brother can have from me.   I^{mo} a Septet *per il Violino, Viola, Violoncello, Contrabasso, Clarinetto, Corno, Fagotto—tutti obligati.* (I cannot write anything not obligato for I came into this world with an obligato accompaniment.)   This Septet has pleased greatly.   For more frequent use the three wind-instruments, namely *Fagotto, Clarinetto* and *Corno* might be transcribed for another violin, viola and violoncello.   II° A grand Symphony for full orchestra. III° A Concerto for pianoforte which I do not claim to be one of my best, as well as another one which will be published here by Mollo (this for the information of the Leipzig critics) because I am for the present keeping the better ones for myself until I make a tour; but it will not disgrace you to publish it.   IV° A grand Solo Sonata.[1]   That is all that I can give you at this moment.   A little later you may have a Quintet for stringed instruments as well as, probably, Quartets and other things which I have not now with me.   In your reply you might set the prices and as you are neither a Jew nor an Italian, nor I either one or the other, we shall no doubt come to an understanding.

The reference to the Quartets, Op. 18, in this letter, taken in connection with the apologies for long delay in writing, indicates conclusively enough that at least the first set, the first three, had been placed in the hands of Mollo and Co. early in the autumn, and it is barely possible, not probable, that they had already been issued from the press.[2]   The importance of these Quartets in the history both of Beethoven and of chamber music renders very desirable more definite information upon their origin and dates of composition than the incomplete, unsatisfactory and not always harmonious data already known, afford.   The original manuscripts appear to have been lost.

Von Lenz quotes in his "Critical Catalogue of Beethoven's Works" an anecdote from a pamphlet printed at Dorpat in which is related:

After Beethoven had composed his well-known String Quartet in F major he played for his friend (Amenda) (on the pianoforte?) the glorious *Adagio* (D minor, 9-8 time) and asked him what thought had been awakened by it.   "It pictured for me the parting of two lovers,"

---

[1]In B-flat, Op. 22.

[2]The Pianoforte Concerto offered to Hoffmeister was that in B-flat.   It was published by Hoffmeister and Kühnel toward the end of 1801 and advertised on January 16, 1802.   The Concerto published by Mollo was that in C major.   A letter written to Breitkopf and Härtel on the same day contains the equivalent of the remark: "I am for the present keeping the better ones for myself until I make a tour," which is significant, since it makes it sure that other concertos were at least planned and that the one in C minor was looked upon as finished by Beethoven.

was the answer. "Good!" remarked Beethoven, "I thought of the scene
in the burial vault in 'Romeo and Juliet'."

This Quartet existed, then, before Amenda left Vienna. Czerny
says in his notes for Jahn: "Of the first six Violin Quartets that
in D major, No. 3 in print, was the very first composed by Beethoven. On the advice of Schuppanzigh he called that in F major
No. 1, although it was composed later." Ries confirms this: "Of
his Violin Quartets, Op. 18, he composed that in D major first of
all. That in F major, which now precedes it, was originally the
third."[1] *Nota bene* that neither Czerny nor Ries spoke from personal
observation at the time of composition; they must both have
learned the fact from Beethoven himself, or, more probably, from
dates on the original manuscripts. A criticism of three quartets
which appeared in the "Allg. Mus. Zeitung" in 1799, which failed
to give the name of the composer, has been applied by some writers
(by Langhans in his History of Music, for instance) to Beethoven's
Op. 18; but erroneously. They were the works of Emanuel Aloys
Förster (born January 26, 1748, in Neurath, Upper Silesia, died
November 12, 1823, in Vienna), a musician who was so highly
esteemed by Beethoven that, on one occasion at least, he called
him his "old master." The phrase can easily be interpreted to
mean that Beethoven found instruction in Förster's chamber
music which he heard at the soirées of Prince Lichnowsky and
other art-patrons. Förster's compositions, not many of which
have been preserved in print, are decidedly Beethovenish in character. His eldest son, who in 1870 was still living in Trieste,
remembered Beethoven perfectly well from 1803 to 1813, and
communicated to the author of this biography some reminiscences
well worth preserving. It is known from other sources that Beethoven, after the retirement of Albrechtsberger, considered Förster
to be the first of all the Vienna teachers of counterpoint and
composition, and this is confirmed by the son's statement that it
was on Beethoven's advice that he sent to press the compendious
"Anleitung zum Generalbass" which Breitkopf and Härtel published in 1805. A year or two later, Count Rasoumowsky applied
to Beethoven for instruction in musical theory and especially in
quartet composition. Beethoven absolutely refused, but so
strongly recommended his friend Förster, that the latter was engaged. Förster's dwelling in all those years was a favorite resort
of the principal composers and dilettanti. Thither came Beethoven; Zmeskall, a very precise gentleman with abundant white

[1] In reality it was the second, as the Amenda parts show.

hair; Schuppanzigh, a short fat man with a huge belly; Weiss, tall and thin; Linke, the lame violoncellist, Henry Eppinger, the Jewish violin dilettante, the youthful Mayseder, J. N. Hummel, and others. The regular periods of these quartet meetings were Sunday at noon, and the evening of Thursday; but Beethoven in those years often spent other evenings with Förster, "when the conversation usually turned upon musical theory and composition." Notwithstanding the wide difference in their ages (22 years), their friendship was cordial and sincere. The elder not only appreciated and admired the genius of the younger, but honored him as a man; and spoke of him as being not only a great musical composer, but, however at times rough in manner and harsh, even rude, in speech, of a most honorable and noble nature. Add to all this the fact, that Beethoven in later years recommended Förster to pupils as his own "old master," and it is no forced and unnatural inference, that he (Beethoven) had studied quartet composition with him, as he had counterpoint with Albrechtsberger, and operatic writing with Salieri. Nor is this inference weakened—it is rather strengthened—by some points in what now follows:

The earliest mention of a string quartet in connection with Beethoven is that proposal by Count Appony cited from Wegeler which led to no instant result. Then comes a passage from a letter to Amenda: "Do not give your Quartet to anybody, because I have greatly changed it, having learned how to write quartets properly." Had he learned from study under Förster?

The original manuscripts being lost, further chronological notices concerning them must be sought for in the sketchbooks. Here Nottebohm comes to our assistance. In the Petter collection at Vienna there are sketches for the last movement of the G major Quartet, the last movement of the B-flat Quartet (among them one which was discarded), both deviating from the printed form more or less, and one for the last movement of the F major Quartet, this approaching pretty closely the ultimate form; thus this quartet was farther advanced than the others. Associated with this sketch are sketches for the Sonata in B-flat, Op. 22, and for the easy Variations in G major which were begun while work was in progress on the last movement of the Quartet in G. Beethoven worked simultaneously on the first movement of Op. 22 and the scherzo of the first Quartet; while working on the last movement of the Quartet in B-flat the rondo of the Sonata was begun. The sketches date from 1799 and 1800. Inasmuch as they occur before those for the Horn Sonata, which was composed very hurriedly and performed on April 18, 1800, the sketches were doubtless written earlier. One of the variations of the Quartet in A major was sketched much earlier—in 1794 or 1795. A little sketch for the first movement of the F major Quartet found beside sketches for the Violin Sonata, Op. 24, no doubt belongs to the revised form of the Quartet. In a sketchbook formerly in the possession of Grassnick in Berlin, there are sketches for the Quartet in D major which are near the ultimate form, except that there is a different theme for the last movement. Then comes a beginning in G major inscribed "Quartet 2," the germ of the theme of the second Quartet. There was, therefore, at the time no second Quartet, and that in D is the first. There follows "Der Kuss," sketches for the "Opferlied," the Rondo in G major, Op. 51, No. 2, to a passage from Schiller's "Ode to Joy," to Gellert's "Meine Lebenszeit verstreicht," in G minor, to an intermezzo for pianoforte, to the revised form of the B-flat Concerto (which he played in Prague in 1798), and to various songs. The indications are, therefore, that the sketches were written in 1798. Then come sketches for the variations on "La stessa, la stessissima," which originated and were published in the beginning of 1799, and after them extended sketches for the first movement of the F major Quartet, of which those belonging to the first movement are in an advanced stage, those for the second movement less so. A few sketches for a "third" quartet (thus specified) which were not used show that there was no third at the time; therefore, the Quartet in F is the second and was planned in 1799. Another sketchbook contains the continuation of the sketches for the F major Quartet, and, indeed, for all the movements; then an unused sketch for a "third" quartet (still not yet in existence), then to two songs by Goethe (one "Ich denke dein"), then to the movements of the G major Quartet, which is thus indicated to have been the third (the intermezzo in the second movement was conceived later), further sketches for the A major Quartet, which, it follows, was the fourth. Among these sketches are others for the Septet and the Variations on "Kind, willst du ruhig schlafen?" which appeared in December in 1799, and was therefore not composed earlier. All these sketches date from 1798 and 1799; but the Quartets were not finished. In an unused sketch for the Adagio of the quartet in F occur the words: "Les derniers soupirs," which confirm the story told by Amenda. The continuation of the G major Quartet dates to 1800. Up to now no sketches for the Quartet in C minor have been found.

The results of this chronological investigation may be summed up as follows: The composition of the Quartets was begun in

1798, that in D, the third, being first undertaken. This was followed by that in F and soon after, or simultaneously, work was begun on that in G, which was originally designed as the second; but, as that in F was completed earlier, this was designated as the second by Beethoven, and that in G became in point of time the third. The Quartet in F was finished in its original shape by June 25, 1799, on which day he gave it to Amenda; he revised it later. Whether or not this was also done with the others cannot be said; there is no evidence. The remark made in 1801, that he had just learned to write quartets, need not be read as meaning that he had formal instruction from Förster, but is amply explained by his practice on the six Quartets; yet Förster may have influenced him strongly. He then wrote the one in A (now No. 5), intending it to be the fourth; in this he seems to have made use of a *motif* invented at an earlier period. The Quartets in B-flat and C minor followed, the latter being, perhaps, the last. The definitive elaboration of the Quartets lasted certainly until 1800, possibly until 1801. The Quartets then appeared in two sets from the press of Mollo. It is likely that the first three, at least, were in the hands of the publisher before the end of 1800, as is proved by the letter to Hoffmeister. The first three appeared in the summer of 1801 and were advertised as on sale by Nägeli in Zurich already in July; they were mentioned in the "Allg. Musik. Zeitung" on August 26, and in Spazier's "Zeitung für die Elegante Welt." In October of the same year the last three appeared and Mollo advertised them in the "Wiener Zeitung" of October 28. The Quartets are dedicated to Prince Lobkowitz.

Notice of a valuable present to Beethoven from his lenient and generous patron, Prince Carl Lichnowsky, naturally connects itself with the story of the Quartets—a gift thus described by Alois Fuchs, formerly violinist in the Imperial Court Orchestra, under date of December 2, 1846:

Ludwig van Beethoven owned a complete quartet of excellent Italian instruments given to him by his princely patron and friend Lichnowsky at the suggestion of the famous quartet-player Schuppanzigh. I am in a position to describe each of the instruments in detail.

1. A violin made by Joseph Guarnerius in Cremona in the year 1718 is now in the possession of Mr. Karl Holz, director of the *Concerts spirituels* in Vienna.

2. The second violin (which was offered for sale) was made by Nicholas Amati in the year 1667, and was in the possession of Dr. Ohmeyer, who died recently in Hütteldorf; it has been purchased by Mr. Huber.

3. The viola, made by Vincenzo Ruger in 1690, is also the property of Mr. Karl Holz.

4. The violoncello, an Andreas Guarnerius of the year 1712, is in the possession of Mr. P. Wertheimber of Vienna.

The seal of Beethoven has been impressed under the neck of each instrument and on the back of each Beethoven scratched a big B, probably for the purpose of protecting himself against an exchange. The instruments are all well preserved and in good condition. The most valuable one, without question, is the violin by Joseph Guarnerius, which is distinguished by extraordinary power of tone, for which, indeed, Mr. Holz has refused an offer of 1000 florins.

The four instruments were bought by Peter Th. Jokits in 1861, who gave them to the Royal Library at Berlin. Beethoven received them from Lichnowsky certainly before 1802, but in what year is unknown.[1] Another proof of the Prince's regard and generosity, however, belongs to this, namely, an annuity of 600 florins to be continued until the composer should find some suitable permanent employment.

The only known publication of the year 1800 is the Rondo in G major, Op. 51, No. 2, which came from the press of Simrock. As for the compositions of the year it is safe to assume that Beethoven put the finishing touches to the first Symphony, the Septet, Op. 20, and the Quartets, Op. 18. Furthermore, there can be little doubt but that the Sonata for Horn, Op. 17, the Pianoforte Sonata, Op. 22, the Concerto in C minor, and the Variations for Four Hands on the melody of the song "Ich denke dein," belong to this year. The "Variations très faciles" on an original theme in G were sketched and probably completed. The only chronological clues to the Horn Sonata are the date of its first performance, April 18, 1800, and the anecdote by Ries concerning the rapid completion of the work. No sketches have been found and nothing is known of the autograph; but according to Nottebohm the beginning of a clean copy of the Adagio is to be found among the sketches for the Sonatas Op. 22 and 23. Punto was still in Munich in 1800, and since the work seems assuredly to have been designed for him, there is equal certainty that it was composed in that year. It was published by Mollo in March, 1801. The Septet, for four strings and three wind-instruments, dedicated

---

[1] Holz sold the Guarnerius Violin in 1852 (see the "Allgemeine Deutsche Musikzeitung" of 1888). When the Beethoven Museum in Bonn was dedicated, the instruments were borrowed from the authorities of the Royal Library, and exhibited in a glass case, where they remain by sufferance of the Prussian authorities.

to the Empress Maria Theresia, was played at the concert at which
the Symphony in C major was brought forward, April 2, 1800;
but it had been heard previously in the house of Prince Schwarzenberg. Inasmuch as sketches for it are found among those for
the Quartets, specially the one in A major, which belong to the
year 1799, its inception may be placed in that year, though it
was probably finished in 1800 shortly before its performance.
There is no date on the autograph. It was offered to Hoffmeister
in the letter of December 15, 1800, and was published by him in
1802. The Septet speedily won great popularity and was frequently transcribed. Hoffmeister had an arrangement for string
quintet which he advertised on August 18, 1802. Ries thought
that Beethoven had made it, but he was in error; nevertheless,
Beethoven gave Hoffmeister permission to publish an arrangement in which strings were substituted for the wind-instruments,
and himself transcribed it as a pianoforte trio with violin or
clarinet *ad lib*. This arrangement was made as a tribute of gratitude from the composer to his new physician, Dr. Johann Schmidt.
The doctor played the violin and his daughter the pianoforte,
both fairly well, and Beethoven arranged his popular piece for
family use and, as was customary at the time, gave Dr. Schmidt
the exclusive possession of the music for a year.[1]

The theme of the minuet in the Septet was borrowed from
the Pianoforte Sonata, Op. 49, No. 2, but its treatment is original.
There has been considerable controversy without absolutely definitive result touching the melody which is varied in the Andante.
Kretschmer, in his "Deutsche Volkslieder" (Berlin, 1838; Vol. I,
No. 102, p. 181), prints the melody in connection with a Rhenish
folksong ("Ach Schiffer, lieber Schiffer"), and there is a tradition
that Czerny said that it was taken by Beethoven from that
source. Nottebohm offers evidence deserving of consideration
that the melody is a folktune; but Ries and Wegeler, who lived
on the Rhine, had nothing to say on the subject. Erk and Böhme
("Deutscher Liederhort," Vol. I, p. 273) publish folksongs dealing
with the legend which is at the base of "Ach Schiffer, lieber
Schiffer," but the melody of the Andante is not to be found among
them, and Böhme gives it as his opinion that the song printed
by Kretschmer was written to Beethoven's melody by Kretschmer's collaborator Zuccalmaglio. It is not likely that the melody,
had it lived in the mouths of the people, would have escaped so
industrious a collector as Erk, who, moreover, was a native of

---

[1]See the dedication in Kalischer's collection of Beethoven's letters translated by
J. S. Shedlock, Vol. I, p. 94.

the Rhine country. The evidence would seem to indicate that the melody was original with Beethoven.

The Pianoforte Sonata in B-flat, Op. 22, also belongs to this year, as appears from the fact that it was offered to Hoffmeister in the letter of December 15. It was still in an unfinished state on the completion of the Sonata for Horn, as is shown by the circumstance that sketches of it are mingled with a fair transcript of a passage from the latter work. There are also sketches for Op. 22, among those for the Quartet in B-flat, Op. 18, No. 6, and the later movements of the Quartet in F—no doubt the revision. The sketches therefore belong to the year 1800, but may date back to 1799, from which it would appear that Beethoven worked an unusually long time on the Sonata. The principal labor was performed most likely in the summer of 1800, which Beethoven spent at Unterdöbling. It was published in 1802 by Hoffmeister and Kühnel. Sketches from the "Six Easy Variations" are found amongst some for the last movement of the Quartet in G, which seem to be nearly finished. Again we can fix the year as 1799 or 1800. Of special importance is the fact that the theme of the Variations is the same as the first episode of the rondo of the Sonata in B-flat, and the circumstance that the sketches are of almost the same date indicates that the identity was not accidental. The Variations were advertised as new by Traeg on December 16, 1800.

The Variations in D for four hands on the melody of Goethe's poem, "Ich denke dein," were conceived at practically the same time as those just described. Beethoven at first intended to give each stanza a separate setting, and to this end made two sketches, which are associated with the Quartet sketches and belong to the year 1799. He then took the melody of the first stanza as a theme for variations for four hands in the same year and wrote them into the autograph album of two sisters, the countesses Therese Brunswick and Josephine Deym. On September 22, 1803, he offered them to Hoffmeister in the place of the Trio Variations, Op. 44, with the remark that he considered them better than the latter. Hoffmeister, however, published the Trio Variations (in 1804). The Variations in D were not published until the beginning of 1805, and were described as having been written in 1800 for the two countesses mentioned, and dedicated to them.

An autograph preserved in the Royal Library in Berlin contains four of the variations on "Ich denke dein," an Adagio in F major noted on four staves (three with treble, one with the bass clef), a Scherzo in G major, $\frac{3}{4}$ time, and an Allegro in G major, $\frac{2}{4}$. Albert Kopfermann, who published the Adagio for the first time in No. 12, Vol. I, of "Die Musik," considers, no doubt correctly, that the three compositions were written for an automatic musical instrument. Though the number of new compositions produced in 1800 was small, attention must be directed to the fact that the revision and completion of works for publication, together with the planning of new works, gave a deal of occupation to Beethoven. Amongst the compositions made ready for the printer were the Quartets, which were not ready till near the end of the year. To them must be added the Sonata in E-flat, Op. 27, No. 1, and the Concerto in C minor, the autograph of which distinctly bears the date 1800. It is certain, moreover, that Beethoven began working on "Prometheus" in this year, and the summer must have been a busy one for him.

Chapter XIX

The Year 1801—Concerts for Wounded Soldiers—Vigano and the Ballet "Prometheus"—Stephan von Breuning—Hetzendorf—"Christus am Ölberg"—Compositions and Publications of the Year—The Funeral March in the Sonata, Op. 26—The "Moonlight" Sonata—The Quintet, Op. 29.

THE tone of Beethoven's correspondence and the many proofs of his untiring industry during the winter 1800–1 and early part of the succeeding spring, suggest a mind at ease, rejoicing in the exercise of its powers, and a body glowing with vigorous health. But for his own words to Wegeler: "I have been really miserable this winter," the passing allusions to ill health in his replies to Hoffmeister's letters would merely impress the reader as being half-groundless apologies for lack of punctuality in writing. This chapter will exhibit the young master both as he appeared to the public and as he showed himself in confidential intercourse to the few in whose presence he put aside the mask and laid open his heart; and will, therefore, it is believed, be found fully to justify what has been said of his heroic energy, courage and endurance under a trouble of no ordinary nature.

In the beginning of the year he wrote to Hoffmeister[1] as follows under date "January 15 (or thereabouts), 1801":

. . . . Your enterprises delight me also and I wish that if works of art ever bring profit that it might go to real artists instead of mere shopkeepers.

The fact that you purpose to publish the works of *Sebastian Bach* does good to my heart which beats only for the lofty and magnificent art of this patriarch of harmony, and I hope soon to see them in vigorous sale. I hope, as soon as golden peace has been declared, to be helpful in many ways, especially if you offer the works for subscription.

---

[1]Beethoven's carelessness in respect of dates, or a characteristic indifference to the almanac, as exemplified in this date-line, plays an important rôle in one of the most puzzling questions in his personal history, namely, the identity of the woman whom in the famous love-letters he called "The Immortal Beloved."

As regards our real business, since you ask it I meet your wishes by offering you the following items: Septet (concerning which I have already written you), 20 ducats; Symphony, 20 ducats; Grand Solo Sonata—Allegro, Adagio, Minuetto, Rondo—20 ducats. This Sonata is a tidy piece of work (*hat sich gewaschen*), my dearest Mr. Brother.

Now for an explanation: You will wonder, perhaps, that I have made no distinction here between Sonata, Septet and Symphony. I have done this because I have learned that a septet or symphony has a smaller sale than a sonata, though a symphony ought unquestionably to be worth more. (N. B. The Septet consists of a short introductory *Adagio*, then *Allegro, Adagio, Minuetto, Andante* with variations, *Minuetto* again, a short *Adagio* introduction and then *Presto*.) I put the price of the Concerto at only 10 ducats because, as I have already written, I do not give it out as one of my best. I do not think the amount excessive on the whole; I have tried, at least, to make the price as moderate as possible for you. As regards the bill of exchange you may, since you leave the matter to me, issue it to Geimüller or Schüller. The whole sum amounts to 70 ducats for the four works. I do not understand any money except Viennese ducats; how many thalers in gold that amounts to does not concern me, I being a really bad negotiator and mathematician.

This disposes of the disagreeable (*saure*) business; I call it so because I wish things were different in the world. There ought to be only one art warehouse in the world to which an artist would only need to carry his art-works to take away with him whatever he needed; as it is one must be half tradesman; and how we adjust ourselves—good God!—that is what I again call disagreeable. As regards the L... O...,[1] let them talk; they will certainly never make anybody immortal by their twaddle, and as little will they rob anybody of immortality to whom Apollo has decreed it.

The next letter requires a word of introduction. That military campaign which included the disastrous field of Hohenlinden (December 3, 1800), had filled the hospitals at Vienna, and among the various means of raising funds for the benefit of the wounded, was a series of public concerts. The two in which they reached their climax took place in the large Ridotto room (*Redouten-Saal*) of the imperial palace. The one arranged by Baron von Braun as Director of the Court Opera, was a performance of Haydn's "Creation" conducted by the composer, on January 16th; the other was arranged by Mme. Frank (Christine Gerhardi) for January 30th. That lady, Mme. Galvani (Magdalena Willmann) and Herr Simoni were the singers, Beethoven and Punto the instrumental solo performers; Haydn directed two of his own symphonies, Paër and Conti directed the orchestra in the accompaniments to the vocal music. In the first public announcement printed in the "Wiener Zeitung" the only artist mentioned was

[1]"L . . . O . . .", according to Schindler as reported by Nohl, stands for "Leipsic Oxen," the reference being to the critics of the "Allgemeine Musikalische Zeitung."

"the famous amateur singer Frau von Frank, *née* Gerhardi," as the giver of the concert. This called out from Beethoven the following letter:

Pour Madame de Frank.

I think it my duty, best of women, to ask you not to permit your husband again in the second announcement of our concert to forget that those who contribute their talents to the same also be made known to the public. This is the custom, and I do not see if it is not done what is to increase the attendance at the concert, which is its chief aim. Punto is not a little wrought up about the matter, and he is right, and it was my intention even before I saw him to remind you of what must have been the result of great haste or great forgetfulness. Look after this, best of women, since if it is not done dissatisfaction will surely result.

Having been convinced, not only by myself but by others as well, that I am not a useless factor in this concert, I know that not only I but Punto, Simoni, Galvani will ask that the public be informed also of our zeal for the philanthropic purposes of this concert; otherwise we must all conclude that we are useless.

Wholly yours

L. v. Bthvn.

Whether this sharp remonstrance produced the desired effect cannot now be ascertained, but the original advertisement was repeated in the newspaper on the 24th and 28th *verbatim*.

In the state of affairs then existing it was no time to give public concerts for private emolument; moreover, a quarrel with the orchestra a year before might have prevented Beethoven from obtaining the Burgtheater again, and the new Theater-an-der-Wien was not yet ready for occupation; but there is still another adequate reason for his giving no *Akademie* (concert) this spring. He had been engaged to compose an important work for the court stage.

Salvatore Vig'ano, dancer and composer of ballets, both action and music, the son of a Milanese of the same profession, was born at Naples, March 29, 1769. He began his career at Rome, taking female parts because women were not allowed there to appear upon the stage. He then had engagements successively at Madrid—where he married Maria Medina, a celebrated Spanish danseuse—Bordeaux, London and Venice, in which last city, in 1791, he composed his "Raoul, Sire de Croqui." Thence he came to Vienna, where he and his wife first appeared in May, 1793. His "Raoul" was produced on June 25th at the Kärnthnerthor-Theater. After two years of service here he accepted engagements in five continental cities and returned to Vienna again in 1799. The second wife of Emperor Franz, Maria Theresia, was a woman of much and true musical taste and culture, and Vigano determined to compliment her in a ballet composed expressly for that purpose. Haydn's gloriously successful "Creation" may, perhaps, have had an influence in the choice of a subject, "The Men of Prometheus," and the dedication of Beethoven's Septet to the Empress may have had its effect in the choice of a composer. At all events, the work was entrusted to Beethoven.

If the manner in which this work has been neglected by Beethoven's biographers and critics may be taken as a criterion, an opinion prevails that it was not worthy of him in subject, execution or success. It seems to be forgotten that as an orchestral composer he was then known only by two or three pianoforte concertos and his first Symphony—a work which by no means rivals the greater production of Mozart and Haydn—and that for the stage he was not known to have written anything. There is a misconception, too, as to the position which the ballet just then held in the Court Theatre. As a matter of fact it stood higher than ever before and, perhaps, than it has ever stood since. Vigano was a man of real genius and had wrought a reform which is clearly, vigorously and compendiously described in a memoir of Heinrich von Collin, from which we quote:

In the reign of Leopold II the ballet, which had become a well-attended entertainment in Vienna through the efforts of Noverre, was restored to the stage. Popular interest turned at once to them again, and this was intensified in a great degree when, beside the ballet-master Muzarelli, a second ballet-master, Mr. Salvatore Vigano, whose wife disclosed to the eyes of the spectators a thitherto unsuspected art, also gave entertainments. The most important affairs of state are scarcely able to create a greater war of feeling than was brought about at the time by the rivalry of the two ballet-masters. Theatre-lovers without exception divided themselves into two parties who looked upon each other with hatred and contempt because of a difference of conviction. . . . . The new ballet-master owed his extraordinary triumph over his older rival to his restoration of his art back from the exaggerated, inexpressive artificialities of the old Italian ballet to the simple forms of nature. Of course, there was something startling in seeing a form of drama with which thitherto there had been associated only leaps, contortions, constrained positions, and complicated dances which left behind them no feeling of unity, suddenly succeeded by dramatic action, depth of feeling, and plastic beauty of representation as they were so magnificently developed in the earlier ballets of Mr. Salvatore Vigano, opening, as they did, a new realm of beauty. And though it may be true that it was especially the natural, joyous, unconstrained dancing of Madame Vigano and her play of features, as expressive as it was fascinating, which provoked the applause of the many, it is nevertheless true that the very subject-matter of the ballets, which differentiate themselves very favorably from his later conceits, and his then wholly classical, skilful and manly dancing, were well calculated to inspire admiration and respect for the master and his creations.

Two or three pages might be compiled of spicy matter upon the beautiful Mme. Vigano's lavish display of the Venus-like graces and charms of her exquisite form; but her name, long before the "Prometheus" ballet, had disappeared from the roll of the theatre and Fräulein Cassentini reigned in her stead. There was nothing derogatory to Beethoven in his acceptance of the commission to compose the music to a ballet by Vigano; but by whom commissioned, upon what terms, and when—concerning these and similar particulars, we know nothing. We only know, that at the close of the season before Easter, on the 28th of March, "Die Geschöpfe des Prometheus" was performed for the first time for the benefit of the prima ballerina of the ballet corps, Fräulein Cassentini, and that the whole number of its performances this year was sixteen, and in 1802 thirteen. The pecuniary result to Beethoven must therefore have been satisfactory. True, the full score did not appear in print in Beethoven's lifetime or for a long time thereafter; it was not published, indeed, until the appearance of the critical Complete Edition, in which it figures as No. 11 of Series II; nothing is known of the original manuscript. A copy revised except as to two numbers, is in the Royal Imperial Court Library at Vienna. A pianoforte arrangement of the score was published in June, 1801, by Artaria with the opus number 24 and a dedication to Prince Lichnowsky. Hoffmeister printed the orchestral parts and a pianoforte score in 1804 as Op. 43 (the number 24 having meanwhile been assigned to the Violin Sonata in F). Mention ought, perhaps, also to be made of a pianoforte arrangement of No. 8 for four hands "composé pour la famille Kobler par Louis van Beethoven. Cette pièce se trouve aussi à gr. Orchestre dans le même Magazin." The Kobler family was frequently in Vienna, among other times in 1814; it had nothing to do with the "Prometheus" music.

Alois Fuchs has preserved a characteristic anecdote which came to him "from the worthy hand of a contemporary":

When Beethoven had composed the music to the ballet "Die Geschöpfe des Prometheus" in 1801, he was one day met by his former teacher, the great Joseph Haydn, who stopped him at once and said: "Well, I heard your ballet yesterday and it pleased me very much!" Beethoven replied: "O, dear Papa, you are very kind; but it is far from being a 'Creation!'" Haydn, surprised at the answer and almost offended, said after a short pause: "That is true; it is not yet a 'Creation' and I can scarcely believe that it will ever become one." Whereupon the men said their adieus, both somewhat embarrassed.

From the period immediately following we have another letter from Beethoven to Hoffmeister, dated April 22, 1801, in which he says:

Perhaps, too, it is the only sign of genius about me that my things are not always in the best of order, and nobody can mend the matter except myself. Thus, for instance, the pianoforte part, as is usual with me, was not written out in score and I only now have made a fair copy of it so that because of your haste you might not receive my too illegible manuscript. So that the works may appear in the proper sequence as far as possible I inform you that the following opus numbers ought to be placed on the compositions:

On the Solo Sonata . . . . Opus 22
On the Symphony . . . . " 21
On the Septet . . . . " 20
On the Concerto 19

The titles I will send you soon.

Set me down as a subscriber for the works of Johann Sebastian Bach, also Prince Lichnowsky. The transcription of the Mozart sonata (or sonatas) as quartets and quintets will do you honor and certainly prove remunerative. In this also I should like to be of greater service, but I am a disorderly individual and with the best of intentions I am continually forgetting everything; yet I have spoken about the matter here and there, and everywhere have found inclination towards it. It would be a handsome thing if Mr. Brother besides doing this were to publish an arrangement of the Septet for flute, as quintet, for example; by this means the amateur flautists, who have already approached me on the subject, would be helped and they would swarm around it like hungry insects. To say something about myself, I have just written a ballet in which the ballet-master did not do as well as he might have done. Baron von Liechtenstein has endowed us with a product not commensurate with the ideas which the newspapers have spread touching his genius; another bit of evidence against the newspapers. The Baron seems to have formed his ideal on Herr Müller in the marionette show, without, however, having attained it.

These are the beautiful prospects under which we poor fellows in Vienna are expected to flourish. . . .

Under the same date Beethoven wrote to Breitkopf and Härtel:

. . . . As regards your request for compositions by me I regret that at this time I am unable to oblige you; but please tell me what kind of compositions of mine you want, viz., symphonies, quartets, sonatas, etc., so that I may govern myself accordingly, and in case I have what you need or want I may place it at your service. If I am right, 8 works of mine are about to appear at Mollo's in this place; four pieces at Hofmeister's in Leipsic; in this connection I wish to add that *one of my first concertos*[1] *and therefore not one of* the best of my compositions, is to be published by Hofmeister, and that Mollo is to publish a Concerto which, indeed, was written later[2] *but nevertheless does not rank among the best of my works in this form.* This is only a hint for your musical journal in the matter of criticism of these works, although if one might hear them (well-played, that is), one would best be able to judge them. Musical policy requires that one should keep possession for a space of the best concertos. You should recommend to Messrs. your critics great care and wisdom especially in the case of the products of younger authors; many a one may be frightened off who otherwise might, probably, accomplish more; so far as I am concerned I am far from thinking that I am so perfect as not to be subject to blame, yet the howls of your critics against me were at first so humiliating that after comparing myself with others I could not get angry, but remained perfectly quiet, and concluded they did not understand their business; it was the easier to remain quiet since I saw the praise lavished on people who have no significance *in loco* in the eyes of the better sort, and who disappeared from sight here no matter how good they may otherwise have been—but *pax vobiscum*— peace for me and them—I would not have mentioned a syllable about the matter had not you yourself done so.

Coming recently to a friend who showed me the amount which had been collected *for the daughter of the immortal god of harmony*, I marvel at the smallness of the sum which Germany, especially *your Germany*, had contributed in recognition of the individual who seems to me worthy of respect for her father's sake, which brings me to the thought how would it do if I were to publish a work for the benefit of this person by subscription, acquaint the public each year with the amount and its proceeds in order to assure her against possible misfortune. Write me quickly how this might best be accomplished so that something may be done before *this Bach* dies, before this brook[3] dries up and we be no longer able to supply it with water. That you would publish the work is self-evident.

Poor Maximilian's health having become precarious, the welfare of the Teutonic Order in those revolutionary times demanded that a wise and energetic successor to him as Grand Master should be secured in the person of an efficient coadjutor. The thoughts of all parties concerned fixed upon a man who was then not even a member of the order, in case he would join it and accept the position, namely, the famous Archduke Karl. A Grand Chapter was therefore called at Vienna, which opened June 1st, and which unanimously admitted him to membership, he receiving a dispensation from taking the oaths for the time being. On

---

[1] The Concerto in B-flat, Op. 19.

[2] The Concerto in C major, Op. 15.

[3] Bach is the German equivalent of brook. The daughter of Bach referred to was Regina Johanna, in whose behalf Friedrich Rochlitz had issued an appeal. She was the youngest of Bach's children and died on December 14, 1809, her last days having been spent in comfort by reason of the subscription alluded to.

June 3rd, he was elected coadjutor and on the 11th he received the accolade. The circular which called the meeting brought to the Austrian capital the whole body of officials employed at Mergentheim, and thus it happened that Stephan von Breuning, whose name appears in the Calendar of the order from 1797 to 1803, inclusive, as Hofrathsassessor, came again to Vienna and renewed intimate personal intercourse with Beethoven. Another of our old Bonn acquaintances had also recently come thither, he of whom (in the opinion of the present writer) Beethoven writes to Amenda: "Now to my comfort a man has come again"— namely, Anton Reicha. In the spring of this year Beethoven removed from the Tiefer Graben into rooms overlooking one of the bastions—there is little if any doubt, the Wasserkunstbastei— and in one of those houses the main entrances to which are in the Sailerstätte. At a later period of his life he came thither again, and with good reason; for those houses not only afforded a beautiful view over the Glacis and the Landsstrasse suburb, but plenty of sun and fresh air. In the Hamberger house, where now stands No. 15, he had often gone with his exercises to Joseph Haydn, and hard by lived his friend Anton von Türkheim, Royal Imperial Truchsess—that is, carver.

This year he chose Hetzendorf for his summer retreat. Those who know well the environs of Vienna, are aware that this village offers less attraction to the lover of nature than a hundred others within easy distance of the city. There is nothing to invite one, who is fond of the solitude of the forest, but the thick groves in the garden of Schönbrunn some ten minutes' walk distant. It is certainly possible that Beethoven's state of health may have forbidden him to indulge his taste for long rambles, and that the cool shades of Schönbrunn, so easily and at all times accessible, may have determined his choice. It would be pleasant to believe, though there is no evidence to support such a belief, that some feeling of regard for his former patron Maximilian, who had sought retirement at Hetzendorf, was one of the causes which induced the composer to spend this summer there.

That was a period at Vienna fruitful in short sacred cantatas. On certain days in the spring and late autumn no theatrical performances were allowed and the principal composers embraced the opportunity to exhibit their skill and invention in this branch of their art; sometimes in concerts for their own benefit, more commonly in those for public charities. Haydn, Salieri, Winter, Süssmayr, Paër, are names that will occur in this connection to every student of Vienna's musical annals. Beethoven, ever ready to

compete with the greatest talent in at least one work, and desirous
of producing at his next concert the novelty of an extensive vocal
composition by himself, determined to compose a work of this
class.   The subject chosen was "Christus am Ölberg."[1]   Its
composition was the grand labor of this summer.   "The text
was written by me in collaboration with the poet within 14 days,"
writes Beethoven in one of his letters, "but the poet was musical
and had already written many things for music; I was able to
consult with him at any moment."   This poet was Franz Xaver
Huber, fertile writer in general literature and a popular author
for the Vienna stage, who occupied so high a place in public
esteem, that his consent to prepare the text of the "Christus"
is another indication of the high reputation of Beethoven.   The
merits and demerits of the poem need not be expatiated upon;
Beethoven's own words show that he was in part responsible for
them.   Schindler says:

> Beethoven also lived in Hetzendorf in 1805 and composed his
> "Fidelio."   A coincidence touching the two works, one that remained
> in the lively memory of Beethoven for many years, was that he composed
> both of them in the thicket of the forest in the Schönbrunner Hofgarten,
> sitting on the hill between two oaks which branched out from the trunk
> about two feet from the ground.   This oak, which always remained
> remarkable in his eyes (it is to the left of the Gloriet), I found again
> with Beethoven as late as 1823, and it awakened in him interesting
> memories of the early period.

So far as has been determined, the compositions completed
in 1801 were the Sonatas for Pianoforte and Violin, Op. 23 and 24;
the Pianoforte Sonatas in A-flat, Op. 26, E-flat, Op. 27, No. 1,
and C-sharp minor, Op. 27, No. 2, and D major, Op. 28; and
the Quintet in C major, Op. 29.   "The Andante in D minor of
the Sonata, Op. 28," says Czerny, "was long his favorite and he
played it often for his own pleasure."   The twelve Contradances
and six Rustic Dances (*Ländler*) are sketched in part on the first
staves of the Kessler sketchbook.   If we are justified in assuming
that they were composed for the balls of the succeeding winter
and were played from manuscript, it would follow that they also
are to be counted among the compositions completed in this year.
   The published works were the Concerto for Pianoforte and
Orchestra, Op. 15, dedicated "À son Altesse Madame la Princesse

---

[1]Known in English as "The Mount of Olives."

Odescalchi née Keglevics'"; the Sonata for Pianoforte and Horn, Op. 17, dedicated "À Madame la Baronne de Braun"; the Quintet for Pianoforte, Oboe, Clarinet, Horn and Bassoon, Op. 16, dedicated "À son Altesse Monseigneur le Prince Régnant de Schwarzenberg." These three works were announced by Mollo and Co. on March 21. Furthermore, the music to "Prometheus," arranged for Pianoforte (according to Czerny by the composer) and dedicated "A sua Altezza la Signora Principessa Lichnowsky, nata Contessa Thun," published in June by Artaria as Op. 27; "6 Variations très faciles" on an original theme in G, announced by Johann Traeg as absolutely new on August 11, sketched in the preceding year but probably completed in this; the Sonatas, Op. 23 and 24, dedicated "À Monsieur le Comte Maurice de Fries," announced on October 28; the six Quartets, Op. 18, dedicated "À son Altesse Monseigneur le Prince Régnant de Lobkowitz," announced (second series) on October 28 by Mollo. The Pianoforte Concerto in B-flat, Op. 19, dedicated "À Monsieur Charles Nikl Noble de Nikelsberg,'" and the Symphony in C, Op. 21, dedicated "À son Excellence Monsieur le Baron van Swieten," were published by Hoffmeister and Kühnel of Leipsic certainly before the end of the year, since they reached Vienna on January 16, and were advertised there. An earlier Leipsic edition has not been found. The two Violin Sonatas in A minor and F major were dedicated to Count Moritz von Fries and were originally intended to be coupled in a single opus number (23), as appears from the preliminary announcement by Mollo in the "Wiener Zeitung" of October 28, 1801, and also by the designation of the second as "No. 2," on a copy of Op 24. Sketches of the two found in the Petters sketchbook are evidence of their simultaneous origin.

The Pianoforte Sonata, Op. 26, had its origin, according to Nottebohm's study of the sketches, in the year 1800; but Shedlock (in the "Musical Times" of August, 1892) prints a few beginnings of the first movement in B minor (!) which probably date farther back, perhaps to the Bonn period. A young composer,[1] Ferdinand Paër (born at Parma in 1771), since the beginning of 1798 had produced on the court stage a series of pleasing and popular works. Laboring in a sphere so totally different from that of Beethoven, there was no rivalry between them and their relations were cordial and friendly. On June 6th of this summer Paër brought out a heroic opera, "Achilles," which "was received

---

[1] Here, for a space, the Editor reverts to the original manuscript not employed by the German reVisers, except as a foot-note.

with a storm of approval and deserved it," says the correspondent of the "Zeitung für die Elegante Welt." Paër in his old age told Ferdinand Hiller a characteristic anecdote of Beethoven which cannot possibly be true in connection with his "Leonore," as he, by a lapse of memory, related it, but is, undoubtedly, in connection with "Achilles." It was to the effect that Beethoven went with Paër to the theatre where an opera by the latter was performing. He sat beside him and after he had time and again cried out, "Ah, que c'est beau, que c'est intéressant!" had finally said: "Il faut que je compose cela." The correspondent just cited complains of the "want of character" in the marches in "Achilles" and incidentally confirms one of Ries's "Notizen": "The funeral march in A-flat minor in the Sonata dedicated to Prince Lichnowsky (Op.26) was the result of the great praise with which the funeral march in Paër's 'Achilles' was received by Beethoven's friends." Of that Sonata, completed this year, Czerny says: "When Cramer was in Vienna and was creating a great sensation not only by his playing but also by the three sonatas which he dedicated to Haydn (of which the first in A-flat, ¾ time, awakened great amazement), Beethoven, who had been pitted against Cramer, wrote the A-flat Sonata, Op. 26, in which there is purposely a reminder of the Clementi-Cramer passage-work in the Finale. The *Marcia funebre* was composed on the impulsion of a very much admired funeral march of Paër's, and added to the Sonata."

Whether or not this funeral march was really occasioned by Paër's "Achilles" or one from another opera by Paër (since "Achilles" was performed for the first time in 1801, and the older first sketches already contemplated a "pezzo caracteristico p. e. una marcia in as moll"), is of subordinate interest, since the legend has nothing whatever to do with reminiscences, but only with its tremendous superiority to the music by Paër.

The enigmatic "Sonate pour M." in the sketches for this sonata no doubt means "for Mollo" simply. The splendid print in *facsimile*, published by Erich Praeger from the autograph discovered by him, gives information concerning the sketches and also concerning the legends which refer to the origin of the different movements.

Of the two Pianoforte Sonatas, Op. 27, the first (in E-flat) was dedicated to the Princess Johanna von Liechtenstein, *née* the Landgravine Fürstenberg, the second to Countess Giulietta Guicciardi. It is apparent, therefore, that they appeared separately at first. Sketches of the first show that they originated in 1801.

Both are designated "quasi fantasia," which plainly indicates a departure from the customary structure. The C-sharp minor Sonata, Op. 27, No. 2, was dedicated to the Countess Giulietta Guicciardi, who at this time (1801-1802) was Beethoven's pupil and indubitably must be counted amongst the ladies who, for a time at least, were near to his heart. Concerning this, later. As his relationship to the Countess has been exaggerated, so also more significance has been attached to this sonata than is justified from a sober point of view. Beethoven himself was vexed that more importance was attached to it than to other sonatas which he held in higher esteem (Op. 78, for instance), simply because it had become popular. Its popularity was subsequently heightened by the designations "Arbor Sonata" and "Moonlight Sonata" and its creation into a sort of love-song without words, especially after Schindler had identified the Countess Guicciardi with the "Immortal Beloved" of the famous love-letter. It was a long time before attention was paid to a letter written by Dr. G. L. Grosheim, to Beethoven, dated November 10, 1819, in which occur the words: "You wrote me that at Seume's grave (in Teplitz) you had placed yourself among his admirers. . . . It is a desire which I cannot suppress, that you, Mr. Chapelmaster, would give to the world your wedding with Seume—I mean your Fantasia in C-sharp minor and the 'Beterin'."[1]

The autograph of the Sonata in D, Op. 28, bears the inscription "Gran Sonata, Op. 28, 1801, da L. van Beethoven." It

[1] "The Sonata in C-sharp minor has asked many a tear from gentle souls who were taught to hear in its first movement a lament for unrequited love and reflected that it was dedicated to the Countess Giulia Guicciardi, for whom Beethoven assuredly had a tender feeling. Moonlight and the plaint of an unhappy lover. How affecting! But Beethoven did not compose the Sonata for the Countess, though he inscribed it to her. He had given her a Rondo, and wishing to dedicate it to another pupil, he asked for its return and in exchange sent the Sonata. Moreover, it appears from evidence scarcely to be gainsaid, that Beethoven never intended the C-sharp minor sonata as a musical expression of love, unhappy or otherwise. In a letter dated January 22, 1892 (for a copy of which I am indebted to Fräulein Lipsius [La Mara] to whom it is addressed), Alexander W. Thayer, the greatest of Beethoven's biographers, says: 'That Mr. Kalischer has adopted Ludwig Nohl's strange notion of Beethoven's infatuation for Therese Malfatti, a girl of fourteen years, surprises me; as also that he seems to consider the C-sharp minor Sonata to be a musical love-poem addressed to Julia Guicciardi. He ought certainly to know that the subject of that sonata was or rather that it was suggested by—Seume's little poem 'Die Beterin'.' The poem referred to describes a maiden kneeling at the high altar in prayer for the recovery of a sick father. Her sighs and petitions ascend like the smoke of incense from the censers, angels come to her aid, and, at the last, the face of the suppliant one glows with the transfiguring light of hope. The poem has little to commend it as an example of literary art and it is not as easy to connect it in fancy with the last movement of the sonata as with the first and second; but the evidence that Beethoven paid it the tribute of his music seems conclusive."—"The Pianoforte and its Music," by H. E. Krehbiel, Charles Scribner's Sons, pp. 163, 164.

On page 174, Vol. IV, of the German edition of this biography Dr. Deiters remarks: "The venerated Thayer, it is true, conceived the idea that Beethoven's Fantasia and

appeared in print in 1802, having been advertised in the "Wiener
Zeitung" of August 14, from the Industriekontor, with the dedication, "À Monsieur Joseph Noble de Sonnenfels, Conseiller
aulique et Sécrétaire perpétuel de l'Académie des Beaux Arts."
Touching the personality of Joseph Noble de Sonnenfels something may be learned from W. Nagel's book, "Beethoven und
seine Klaviersonaten," and also from Willibald Müller's biography
of him.   At the time, Sonnenfels was nearly 70 years old and, so
far as is known, was not an intimate friend of Beethoven's; the
dedication was probably nothing more than a mark of respect
for the man of brains with whose ideas Beethoven was in sympathy.
The single clue as to the origin of the work is the date (1801) on
the autograph; sketches seem to be lacking.   The sunny disposition of the music is the only evidence, and this is internal.   The
work early acquired the sobriquet "Sonata pastorale" (it was
first printed by A. Cranz), and the designation is not inept.

The String Quintet, Op. 29, as is evidenced by an inscription
on the score, was composed in 1801 and published by Breitkopf
and Härtel in 1802, towards the close of the year.   Simultaneously
it appeared from the press of Artaria.   This second edition has
a history.   According to Ries the Quintet

was stolen in Vienna and published by A. (Artaria) and Co.   Having
been copied in a single night, it was full of errors. . . . .   Beethoven's
conduct in the matter is without parallel.   He asked A. to send the
fifty copies which had been printed to me for correction, but at the same
time instructed me to use ink on the wretched paper and as coarsely
as possible; also to cross out several lines so that it would be impossible
to make use of a single copy or sell it.   The scratching out was particularly in the Scherzo.   I obeyed his instructions implicitly, etc.

Nottebohm has proved that the further statements of Ries
touching the melting of the plates, etc., are wrong; but the enraged composer did make a public statement—and very properly:

Sonata, Op. 27, No. 2, had been inspired by Seume's 'Beterin.'   Whoever compares the
sonata with the poem will soon realize that there can be no thought of this.   We have
here, no doubt, a confusion of pieces.   It would be easier to think of the Fantasia, Op.
77.   Kalischer, who first recognized Thayer's error, thought of the C-sharp minor
Quartet; but this cannot have been in Beethoven's mind, for it was composed much
later."   Grossheim's letter was written in 1819; the C-sharp minor quartet was composed in 1826.   So Kalischer was ridiculously in error.   But why does Dr. Deiters
suggest the Fantasia, Op. 77?   Grossheim was a musician—composer, teacher and conductor—as well as philologist, and when he said "C-sharp minor" it is not likely that he
was thinking of a work in G minor.   Moreover, the most admirable Dr. Deiters to the
contrary notwithstanding, it is not at all difficult to associate the sonata with the poem
whose picture of lamentable petition and rising clouds of incense is strikingly reproduced in suggestion by the music of the first movement.   Serene hopefulness can be
said to be the feeling which informs the second movement; and why should the finale
not be the musician's continuation of the poet's story?

To the Lovers of Music.

In informing the public that the original Quintet in C long ago advertised by me as having been published by Breitkopf and Härtel in Leipsic, I declare at the same time that I have no interest in the edition published simultaneously by Messrs. Artaria and Mollo in Vienna. I am the more compelled to make this declaration since this edition is very faulty, incorrect and utterly useless to players, whereas Messrs. Breitkopf and Härtel, the legal owners of this Quintet, have done all in their power to produce the work as handsomely as possible.

Ludwig van Beethoven.

A year later Beethoven revoked this declaration so far as it concerned Mollo in the following

Announcement to the Public.

After having inserted a statement in the "Wiener Zeitung" of January 22, 1803, in which I publicly declared that the edition of my Quintet published by Mollo did not appear under my supervision, was faulty in the extreme and useless to players, the undersigned hereby revokes the statement to the extent of saying that Messrs. Mollo and Co. have no interest in this edition, feeling that I owe such a declaration to do justice to Messrs. Mollo and Co. before a public entitled to respect.

Ludwig van Beethoven.

As Nottebohm has shown, Beethoven eventually agreed to revise and correct this edition also. A long letter to Breitkopf and Härtel, dated November 13, 1802, gives a lively picture of the excitement which the incident aroused in Beethoven:

I write hurriedly to inform you of only the most important things— know then, that while I was in the country for my health, the arch- scoundrel Artaria borrowed the Quintet from Count Friess on the pretence that it was already published and in existence here and that they wanted it for the purpose of reëngraving because their copy was faulty and as a matter of fact intended to rejoice the public with it in a few days—good Count Fr., deceived and not reflecting that a piece of rascality might be in it, gave it to them—he could not ask me, I was not here, but fortunately I learned of the matter in time, it was on Tuesday of this week, and in my zeal to save my honor and as quickly as possible to prevent your suffering injury, I offered two new works to these con- temptible persons if they would suppress the entire edition, but a cooler- headed friend who was with me asked, Do you want to reward these rascals? The case was finally closed under conditions, they assuring me that no matter what you printed they would reprint it, these generous scoundrels decided therefore to wait three weeks after the receipt here of your copies before issuing their own (insisting that Count F. had made them a present of the copy). For one term the contract was to be closed and for this boon I had to give them a work which I value at at least 40 ducats. Before this contract was made comes my good brother as if sent by heaven, he hurries to Count Fr., the whole thing is the biggest swindle in the world, how neatly they kept themselves out of Count F.'s way and so on, and I go to F. and as the enclosed *Revers* may show that I did all in my power to protect you from injury—and my statement of the case may serve to prove to you that no sacrifice was too great for me to save my honor and save you from harm. From the *Revers* you will see the measures that must be adopted and you should make all possible haste to send copies here and if possible at the same price as the rascals—Sonnleithner and I will take all further measures which seem to us good, so that their entire edition may be destroyed—please take good notice that Mollo and Artaria combined are already only a shop, that is, a combined lot of scoundrels. The dedication to Friess I hope was not forgotten inasmuch as my brother wrote it on the first sheet —I wrote the *Revers* myself since my poor brother is very much occupied with work yet did all he could to save you and me, in the confusion he lost a faithful dog which he called his favorite, he deserves that you thank him personally as I have done on my own account—recall that from Tuesday to late last night I devoted myself almost wholly to this matter and the mere thought of this rascally stroke may serve to make you realize how unpleasant it is for me to have anything to do with such miserable men.

"Revers.

"The undersigned pledges himself under no circumstances to send out or sell here or elsewhere the Quintet received from Mr. Count Friess composed by Lud. v. Beethoven until the original edition shall have been in circulation in Vienna 14 days.

"Vienna, 9th month, 1802.   Artaria Comp."

This *R.* is signed with its own hand by the *Comp.* Use the following: Is to be had à Vienne chez Artaria Comp., à Münich chez F. Halm, à Francfort chez Gayl et Nädler, perhaps also in Leipsic chez Meysel— the price is 2 florins Viennese standard. I got hold of twelve copies, which they promised me from the beginning, and corrected them— *the engraving is abominable.* Make use of all this, you see that on every side we have them in our hands and can proceed against them in the courts.—*N.B.* Any personal measures taken against A. will have my approval.

Under date of December 5, 1802, Beethoven's brother Karl wrote to Breitkopf and Härtel on the same subject:

Finally I shall inform you touching the manner in which my brother sells his works. We already have in print 34 works and about 18 numbers. These pieces were mostly commissioned by amateurs under the following agreement: he who wants a piece pays a fixed sum for its exclusive possession for a half or a whole year, or longer, and binds himself not to give the manuscript to *anybody;* at the conclusion of the period it is the privilege of the author to do what he pleases with the work. This was the understanding with Count Friess. Now the Count has a certain Conti as violin teacher, and to him Artaria turned and he probably for a consideration of 8 or 10 florins said that the quartet (*sic*) had already been printed and was to be had everywhere. This made Count Friess think that there was nothing more to be lost in the matter and he gave it up without a word to us about it. . . . . Count Friess is not here just now, but he will return in 6 days and then we shall see that you are recompensed in one way or another.   I send you the accompanying *Revers* signed by Artaria for inspection; please return it.   This *Revers* cost my brother 7 days during which time he could do nothing, and me innumerable trips, many unpleasantnesses and the loss of my dog.[1]

Beethoven's declaration not having been published until more than two months after his letter containing the *Revers*, the incidents touching which Ries makes report, and the partial reëngraving of the plates, must have taken place after January, 1803, and the end of the quarrel in 1804.   Sketches of the Quintet have not been found and the question naturally arises whether or not it might have had an earlier origin or been developed from earlier sketches.   A note in a Conversation Book of 1826, indicates that one of the Quintet's themes was written by Schuppanzigh.

[1]Appendix II to the second volume of the German edition of this work contains copies of all the documents in the legal controversies which arose out of Beethoven's charges against Artaria and Co. and Mollo in the matter of the unauthorized publication of the Quintet.   They do not add much that is essential to the story as it has been told, though they show that the legal authorities upheld the publishers against the composer.

Chapter XX

Letters of 1801—The Beginning of Beethoven's Deafness—
The Criticisms of a Leipsic Journal—Bonn Friends in
Vienna—Reicha, Breuning, Ries, Czerny—Chronology
Adjusted.

L ET us now turn back to the important letters written in the
summer of 1801, beginning with two written to his friend
Amenda, which were first published in the "Signale" of 1852,
No. 5. The first, without date or record of place, is as follows:

How can Amenda doubt that I shall always remember him[1] because
I do not write or have not written to him—as if memory could only
be preserved in such a manner.

A thousand times the best of all men that I ever learned to know
comes into my mind—yes, of the two men who had my entire love, of
which one still lives, you are the third—how can recollection of you die
out of my mind. You shall soon receive a long letter from me concerning
my present condition and everything about me that might interest you.
Farewell, dear, good, noble friend, keep me always in your love, your
friendship, as I shall forever remain

Your faithful   Beethoven.

The longer letter which he had promised to send to his friend
is dated June 1, 1801:

My dear, good Amenda, my cordial friend, I received and read
your last letter with mixed pain and pleasure. To what shall I compare
your fidelity, your attachment to me. Oh, it is so beautiful that you
have always been true to me and I know how to single you out and
keep you above all others. You are not a Viennese friend, no, you
are one of those who spring from the ground of my native land. How
often do I wish you were with me, for your Beethoven is living an unhappy
life, quarreling with nature and its creator, often cursing the latter
because he surrendered his creatures to the merest accident which sometimes broke or destroyed the most beautiful blossoms. Know that my
noblest faculty, my hearing, has greatly deteriorated. When you were
still with me I felt the symptoms but kept silent; now it is continually
growing worse, and whether or not a cure is possible has become a

[1]Beethoven writes: "How can Amenda doubt that I should ever forget him?"

question; but it is said to be due to my bowels and so far as they are concerned I am nearly restored to health. I hope, indeed that my hearing will also improve, but I am dubious because such diseases are the most incurable. How sad is my lot! I must avoid all things that are dear to me and live amongst such miserable and egotistical men as . . . and . . . and others. I must say that amongst them all Lichnowsky is the most satisfactory, since last year he has settled an income of 600 florins on me and the good sale of my works enables me to live without care. I could sell everything that I compose five times over and at a good price. I have written considerably of late, and as I hear that you have ordered a pianoforte from . . . . I will send you various things in the box of the instrument so that it need not cost you much. To my comfort there has lately come a man with whom I can share the pleasures of association, an unselfish friendship; he is one of the friends of my youth. I have often spoken of you to him and told him that since I left my fatherland you have been the only choice of my heart . . . . . is not very satisfactory to him—he is and always will be too weak for friendship. I use him and . . . . . only as instruments on which I play when I please but they can never become witnesses of my whole internal and external activities or real participants (in my feelings). I estimate them at only what they are worth to me. Oh, how happy would I be if my hearing were completely restored; then would I hurry to you, but as it is I must refrain from everything and the most beautiful years of my life must pass without accomplishing the promise of my talent and powers. A sad resignation to which I must resort although, indeed, I am resolved to rise superior to every obstacle. But how will that be possible? Yes, Amenda, if my infirmity shows itself to be incurable in half a year, I shall appeal to you; you must abandon everything and come to me. My affliction causes me the least trouble in playing and composing, the most in association with others, and you must be my companion. I am sure my fortune will not desert me. What might I not essay? Since you have been gone I have composed everything except operas and church-music. You will not deny me; you will help your friend bear his cares and affliction. I have also greatly bettered my pianoforte playing and I hope the journey will, perhaps, make your fortune; afterward you will remain with me. I have received all of your letters and despite the fact that I answered so few you were always with me and my heart still beats as tenderly for you as ever it did. I beg of you to keep the matter of my deafness a profound secret to *be confided to nobody no matter who it is.* Write to me very often. Your letters, no matter how short, comfort me, do me good, and I shall soon expect another from you, my dear fellow. Do not lend your quartet to anybody because I have changed it greatly having just learned how properly to write quartets, as you will observe when you receive it. Now, farewell, my dear, good fellow; if you think I can do something for you here, command me as a matter of course.

Your faithful, and truly affectionate

L. v. Beethoven.

In the same month Beethoven wrote again to the publisher Hoffmeister to this effect:

I am a little amazed at what you have communicated to me through
the local representative of your business. I am almost vexed to think
that you consider me capable of such a trick.

It would be a different matter if I had sold my wares only to avaricious tradesmen hoping that they would make a good speculation on
the sly, but *as artist towards artist* it is a bit harsh to think such things
of me. It looks to me as if the whole matter had been planned to test
me or to be merely a suspicion; in either case I inform you that before
you received the Septet from me I sent it to London to Mr. Salomon
(for performance at his concerts out of mere friendship) but with the
understanding that he should have a care that it should not fall into the
hands of strangers, because I intended that it should be published in
Germany, concerning which, if you think it necessary, you may make
inquiry of him. But in order to prove my honesty *I give you the assurance herewith that I have not sold the Septet, Concerto, the Symphony and
the Sonata to anybody but you, Hoffmeister and Kühnel, and that you may
consider it (sic) as your exclusive property and to this I pledge my honor.*
You may make such use of this assurance as you please.

As for the rest I believe as little that Salomon is capable of being
guilty of having the Septet printed as I am of having sold it to him. I
am so conscientious that I have denied the applications of *various publishers* to print the pianoforte arrangement of the Septet, and yet I
do not know whether or not you intend to make such use of it.

On June 29, he sent the following longer letter to Wegeler,
who published it in his "Notizen":

Vienna, June 29.

My good, dear Wegeler!

How greatly do I thank you for thinking of me; I have so
little deserved it and so little tried to deserve anything from you, and
yet you are so very good and refuse to be held aloof by anything,
not even by my unpardonable remissness, remaining always my true,
good, brave friend. Do not believe that I could forget you who were
always so dear to me. No. There are moments when I long for you
and would like to be with you. My fatherland, the beautiful region in
which I first saw the light, is still as clear and beautiful before my eyes
as when I left you. In short, I shall look upon that period as one of the
happiest incidents of my life when I shall see you again and greet Father
Rhine. When this shall be I cannot now tell you—but I want to say
that you will see me again only as a great man. You shall receive me as
a great artist but as a better and more perfect man, and if the conditions
are improved in our fatherland my art shall be employed in the service
of the poor. O happy moment! How happy am I that I created thee—
can invoke thee! . . . You want to know something about my situation.
It is not so bad. Since last year, unbelievable as it may sound, even
after I tell you, Lichnowsky, who has always remained my warmest
friend (there were little quarrels between us, but they only served to
strengthen our friendship), set aside a fixed sum of 600 florins for me to
draw against so long as I remained without a position worthy of me.
From my compositions I have a large income and I may say that I have
more commissions than it is possible for me to fill. Besides, I have 6

or 7 publishers and might have more if I chose; they no longer bargain
with me—I ask, and they pay. You see it is very convenient. For instance,
I see a friend in need and my purse does not permit me to help him at once.
I have only to sit down and in a short time help is at hand. Moreover, I am
a better business man than formerly. If I remain here always I shall bring
it to pass that I shall always reserve a day for my concert of which I give
several. The only pity is that my evil demon, my bad health, is continually putting a spoke in my wheel, by which I mean that my hearing
has grown steadily worse for three years for which my bowels, which
you know were always wretched and have been getting worse, since I
am always troubled with a dysentery, in addition to unusual weakness,
are said to be responsible. Frank wanted to tone up my body by tonic
medicines and restore my hearing with almond oil, but, *prosit*, nothing
came of the effort; my hearing grew worse and worse, and my bowels
remained as they had been. This lasted until the autumn of last year
and I was often in despair. Then came a medical ass who advised me
to take cold baths, a more sensible one to take the usual lukewarm
Danube bath. That worked wonders; my bowels improved, my hearing
remained, or became worse. I was really miserable during this winter;
I had frightful attacks of colic and I fell back into my previous condition,
and so things remained until about four weeks ago, when I went to Vering,
thinking that my condition demanded a surgeon, and having great
confidence in him. He succeeded almost wholly in stopping the
awful diarrhœa. He prescribed the lukewarm Danube bath, into
which I had each time to pour a little bottle of strengthening stuff,
gave me no medicine of any kind until about four weeks ago, when
he prescribed pills for my stomach and a kind of tea for my ear. Since
then I can say I am stronger and better; only my ears whistle and buzz
continually, day and night. I can say I am living a wretched life; for
two years I have avoided almost all social gatherings because it is impossible for me to say to people: "I am deaf." If I belonged to any other
profession it would be easier, but in my profession it is an awful state,
the more since my enemies, who are not few, what would they say?
In order to give you an idea of this singular deafness of mine I must
tell you that in the theatre I must get very close to the orchestra in
order to understand the actor. If I am a little distant I do not hear
the high tones of the instruments, singers, and if I be but a little farther
away I do not hear at all. Frequently I can hear the tones of a low
conversation, but not the words, and as soon as anybody shouts it is intolerable. It seems singular that in conversation there are people who do
not notice my condition at all, attributing it to my absent-mindedness.[1]
Heaven knows what will happen to me. *Vering says that there will be
an improvement if no complete cure.* I have often—cursed my existence; *Plutarch* taught me resignation. If possible I will bid defiance
to my fate, although there will be moments in my life when I shall be
the unhappiest of God's creatures. I beg of you to say nothing of my
condition to anybody, not even to Lorchen;[2] I entrust the secret only
to you; I would be glad if you were to correspond with Vering on the

---

[1] We shall see that even Ries took no note of his friend's infirmity for two years.

[2] Eleonore von Breuning, wife of Wegeler.

subject. If my condition continues I will go to you next spring; you could hire a house for me in some pretty place in the country and for half a year I would be a farmer. This might bring about a change. Resignation! What a wretched refuge—and yet the only one open to me. Forgive me that I add these cares of friendship to yours which is sorrowful enough as it is. Steffen Breuning is here now and we are together almost daily; it does me so much good to revive the old emotions. He is really become a good, splendid youngster, who knows a thing or two, and like us all has his heart in the right place. I have a pretty domicile on the bastion which is doubly valuable because of my health. I believe I shall make it possible for Breuning to come to me. You shall have your Antioch[1] and also many musical compositions of mine if you do not think they will cost you too much. Honestly, your love for art still delights me much. Write to me how it is to be done and I will send you all my compositions, already a goodly number and increasing daily. . . . In return for the portrait of my grandfather which I beg of you to send me as soon as possible by mail-coach, I am sending you that of his grandson, your good and affectionate Beethoven, which is to be published here by Artaria, who, like many others, including art-dealers, have often asked me for it. I shall soon write to Stoffel[2] and give him a piece of my mind concerning his stubborn disposition. I will make his ears ring with the old friendship, and he shall promise me by all that is holy not to offend you further in your present state of unhappiness. I shall also write to good Lorche. I have never forgotten one of you good people even if I did not write to you; but you know that writing was never my forte; the best of my friends have not had a letter from me in years. I live only in my notes and when one composition is scarcely ended another is already begun. As I compose at present I frequently work on three or four compositions at the same time. Write to me often, hereafter. I will try occasionally to find time to write to you. Give greetings to all, including the good Madame Councillor,[3] and tell her that I still occasionally have a "raptus." As regards K. I do not at all wonder over his change. Fortune is round, like a ball, and therefore does not always drop on the noblest and best. A word about Ries, whom I greet heartily; so far as his son is concerned I shall write you more in detail, although I think that he would be more fortunate in Paris than in Vienna. Vienna is overcrowded and the most meritorious find it extremely difficult to maintain themselves. In the autumn or winter I shall see what I can do for him, for at that time the public hurries back to the city. Farewell, good, faithful Wegeler! Be assured of the love and friendship of

Your   Beethoven.

On November 16, he wrote in greater detail to Wegeler:

My good Wegeler!

     I thank you for the new evidence of concern in my behalf, all the more since I deserve so little at your hands. You want to know

---

[1] A well-known picture by Füger, Director of the Academy of Painting in Vienna.

[2] Christoph von Breuning.

[3] Breuning's mother. (Wegeler.)

how it goes with me, what I need; as little as I like to discuss such matters I would rather do it with you than with others.

For several months Vering has had vesicatories placed on both arms, which consist, as you know, of a certain bark.[1] This is a very unpleasant remedy, inasmuch as I am robbed of the free use of my arms (for a few days, until the bark has had its effect), to say nothing of the pain. It is true I cannot deny that the ringing and sounding in my ears has become less than usual, especially in the left ear, where my deafness began; but my hearing has not been improved and I dare not say that it has not grown worse rather than better. My bowels are in a better condition, especially after the lukewarm baths for a few days when I feel quite well for 8 or 10 days, seldom needing a tonic for my stomach. I am beginning to use the herbs on the belly as suggested by you. Vering will hear nothing of plunge baths, and I am thoroughly dissatisfied with him; he has much too little care and consideration for such a disease; if I did not go to him, which costs me a great deal of trouble, I should not see him at all. What do you think of Schmidt? I do not like to change, but it seems to me Vering is too much of a practitioner to acquire new ideas. Schmidt seems to me a very different sort of man and, perhaps, would not be so negligent. Miracles are told of *galvanism;* what have you to say about it? A doctor told me that he had seen a deaf and dumb child recover his hearing (in Berlin) again— and a man who had been deaf 7 years got well. I am living more pleasantly since I live more amongst men. You will scarcely believe how lonely and sad my life was for two years; my bad hearing haunted me everywhere like a ghost and I fled from mankind and seemed like a misanthrope, though far from being one. This change has been wrought by a *dear, fascinating* girl who loves me and whom I love. There have been a few blessed moments within the last two years and it is the first time that I feel that marriage might bring me happiness. Alas! she is not of my station—and now—it would be impossible for me to marry. I must still hustle about most actively. If it were not for my deafness, I should before now have travelled over half the world, and that I must do. There is no greater delight for me than to practise and show my art. Do not believe that I would be happy with you. What is there that could make me happier? Even your care would give me pain. I would see pity on your faces every minute and be only the unhappier. What did those beautiful native regions bestow upon me? Nothing except the hope of a better state of health, which would have come had not this affliction seized upon me. Oh, if I were rid of this affliction I could embrace the world! I feel that my youth is just beginning and have I not always been ill? My physical strength has for a short time past been steadily growing more than ever and also my mental powers. Day by day I am approaching the goal which I apprehend but cannot describe. It is only in this that your Beethoven can live. Tell me nothing of rest. I know of none but sleep, and woe is me that I must give up more time to it than usual. Grant me but half freedom from my affliction and then—as a complete, ripe man I shall return to you and renew the old feelings of friendship. You must see me as happy as it is possible to be here below—not unhappy. No! I cannot endure it.

[1]The bark of *Daphne Mezereum.*

I will take Fate by the throat; it shall not wholly overcome me.   Oh,
it is so beautiful to live—to live a thousand times!   I feel that I am not
made for a quiet life.   You will write to me as soon as you can.   See
that Steffen secures an appointment of some kind in the *Teutonic Order*.
Life here is connected with too many hardships for his health.   Besides,
he lives so isolated an existence that I cannot see how he is to get along
in this manner.   You know the state of affairs here.   I will not say that
social life may not lessen his moodiness; but it is impossible to persuade
him to go anywhere.   A short time ago I had a *musicale* at my home;
yet our friend Steffen did not come.   Advise him to seek more rest
and composure.   I have done my best in this direction; without these
he will never be again happy or well.   Tell me in your next letter whether
or not it will matter if I send you a great deal of my music; you can sell
what you do not need and so get back the post-money—and my portrait.
All possible lovely and necessary greetings to Lorchen, Mama and
Christoph.   You love me a little, do you not?   Be assured of the love
and friendship of

Your

Beethoven.

A commentary upon these letters—the first two excepted,
which need none—might be made, by a moderate indulgence of
poetic fancy, to fill a volume of respectable size; but rigidly confined to prosaic fact may be reduced to reasonable dimensions.
Taking up the letters in their order, the first is that to Hoffmeister
of April 22nd.

I. One of the earliest projects of the new firm of Hoffmeister
and Kühnel was the publication of "J. Sebastian Bach's Theoretical
and Practical Clavier and Organ Works."   The first number contained: 1, Toccata in D-flat; 2, fifteen inventions; 3, "The Well-
Tempered Clavichord"—in part; the second number: 1, 15 symphonies in three voices; 2, continuation of "The Well-Tempered
Clavichord."   Now compare what Schindler says (third edition,
II, 184):

> Of the archfather Johann Sebastian Bach the stock was a very
> small one except for a few motets which had been sung at the house of
> van Swieten; besides these the majority of pieces were those familiarly
> known, namely, the "Well-Tempered Clavichord," which showed signs
> of diligent study, three volumes of exercises, fifteen inventions, fifteen
> symphonies and a toccata in D minor.   This collection of pieces in *a
> single volume* is to be found in my possession.   Attached to these was a
> sheet of paper on which, in a strange handwriting, was to be read the
> following passage from J. N. Forkel's book "On the Life and Artwork
> of Johann Sebastian Bach"; "The pretence that the musical art is an art
> for *all* ears cannot be substantiated by Bach, but is disproved by the mere
> existence and uniqueness of his works, which seem to be destined only
> for connoisseurs.   Only the connoisseur who can surmise the inner or-
> ganization and feel it and penetrate to the intention of the artist, which

does nothing needlessly, is privileged to judge here; indeed, the judgment of a musical connoisseur can scarcely be better tested than by seeing how rightly he has learned the works of Bach." On both sides of this passage there were interrogation points from the thickest note-pen of Beethoven as a gloss on the learned historian and most eminent of all Bachians. No Hogarth could have put a grimmer look, or a more crushing expression, into an interrogation point.

Nägele, who professed long to have entertained the design to publish Bach's "most admirable works," issued his proposals in February, written with some degree of asperity against "the double competition" which, he had already learned, "was confronting" him. Of his edition of "The Well-Tempered Clavichord" Beethoven also possessed a part.

The names left blank in publishing this letter are easily supplied. Baron Carl August von Liechtenstein, the same to whom, from 1825 to 1832, was confided the management of the opera in Berlin, who died there in 1845, had been so extravagantly praised as head of the Princely Music at Dessau that he was called to assume the chapelmastership of the Imperial Opera in Vienna near the end of 1800. The contemporary reports of his efficiency as conductor are highly favorable. He deserves the credit of determining to add to the repertory of the Imperial Opera Mozart's "Zauberflöte" which, till then, had been heard by the Viennese only in the little theatre Auf-den-Wieden. It is worth mentioning that Liechtenstein brought with him from Dessau poor Neefe's daughter Felice, now Mme. Rösner, and that she was the *Pamina* of this performance. In the first new work produced (April 16th) upon the imperial stage after Beethoven's "Prometheus" music, Liechtenstein introduced himself to the Vienna public in the character of a composer. It was in his opera "Bathmendi," completely revised. The result was a wretched failure. Hoffmeister's long and familiar acquaintance with Vienna, its musicians and its theatres, would cause him readily to appreciate the fun and wit of Beethoven's remark that the newly engaged chapelmaster and composer of the Imperial Opera "seems to have taken for an ideal Mr. M. (Müller)"—the Offenbach of that time—but without reaching "even him." Considering that the Baron was yet a young man, at the most but three years older than Beethoven, the somewhat bitter remark which follows the jest appears natural enough.

II. Beethoven had just cause for indignation in the treatment which he had received at the hands of the writers for the "Allgemeine Musikalische Zeitung" (the "Leipsic oxen" of his letter of January 15th). Hoffmeister had evidently written him on the subject, and his reticence in confining himself in reply to a single contemptuous sentence, though writing in the confidence of private correspondence, is something unexpected; not less so is the manly, dignified and ingenuous style of his answer to Breitkopf and Härtel upon the same topic in the letter of April 22nd. The first number of that famous musical journal (take it for all in all, the noblest ever published) appeared October 3rd, 1798, edited by Rochlitz, published by Breitkopf and Härtel. In the second number, "Z......" eulogizes the Six Fughettos of the lad, C. M. von Weber; in the tenth young Hummel's sonatas, Op. 3, are reviewed; in the fifteenth the name of Beethoven first appears, viz.: in the title of three sonatas dedicated to him by Wölffl. At length, in No. 23, March 17th, 1799, he is introduced to the readers of the journal as an author—not of one or more of the eight Trios, ten Sonatas, the Quintet and Serenade, which make up the *opera* 1 to 11 then published—but as the writer of the Twelve Variations on "Ein Mädchen oder Weibchen," and eight on "Une fièvre brûlante."

The criticisms are a perfect reflex of the conventional musical thought of the period and can be read now with amused interest, at least. There is no room here for their production in full. The writer, "M....," recognizes the clever pianoforte player in the Variations but cannot see evidences in them of equal capacity as a composer. He likes some of them and "willingly admits" that those on "Une fièvre brûlante" are "more successful than those of Mozart, who in his early youth also treated the same subject." But Mozart did not write the variations referred to, and when Grétry's "Richard Cœur de Lion," from which the theme was borrowed, was first performed in Paris, Mozart was not in his "early youth" but 28 years old. The critic descants with disapproval on "certain harshnesses in the modulations," illustrating them; holds up Haydn as a model chooser of themes, and commends the comments of Vogler on a set of variations on "God save the King" printed in a little book on the subject. Thus Beethoven found, in the first recognition of himself as a composer in that journal, two compositions which he did not think worthy of opus numbers, to the neglect of all his better works, made the subject of censure and ridicule for the purpose of puffing and advertising a pamphlet by Vogler. Were his own subsequent Variations on "God save the King" an effect of this article?

No. 23 of the "Allgemeine Musikalische Zeitung" contains nearly two pages from the pen of Spazier on Liechtenstein's opera, "Die steinerne Braut," and a parallel between Beethoven and

Wölffl as pianists.   Then in the next number the beautiful Trio, Op. 6, finds a reviewer.   Here is the whole of his article:

This Trio, which in part is not easier but more flowing than many other pieces by the same author, makes an excellent ensemble on the pianoforte with accompaniment.   The composer with his unusual harmonic knowledge and love for serious composition would provide us many things which would leave many hand-organ things far in the rear, even those composed by famous men, if he would but try to write more naturally.

Could one say less?

The "Leipsic oxen" are now ruminating upon the noble Sonatas for Pianoforte and Violin, Op. 12, and No. 36 (June, 1799), contains the result:

The critic, who heretofore has been unfamiliar with the pianoforte pieces of the author, must admit, after having looked through these strange sonatas, overladen with difficulties, that after diligent and strenuous labor he felt like a man who had hoped to make a promenade with a genial friend through a tempting forest and found himself barred every minute by inimical barriers, returning at last exhausted and without having had any pleasure.   It is undeniable that Mr. Beethoven goes his own gait; but what a bizarre and singular gait it is!   Learned, learned and always learned—and nothing natural, no song.   Yes, to be accurate, there is *only a mass of learning here, without good method*; obstinacy, but for which we feel but little interest; a striving for strange modulations, an objection to customary associations, a heaping up of difficulties on difficulties till one loses all patience and enjoyment.   Another critic (M. Z., No. 24) has said almost the same thing, and the present writer must agree with him completely.

Nevertheless, the present work must not be rejected wholly.   It has its value and may be of excellent use for already practised pianoforte players.   There are always many who love difficulties in invention and composition, what we might call perversities, and if they play these Sonatas with great precision they may derive delight in the music as well as an agreeable feeling of satisfaction.   If Mr. v. B. wished to deny himself a bit more and follow the course of nature he might, with his talent and industry, do a great deal for an instrument which he seems to have so wonderfully under his control.

Let us pass on to No. 38 of the journal, where we find half a dozen notices to arrest our attention.   Variations by Schuppanzigh for two violins are "written in good taste and conveniently for the instrument"; variations for the pianoforte by Philip Freund are very satisfactory and "some among them belong to the best of their kind"; variations by Heinrich Eppinger for violin and violoncello "deserve honorable mention"; but "X Variations pour le clavecin sur le Duo 'La stessa, la stessissima' par L. v. Beethoven" the critic "cannot at all be satisfied with, because they are stiff and strained; and what awkward passages are in them, where harsh tirades in continuous semitones create an ugly relationship and the reverse! No; it is true; Mr. van Beethoven may be able to improvise, but he does not know how to write variations."

Now, however, the tide begins to turn. After an interval of nearly four months, in No. 2 of Vol. II (October, 1799), the Sonatas, Op. 12, for Pianoforte and Violin have a page allotted to them. A few sentences to show the tone of the article will suffice; for the praise of Beethoven needs no repetition:

It is not to be denied that Mr. v. B. is a man of genius, possessed of originality and who goes his own way. In this he is assured by his extraordinary thoroughness in the higher style of writing and his unusual command of the instrument for which he writes, he being unquestionably one of the best pianoforte composers and players of our time. His abundance of ideas, of which a striving genius never seems to be able to let go so soon as it has got possession of a subject worthy of his fancy, only too frequently leads him to pile up ideas, etc. Fancy, in the extraordinary degree which Beethoven possesses, supported, too, by extraordinary knowledge, is a valuable possession, and, indeed, an indispensable one for a composer, etc. The critic, who, after he has tried to accustom himself more and more to Mr. Beethoven's manner, has learned to admire him more than he did at first, can scarcely suppress the wish that . . . . it might occur to this fanciful composer to practise a certain economy in his labors. . . . . This tenth collection, as the critic has said, seems deserving of high praise. Good invention, an earnest, manly style, ... well-ordered thoughts in every part, difficulties not carried to an excess, an entertaining treatment of the harmony—lift these Sonatas above the many.

In No. 21 (February, 1800) justice is done to the "Sonate pathétique." Except a passing notice of the publication of the Quartets, Op. 18, made by a correspondent, Vol. III of the "Allg. Mus. Zeitung" contains *nothing* on the works of Beethoven. So that more than a year passed between the favorable review of the "Sonate pathétique" and the letter to Breitkopf and Härtel of April 22nd. The mild tone of that missive is, therefore, easily explained. The tone of the journal had completely changed; this fact, and time, had assuaged Beethoven's wrath, and finally the publishers in applying to him for manuscripts had made the *amende honorable*.

In the number of May 26th begins, with a notice of the two Sonatas for Pianoforte and Violin, Op. 23 and Op. 24, that long series of fair, candid and generously eulogistic articles on Beethoven's works which culminated in July, 1810, in the magnificent review of the C minor Symphony by E. T. A. Hoffmann—a labor of love that laid the foundation of a new school of musical criticism.

III. Upon the last topic of the letter to Breitkopf and Härtel something remains to be said. It was in the "Intelligenzblatt" of the "Allg. Mus. Zeit." for May, 1800, that Rochlitz made a touching appeal for aid for the last survivor of Sebastian Bach's children. "This family," says he, "has now died out down to the single daughter of the great Sebastian Bach, and this daughter is now very old. . . . This daughter is starving. . . . The publishers of the 'Musik Zeitung' and I offer to obligate if anybody shall entrust us with money to forward it in the most expeditious and careful manner, and to give account of it in the 'Intelligenzblätter'." The first account is in the paper for December. Regina Susanna Bach publishes her "thanks" for 96 thalers and 5 silbergroschens contributed, as the "careful account" which is appended shows, by sixteen persons, four of whom, in Vienna, sent more than 80 florins, leaving certainly but a small sum as the offering of "her Germany." One other—and only one—account appears, in June, 1801. It is an acknowledgment by Rochlitz, Breitkopf and Härtel and Fräulein Bach of having received on May 10th the considerable sum of 307 florins Viennese (the equal of 200 thalers)

through the Viennese musician Andreas Streicher, collected by Streicher and Count Fries. At the same time the famous Viennese composer Herr van Beethoven declares that he will publish one of·his newest works solely for the benefit of the daughter of Bach . . . . so that the good old lady may derive the benefit of it from time to time. Therefore he nobly urges that the publication be hastened as much as possible lest the daughter of Bach die before his object be attained.

Whether or not any such work was published is not known. Unsupported conjectures as to the names left blank in the letter to Amenda when originally printed in the "Signale" are of no use, and if made might hereafter expose the conjecturer to just ridicule; there remain, then, but two topics which require a word of comment—the year omitted in the date, and the friend of his youth of whom Beethoven speaks in such strong terms of affection—both of which, however, may better be disposed of, in what is to be said upon the letter to Wegeler of June 29th.

This long, important and very interesting paper affords an illustration of the readiness with which a conjecture may be accepted as a truth, until one is compelled to subject it to rigid examination. Thus, in using this letter for a particular purpose,[1] Wegeler's date "most probably 1800" was accepted, as it had universally been for forty years, without question; but the moment

[1]The attempt to fix the chronology of Beethoven's works.

it became necessary to subject its entire contents to careful scrutiny, for the purposes of this biography, the error became at once so apparent as really to awaken a feeling of mortification for the temporary blindness that allowed it to pass unquestioned. The allusions to Susanna Bach ("You see it is very convenient, etc."), to his change of lodgings, to the publication of his portrait by Artaria, and (in the second letter) to the change of his physicians, are all more or less indicative of the true date, 1801, while the mention of Breuning's return to Vienna is proof positive.   Finally, the similarity, almost identity, of passages in the Amenda letter to portions of this, shows that the two belong to the same June. Thus we at last have the gratification of seeing these two valuable documents fall easily and naturally into their true place in Beethoven's history.   It is worth noting that this Wegeler letter offers —at the least, appears to offer—an example of Beethoven's occasional loose way of making statements; as in the letter to Breitkopf and Härtel he writes as if he had half a dozen unpublished concertos on hand, so now he speaks of having "already given several" *Akademien;* and yet the most careful research has failed to show that his concerts were at this time more than three in number in all; or that he had ever even given more than one public concert in Vienna.   Perhaps, however, he may have included those given in Prague in his "several."   As nothing can be added to his account of his bad health and incipient deafness, we pass to the passages upon Breuning and Ries.

IV. The opinion was before expressed, that the "man" spoken of in the Amenda letter as having come to Vienna, to Beethoven's comfort, was Anton Reicha.[1]   They were alike in age—Reicha being but a few months the elder—and alike in tastes and pursuits. Reicha was superior in the culture of schools and in what is called musical learning; Beethoven in genius and originality as a composer and in skill as a pianist.   The talents of each commanded the respect of the other.   Both were aspiring, ambitious, yet diverged sufficiently in their views of art to prevent all invidious rivalry.   Reicha gained a reputation which, in process of time, secured him the high position which he held during the last twenty years of his life—that of Méhul's successor in the Paris Conservatoire.

To Beethoven, who was still digesting plans for musical tours, the experience of his friend must have been of great value; not less to Reicha the experience of Beethoven in Vienna.   But he

---

[1] The German editor of Vol. II insists that it was not Reicha but Stephan von Breuning—though he permits all of Thayer's argument to stand.

was by no means dependent upon Beethoven for an introduction into the highest musical circles of the capital.   It has been shown in a previous chapter how freely the salons were opened to every talented young musician, but beyond this he bore a well-known name and the veteran Haydn kindly remembered him as one of the promising young men who had paid him their respects in Bonn.   His opera "Ubaldi" was performed in Prince Lobkowitz's palace, and this probably led to his introduction to the Empress Maria Theresia, who gave him an Italian libretto, "Argene Regina di Granata," for composition, in which the Empress herself sang a part at the private performance in the palace.

Thus Beethoven and Reicha again met and lived on equal terms.   "We spent fourteen years together,"[1] said the latter, "as closely united as Orestes and Pylades, and were always together in our youth.   After an eight years' separation we met each other again in Vienna and confided all our experiences to each other."

V. When Wegeler says of Stephan von Breuning, "But he had, with short interruptions, spent his life in closest association with Beethoven from his tenth year to his death," he says too much; and too little when he writes that Beethoven "had once broken for a considerable space with Breuning (and with what friend did he not?)"   For besides the quarrel, which Ries describes, there came at last so decided a separation that Breuning's name disappears from our history for a period of eight to ten years— and that, too, not from *his* fault.

It was impossible that the two should have met in 1801 on such terms as those on which they had parted in 1796.   Breuning had passed this interval of five years in a small provincial town, Mergentheim, in the monotonous routine of a petty office, in the service of a semi-military, semi-religious institution which had so sunk in grandeur and power as to be little more than a venerable name—a relic of the past.   In the same service he had now returned to Vienna.   How Beethoven had been employed, and how he had risen, we have seen.   Thus, their relative positions in society had completely changed.   Beethoven now moved familiarly in circles to which Breuning could have access only by his or some other friend's protection.

In view of the relation in which Wegeler stood to the Breuning family, Beethoven might well have said more about "Steffen," but not easily less.   Even here something of patronizing condescension in the tone makes itself felt, which becomes far too

[1]From 1785 to the end of October, 1792; and from the winter 1800-'01 to 1808; two periods of seven years each, separated by the eight years' interval.

pronounced when he speaks of him in the second letter—that of November. Reading these passages in connection with those unlucky sentences in the Amenda letter, which have been censured in another place, one feels that Breuning had been made sensible, to a painful degree, how great his friend had grown. Wegeler himself is struck by Breuning's non-appearance at Beethoven's private concert, and remarks: "He must have felt his disappointment with this old friend all the more, since Breuning had been developed by Father Ries from an amateur to a most admirable violinist, and had several times played in electoral concerts."

The more thoroughly the character of Breuning is examined, not only in his subsequent relations to Beethoven but also in the light of all that is known of him as a public official, as a husband, father and friend, the higher he stands as a man. Under circumstances, in his office, fitted to try his patience beyond the ordinary limits of endurance, he never failed to bear himself nobly, as a man of high principle, ever ready to sacrifice private and personal considerations to the call of duty. In private life he was invariably just, generous, tenacious of the right. Whatever causes he may have had on divers occasions to complain of Beethoven, we learn nothing of them from his correspondence so far as it has been made public, unless a single passage cited by Wegeler be thought an exception; yet this is but the expression of heartfelt sorrow and compassion—not one word of anger. And we know that Beethoven, when in distress, never turned to him in vain for sympathy nor for such aid as was in his power to give. In the miserable years to come the reader will learn enough of Breuning, though by no means a prominent figure, to feel respect and admiration for his character, and to see for himself how unjust to him were those letters—written by Beethoven under the impulse of short-lived choler—which Ries has contributed to the "Notizen." There is some temptation to think that Breuning was of those whom Beethoven "estimated at only what they were worth to him"; but let us trust that, should ever the blanks in the Amenda letter be filled from the autograph, his name will not be found—certainly not, if the conjecture as to the time of Amenda's residence in Vienna prove correct. It is difficult to avoid saying either too much or too little on such a topic as this of Breuning and Beethoven—to strike the just medium in the strength of the language used; but the subject has been made the occasion of so much injudicious comment, it was not possible to pass it over.

VI. The "Intelligenz-Blatt" of Bonn, under date of November 30, 1784, announces the baptism, on the preceding day, of Ferdinand, son of Franz Ries.

Like many others who have become eminent musicians, his taste and capabilities manifested themselves very early; as, at five years old, he began his musical education under his father, and afterwards under Bernhard Romberg, the celebrated violoncello player.

The French invasion, the departure of Romberg in consequence (1794) from Bonn, and the pecuniary straits to which Franz Ries was reduced,

prevented much attention being, for some time, paid to the instruction of his son. . . . . At last, when he was about thirteen ("he had reached the age of 13 years", says the "Rheinischer Antiquarius"), a friend of his father took him to Arnsberg in Westphalia, for the purpose of learning thoroughbass and composition from an organ-player in that neighborhood. . . . . The pupil proved so much the more able to teach of the two, that the organist was obliged to give the matter up at once and proposed to young Ries to teach him the violin instead. As a *pis-aller*, this was accepted; and Ries remained at Arnsberg about nine months, after which he returned home. Here he remained upwards of two years, improving himself in his art with great industry. . . . At length, in the year 1801, he went to Munich with the same friend who had formerly taken him to Arnsberg. Here he was thrown upon his own resources; and throughout the trying and dispiriting circumstances which, with slight exception, attended the next years of his life, he appears to have displayed a firmness, an energy, and an independence of mind, the more honorable, perhaps, from the very early age at which they were called into action. At Munich, Mr. Ries was left by his friend, with little money and but very slender prospects. He tried for some time to procure pupils, but was at last reduced to copy music at three-pence per sheet. With this scanty pittance, he not only continued to keep himself free from embarrassments, but saved a few ducats to take him to Vienna, where he had hopes of patronage and advancement from Beethoven. . . . . He set out from Munich with only seven ducats and reached Vienna before they were exhausted!

The citations are from that noble musical journal the London "Harmonicon," and belong to an article on Ries published in March, 1824. They correspond perfectly to a sketch of Ries's life in the "Rheinischer Antiquarius," although there are sufficient differences to show that the materials of the two articles were drawn from independent sources. The "Antiquarius" (Part III, Vol. II, p. 62), however, dates Ries's arrival in Munich 1800, the "Harmonicon" giving it 1801. But the difference is rather apparent than real, since the winter of 1800-1801 includes them both, and is therefore of very little import. But when Ries, in the "Notizen" (p. 75), says: "On my arrival in *Vienna* in 1800," the discrepancy is one not to be passed over without investigation; not that it is a matter of much interest in itself when a boy of fifteen or sixteen years became a pupil of Beethoven, but because of its bearing upon other and weightier questions in the chronology of the master's life and works.   Which, then, is correct?

Ayrton, the editor of the "Harmonicon," could have obtained (in 1824) the date for his article only from Ries himself, as in fact the internal evidence proves him to have done.   It was published after the announcement of Ries's farewell concert in London, with the evident intention of aiding in securing its success, and must have been presented to Ries for revision before it was sent to press.   Ries, therefore, must have erred by a lapse of memory, in 1824 as he admitted he may have done, or in December, 1837, when he wrote the "Notizen."   As for the writer, he has no hesitation in accepting September or October, 1801, as the date of Ries's advent in Vienna.   Thus the last of these errors—that of Wegeler in his date of the letter of June 29; that of Schindler (in his first editions) in the date of the "Christus am Ölberg"; and this of Ries—which had thrown all this period of Beethoven's history into a confusion that seemed inextricable, is satisfactorily rectified, and the current of the narrative now flows as clear and unimpeded here as in any other part.

Let us return to it.   The "Harmonicon" proceeds:

Ries' hopes from his father's early friend, were not disappointed; Beethoven received him with a cordial kindness, too rare, alas! from men who have risen to eminence and distinction towards those whose claim upon them is founded on the reminiscences of their humble state.   He at once took the young man under his immediate care and tuition; advanced him pecuniary loans, which his subsequent conduct converted to gifts; and allowed him to be the first to take the title of pupil and appear in public as such.

So also the "Notizen":

In the letter of recommendation from my father there had been opened a small credit account to be used in case of need.   I never made use of it but, when a few times Beethoven discovered that I was short of funds, he sent me money without being asked and never wanted to take it back.   He was really very fond of me, of which fact he once in his absent-mindedness gave me a very comical proof.   Once when I returned from Silesia, where I had spent some time at the country-seat of Prince Lichnowsky as pianist on the recommendation of Beethoven, and entered his room he was about to shave himself and had lathered his face up to his eyes—for so far his fearfully stiff beard reached.   He jumped up, embraced me cordially and thereby transferred so much of the lather

from his left cheek to my right that he had none left.   Did we laugh?
Beethoven must also have learned privately how matters had gone with
me; for he was acquainted with many of my youthful escapades, with
which he only teased me.   In many cases he disclosed a really paternal
interest in me.

"But with all his kindness" continues the "Harmonicon,"

Beethoven would not give Ries instruction in thoroughbass or composition.   He said it required a particular gift to explain them with
clearness and precision, and, besides that, Albrechtsberger was the
acknowledged master of all composers.   This latter had almost given up
teaching, being very old, and was persuaded to take a new pupil only by
the strong recommendation of Beethoven and by the temptation of a
ducat a lesson.   Poor Ries' ducats ran only to the number of 28; after
this he was driven to his books again.

So it appears that he was Beethoven's pupil only upon the
pianoforte.   The manner in which he was taught is also described
in the "Notizen":

When Beethoven gave me a lesson I must say that contrary to
his nature he was particularly patient.   I was compelled to attribute
this and his friendly disposition, which was seldom interrupted, chiefly
to his great affection and love for my father.   Thus, sometimes, he would
permit me to repeat a thing ten times, or even oftener.   In the Variations
dedicated to the Princess Odescalchi (Op. 34), I was obliged to repeat
the last *Adagio* variations almost entirely seventeen times; yet he was
still dissatisfied with the expression of the little cadenza, although I
thought I played it as well as he.   On this day I had a lesson which
lasted nearly two hours.   If I made a mistake in passages or missed
notes and leaps which he frequently wanted emphasized he seldom said
anything; but if I was faulty in expression, in *crescendos*, etc., or in the
character of the music, he grew angry because, as he said, the former was
accidental while the latter disclosed lack of knowledge, feeling, or atten-
tiveness.   The former slips very frequently happened to him even when
he was playing in public.

"I often played on two fortepianos with Ries," says Czerny,
"among other things the Sonata, Op. 47, which had been arranged
for two pianofortes.   Ries played very fluently, clear but cold."[1]

Here we have a key to the identity of so many of Ries's and
Czerny's facts and anecdotes of those years, written out by them
independently; the latter, as he assures us, having first become
acquainted with the "Notizen" through the quotations of Court
Councillor Lenz.   The two brilliant boys, thrown so much together,
would never weary of talking of their famous master.   The stories
of his oddities and eccentricities, minute facts relating to his

[1] From O. Jahn's posthumous papers.

compositions, were, therefore, common property; and it is clear that some which in this manner became known to Ries at last assumed in his memory the aspect of personal experiences and, as such, are related in the "Notizen." The author of this work once introduced an incident into something that he was writing, under the full conviction of having been an actor in it, which he now knows was only related to him by his brother. Yet only some six or seven years had elapsed, whereas Ries wrote of a period which ended thirty-five years before.

Another remark of Czerny's is as follows:

When the French were in Vienna for the first time, in 1805, Beethoven visited a number of officers and generals who were musical and for whom he played Gluck's "Iphigenia in Tauris" from the score, to which they sang the choruses and songs not at all ill. I begged the score from him and at home wrote out the pianoforte score as I had heard him play it. I still have this arrangement (November, 1852). From that time I date my style of arranging orchestral works, and he was always wholly satisfied with my arrangements of his symphonies, etc.

A lad who, though not yet fifteen years old, was able to write a pianoforte score of such an opera after a single hearing, certainly deserved the testimonial to his talent which, though written by another hand, was signed at the time by Beethoven and sealed. The testimonial, in the possession of the Gesellschaft der Musikfreunde in Vienna, runs as follows:

We, the undersigned, cannot withhold from the lad Carl Czerny, who has made such extraordinary progress on the pianoforte, far surpassing what might be expected from a boy of fourteen years, that for this reason, and also because of his marvelous memory, he is deserving of all possible support, the more since his parents have expended their fortune in the education of this promising son.

Vienna, December 7, 1805.

Ludwig van Beethoven. (Seal)

The master had early and wisely warned him against a too free use of his extraordinary memory. "My musical memory," Czerny writes,

enabled me to play the Beethovenian works by heart without exception, and during the years 1804-1805 I was obliged to play these works in this manner at Prince Lichnowsky's once or twice a week, he calling out only the desired opus number. Beethoven, who was present a few times, was not pleased. "Even if he plays correctly on the whole," he remarked, "he will forget in this manner the quick survey, the *a vista*-playing and, occasionally, the correct expression."

Very neat is the anecdote which Czerny relates in the "Wiener Musikzeitung" of September 28th, 1845, how, after he had outgrown his studies, he was deservedly reprimanded for a few additions which he made on his own account in one of his master's works.

On the whole he was pleased with my performance of his works .... but he scolded me for every blunder with a kind freedom which I shall never forget.   When once, for instance, I played the Quintet with Wind-Instruments with Schuppanzigh, I permitted myself, in a spirit of youthful carelessness, many changes, in the way of adding difficulties to the music, the use of the higher octave, etc.—Beethoven took me severely to task in the presence of Schuppanzigh, Linke and the other players. The next day I received the following letter from him, which I copy carefully from the original draft:

"Dear Czerny:
    "To-day I cannot see you, but to-morrow I will call on you myself to have a talk with you.   I burst forth so yesterday that I was sorry after it had happened; but you must pardon that in an author who would have preferred to hear his work exactly as he wrote it, no matter how beautifully you played in general.   I will make *loud* amends at the Violoncello Sonata (I was to play his Violoncello Sonata with Linke the next week).   Be assured that as an artist I have the greatest wishes for your success and will always try to show myself,
                        Your
                            true Friend
                                Beethoven."

This letter did more than anything else to cure me of the desire to make any changes in the performance of his works, and I wish that it might have the same influence on all pianists.

Chapter XXI

Beethoven's Love-Affairs—The Letter to the "Immortal Beloved"—Giulietta Guicciardi—Therese Brunswick—Countess Erdödy—Therese Malfatti—Confused Chronologies—Many Contradictory Theories and Speculations.

IN the letter dated November 16, Beethoven's strong expressions of desire and intention to exhibit his powers as pianist and composer in other cities, are striking and worthy of the reader's attention, yet need no comment; but a new topic there introduced must be treated at some length, not because it is of very great importance in itself, but as an episode in the master's life which has employed so many pens and upon which biographer and novelist seem to have contended which could make the most of it and paint it in the highest romantic colors.[1]

The sentences referred to are: "I am living more pleasantly since. I live more amongst men. . . . This change has been wrought by a *dear fascinating* girl, etc." Notwithstanding all that has been written on this text there is little reason to think that Beethoven's passion for this particularly fascinating girl was more engrossing or lasting than at other periods for others, although peculiar circumstances subsequently kept it more alive in his memory. The testimony of Wegeler, Breuning, Romberg, Ries,

[1] The Editor of this English edition of Thayer's "Life of Beethoven" is unwilling to admit that the author's argument against the Countess Guicciardi as the lady to whom the famous love-letter which is the basis of the episode referred to by the author, has been disproved; or that the burden of proof is against Thayer's theory (never put forward as a demonstrated fact, but rather as what the scientists call a "working hypothesis") that the object of his love at the time the letter was written was the Countess Therese Brunswick (or Brunsvik, as the Hungarian branch of the family wrote the name). The question is one of great difficulty, however, and the Editor has thought it wise, expedient and only fair to the memory of Mr Thayer, to bring together the *disjecta membra* of his argument as they are to be found in the body of Vol. II and the body and Appendices of Vol. III of the original German edition, in a continuous chapter, and then to add, in the form of a comprehensive postscript, an abstract of the opinion of others and some suggestions of his own touching the woman who, though not yet definitively identified, wears the halo which streams from the title which Beethoven bestowed upon her—his "Immortal Beloved." It will be observed that the question turns largely on an adjustment of dates—a necessary procedure in other affairs of Beethoven's besides those of his heart.

has been cited to the point that Beethoven "was never without
a love, and generally deeply engrossed in it."

In Vienna (says Wegeler) at least as long as I lived there, Beethoven
always had a love-affair on his hands, and occasionally made conquests
which, though not impossible, might have been difficult of achievement
to many an Adonis. . . . . I will add that, so far as I know, every one
of his sweethearts belonged to the higher social stations.

So, also, friends of Beethoven with whom Jahn conversed
in 1852. Thus according to Carl Czerny he was said to have been
in love with a Countess Keglevics, who was not generally considered
handsome. The Sonata in E-flat, Op. 7 (dedicated to her), was
called "Die Verliebte" ("The Maiden, or Woman, in Love"). Dr.
Bertolini, friend and physician of Beethoven from 1806 to 1816,
said: "Beethoven generally had a flame; the Countess Guicciardi,
Mme. von Frank, Bettina Brentano and others." He was not
insensible to ladies fair and frail. Doležalek, a music teacher
who came to Vienna in 1800 and was the master's admirer and
friend to the last, adds the particular that "he never showed that
he was in love."

In short, Beethoven's experience was precisely that of many
an impulsive man of genius, who for one cause or another never
married and therefore never knew the calm and quiet, but un-
changing, affection of happy conjugal life. One all-absorbing but
temporary passion, lasting until its object is married to a more
favored lover, is forgotten in another destined to end in like
manner, until, at length, all faith in the possibility (for them) of
a permanent, constant attachment to one person is lost. Such
men after reaching middle age may marry for a hundred various
motives of convenience, but rarely for love.

Upon this particular passion of Beethoven, the present writer
labors under the disadvantage of being compelled to subordinate
his imagination to his reason and to sacrifice flights of fancy
to the duty of ascertaining and imparting the modicum of truth
that underlies all this branch of Beethoven literature, of extract-
ing the few grains of wheat from the immense mass of chaff. With
what success remains to be seen.

When Schindler, in perusing the "Notizen," came to the
passages above quoted, with his usual agility in jumping at conclusions he decided at once, that Beethoven here refers to the
Countess Julia Guicciardi, and so states in his book; probably
hitting the truth nearer than on the next page, where he makes
Fräulein Marie Koschak the object of Beethoven's "autumnal

love," some half a dozen years before the two had ever met. In this case, however, there is no reason to suppose him mistaken.

On the 16th of November, 1801—the date of Beethoven's letter—the Countess Guicciardi was just one week less than seventeen years of age. She is traditionally described as having had a good share of personal attractions, and is known to have been a fine looking woman even in advanced years. She appears to have possessed a mind of fair powers, cultivated and accomplished to the degree then common to persons of her rank; but it is not known that she was in any way eminently distinguished, unless for musical taste and skill as a pianist, which may perhaps be indicated in the dedication to her of a sonata by Kleinheinz as well as by Beethoven.

Julia Guicciardi's near relationship to the Brunswicks would naturally throw her into the society of Beethoven immediately upon the transfer of her father from Trieste to Vienna; their admiration of his talents, their warm affection for him as a man, would awaken her curiosity to see him and create a most natural prejudice in his favor. Coming to the capital from a small, distant provincial town when hardly of an age to enter society, and finding herself so soon distinguished by the particular attentions and evident admiration of a man of Beethoven's social position and fame, might well dazzle the imagination of a girl of sixteen, and dispose her, especially if she possessed more than common musical taste and talents, to return in a certain degree the affection proffered to her by the distinguished author of the Symphony, the Quartet, the Septet, the "Prometheus" music, and so many wonderful sonatas, by the unrivalled pianist, the generous, impulsive, enthusiastic artist, although unprepossessing in person and unable to offer either wealth or a title. There was romance in the affair. Besides these considerations there are traditions and reminiscences of old friends of the composer all tending to confirm the opinion of Schindler, that the "fascinating girl" was indeed the young Countess Guicciardi. That writer, however, knew nothing of the matter until twenty years afterwards; but what he learned came from Beethoven himself.

It happened, when the topic came up between them, "that, being in a public place where he did not like to trust himself to speak," says Schindler, Beethoven also wrote his share in the conversation, so far as it related to this subject; hence his words may still be read in a Conversation Book of February, 1823, preserved in the Royal Library at Berlin. His statements have certainly gained nothing in clearness from his whim of writing them in part in bad French.

It is proper to state, before introducing the citation from this book, that the young lady married Count Wenzel Robert Gallenberg, a prolific composer of ballet and occasional music, on the 3rd of November, 1803. The young pair soon left Vienna for Italy and were in Naples in the spring of 1806; for Gallenberg was one of the composers of the music for the fêtes, on the occasion of Joseph Bonaparte's assumption of the crown of the Two Sicilies. When the Neapolitan Barbaja took charge of the R. I. Opera at Vienna, toward the close of 1821, he made the Count an associate in the administration, and thus it happened that Schindler had occasion to call upon him with a message from Beethoven.

The Conversation Books of those years show, that the question of selling the opera, "Fidelio," to various theatres, was one often discussed by Beethoven and his friends, and, also, that the author had no complete copy of the score. It thus became necessary to borrow one for the purpose of copying the whole or parts; and at this point we turn to the Conversation Book. Schindler, in the midst of a long series of remarks upon heterogeneous topics, expresses surprise that the Dresden theatre has never purchased "Fidelio," and adds his opinion, that Weber will do all in his power to further Beethoven's interest, both in regard to the opera and to the Mass in D. Then follows political news—Spain, England, etc.—and the sale or hypothecation by Dr. Bach of certain bank shares on which Beethoven wishes to raise money; and then:

Schindler: Now as to "Fidelio"; what shall, what can I do to expedite that?

Beethoven: Steiner has the score.

Schindler: I shall go to Count Gallenberg, who will lend it to you for a time with pleasure. It would be best if you were to have it copied at your own expense. You may ask 40 ducats. (After a farther remark or two he promises to see Gallenberg "to-morrow morning"; some pages farther is the report):

Schindler: Gallenberg presents his compliments; he will send the score, provided they have two copies. If this is not the case he will have the score copied for you. I am to call on him again in two days. (The conversation then turns upon copying certain songs and upon lithographing the Mass in D; after which):

Schindler: He (Gallenberg) did not inspire me with much respect to-day.

Beethoven: I was his invisible benefactor through others.

Schindler: He ought to know that, so that he might have more respect for you than he seems to have. (Kitchen affairs follow here for a space; then Beethoven takes the pencil and writes):

Beethoven: So it seems you did not find G. favorably disposed toward me; I am little concerned in the matter, but I should like to know what he said.

Schindler: He replied to me that he thought that you must have the score yourself; but when I assured him that you did not have it he said that its loss was a consequence of your irregular habits and many changes of lodgings. What affair is that of the public? And, moreover, who will care what such persons think? What have you decided to do in the matter at Steiner's? To keep quiet still longer? Dr. Bach recently asked me about it. I thought you wanted to keep the score because you had none. Do you want to give the five-part fugue also for nothing? My dearest friend and master, that is too much generosity towards such unworthy persons. You will only be laughed at. (Steiner had bought some compositions of B. and not published them.)

Beethoven: (having asked Schindler if he had seen Gallenberg's wife, proceeds): *J'étois bien aimé d'elle et plus que jamais son époux. Il étoit pourtant plutôt son amant que moi, mais par elle j'apprenois de son misère et je trouvais un homme de bien, qui me donnait la somme de 500 fl. pour le soulager. Il étoit toujours mon ennemi, c'étoit justement la raison, que je fusse tout le bien que possible.*

Schindler: It was for this reason that he added "He is an intolerable fellow." Probably because of pure gratitude. But forgive them, Lord, they know not what they do. *Est-ce qu'il y a longtemps qu'elle est mariée avec Mons. de Gallenberg?—Mad. la Comtesse? Était-elle riche? Elle a une belle figure jusqu'ici!*

Beethoven: Elle est née Guicciardi. Elle étoit l'épouse de lui avant son voyage en Italie—arrivé à Vienne elle cherchoit moi pleurant, mais je la méprisois.[1]

Schindler: Hercules at the crossways!

Beethoven: And if I had wished to give my vital powers with that life, what would have remained for the nobler, the better (things)?

Reverence for the composer, and admiration for his compositions, must have led many who will read this to the perusal of the constantly accumulating literature of which Beethoven and

---

[1] Jahn transcribes the last words ("*je la méprisois, etc.*) as follows: *Elle est née Guicciardi elle étoit* (an illegible word marked with an interrogation point) *qu epouse de lui (avant son voyage) de l'Italie. Arrivée à Vienne et elle cherchoit moi pleurant, mais je la méprisois.*

Ludwig Nohl asserts that the words "*arrivée à Vienne*" had been "added" by Schindler. But Schindler printed the passage in 1845 as well as in 1860 thus: *Elle étoit l'épouse de lui avant son voyage en Italie . . . . Arrivée à Vienne elle cherchoit moi pleurant, etc.* In the edition of 1860 of his biography of Beethoven he adds the following remark: "One of the conversation books of 1823, all of which are preserved in the Royal Court Library at Berlin, contains these revelations." If Nohl's assertion is correct it follows that Schindler lied and deceived the public, being guilty of a forgery which escaped the eyes of both Jahn and Thayer; and that, furthermore, he was guilty of the folly of calling attention to the very book whose contents he had falsified. Nohl asserts further that Giulietta had sought an interview with Beethoven before her journey to Italy. On such an act he founds the assertion that the young woman, married only a few months, was already willing to leave her husband. From circumstances unknown to Nohl it is certain that the visit did not take place until after her return to Vienna in 1822.

his works are the subject; and they must remember the prominence accorded to the Guicciardi affair. Will they believe that all the *established* facts, which have ever been made public, are exhausted in these pages already? This is literally true. All else is but conjecture or mistake. There is nothing in the present state of knowledge on this subject to relieve the great mass of turgid eloquence expended upon it from being described in one word as— nonsense. The foundation for a tragedy is certainly small in a case where the lover writes: "It is the first time that I feel as if marriage *might* make me happy"; and immediately adds "now, of course, I could not marry!" because the gratification of his ambition was more to him than domestic life with the beloved one.

In November, 1852, Jahn had an interview with the Countess Gallenberg. On so delicate a topic as Beethoven's passion for her fifty years before, reticence was natural; but had the affair in truth been of the importance that others have given it, some hint must have confessed it. Yet there is nothing of the kind in his notes of the conversation. Here they are:

Beethoven was her teacher; he had his music sent to her and was extremely severe until the correct interpretation was reached down to the smallest detail; he laid stress upon a light manner of playing; he easily became angry, threw down his music and tore it; he would take no pay but linen, although he was very poor, under the pretence that the Countess had sewed it. He also taught Princess Odescalchi and Baroness Erdmann; sometimes he went to his pupils, sometimes they came to him. He did not like to play his own compositions, but would only improvise. At the slightest disturbance he would get up and go away. Count Brunswick, who played the violoncello, adored him as did (also) his sisters, Therese and Countess Deym. Beethoven had given her (the Countess Guicciardi) the Rondo in G, but begged its return when he had to dedicate something to the Countess Lichnowsky, and then dedicated the Sonata to her. B. was very ugly, but noble, refined in feeling and cultured.

In this simple record the lady's memory evidently mistakes by overrating the poverty of Beethoven at the time she was his pupil and in making him then so negligent in dress. "In his earlier years Beethoven dressed carefully, even elegantly; only later did he grow negligent, which he carried to the verge of uncleanliness," says Grillparzer; and Czerny: "About the year 1813–'14, when B. looked well and strong, he also cared for his outward appearance." But what a blow to all the supposed romantic significance is the short, prosaic account of the dedication of the C-sharp minor Sonata to her—a composition which was not a favorite with the composer himself. "Everybody is always talking about the C-sharp minor Sonata! Surely I have written better things. There is the Sonata in F-sharp major—that is something very different," he once said to Czerny.

There is but one well-authenticated fact to be added, namely, that Beethoven kept up his intercourse with the family Guicciardi certainly as late as May or June, 1823, that is, to within six months of the young lady's marriage. A careful survey and comparison both of the published data and of the private traditions and hints gleaned during a residence of several years at Vienna, result in the opinion (an opinion, note, not a statement resting on competent evidence) that Beethoven at length decided to offer Countess Julia his hand; that she was not indisposed to accept it; and that one of her parents consented to the match, but the other, probably the father, refused to entrust the happiness of his daughter to a man without rank, fortune or permanent engagement; a man, too, of character and temperament so peculiar, and afflicted with the incipient stages of an infirmity which, if not arrested and cured, must deprive him of all hope of obtaining any high and remunerative official appointment and at length compel him to abandon his career as the great pianoforte virtuoso. As the Guicciardis themselves were not wealthy, prudence forbade such a marriage. Be all this as it may, this much is certain: Beethoven did not marry the Countess Julia Guicciardi; Count Wenzel Robert Gallenberg did. The rejected lover—true to a principle enunciated in a letter to Zmeskall of March 29, 1799, "there is no use in quarrelling with what cannot be changed"—made the best of it, and went to work on the "Sinfonia eroica"!

Every reader acquainted with Schindler's book will have noticed that two grave matters, connected by him with the Guicciardi affair, have been silently passed over, notwithstanding the very great importance given to them by him and his copyists. They must now be considered. Schindler's honest and conscientious desire to ascertain and impart the truth concerning Beethoven admits no doubt. The spirit was willing, but his weakness as an investigator was something extraordinary. His helplessness in finding and following the clue out of a difficulty is sometimes pitiable, sometimes ludicrous. He reminds us, now and then, of the character described by Addison: "He is perpetually puzzled and perplexed amidst his own blunders."

Take the present matter for an instance. In his first editions of the biography the date given to the Guicciardi affair is 1806. With Wegeler's letter before him giving him one fixed point —November, 1801—and the "Gräfliches Taschenbuch" to be

consulted in every respectable bookstore and public library for the
day of Gallenberg's marriage, November 3, 1803, he is still at a loss.
"I had first to come to Paris, there make the acquaintance of
Cherubini, in order to hit, quite accidentally, upon a certain clue
for this date for which I had vainly searched in Vienna.   Cherubini
and his wife, soon after their arrival in Vienna in 1805, heard of
this affair as of something that had happened two years before."
Following this hint, in his edition of 1860, he changes the 1806
to 1803—that is, he adopts the new date because, twenty years
before, he heard from an old gentleman of 80 years and his wife,
nearly as old, that, thirty-five years before, they had heard that
some two years before that time Beethoven had been jilted! They
also "could say with certainty that the effect upon Beethoven's
, mood had already been overcome";—which we are very willing to
hear from them, although the fact needed no confirmation. Again;
his conversation with Beethoven, given as an appendix to the
edition of 1845, was suppressed in the first because the Countess
Gallenberg was then living; the "Taschenbuch" would have
taught him that this objection remained in force until March
22nd, 1856!   How is it possible to read with confidence the opinions
and statements of so helpless a writer—even when we grant him,
as we do Schindler, the utmost rectitude of intention—except
when he speaks from personal knowledge, or upon evidence
which he shows to be good?

Having in a manner so extraordinary fixed the date to his
satisfaction, Schindler proceeds to the catastrophe:

Yet touching the results of this break upon the spirits of our master,
so highly blessed by this love, something more may be said.   In his
despair he sought comfort with his approved and particularly respected
friend Countess Marie Erdödy—at her country-seat at Jedlersee, in
order to spend a few days in her company.   Thence, however, he disappeared and the Countess thought he had returned to Vienna, when,
three days later, her music-master, Brauchle, discovered him in a distant
part of the palace gardens.   This incident was long kept a close secret,
and only after several years did those familiar with it confide it to the
more intimate friends of Beethoven, long after the love-affair had been
forgotten.   It was associated with a suspicion that it had been the purpose
of the unhappy man to starve himself to death.   Those friends who made
close observation of the attitude of Beethoven towards the music-master
noticed that he treated him with extraordinary attention thereafter.

Jedlersee is so near Vienna, that a stout walker like Beethoven would think nothing of the distance; and for *him* to obey
the whim or necessity of the moment, and disappear for two or
three days, is the very weakest of all grounds for the astounding

conjecture here gravely related. But grant for a moment that something of the kind, some time or other, really occurred; what reason is there to suppose that it happened then, and in connection with the Guicciardi matter? None. *Credat Judæus Apella, non ego.* Indeed the whole story, whatever its date and connection, is told on such mere hearsay evidence as would not justify the police in arresting a beggar. To prevent it from passing into the category of established facts—at least in connection with this particular love-affair, and until some new and competent proof be discovered—it may be remarked:

I. Schindler's first knowledge of the passion of Beethoven for Julia Guicciardi was obtained in 1823. Whatever he heard from other sources could only have been afterwards; and in all probability was after Beethoven's death, when his attention was recalled to the subject by a paper presently to be noticed. He does not pretend to have heard this Jedlersee story from any party to it; nor could he, for the Countess Erdödy had been banished from the Austrian dominions long before it could have come to his ears. He is, in fact and upon his own showing, gravely detailing a mere private rumor, current (he says) among certain friends of Beethoven, of an event which happened (if at all) fifteen, twenty or thirty years before, and which was *surmised* by them, or by him, to have occurred at the time he was jilted by the young Countess Guicciardi.

II. There is nothing whatever in Ries's reminiscences, most of which are of the precise period of that affair, which, by any stretch of fancy, can be made to confirm the story; nay, more, they are utterly inconsistent with it. There is nothing even to show that he ever observed that his master's relations to the Guicciardis were in any way remarkable; yet Beethoven's inclination to the society of women was a point in his character that particularly impressed him. "Beethoven," he says,

was fond of the company of women, especially if they had young and pretty faces, and generally when we passed a somewhat charming girl he would turn back and gaze at her through his glasses keenly, and laugh or grin if he noticed that I was looking at him. He was frequently in love, but generally only for a short period. Once when I twitted him concerning his conquest of a pretty woman he admitted that she had held him in the strongest bonds for the longest time, viz., fully seven months.

III. And so too with Breuning. There is no letter, or part of a letter by him (so far as made known by Wegeler), nor any tradition derived from him, that relates to this passion or its supposed consequences; and yet, it is only from one of his letters that we know of the proposal of marriage in 1810; nay, more, we shall find, in 1803, Beethoven inviting a friend to dine with "Countess Guicciardi," at a time when he and Breuning lodged together!

IV. If the Jedlersee story be true at all in connection with this particular lady, the time must have been 1803. But it is totally inconsistent with what is known of the composer's history during that year.

V. Brauchle was not the Countess Erdödy's music-teacher, but the tutor of her children, in which capacity he could hardly have been employed at a time when the eldest was not six years of age! If we are correctly informed, he was not in that service until after the year 1803; nor is it known that Beethoven's intimacy with the Countess had then been formed. In any case, the starvation story may be considered as disposed of for the present.

The force of these arguments will be incidentally but materially increased by the views—if they find favor and acceptance— advanced and supported in a short discussion of the single remaining question belonging to the Guicciardi affair, to which we now come.

It was well known to Beethoven's friends, that he died possessed of a few bank-shares; but where the certificates were deposited neither his brother, Breuning nor Schindler knew. "B. kept his bank-shares in a secret drawer of a cabinet known only to Holz," is one of Jahn's notes of a conversation with Carl Holz. When Schindler read Jahn's manuscript notices and memoranda upon Beethoven and added his comments, he remarked here:

Johann Beethoven first devoted himself to the disappearance of the shares, and not finding them he cried out: "Breuning and Schindler must find them." Holz was asked to come, by Breuning, and requested to say if he did not know where they were concealed. He knew the secret drawer in the old cabinet in which they were kept.

In that "secret drawer" Breuning found not only the bank-certificates, but also various "letters of importance to his friend," as Schindler describes them. One of these was a letter with two postscripts written by Beethoven on two pieces of note-paper with a lead pencil, at some watering-place not named, in the July of a year not given and to a person not indicated. It is couched in terms of enthusiastic love rarely equalled even in romance, being like a translation into words of the most tender and touching passages in his most impassioned musical compositions. This document, placed in Schindler's possession by Breuning, is the original of what was first printed in 1840, as, "three autograph letters written by Beethoven to his Giulietta from a bathing-place in Hungary"[1] and which have so often been reprinted at various times. The letter is as follows:

July 6, in the morning.

My angel, my all, my very self—only a few words to-day and at that with pencil (with yours)—not till to-morrow will my lodgings be definitively determined upon—what a useless waste of time. Why this deep sorrow where necessity speaks—can our love endure except through sacrifices—except through not demanding everything—can you change it that you are not wholly mine, I not wholly thine. Oh, God! look out into the beauties of nature and comfort yourself with that which must be—love demands everything and that very justly—*thus it is with me so far as you are concerned, and you with me.* If we were wholly united you would feel the pain of it as little as I. My journey was a fearful one; I did not reach here until 4 o'clock yesterday morning; lacking horses the post-coach chose another route—but what an awful one. At the stage before the last I was warned not to travel at night—made fearful of a forest, but that only made me the more eager and I was wrong; the coach must needs break down on the wretched road, a bottomless mud road—without such postilions as I had with me I should have stuck in the road. Esterhazy, travelling the usual road hitherward, had the same fate with eight horses that I had with four—yet I got some pleasure out of it, as I always do when I successfully overcome difficulties. Now a quick change to things internal from things external. We shall soon surely see each other; moreover, I cannot communicate to you the observations I have made during the last few days touching my own life—if our hearts were always close together I would make none of the kind. My heart is full of many things to say to you—Ah!—there are moments when I feel that speech is nothing after all—cheer up—remain my true, my only treasure, my all as I am yours; the gods must send us the rest that which shall be best for us.

Your faithful Ludwig.

Evening, Monday, July 6.

You are suffering, my dearest creature—only now have I learned that letters must be posted very early in the morning. Mondays, Thursdays,—the only days on which the mail-coach goes from here to K. You are suffering—Ah! wherever I am there you are also. I shall arrange affairs between us so that I shall live and live with you, what a life! ! ! ! thus! ! ! ! thus without you—pursued by the goodness of mankind hither and thither—which I as little try to deserve as I deserve it. Humility of man towards man—it pains me—and when I consider myself in connection with the universe, what am I and what is he whom we call

---

[1]The Editor of this English edition takes the liberty of inserting the letter in the body of the text. Mr. Thayer, or his first German Editor, Dr. Deiters, put it in the appendix to the third Volume, following it with an argument advanced to show that it was not addressed to the Countess Guicciardi. This argument the English Editor has also transferred to the body of the text so that the discussion may be read continuously.

the greatest—and yet—herein lies the divine in man. I weep when I reflect that you will probably not receive the first intelligence from me until Saturday—much as you love me, I love you more—but do not ever conceal your thoughts from me—good-night—as I am taking the baths I must go to bed. Oh, God! so near so far! Is our love not truly a celestial edifice—firm as Heaven's vault.

Good-morning, on July 7.

Though still in bed my thoughts go out to you, my Immortal Beloved, now and then joyfully, then sadly, waiting to learn whether or not fate will hear us. I can live only wholly with you or not at all— yes, I am resolved to wander so long away from you until I can fly to your arms and say that I am really at home, send my soul enwrapped in you into the land of spirits.—Yes, unhappily it must be so—you will be the more resolved since you know my fidelity—to you, no one can ever again possess my heart—none—never—Oh, God, why is it necessary to part from one whom one so loves and yet my life in W (Vienna) is now a wretched life—your love makes me at once the happiest and the unhappiest of men—at my age I need a steady, quiet life—can that be under our conditions? My angel, I have just been told that the mail-coach goes every day—and I must close at once so that you may receive the L. at once. Be calm, only by a calm consideration of our existence can we achieve our purpose to live together—be calm—love me—to-day— yesterday—what tearful longings for you—you—you—my life—my all— farewell—Oh continue to love me—never misjudge the most faithful heart of your beloved L.

> ever thine
> ever mine
> ever for each other.

Among the many persons before whom at various times Schindler kindly placed the original for examination were Otto Jahn and the present writer, neither of whom ever discovered any other reason to suppose this paper to have been intended for the Countess Guicciardi than Schindler's conjecture and the grounds upon which he had formed it. Bearing in mind that the existence of this paper was utterly unknown to either Breuning or Schindler until after the death of its writer, who alone could have imparted its history, the mental process by which it came to be described in the words just quoted, "three autograph letters written by Beethoven to his Giulietta from a bathing-place in Hungary," is perfectly easy to trace; thus:

In the first of the three parts, or letters, Beethoven speaks of the very disagreeable journey which he had performed with four post-horses, and Esterhazy with eight; in the second he writes of the "mail-coach from here to K." and again, "As I am taking the baths I must go to bed." Now, of the 218 places in the

Austrian postal-guide whose names begin with K, a large number
are in Hungary; the bathing-places in that kingdom are also
numerous; and Esterhazy's possessions were there; hence
Schindler's assumption that Beethoven wrote from a Hungarian
watering-place—which may stand for the present.   His conjecture
as to whom he wrote was of course suggested by his conversation
in 1823 upon the Countess Gallenberg. This assumption, so
obvious and natural for him to make that it was accepted unquestioned and even unsuspected for thirty years, must nevertheless
be tested.

The document presents three incomplete dates, the year being
omitted in each:

> "July 6, in the morning."
> "Evening, Monday, July 6."
> "Good-morning on July 7."

A reference to the almanacs of 1795, 1801, 1807, and 1812,
shows that July 6th fell upon a Monday in those years. The
year 1795 is of course excluded, for Julia Guicciardi had not then
completed her eleventh year, and we turn at once to 1801. The
main subjects of Beethoven's letter to Wegeler of June 29th were
his ailments and the modes of treatment adopted by his medical
advisers; to which he adds his desire for his friend's counsel,
Wegeler being a physician of eminent ability and skill. It was
Wegeler's reply which drew forth the second letter of November
16, only four and a half months after the first, which continues
the subject with equal minuteness of detail. If now the reader
will turn back and carefully reperuse the two, he will see that all
possibility of a journey to some distant watering-place, requiring
the use of four post-horses, whether in Hungary or elsewhere, in
the interval between those letters is absolutely excluded by their
contents. The conclusion is unavoidable that the diary was not
written in 1801.

But may there not be an error either in the day of the month
or of the week in the words: "Evening, Monday, July 6?" If there
be, the inquiry is extended to the years 1800 and 1802.

On July 6th, 1800, the Guicciardi family had hardly reached
Vienna from Trieste. But suppose Julia had been previously
sent thither to complete her education, and thus had become
known to Beethoven. In that case, what is to be thought of
guardians and friends who could allow her such liberty, or rather
license, that she, at the age of fifteen and three-quarter years,
should already have formed the relations necessarily implied by

the language of the diary with a man twice her age? What, too, must be thought of Beethoven! · Granting him to have been, as Magdalena Willmann and others said, "half crazy," the man certainly was not a fool!

The year 1800 may also be safely discarded. As to 1802, it is superfluous to say more than that in the next chapter will be found part of a letter by Beethoven, dated "Vienna, July 13, 1802." His stay at the bath must, indeed, have been short if he reached it with four post-horses on the 5th and is in Vienna again writing letters on the 13th!

In 1803, July 6th fell upon Wednesday. But there was no such error in the date; Beethoven gives the day of the month three times in twenty-four hours—twice on the 6th, once on the 7th. A mistake here is inconceivable. The day of the week, indeed, is written but once; but then it is Monday, and Sunday and Monday are precisely the two days of the week which one most rarely or never mistakes. But that part of the document which bears the date "Evening, Monday, July 6" contains certain words that are decisive. This part is a postscript to the writing of the morning and is written, he says, because he was too late for the post on that day, and "Mondays, Thursdays, the only days on which the mail-coach goes from here to K." The conclusion is irresistible: Schindler and his copyists are all wrong; the document was not written in the years 1800–1803; the "Immortal Beloved" for whom it was written was *not* the Countess Julia Guicciardi. Therefore, they who have wept in sympathy over this Werther's sufferings caused by this Charlotte, may dry their tears. They can comfort themselves with the assurance, that the catastrophe was by no means so disastrous as represented. The affair was but an episode; not the grand tragedy of Beethoven's life. But, being a love adventure, it has been treated with fact in ratio to fancy like Falstaff's bread to his sack. One author in particular, who accepts all Schindler's assumptions and conjectures without question or suspicion, has elaborated the topic at great length, though perhaps (to borrow Sheridan's jest) less luminously than voluminously. Having wrought up the feelings of "his lovely readers, his dear lady friends of Beethoven," to the highest pitch possible in a tragedy where the hero, after the catastrophe, still lives and prospers, he consoles them a few chapters farther on by giving to Beethoven for his one "Love's Labor Lost" two new ones gained—the one, a married woman, the other, a young girl of fourteen years; and, moreover—if, in the confusion of his dates, the reader is not greatly misled—both at the same time! "Also the Lord gave Job twice as much as he had before," saith the ancient Hebrew poet.[1]

Even if one were disposed to attach no great importance to the arguments thus far advanced, there are two passages in the letter which could not have been written in that brilliant period of Beethoven's life (1800–1802) and therefore are conclusive; viz.: "My life in W (Wien = Vienna) is now a wretched life," and "At my age I need a quiet, steady life." In fact, the severest critical discussion of my argument against the accuracy of Schindler's statement has failed to find a flaw in it beyond the unessential assertion that Beethoven could scarcely be conceived as having erred in the matter of the day of the week. Since then the author has himself accidentally learned by experience how a mistake of this kind, made in the morning, can easily be perpetuated in private letters; he learned it by being compelled to prove the absolute accuracy of an official document.

Every attentive and thoughtful reader of the letter must realize that it is irreconcilable with the notion that Beethoven's passionate devotion to the lady was a new and sudden one; also that Beethoven had parted with his beloved, whoever she may have been, only a short time before; that he writes in the full conviction that his love is returned and the desire for a union of their fates was mutual, and that by patient waiting the obstacles then in the way of their purpose to live together would be overcome.

In the effort to determine when Beethoven wrote in this strain his own inaccurate dates cannot be overlooked, but must be discussed at the outset of the inquiry. If the words "Evening, Monday, July 6," are to be considered conclusive, the investigation will have to be confined to the years 1807 and 1812, both 1801 and 1818 being out of the question. But if an error of a day be assumed, inquiry may be extended to the following years. In the first three years

	1806	1807	1808
the 5th of July fell on a	Saturday	Sunday	Tuesday
the 6th of July on a	Sunday	Monday	Wednesday
the 7th of July on a	Monday	Tuesday	Thursday

In the three later years

	1811	1812	1813
July 5th fell on a	Friday	Saturday	Monday
July 6th on a	Saturday	Monday	Tuesday
July 7th on a	Sunday	Tuesday	Wednesday

[1]From here on the Editor of this English edition presents Mr. Thayer's further contentions as they are set forth in the first appendix to Vol. III of the first German edition, though in the form of a translation—the original manuscript not having reached his hands.

To pass by other reasons, the years 1808 and 1811 are to be excluded because they presuppose an error of two days. There remain, then, the years 1806, 1807, 1812 and 1813, which can be best studied in their reverse order. The year 1813 shows itself at once impossible because of the date of a letter to Varena: "Baden, July 4, 1813," besides other circumstances which prove that Beethoven spent the months of June and July of this year in Vienna and Baden. In a similar manner 1812 must be rejected because he wrote a letter to Baumeister on June 28 from Vienna and arrived in Teplitz on July 7.

There remain, then, only the years 1806 and 1807. If we are willing to attach too great weight to the improbability of an error in Beethoven's dates (July 6 and 7) it would certainly be impossible to decide in favor of the year for which other considerations plead with almost convincing force—viz., 1806. There is a letter from Beethoven to Brunswick proposing to visit him in Pesth *printed* with the date "May 14, 1806" which might be strong evidence in favor of that year; but, unfortunately, the true date is 1807, and so adds to our difficulty. For it is known that on July 22nd, 1807 (and for several days at least before), he was in Baden, and there is nothing thus far to prove that he did not make the proposed visit and return from Hungary in season to have written the love-letter on the 6th and 7th of that month; this is, it is true, a very unsatisfactory assumption. There is a date in a correspondence with Simrock touching the purchase of certain works, which, if it could be established with certainty, would remove all doubt and provide a satisfactory conclusion. If the correspondence took place in 1806 it would be impossible to avoid the unsatisfactory assumption.

The head of the famous house of Simrock once told the author that the letters written to his father by Beethoven had been stolen (they have since been recovered), and that the only possible information on the point might be obtained from the old business books of the house. The author asked that they be examined for him and his request was most courteously complied with, with the result that he was provided with the excerpts from the letters of which he has made use in a later chapter. To his great satisfaction the most important of the letters bears date May 31, 1807. This and the letter following show that Beethoven spent the months of June and July 1807 in Baden.

The result would, then, seem to be irrefutable:—there is an error of one day in Beethoven's date. The letter was written in the summer which he spent partly in Hungary, partly in Silesia—

the summer of 1806. In all the years from 1800 to 1815 there is no other summer in which he might have written the letter within the first ten days of July unless we choose to assume a state of facts which would do violence to probability.

But our contention has a much more serious purpose than the determination of the date of a love-letter; it is to serve as the foundation for a highly necessary justification of Beethoven's character at this period in his life. The editor of Beethoven's letters to Gleichenstein which appeared in "Westermann's Monatsheften" (1865)[1] learned from Gleichenstein's widow that the composer had once made a proposal of marriage to her sister Therese Malfatti. On the strength of this information, and certain references in the letters themselves, the editor founded a singular theory;—Beethoven, says the editor in question, fell in love with "the dark-brown Therese," who, despite the fact that she was "then only 14 years old (in 1807), was fully developed." "His love for her was as rapid in its growth as it was in its passionateness, but *was not returned then or later.*" "The affair was plainly embarrassing to the family, for the passion of the half-deaf, very eccentric man of 36 for a girl of fourteen could not fail in the long run to become dangerous (*misslich*)."

"Why, very well; I hope here be truths," as the *Fool* says in "Measure for Measure."

Reflect that this was the year of the Mass in C and the C minor Symphony, and imagine the picture: Beethoven, the mighty master, occupied in developing works which stirred the deepest depths of the soul. Such on one hand; on the other "the lover, sighing like a furnace, with a woeful ballad made to his mistress' eyebrow." Or, if one prefer, instead of the first picture, a half-deaf, eccentric, 36-year old Corydon, wandering about by the side of mossy brooks vainly piping tunes to a melancholy early-developed and early-loved Phyllis! Let us admit for the nonce that the amiable picture of Beethoven in 1807 is the correct one; there is yet no excess of reason based on sense or probability, no boundlessness of imagination or immature logic which can assert that the letter of July 6 and 7 was written to Therese Malfatti, then 13 years old.

There is still another assumption or suspicion which must be touched upon here and if possible refuted; it is that, even in 1806, Beethoven's letter was addressed to the Countess Guicciardi, then already the wife of Count Gallenberg. Moreover, a more

[1] Ludwig Nohl.

natural solution of the difficulties could scarcely be found if it could but be proved or accepted as true that the composer was one of those exalted musical geniuses, recently lauded by a writer, who are "no longer subject to once accepted notions of morals and ordinary duties," and who refuse to permit "narrow-minded ethics to be lifted to the real laws of existence." If Beethoven had been a man of this character, what more should we need to believe that in the summer of 1806 he and the lady were impatiently awaiting the moment when they might steal away from husband and children and thus attain "their purpose to live together," heart closely pressed to heart? Here a single objection will suffice: Count Gallenberg and his wife had at this time long been in Naples. No! This disgrace does not attach to the name of Beethoven.

Those who have thought it worth while to follow the discussion thus far will now understand why so much time and labor were spent on removing all doubt as to the dates of the letters of June 29, 1801, and July 6 and 7, 1806, and this after a long time had passed during which there had never arisen a doubt in the mind of the writer. For if these dates remain fixed, the extended romantic structures which have been reared on the sandy foundation of conjecture must fall in ruins.

The conclusions reached by the study seem as natural as they are satisfactory and indubitable. Young Beethoven, possessed of a temperament susceptible and excitable in the highest degree and endowed not only with extraordinary genius but, leaving out of consideration his physical misfortunes, with other attractive qualities—the great pianist, the beloved teacher, the highly promising composer, admired and accepted gladly in the highest circles of society of the metropolis—this Beethoven, as Wegeler expresses it, was always in love and generally in the highest degree. As he took on years, however, his passions cooled, and it is a truth of daily observation that at the last a strong and lasting attachment can obtain mastery over the most vacillating and fickle lover. According to our conviction this was also the case with Beethoven, and most assuredly the famous love-letter was addressed to the object of a wise and honorable love which had taken control over him. If this be true, and if he was so violently in love in 1806, it follows that the references in the Gleichenstein correspondence which their editor applies to a "completely developed girl of fourteen years of age," in 1807, were aimed at an entirely different individual; and this, too, is the conviction of the author.

But who is the lady? it is asked.[1]   The secret was too well guarded; and she is still unknown.   This, only, is certain: that 1st. Of all Beethoven's friends and acquaintances of the other sex whose names are on record one only could have been the "Immortal Beloved" of the letter and the party to this project of marriage; 2nd, all the circumstantial evidence points to her and to her only; 3rd, long after these two points were determined, Robert Volkmann, the fine musician and composer, in conversation with the author, mentioned a local tradition at Pesth which directly names her as having been once the' beloved and even (if our memory serve) the bride *in spe* of Beethoven.   This lady was the Countess Therese von Brunswick.

The scattered notices of the Brunswicks in these volumes, if taken connectedly, may appear of deeper significance than has been suspected.   They were of the earliest and warmest friends of Beethoven in Vienna; they "adored him," said their cousin, the Countess Gallenberg; Beethoven wrote the song "Ich denke dein" in the album of the sisters and dedicated it to them when he published it in 1805; he received from Therese her portrait in oil;[2] visited the Brunswicks in the autumn of 1806 and composed the Sonata, Op. 57, which he dedicated to the brother; and immediately after his departure wrote the passionate love-letter,—to whom?—wrote to Count Franz, "Kiss your sister Therese," and in the autumn of 1809, while on another visit to them, composed the Sonata, Op. 78, dedicated to the sister.   A few months later the marriage project fell through.

Two remarks may be noted here which, if of no great importance, are worth the space they will occupy: 1st. After the

---

[1]These concluding remarks, from chapters V and VI of Vol. III of the first German edition, are brought in here to complete the author's public utterances on the subject of the identity of the "Immortal Beloved." Thayer is discussing the failure of Beethoven's marriage project.

[2]Amongst Beethoven's posthumous effects was found a portrait in oil by J. B. von Lampi with the following inscription on the back of the frame:

<blockquote>
To the Unique Genius
To the Great Artist
To the Good Man   (Dem seltenen Genie, Dem grossen
    from T. B.   Künstler, Dem guten Menschen)
</blockquote>

This picture went from the possession of the widow of Beethoven's nephew Karl into that of Georg Hellmesberger Sr. in 1861 and was presented by his grandson to the Beethoven-Haus Verein in Bonn, where it is now preserved. It is, in all probability, the portrait of which Beethoven speaks in a letter to Count Franz von Brunswick, dated July 11, 1811: "Since I do not know how the portrait fell into your hands, it would be best were you to bring it with you; an amiable artist will no doubt be found who will copy it for the sake of friendship." Besides the portrait of the Countess Therese there was also a medallion picture of the Countess Guicciardi amongst the effects left by Beethoven. It was identified as such by her son, who died in 1893 (See Breuning, "Aus dem Schwarzspanierhause," p 124) appearance of the dedication of Op. 78, Therese von Brunswick's name disappears from all papers, notes and memoranda concerning Beethoven collected by Jahn or the author; yet the friendship between him and the brother remained undisturbed. 2nd. This friendship of thirty years' duration was broken only by death; yet, although in the later years long periods of separation were frequent, their known epistolary correspondence is comprised in some half dozen letters, and the half of these with false dates. Were these all? If not, why should all, except just these which are neither of particular interest nor importance, have been destroyed or concealed? Unless, indeed, there was a secret to be preserved. Therese von Brunswick lived to a great age, having the reputation of a noble and generous but eccentric character. In regard to Beethoven, so far as is known, she, like Shakespeare's *Cardinal*, "died and made no sign." Because she could not?[1]

(Postscript by the Editor of the English Edition.)

There are other candidates than the Countesses Guicciardi and Brunswick for the honor of having been the object of what, it must be admitted, was Beethoven's supreme love;—or, at least, there are other women for whom writers have put in pleas. Though Dr. Kalischer professed to believe that he had effectually disposed of the Thayer hypothesis, it is significant that by far the most notable champions who fought for their respective lady-loves are those who entered the lists for the Countess Therese. I mention only the American Thayer; the Englishman Grove; the Germans La Mara, Storck, and Prelinger (like Kalischer, the editor of a collection of Beethoven's letters); the Frenchmen

[1]Riemann in his revision of Vol. II of this biography says, "The statement in the second and third Volumes of the first edition were based on the belief that the serious marriage project of Beethoven which led him to ask Wegeler to get for him [a transcript of] his baptismal certificate, but which fell through soon after, must needs be connected with the person to whom the love-letter was addressed. But since it has been determined by a careful study of Clementi's letters that Beethoven's offer of marriage, in 1810, most certainly referred to Therese von Malfatti, who, however, as we shall see, cannot be considered in connection with the love-letter, this combination is become untenable. A large number of Beethoven's letters must be assigned to entirely different years, because Clementi's correspondence with his partner Collard makes it certain that the honorarium for the works sold in 1807 was not paid out till the spring of 1810. The relations of Beethoven to Therese Malfatti are thus transferred from 1807 to 1809-1810, and it can no longer be maintained that 1810 was the year in which Beethoven's prospect of a marriage with Therese Brunswick came to an end." This means that Dr. Riemann believes that while a man of 38 years of age would not write a love-letter like Beethoven's to a girl of less than 14 years he would try to marry her when he was 40 and she a trifle under 16.

Rolland and Chantavoine, both biographers of Beethoven.
Schindler, Nohl and Kalischer carried the sleeve of the Countess
Guicciardi; Frimmel and Volbach seemed gently inclined to
Magdalena Willmann, the actress who said that Beethoven wanted
to marry her but she would not have him because he was so ugly
and "half crazy"; Dr. Wolfgang A. Thomas-San-Galli is the
champion of Amalia Sebald as the "Immortal Beloved" and of
1812 as the year in which the love-letter was written. Of his
book ("Die Unsterbliche Geliebte Beethovens, Amalia Sebald,"
Halle, 1909) it may be said that its merit lies in its close, pertinent
and dispassionate reasoning—the quality in which all of Dr.
Kalischer's arguments are most deficient.

Schindler's story touching the letter and Giulietta Guicciardi
was unquestioned for thirty years, when doubt was cast upon it
by Thayer's investigations, which fixed the date as 1806 and
thereby eliminated the Countess as the composer's inamorata.
In Vol. II, Thayer contented himself with a demonstration that
the Countess could not be the "Immortal Beloved." In Vol. III,
in the body of the book, he suggested that in "greatest probability"
the lady was the Countess Therese von Brunswick. It does not
appear that he ever went further than this, but he died, in 1897,
in full conviction that by no possibility could the Guicciardi be
rehabilitated in the place she had so long occupied in the minds of
historians and romancers. His first contribution to the question
(the first portion of this chapter) immediately called forth a
defence of Schindler's story, Dr. Alfred Christian Kalischer being
in the van of Schindler's defenders. Instead of traversing the
evidence in the case as Thayer had done, Kalischer proposed
and followed the "inductive method" thus: Beethoven could not
have indulged in such transports at as late a date as 1806 or 1807.
They were the outpourings of a sentimentalist, one of the
Werther sort. Beethoven had said in the letter that he could
only live wholly with his love or not at all—an expression not to
be thought of in connection with a genius who had created the
"Eroica" symphony, "Fidelio," the Sonatas in D minor and F
minor (Op. 57), the Pianoforte Concertos in C minor and G major,
the Quartets, Op. 59, had finished the fourth Symphony and
sketched the C minor and the "Pastoral"—could such a genius
believe for a moment that he could not live without the object
of his love? etc. The whole argument was merely rhetoric and
psychologically speculative.

In a criticism of Thayer's third volume, written for "Der
Clavierlehrer" in 1879, Kalischer took up the subject of Therese

Brunswick and, pursuing his old style of argumentation, urged that the "Immortal Beloved" was Giulietta and not Therese because, forsooth, Beethoven had dedicated the C-sharp minor Sonata to the former and nothing better than the Sonata in F-sharp major, Op. 78, composed in 1809, to the latter. Kalischer saw no force in the fact that sketches for the so-called "Moonlight" Sonata antedated the dedication by a considerable period; the essential things in his mind were the dedication and that Lenz thought highly of the C-sharp minor and little of the Fantasia for Pianoforte, Op. 77, dedicated by Beethoven "to his friend" Brunswick, and still less of the F-sharp Sonata dedicated to "another member of the house of Brunswick"; and that while Marx had described the C-sharp minor Sonata as "the low hymn of love's renunciation" he did not consider the F-sharp major Sonata as worthy even of mention.

These essays, together with another in which Dr. Kalischer performed with great energy the work of disposing of the romantic vaporings of a writer who called herself Mariam Tenger, who had published a book ("Beethoven's Unsterbliche Geliebte, nach persönlichen Erinnerungen") at Bonn in 1890, in which she affected to prove what Thayer had set down as merely a probability. This writer (who had most obviously taken her cue from Thayer, though she protested that she had not read his biography when she wrote her book) professed to have had the tale from the lips of the Countess Brunswick herself, that Beethoven, while visiting at Martonvásár, the country-seat of the Brunswicks, in May, 1806, had become secretly engaged to the Countess, no one else knowing the fact except Beethoven's friend Count Franz von Brunswick. Dr. Kalischer found little difficulty in demolishing a large portion of the fantastic fabric reared by Mariam Tenger, especially that portion which professed to rest upon the alleged testimony of a "Baron Spaun" who was plainly a creation of the romancer's, though a veritable Spaun did figure, largely and creditably, in the life-history of Schubert. Not content with this the critic went further, and reviewing the sentimental career of Beethoven from 1806 to 1810 (in which latter year it is supposed the relations between him and the Countess Brunswick came to an end), he protested that, in 1807, Beethoven was in love with Therese Malfatti, then a girl of 14 years.

That question had already been discussed by Thayer, as we have seen. So also had the identity of Baron Spaun by Marie Lipsius, known in musical literature by her pen-name La Mara, who called attention to inaccuracies in the Tenger story in the first of a collection of essays entitled "Classisches und Romantisches aus der Tonwelt," published in Leipsic in 1891. The same author who, in all her writings on the subject, has stoutly maintained the correctness of Thayer's theory, made the most valuable contribution yet offered to the controversy by her book, "Beethoven's Unsterbliche Geliebte. Das Geheimniss der Gräfin Brunsvick und ihre Memoiren," published by Breitkopf and Härtel in 1909. To this book it is necessary to pay rather extended attention; but before its contents are passed in review it deserves to be noted that Thayer, who followed the multitude of arguments for and against his hypothesis with the greatest interest and with a characteristically open mind, went down to his grave with his strong conviction unshaken that "in greatest probability" the Countess Therese was the "Immortal Beloved." To La Mara he sent a letter dated January 22, 1892, to which attention was called in a foot-note on the history of the C-sharp minor Sonata in an earlier chapter of this work, and which, through the courtesy of the lady to whom it was addressed, is now given in substance:

. . . . That Mr. Kalischer has adopted Ludwig Nohl's strange notion of Beethoven's infatuation for Therese Malfatti, a girl of *fourteen years*, surprises me; as also that he seems to consider the Cis moll Sonata to be a musical love poem addressed to Julia Guicciardi. He ought certainly to know that the subject of that Sonata was, or rather that it was suggested by, Seume's little poem "Die Beterin."

I pray you to stop here and read before proceeding the first part of the *Liebesbrief*. Note well that it was written from a *Badeort* so far away from Vienna that he journeyed thither in a coach with four horses and Esterhazy with eight. And now to the essential points.

During the summer of 1801, we know that Beethoven lodged in Hetzendorf—where ex-Kurfürst Franz resided and died July 26, that year—and composed his "Christus am Ölberg" in great part in the near Schönbrunn garden. We know that he wrote on June 29, a very full account of his increasing deafness to Dr. Wegeler. Was he, only seven days later, in a distant *Badeort*, writing *such* a love-letter to a young *Grafin* not yet seventeen years old? In November he again wrote to Wegeler. "Du willst wissen," he says, "wie es mir geht, was ich brauche," and proceeds to describe his physician's treatment. In neither of these letters is there the remotest hint that the doctor sent him to a distant *Badeort*. In 1802, Beethoven's summer lodging was in Heiligenstadt where young Ries came often to receive his master's instructions. There is not the slightest intimation from him, nor anywhere else, of any absence of Beethoven during that summer. Did Beethoven write the *Liebesbriefe* in July and the so-called Testament—that document of despair—in October? Observe these dates. In the *Liebesbriefe* from the *Badeort* July 6: "Ich kam erst Morgens 4 Uhr gestern hier an." Seven days later, July 13, he was in Vienna writing to Breitkopf and Härtel!

In the Testament we read: "Dieses halbe Jahr was ich auf dem Lande zubrachte," but in no known letter or writing of Beethoven's of that summer is there any reference to the distant *Badeort*.

All that is known of Beethoven in the summer of 1801 and 1802, is against the journey to the *Badeort;* what is known of the summer of 1806 is for it. The burden of proof lies upon Mr. Kalischer. When he *can* prove such a journey in 1801 or 1802, and does so, it will be *one* point in his favor.

The method pursued by La Mara in her investigation, which extended over several years, was much like that of Thayer: in every case in which it seemed that testimony might be had from the mouths of living persons she sought to obtain it. First she visited the Countess Marie Brunswick (or Brunsvik, as the Hungarian branch of the Braunschweigers, or Brunswicks, spelled the name), daughter of Count Franz. There was an interview followed by a correspondence. The Countess said that the family knew nothing whatever of the alleged romantic attachment between her aunt and Beethoven. She recalled that Beethoven had a "grosse Schwärmerei" for her father's cousin, the Countess Guicciardi, afterwards Gallenberg, but the feeling was not reciprocated on the part of the Countess so far as had been learned. The family was still in possession of three or four letters from Beethoven to her father. In November, 1899, she sent four letters to La Mara which were then owned by her brother, Count Géza Brunswick. Three of these letters had already been printed in the first edition of this biography. The only one bearing on the subject of this study was that in which Beethoven begs the Count to kiss his sister Therese. (This letter La Mara presents in *facsimile* in her book.) Count Gallenberg (son of the Countess Giulietta and the last of the family) had died in Vienna in 1893, two years after he had denied that there had been any talk of marriage or *mutual* love between his mother and Beethoven. The testimony of two grand-children of the Countess Giulietta was asked. "Beethoven wanted to marry grandmamma," said the Countess Bertha Kuenburg, *née* Countess Stolberg-Stolberg, in Salzburg, "but she loved Gallenberg." Baroness Hess-Diller, *née* Countess Gallenberg, in Baden said:

Among our family papers there is absolutely nothing bearing on the matter—*no* letters, *no* diary. The prejudices of the period, the incredible point of view held by persons of our station towards artists, even towards artists of Beethoven's greatness, may have been responsible for the fact that no interest was felt in the matter. All that verbal tradition has brought down to me is summed up in the one circumstance that Beethoven figured only as a music-teacher in the house of my great-grand-parents.

On the suggestion of the grand-children of the Countess Giulietta, La Mara called on Fräulein Karoline Languider, a life-long friend of the Gallenbergs, who had lived with them and the Countess Marie Brunswick. This witness testified:

I do not believe that the *Schwärmerei* for Countess Julia Gallen-berg-Guicciardi—though it may have been warm and wonderful, for she was a very beautiful, elegant woman of the world—ever took such possession of the heart of Beethoven as did the later love for Countess Therese Brunsvick, which led to an engagement. That was deci-dedly his profoundest love, and that it did not result in marriage, it is said, was due to the—what shall I call it?—real artistic temperament (*Natur*) of Beethoven, who, in spite of his great love, could not make up his mind to get married. It is said that Countess Therese took it greatly to heart. Having lived during my childhood with my parents in Pressburg, I often heard—with childish ears, of course—persons speak about the matter, and am able to remember that Countess Therese was greatly beloved, and that my mother was always very glad when she came to Pressburg, which was every year.

La Mara having sent Fräulein Languider some of her writings and a copy of Lampi's portrait of the Countess Therese, she wrote on January 24, 1901: "After all that has been said *pro* and *contra* I remain of the unalterable opinion that the Countess Therese was the 'Immortal Beloved' and fiancée of the great master, concerning which fact I heard innumerable conversations in my childhood, and that the portrait is hers. Countess Marie does not see a resemblance, but I do not trust her memory." Countess Marie Brunswick had said to La Mara that she did not consider the painting which is now preserved in the Beethovenhaus in Bonn a portrait of her aunt; "but," says La Mara, "since there was a difference of 57 years, she could no longer judge of a likeness with the youthful picture."

Count Géza Brunswick, son of Beethoven's friend, died in the spring of 1902, having outlived his sister Marie. The direct line of Brunswicks reached its end in him. The castles Korompa and Martonvásár passed into other hands. Count Franz's art collection was sold at auction in Vienna, but the widow of Count Géza retained possession of the Beethoven relics (the letters and an oil portrait) and took them with her to Florence, where sub-sequently she married the Marchese Capponi. She, too, gave her testimony: "It is certain that there were soul-relationships between Beethoven and Therese Brunsvik."

Next, La Mara went to Pressburg (in search of such traditions as Thayer had found in Pesth), working on the hint thrown out by Fräulein Languider. In Pressburg she met Johann Batka, municipal archivist, who bore testimony to the fact that a relative of the Countess Therese Brunswick, who was in possession of her memoirs (a copy, evidently, since La Mara obtained the original from the family of Count Deym), had persuaded him to believe that Therese was the "Immortal Beloved" and secret fiancée of Beethoven. After La Mara had published the results of her investigation in the January number for 1908 of the "Neue Rundschau," the grand-niece of Countess Therese, Isabella, Countess Deym, and her sister Madame Ilka Melichar, confirmed the statement that the letter had been addressed to their illustrious grand-aunt. An estrangement had sprung up between Count Franz and his sister Therese after his marriage; but the intimacy between the sisters Therese and Josephine, Countess Deym, had 'continued, and the romance, never known to the families of Count Franz and his sister Countess Teleky, had come down as a tradition in the family of Count Deym.

The rest of La Mara's book is filled with the memoirs of Therese Brunswick, which she began writing in September, 1846, and called "My Half-Century." In introducing the interesting document, La Mara thought herself compelled to abandon Thayer's contention that the love-letter had been written in 1806, and substituted 1807 (a date urged also by Ladislaw Jachinecki, in an article published in the "Zeitschrift der Internationalen Musikgesellschaft" for July and August, 1908), on the ground that 1806 had become untenable, 1807 agreed with the almanac and that Beethoven's sojourn at Baden in the summer of 1807 did not preclude a visit to Hungary of three weeks' duration between the end of June and July 26. La Mara was persuaded to make the change by her discovery in the memoirs of the fact that on July 5, 1806, Countess Therese was in Transylvania visiting her sister Charlotte, Countess Teleky, and was present when the latter gave birth to a daughter, Blanca, on that date. Having assumed, with Thayer, that Beethoven wrote the love-letter very soon after a visit to the Brunswicks at Korompa (which is her reading of the mysterious "K" in the letter), and sent it from a neighboring watering-place, convinced that Therese was with her sister on July 6, 1806, she adopted the theory that the letter was written in 1807, in which year the much-discussed 6th of July fell on a Monday. She also alludes to other evidence which she does not describe but by which she doubtless means a letter by Beethoven to Breitkopf and Härtel dated "Vienna, July 5, 1806," which became known to the investigators when the well-known publishers of Leipsic made a private publication of the letters from the composer found in their archives.   This was after the death of Mr. Thayer. Touching this letter and the significance of Beethoven's "K" the writer of this note submits, without argument, a few suggestions:

1. There is nothing in the letter, beyond what might be called its atmosphere, to indicate that Beethoven had recently visited the object of his love.   The words "To-day—yesterday—what tearful longings for you," to which such an interpretation might be given, plainly refer only to his mood and his thoughts on the two days when the letter was in his mind; they tell us nothing about the distance or time which lay between him and his "ferne Geliebte."

2. It is plain that Beethoven and Prince Esterhazy started from the same place for the Hungarian watering-place whence the letter was sent (if it ever was sent), Beethoven travelling by an unusual route because of a lack of horses, the Prince by the usual route.   It is anything but likely that this place was Marton-vásár; it is much more probable that it was one of Esterhazy's country-seats.

3. There is no indication in the letter or anywhere else how long Beethoven was *en route*, but the journey extended over several stages, for "at the stage before the last" he was warned not to travel at night, etc.   He may have been as far in the interior of Hungary as a post-coach could carry him in, let us say, two days.

4. We know nothing about the rapidity of travel over Hungarian roads a century ago, but we do know that as early as 1635, i. e., 171 years before Beethoven made the journey, an English post was established which made the trip from London to Edinburgh and back in six days; and Edinburgh is 357 miles from London by road.   The English mail-coach, therefore travelled an average of 119 miles in 24 hours.   At even half of this speed Beethoven might have been comparatively near the place in which Countess Therese spent June and July, 1806.

5. This place was not Korompa, but may have been Klausenburg or Kolosz, the principal town of Transylvania, where Count Teleky lived.   This is at least remotely possible.

6. It is but natural to assume that the post between the important places of Hungary and the metropolis of Transylvania ran fairly often and at fair speed, and if Beethoven expected that a letter which he thought would be detained at the place where it was posted till early on Thursday morning would not reach its destination till Saturday, that destination must have been at a considerable distance (a two days' run) from the watering-place.

"So near, so far!" has little value as evidence; it is an ecstatic commonplace concerning the unattainable, or that which seems to be so.

7. The fact that the Countess Therese was not at Korompa in the early part of July, 1806, is not in itself a sufficient reason for abandoning that date; she was at Klausenburg. The letter to Breitkopf and Härtel, though plainly dated "Vienna, July 5, 1806" (Kalischer, No. 109), might easily be disposed of as convincing evidence against 1806, if it did not bear the publishers' endorsement apparently indicating that it had either been received or answered on July 11 of the year. Nothing could make Beethoven's carelessness in respect of dates plainer than the next letter of Beethoven's in which he replied to the letter which Breitkopf and Härtel had sent him in answer to the proposition which he had made in the letter dated July 5, 1806. The second letter is dated "Grätz, am 3ten Heu-Monat," (i.e., Hay month, otherwise July); yet it refers to the earlier letter and was written at Troppau in Austrian Silesia, where Beethoven spent the fall of 1806 as the guest of Prince Lichnowsky. Breitkopf and Härtel's endorsement shows that the letter was received and answered in September. There is some significance, too, in the fact that Beethoven refers to his journey from Vienna to Troppau, which must have been nearly 200 miles long, as a short one ("Etwas viel zu thun und die *kleine Reise* hierher," etc.). (See Kalischer, Letter No. 110.) Beethoven may have written the letter in Vienna on one of the first two days of July, or even the last of June, making one of his characteristic blunders in the dating, and yet have been deep in Hungary on the dubious date on which he wrote the love-letter. The endorsement of Breitkopf and Härtel, "July 5, 1806," could not have been anything more than a transcript of the date found on the letter.

The editor is well aware that his suggestions do not clear up the mystery; he offers them nevertheless for what they are now or may hereafter be worth. The references to Beethoven in the Memoirs of Therese Brunswick made public by La Mara are to be found in the following excerpts:

During the extraordinary sojourn of 18 days in Vienna my mother desired that her two daughters, Therese and Josephine, receive Beethoven's invaluable instruction in music. Adalbert Rosti, a schoolmate of my brother's, assured us that Beethoven would not be persuaded to accept a mere invitation; but if Her Excellency were willing to climb the three flights of winding stairs of the house in St. Peter's Place, and make him a visit, he would vouch for a successful outcome of the mission. It was done. Like a schoolgirl, with Beethoven's Sonatas for Violin and

Violoncello and Pianoforte under my arm, we entered. The immortal, dear Louis van Beethoven was very friendly and as polite as he could be. After a few phrases *de part et d'autre*, he sat me down at his pianoforte, which was out of tune, and I began at once to sing the violin and the 'cello parts and played right well. This delighted him so much that he promised to come every day to the Hotel zum Erzherzog Carl—then Goldenen Greifen. It was May in the last year of the last century. He came regularly, but instead of an hour frequently staid from 12 to 4 or 5 o'clock, and never grew weary of holding down and bending my fingers, which I had been taught to lift high and hold straight. The noble man must have been satisfied, for he never missed a single day in the 16. . . . . It was then that the most intimate and cordial friendship was closely established with Beethoven, a friendship which lasted to the end of his life. He came to Ofen; he came to Martonvásár; he was initiated into our social republic of chosen people. A round spot was planted with high, noble lindens; each tree had the name of a member, and even in their sorrowful absence we conversed with their symbols, and were entertained and instructed by them. Often after giving the good-morning greeting I asked the tree concerning this and the other thing which I desired to have explained, and it never failed to answer me.

Later, speaking of the loss of caste and poverty of her brother-in-law Count Deym (who had changed his name to Müller because of a duel fought before he had attained his majority, and conducted an art museum, and who after his marriage to Therese's sister Josephine tried in vain to take the position in society to which his rank entitled him), the Countess writes:

The aristocracy turned its back on him because he had gone into business. He could not hunt up his former rich acquaintances. Beethoven was the faithful visitor at the house of the young Countess— he gave her lessons gratis and to be tolerated one had to be a Beethoven. The numerous relatives, the sisters of her father and their children, frequently visited their amiable niece. Tableaux were occasionally given; Deym, being himself an artist, was at home in such matters, they gave him pleasure. . . . There were musical soirées. My brother came in vacation-time and made the acquaintance of Beethoven. The two musical geniuses became intimately associated with each other, and my brother never deserted his friend in his frequent financial troubles until his, alas! too early death.

It was about this time (1814) that Baron C. P. came very often to Martonvásár. He was fond of my brother and wanted to learn the science of agriculture from him and his men. We played chess with each other; he conceived a passion for me and tried to embrace me. From that moment onward he frequently repeated his offers and waited two years for my assent—for I always answered that I should have to ponder the matter and had had no time to do so. I had remained cold, an earlier passion had devoured my heart. Josephine needed me, her children, who were very promising, loved me and I them—how could I withdraw myself from such a magic circle? When I was active with the Women's Association after the great famine of 1819, we met on the

street. I was in a carriage and had the coachman stop at a signal from
him. He came to the carriage and said significantly, "Have you pondered,
dear Therese? it is the last time I shall ask you. I am going to Dresden
and shall there take a bride unless you make up your mind." I laugh-
ingly gave him my old answer, heart and head being occupied with the
widespread misery: "I really haven't had time, dear Carl." We parted
—he became my enemy.

Shortly after the appearance of La Mara's essay in 1909, a
singular contribution to the controversy touching the "Immortal
Beloved" came from France. The essay had been reviewed in
the "Revue des Deux Mondes," whereupon the editor of "Le
Temps" asked one of its contributors to make inquiry as to possible
family traditions of the mother of M. F. de Gerando, a grand-
niece of the Countess Therese. This was done, but the lady
would hear nothing of an identification of her grand-aunt with
the object of Beethoven's passion. Then came journalistic insinuations that family pride had much to do with the denial. This
provoked M. de Gerando, who undertook, in the "Mercure de
France," to answer the arguments of Thayer and La Mara. There
was one ludicrous feature in his argument and a new revelation.
He disposed of the kiss sent to Therese by Beethoven through
her brother Count Franz, by saying it was only such a familiarity
as an old man might be permitted to indulge towards a young
pupil; this notwithstanding that Therese was born in 1775 and
Beethoven in 1770 and at the time he wrote the love-letter was still
laboring under the delusion that the year of his birth was 1772.
The revelation consisted in the circumstance, set forth by him,
that among the letters of the Countess Therese he had found a
thick portfolio inscribed "The Journal of my Heart. No Romance,"
which (I quote now from an article contributed by Mr. Philip
Hale to the "New Music Review," in the numbers for July and
September, 1909)

contained many letters, notes, messages written at all hours, and addressed to a man, whose Christian name was Louis. Mr. de Gerando,
who has been unable to learn the family name of this man, thought at
first, and naturally, that Beethoven was the one; but this Louis, with
whom Therese was passionately in love, to whom she was betrothed,
without the knowledge of others, was a young man of noble family,
much younger than Therese, and had been educated at the Theresianum
in Vienna, a school frequented by young noblemen. "Van Beethoven
was older than the Countess Brunsvik. He was not noble by birth.
He never attended the Theresianum." The letters reveal a strange
and violent passion. They are at times cold and philosophical. When
Therese signed them with her name, they were true love-letters. When
she signed them with the Greek word "Diotima," the name of a priestess

of beauty and love mentioned by Plato, they were metaphysical speculations, long-winded discussions on the end of life and the nature of
love. "I do not think that Beethoven would have been contented with
this correspondence of encyclopædists." There were a few letters from
Louis, one of them sealed with a coat of arms, and thus there is hope
of identification.

One might answer, continues Mr. Hale, that Therese perhaps loved
twice; that there were two Louis in the field. Mr. de Gerando does
not find this probable. Therese was cerebral in her passion. She knew
passion, but her intellectual side revolted at it, and, when her brain
controlled her, she could write phrases like this: "To think that I could
have lowered myself even to the point of marrying him!" (But, one
might reply, the countess might well have said this with reference to
Beethoven, who was beneath her in station.) She rained contempt on
the man who had awakened in her the love that she detested, and when
she had driven him from her mind, she wrote exultantly: "Free! Free!
Free!" Mr. de Gerando argues from this that she would not a second
time have given up her independence, but nothing that a woman like
Therese would have done should surprise even a great-grand-nephew.

Mr. de Gerando does not understand how any love affair between
Therese and Beethoven could have escaped the curious gossips in society,
eager for news and scandal. "The adventure of Therese de Brunsvik
with Louis appears to me to be a sufficient reason to judge the theory
of Thayer inane. At the same time it explains to us the genesis of this
theory. It is now certain, as far as I am concerned, that some resemblance of the affair between the Countess of Brunsvik and Louis had
come down to Thayer. The similarity of the names, the letter in which
the kiss was sent, and other and more vague indices, led the American
biographer to turn the noble Hungarian dame into the 'well-beloved' of
Beethoven." Such was, in substance, the article of Mr. de Gerando.
It is fair to ask him how the love affair between Therese and the
mysterious Louis, young, noble, etc., escaped the curious gossips, escaped
them so completely that even the great-grand-nephew of Therese is
unable to find out the family name of her lover.

Chapter XXII

The Year 1802—The Heiligenstadt Will—Beethoven's Views on Arrangements—A Defence of Beethoven's Brothers— The Slanders of Romancers and Unscrupulous Biographers—Compositions and Publications of the Year.

THE impatient Beethoven, vexed at the tardy improvement of his health under the treatment of Vering, made that change of physicians contemplated in his letter to Wegeler. This was done some time in the winter 1801–1802, and is all the foundation there is for Schindler's story of "a serious illness in the first months of this year for which he was treated by the highly esteemed physician Dr. Schmidt." The remarkable list of compositions and publications belonging to this year is proof sufficient that he suffered no physical disability of such a nature as seriously to interrupt his ordinary vocations; as is also the utter silence of Ries, Breuning, Czerny, Doležalek and Beethoven himself. The tone of the letters written at the time is also significant on this point.

Concerning the failure of his project to follow the example set in 1800 and give a concert towards the close of the winter in the theatre we learn all we know from a letter from his brother Carl to Breitkopf and Härtel dated April 22, 1802. Therein we read:

My brother would himself have written to you, but he is ill-disposed towards everything because the Director of the Theatre, Baron von Braun, who, as is known, is a stupid and rude fellow, refused him the use of the Theatre for his concert and gave it to other really mediocre artists; and I believe it must vex him greatly to see himself so unworthily treated, particularly as the Baron has no cause and my brother has dedicated several works to his wife.

When one looks down from the Kahlenberg towards Vienna in the bright, sweet springtime, the interesting country is almost worthy of Tennyson's description:

It lies
Deep-meadowed, happy, fair with orchard-lawns
And bowery hollows, crown'd with summer sea.

Conspicuous are the villages, Döbling, hard by the city Nussdorfer line, and Heiligenstadt, divided from Döbling by a ridge of higher land in a deep gorge.

Dr. Schmidt, having enjoined upon Beethoven to spare his hearing as much as possible, he removed for the summer to the place last named. There is much and good reason to believe that his rooms were in a large peasant house still standing, on the elevated plain beyond the village on the road to Nussdorf, now with many neat cottages near, but then probably quite solitary. In those years, there was from his windows an unbroken view across fields, the Danube and the Marchfeld, to the Carpathian mountains that line the horizon. A few minutes' walk citywards brought him to the baths of Heiligenstadt; or, in the opposite direction, to the secluded valley in which at another period he composed the "Pastoral" symphony. The vast increase of Vienna and its environs in population, has caused corresponding changes; but in 1802, that peasant house seems to have offered him everything he could desire; fresh air, sun, green fields, delightful walks, bathing, easy access to his physician, and yet a degree of solitude which now is not easy to conceive as having been attainable so near the capital.

Part of a letter written hence to Breitkopf and Härtel, but no longer in the possession of that house, affords another illustration of Beethoven's excellent common sense and discrimination in all that pertained to his art.

. . . . Concerning arrangements I am heartily glad that you rejected them. The unnatural rage now prevalent to transplant even *pianoforte pieces* to stringed instruments, instruments so utterly opposite to each other in all respects, ought to come to an end. I insist stoutly that only Mozart could arrange his pianoforte pieces for other instruments—and Haydn—and, without wishing to put myself in the class of these great men, I also assert it touching my *pianoforte sonatas* too, since not only are whole passages to be omitted and changed, but also—things are to be added, and here lies the obstacle, to *overcome* which one must either be the master himself or at least have the same *skill and inventive power*— I transcribed a single one of my sonatas for string quartet,[1] yielding to great persuasion, and I certainly know that it would not be an easy matter for another to do as well.

[1] The Sonata in E, Op. 14, No 1, transposed to F major, was published in 1802. See W. Altmann, "Ein Vergessenes Streichquartett Beethovens," "Die Musik," 1905.

The difficulties here mentioned, it will be noticed, are those
of transcribing pianoforte music for other instruments; the contrary operation is so comparatively easy, that Beethoven very
rarely performed it himself, but left it for the most part to young
musicians, whose work he revised and corrected.

There are a great many pieces by Beethoven (says Ries), published
with the designation: *Arrangé par l'Auteur même;* but only four of
these are genuine, namely: from his famous Septet he arranged first
a violin quintet, and then a Pianoforte Trio; out of his Pianoforte Quintet
(with four wind-instruments) he made a Pianoforte Quartet with three
string-instruments; finally, he arranged the Violin Concerto which is
dedicated to Stephan von Breuning (Op. 61) as a Pianoforte Concerto.
Many other pieces were arranged by me, revised by Beethoven, and
then sold as Beethoven's by his brother Caspar.

Without calling in question here the general statement in
this citation, it may be remarked, that if Ries is right in respect
to the arrangement of the Septet as a Quintet, the work remained
in manuscript, for the one published was by Hoffmeister.   But
the Trio was begun and, as is believed, finished this year.   Its
history has been told.   Ries's statement is neither exhaustive nor
altogether exact touching the arrangements of the Septet.   Moreover, in 1806, without Beethoven's knowledge or consent, he
arranged the six Quartets, Op. 18, and the three Trios for strings,
Op. 9, as Pianoforte Trios.

An interesting anecdote from the "Notizen" may be introduced here.   "Count Browne," says Ries,

made a rather long sojourn about this time in Baden near Vienna, where
I was called upon frequently to play Beethoven's music evenings in the
presence of enthusiastic Beethovenians, sometimes from notes, sometimes by heart.   Here I had an opportunity to learn how in the majority of
cases a *name* alone is sufficient to characterize everything in a composition as beautiful and excellent, or mediocre and bad.   One day, weary
of playing without notes, I improvised a march without a thought as to
its merit or any ulterior purpose.   An old countess who actually tor-
mented Beethoven with her devotion, went into ecstasies over it, thinking it was a new composition of his, which I, in order to make sport of
her and the other enthusiasts, affirmed only too quickly.   Unhappily
Beethoven came to Baden the next day.   He had scarcely entered
Count Browne's room in the evening when the old countess began to
speak of the most admirable and glorious march.   Imagine my embarrassment!   Knowing well that Beethoven could not tolerate the old
countess, I hurriedly drew him aside and whispered to him that I had
merely meant to make sport of her foolishness.   To my good fortune
he accepted the explanation in good part, but my embarrassment grew
when I was called upon to repeat the march, which turned out worse
since Beethoven stood at my side.   He was overwhelmed with praise

on all hands and his genius lauded, he listening in a perturbed manner and with growing rage until he found relief in a roar of laughter. Later he remarked to me: "You see, my dear Ries, those are the great cognoscenti, who wish to judge every composition so correctly and severely. Only give them the name of their favorite; they will need nothing more." Yet the march led to one good result: Count Browne immediately commissioned Beethoven to compose three Marches for Pianoforte, four hands.[1]

The seclusion of Heiligenstadt was of itself so seductive to Beethoven, that the prudence of Dr. Schmidt in advising him to withdraw so much from society, may be doubted; the more, because the benefit to his hearing proved to be small or none. It gave him too many lonely hours in which to brood over his calamity; it enabled him still to flatter himself that his secret was yet safe; it led him to defer, too long for his peace of mind, the bitter moment of confession; and consequently to deprive himself needlessly of the tender compassion and ready sympathy of friends, whose lips were sealed so long as he withheld his confidence. But, in truth, the secret so jealously guarded was already known—but who could inform him of it?—though not long nor generally, as we learn from Ries.

It was well for Beethoven, when the time came for him to return to the city, and to resume the duties and obligations of his profession. To what depths of despondency he sometimes sank in those solitary hours at Heiligenstadt, is shown by a remarkable and most touching paper, written there just before his return to town, but never seen by other eyes until after his death. Although addressed to and intended for both his brothers, it is, as Schindler has remarked, "surprising and singular," that the name "Johann" is left utterly blank throughout—not even being indicated by the usual. . . . It is couched in terms of energetic expression, rising occasionally to eloquence—somewhat rude and unpolished indeed, but, perhaps, for that reason the more striking. The manuscript[2] is so carefully written, and disfigured by so few

---

[1] Those dedicated to Princess Esterhazy, Op. 45.

[2] This Testament or Promemoria, written on a large foolscap sheet, appears to have been discovered in a mass of loose papers purchased by the elder Artaria at the sale of Beethoven's effects in 1827. Endorsed upon it is an acknowledgement, signed by Jacob Hotschevar, the guardian (after Breuning's death) of the composer's nephew, of having received it from Artaria & Co. Then follows a similar acknowledgement of its reception by Johann van Beethoven. Its next possessor appears to have been Alois Fuchs—the great collector of musical manuscripts and autographs of musicians. In 1855, it was purchased by Ernst, the violinist (of whom is not known?), who presented it to Mr. Otto and Madame Jenny Lind Goldschmidt as a testimony of gratitude for their valuable assistance in one of his concerts. By their kindness the present writer was allowed to make a very careful copy on April 2, 1861. As printed in the "Allg. Musikalische Zeitung," by Schindler and others, it differs little from the original, though

erasures and corrections, as to prove the great pains taken with it before the final copy was made. The closing sentences, in which he discovers his expectations of an early death, have acquired double importance since the publication of Schindler's suicide story, for the decisive manner in which they remove every possible suspicion that, even in his present hypochondria, he could contemplate such a crime.

Ries's paragraph upon Beethoven's deafness, in which he relates a circumstance alluded to in the document, is its most fitting introduction:

As early as 1802, Beethoven suffered from deafness at various times, but the affliction each time passed away. The beginning of his hard hearing was a matter upon which he was so sensitive that one had to be careful not to make him feel his deficiency by loud speech. When he failed to understand a thing he generally attributed it to his absent-mindedness, to which, indeed, he was subject in a great degree. He lived much in the country, whither I went often to take a lesson from him. At times, at 8 o'clock in the morning after breakfast he would say: "Let us first take a short walk." We went, and frequently did not return till 3 or 4 o'clock, after having made a meal in some village. On one of these wanderings Beethoven gave me the first striking proof of his loss of hearing, concerning which Stephan von Breuning had already spoken to me. I called his attention to a shepherd who was piping very agreeably in the woods on a flute made of a twig of elder. For half an hour Beethoven could hear nothing, and though I assured him that it was the same with me (which was not the case), he became extremely quiet and morose. When occasionally he seemed to be merry it was generally to the extreme of boisterousness; but this happened seldom.

Following is the text of the document:

For my brothers Carl and —— Beethoven.

O ye men who think or say that I am malevolent, stubborn or misanthropic, how greatly do ye wrong me, you do not know the secret causes of my seeming, from childhood my heart and mind were disposed to the gentle feeling of good will, I was even ever eager to accomplish great deeds, but reflect now that for 6 years I have been in a hopeless case, aggravated by senseless physicians, cheated year after year in the hope of improvement, finally compelled to face the prospect of a *lasting malady* (whose cure will take years or, perhaps, be impossible), born with an ardent and lively temperament, even susceptible to the diversions of society, I was compelled early to isolate myself, to live

some of Beethoven's peculiar forms of spelling were corrected—such as "Heiglnstadt." "That Beethoven, throughout the document, never mentions the name of his second brother Johann, and indicates it only by points, is surprising and singular, inasmuch as this brother, as we have just seen, had come to Vienna only a short time before in order to take part in the affairs of our Beethoven." Our copy certainly contains no such "points." The other mistake, as to the recent arrival of Johann in Vienna, every reader will note.

in loneliness, when I at times tried to forget all this, O how harshly was I repulsed by the doubly sad experience of my bad hearing, and yet it was impossible for me to say to men speak louder, shout, for I am deaf, Ah how could I possibly admit an infirmity in the *one sense* which should have been more perfect in me than in others, a sense which I once possessed in highest perfection, a perfection such as few surely in my profession enjoy or ever have enjoyed—O I cannot do it, therefore forgive me when you see me draw back when I would gladly mingle with you. my misfortune is doubly painful because it must lead to my being misunderstood, for me there can be no recreation in society of my fellows, refined intercourse, mutual exchange of thought, only just as little as the greatest needs command may I mix with society, I must live like an exile, if I approach near to people a hot terror seizes upon me, a fear that I may be subjected to the danger of letting my condition be observed —thus it has been during the last half year which I spent in the country, commanded by my intelligent physician to spare my hearing as much as possible, in this almost meeting my present natural disposition, although I sometimes ran counter to it yielding to my inclination for society, but what a humiliation when one stood beside me and heard a flute in the distance and *I heard nothing* or someone heard *the shepherd singing* and again I heard nothing, such incidents brought me to the verge of despair, but little more and I would have put an end to my life —only art it was that withheld me, ah it seemed impossible to leave the world until I had produced all that I felt called upon to produce, and so I endured this wretched existence—truly wretched, an excitable body which a sudden change can throw from the best into the worst state—Patience—it is said I must now choose for my guide, I have done so, I hope my determination will remain firm to endure until it pleases the inexorable parcæ to break the thread, perhaps I shall get better, perhaps not, I am prepared. · Forced already in my 28th year to become a philosopher, O it is not easy, less easy for the artist than for any one else—Divine One thou lookest into my inmost soul, thou knowest it, thou knowest that love of man and desire to do good live therein. O men, when some day you read these words, reflect that ye did me wrong and let the unfortunate one comfort himself and find one of his kind who despite all the obstacles of nature yet did all that was in his power to be accepted among worthy artists and men. You my brothers Carl and   as soon as I am dead if Dr. Schmid is still alive ask him in my name to describe my malady and attach this document to the history of my illness so that so far as is possible at least the world may become reconciled with me after my death. At the same time I declare you two to be the heirs to my small fortune (if so it can be called), divide it fairly, bear with and help each other, what injury you have done me you know was long ago forgiven. To you brother Carl I give special thanks for the attachment you have displayed towards me of late. It is my wish that your lives may be better and freer from care than I have had, recommend *virtue* to your children, it alone can give happiness, not money, I speak from experience, it was virtue that upheld me in misery, to it next to my art I owe the fact that I did not end my life by suicide—Farewell and love each other—I thank all my friends, particularly *Prince Lichnowsky* and *Professor Schmid*—I desire that the instruments from Prince L. be preserved by one of you but let no quarrel result from this, so soon as they can serve you a better purpose sell them, how glad will I be if I can still be helpful to you in my grave—with joy I hasten towards death—if it comes before I shall have had an opportunity to show all my artistic capacities it will still come too early for me despite my hard fate and I shall probably wish that it had come later—but even then I am satisfied, will it not free me from a state of endless suffering?   Come when thou wilt I shall meet thee bravely—Farewell and do not wholly forget me when I am dead, I deserve this of you in having often in life thought of you how to make you happy, be so—

Ludwig van Beethoven.

(seal)

Heiglnstadt,
October 6th,
1802.

For my Brothers Carl and to be read and executed after my death.

Heiglnstadt, October 10th, 1802, thus do I take my farewell of thee—and indeed sadly—yes that beloved hope —which I brought with me when I came here to be cured at least in a degree—I must wholly abandon, as the leaves of autumn fall and are withered so hope has been blighted, almost as I came—I go away—even the high courage—which often inspired me in the beautiful days of summer—has disappeared—O Providence—grant me at last but one day of pure *joy*—it is so long since real joy echoed in my heart—O when—O when, O Divine One—shall I feel it again in the temple of nature and of men—Never? no—O that would be too hard.

De profundis clamavit!   And yet in that retirement whence came a paper of such profound sadness was wrought out the Symphony in D; a work whose grand and imposing introduction—brilliant Allegro, a Larghetto "so lovely, so pure and amiab'y conceived," written in the scenes which gave inspiration to the divine "Pastorale" of which its serene tranquility seems the precursor; a Scherzo "as merry, wayward, skipping and charming as anything possible," as even Oulibichef admits; and a Finale, the very intoxication of a spirit "intoxicated with fire"—made it, like the Quartets, an era both in the life of its author and in the history of instrumental music.   In life, as in music, the more profoundly the depths of feeling are sounded in the Adagio, the more "merry to the verge of boisterousness" the Scherzo which follows.   But who, reading that in October that beloved hope had been abandoned and the high courage which had often inspired him in the beautiful days of summer had disappeared, could anticipate that in November, through the wonderful elasticity of his nature, his mind would have so recovered its tone as to leave no trace visible of the so recent depression and gloom? Perhaps the mere act of giving his feelings vent in that extraordinary *promemoria* may have brought on the crisis, and from that moment the reaction may have begun.

The following letter to Zmeskall (to which the recipient appended the date, November, 1802) is whimsically written on both sides of a strip of very ordinary coarse writing paper fourteen and a half inches long by four and three-quarters wide:

You may, my dear Z., talk as plainly as you please to Walter in the affair of mine, first because he deserves it and then because since the belief has gone forth that I am no longer on good terms with Walter I am pestered by the whole swarm of pianoforte makers wishing to serve me—and gratis, morcover, every one wants to build a pianoforte for me just to my liking; thus Reicha was urgently begged by the man who made a pianoforte for him to persuade me to let him make me one, and he is one of the more honest at whose place I have seen good instruments—make him understand therefore that I will pay him 30 florins, whereas I might have one from all the others for nothing, but I will pay 30 florins only on condition that it be of mahogany and I also want the one string (*una corda*) pedal—if he does not agree to this make it plain to him that I shall choose one of the others and also introduce him to Haydn—a Frenchman, stranger, is coming to me at about 12 o'clock to-day *volti*

subito

Herr R(eicha) and I will have the pleasure of *displaying my art on a piano* by Jakesch—*ad notam*—if you want also to come we shall have a good time since afterward we, Reicha, our miserable Imperial Baron and the Frenchman, will dine together—you do not need to don a *black coat* as we shall be *a party of men only*.

Another letter to Zmeskall (who noted the date November 13, 1802, on it) runs as follows:

Dear Z.-*Give up your music at the Prince's, nothing else can be done.* We shall rehearse at your house to-morrow morning early at half past 8 and the production will be at my house at eleven —
ad dio excellent Plenipotentiarius *regni Beethovensis*
The rascals have been jailed as they deserved in their own handwriting.[1]

"Production" of what? The new Quintet, Op. 29, no doubt. "At my house"—no longer in the Hamberger House on the Bastion,

---

[1] The reference is, of course, to Artaria and Co and the *Rerers*.

but in the one pointed out by Czerny: "Beethoven lived a little later (about 1802) on the Petersplatz, the corner house beside the Guard-house, *vis-à-vis* of my present lodgings, in the fourth (?) storey, where I visited him as often as I did (in the Tiefen Graben). If you will give me the pleasure of a visit (No. 576) beside Daum, second storey, I will show you the windows. There I visited several times every week."[1]

What whim could have induced Beethoven to remove to this house with the bells of St. Peter's on one side and those of St. Stephen's sounding down upon him on the other, and he so suffering with his ears? Perhaps because friends were in the house. Förster's earliest recollections of Beethoven date from this winter and this house; for his father's dwelling was in the third storey above him. He remembers that Beethoven volunteered to instruct him in pianoforte playing, and that he was forced to rise at six in the morning and descend the cold stairs, child as he was, hardly six years of age, to take his lessons; and on one occasion going up again crying because his master had whipped his little fingers with one of the iron or steel needles used in knitting the coarse yarn jackets worn by women in service.

The composition of the Marches for Four Hands (Op. 45), ordered by Count Browne, dates also from the house in the Petersplatz.

He composed part of the second march while giving me a lesson on a sonata which I had to play in the evening at the Count's house at a little concert—a thing that still seems incomprehensible to me. I was also to play the marches on the same occasion with him. While we were playing young Count P.... sitting in the doorway leading to the next room spoke so loudly and continuously to a pretty woman, that Beethoven, after several efforts had vainly been made to secure quiet, suddenly took my hands from the keys in the middle of the music, jumped up and said very loudly, "I will not play for such swine!" All efforts to get him to return to the pianoforte were vain, and he would not even allow me to play the sonata. So the music came to an end in the midst of much ill humor.

In composing Beethoven tested his pieces at the pianoforte until he found them to his liking, and sang the while. His voice in singing was hideous. It was thus that Czerny heard him at work on the four-hand Marches while waiting in a side room.

According to Jahn's papers this statement came also from Czerny.

It is now necessary to turn back to November and again undertake the annoying and thankless task of examining a broad

[1]Letter to Ferdinand Luib, May 28, 1852.

tissue of mingled fact and misrepresentation and severing the truth from the error; this time the subject is the relations which existed between Beethoven and his brothers in these years. A letter written by Kaspar is the occasion of taking it up here. Johann André, a music publisher at Offenbach-on-the-Main, following the example of Hoffmeister, Nägeli, Breitkopf and Härtel and others, now applied to Beethoven for manuscripts. Kaspar wrote the reply under date November 23, 1802:

> . . . .At present we have nothing but a Symphony, a grand Concerto for Pianoforte, the first at 300 florins and the second at the same price, if you should want three pianoforte sonatas I could furnish them for no less than 900 florins, all according to Vienna standard, and these you could not have all at once, but one every five or six weeks, because my brother does not trouble himself with such trifles any longer and composes only oratorios, operas, etc.
> Also you are to send us eight copies of *every* piece which you may possibly engrave. Whether the pieces please you or not I beg you to answer, otherwise I might be prevented from selling them to someone else.
> We have also two Adagios for the Violin with complete instrumental accompaniment, which will cost 135 florins, and two little easy Sonatas, each with two movements, which are at your service for 280 florins. In addition I beg you to present our compliments to our friend Koch.
>   Your obedient,
>   K. v. Beethoven.
>   R.I. Treasury official.

This ludicrous display of the young man's self-importance as "Royal Imperial Treasury Official" and Ludwig van Beethoven's factotum is certainly very absurd; but hardly affords adequate grounds for the exceeding scorn of Schindler's remarks upon it. It is in itself sufficiently provocative of prejudice against its writer. But a display of vanity and self-esteem is ridiculous, not criminal.

The general charge brought by Ries against Kaspar and Johann van Beethoven is this:

> His brothers sought in particular to keep all his intimate friends away from him, and no matter what wrongs they did him, of which he was convinced, they cost him only a few tears and all was immediately forgotten. On such occasions he was in the habit of saying: "But they are my brothers, nevertheless," and the friend received a rebuke for his good-nature and frankness. The brothers attained their purpose in causing the withdrawal from him of many friends, especially when, because of his hard hearing, it became more difficult to converse with him.

Two years after the "Notizen" left the press Schindler published his "Biography." In it, although he first knew Beethoven in 1814, Johann some years later and Kaspar probably never, and therefore personally could know nothing of the facts of this period, yet he made the picture still darker. The special charge against Kaspar is that "about this time (in 1800) he began to rule Beethoven and made him suspicious of his most sincere friends and devotees by means of false representations and even jealousy."

There is a class of writers in Germany, whom no regard for the feelings of the living, no veneration for the memories of the great dead, no scruples on the score of truth, and even, in some cases, not respect and admiration for the greatest living genius, talent, and literary or scientific fame, restrain from using, or moderate their use of, whatever can add piquancy to their appeals to the prurient imaginations of certain classes of readers. Delicacy of feeling and nicety of conscience are not to be expected of such heartless traducers of the living and the dead; but that even the most contemptible of the tribe, regardless of the pain which such a slander of her husband's father must have caused to a widowed mother and her amiable children, could venture to represent Karl Kaspar van Beethoven as the seller of his wife's virtue and a sharer in the wages of her shame, is as inconceivable, as that his book should be received with praise by critics and applause by the public; that it should gain its author pecuniary profit instead of a prison. The story is utterly without foundation; a pure invention and a falsehood, and is told, moreover, of poor Kaspar, at a time when as yet he had no wife! Unfortunately, this treatment of Beethoven's brothers is not confined to writers of novels and feuilletonists. They, who profess to write history, no sooner strike upon this topic, than fancy seems to usurp the seat of reason and imagination to take the place of judgment. The lines of Ries expand into paragraphs; the sentences of Schindler into chapters. But the picture, thus overdrawn and exaggerated, in some degree corrects itself; for if the brothers were really as represented, what is to be thought of Beethoven if he in fact was so led, controlled and held in subjection by them as described?

Now, what is really known of Karl Kaspar and Johann, though it sufficiently confutes much of the calumnious nonsense which has been printed about them, is not fitted to convey any very exalted idea of their characters. The same Frau Karth, who remembered Ludwig in his youth as always "gentle and lovable," related that Kaspar was less kindly in his disposition, "proud and presumptuous," and that Johann "was a bit stupid, yet very good-natured." And such they were in manhood. Kaspar, like Ludwig, was very passionate, but more violent in his sudden wrath; Johann, slow to wrath and placable. Notwithstanding the poverty of his youth and early manhood, it is not known that Kaspar was avaricious; but Johann had felt too bitterly the misery of want and dependence, and became penurious. After he had accumulated a moderate fortune, the contests between his avarice and the desire to display his wealth led to very ludicrous exhibitions. In a word, Beethoven was not a phenomenon of goodness, nor were his brothers monsters of iniquity. That both Ries and Schindler wrote honestly has not been doubted; but common justice demands the reminder that they wrote under the bias of strong personal dislike to one or both brothers. Ries wrote impressions received at a very early time of life, and records opinions formed upon incomplete data. Schindler wrote entirely upon hearsay. Ries had not completed his twenty-first year when he departed from Vienna (1805). Howsoever strong were Beethoven's gratitude to Franz Ries and affection for Ferdinand, fourteen years was too great a disparity in age to allow that trustful and familiar intercourse between master and pupil which could enable the latter to speak with full knowledge; nor does a man of Beethoven's age and position turn from old and valued friends, like the Lichnowskys, Breuning, Zmeskall and others of whatever names, to make a youth of from 18 to 20 years, a new-comer and previously a stranger, even though a favorite pupil, his confidential adviser. Facts confirm the proposition in this case. We know that Beethoven in 1801 imparted grave matters to Wegeler and Amenda, of which Ries a year later had only received intimation from Breuning; and other circumstances of which he knew nothing are recorded in the testament of 1802. The charges against the brothers, both of Ries and Schindler, are general in terms; Ries only giving specifications or instances in proof. Schindler may be passed by as but repeating the "Notizen." Now, the onus of Ries's charges is this:

First: that Kaspar thrust himself impertinently into his brother's business; second: that both brothers intrigued to isolate Beethoven from his intimate friends and that their machinations were in many cases successful.

To the first point it is to be remarked: Besides Beethoven's often expressed disinclination to engage personally in negotiations for the sale of his works—although when he did he showed no lack of a keen eye to profits—his physical and mental condition at this period of his life often rendered the assistance of an agent indispensable. Accounts were to be kept with half a dozen publishers; letters received upon business were numerous and often

demanded prompt replies; proof-sheets were constantly arriving
for revision and correction; copyists required supervision; an
abundance of minor matters continually coming up and needing
attention when Beethoven might be on his long rambles over
hill and dale, the last man to be found in an emergency. One
asks with astonishment, how could so obvious a necessity for a
confidential agent have escaped notice? Who should or could
this agent be but his brother Kaspar?[1] He held an honorable place in a public office, the duties of which necessarily implied
the possession of those talents for, and habits of, prompt and
skillful performance of business which his early receipt of salary
and his regular advancement in position show that he really did
possess; his duties detained him in the city at all times, occasional
short vacations excepted, and yet left him ample leisure to attend
to his brother's affairs; he was a musician by education and fully
competent to render valuable service in that "fearful period of
arrangements"—as it is well known he did. What would have
justly been said of Beethoven if he had passed by one so eminently
qualified for the task—one on whom the paternal relation and
his own long continued care and protection had given him so
many claims—and had transferred the burden from his own
shoulders to those of other friends? But if, after adequate trial,
the agent proved unsatisfactory, the case would be changed and
the principal might with propriety seek needed assistance in other
quarters. And precisely this appears to have occurred; for after
a few years Kaspar disappears almost entirely from our history
in connection with his brother's pecuniary affairs. This fact is
stronger evidence than anything in Ries's statements, that Beethoven became dissatisfied with his brother's management, and
would have still more weight had he been less fickle, inconstant
and undecided in matters of business.[2]

---

[1]Under date April 22, 1802, Beethoven writes to Breitkopf and Härtel: "I reserve
the privilege of soon writing to you highborn gentlemen myself—many business matters,
and also many vexations—render me utterly useless for some things for a time—
meanwhile you may trust implicitly in my brother—who, in fact, manages all my affairs."

[2]Hugo Riemann, the editor of Volumes II and III of the second edition of this
"Life," was not disposed to permit the author's defence of Beethoven's brothers to
stand unchallenged, as Dr. Deiters had done in the first edition. Dr. Riemann calls
attention to a letter sent by Beethoven to Johann after the latter had removed to
Linz—the date as written by Beethoven is "March 28, 1089"—another instance of
Beethoven's careless treatment of such matters. Of course the year was 1809. In
the letter the composer says: "God grant to you and the other brother instead of his
unfeelingness, feeling—I suffer infinitely through him, with my bad hearing I always
need somebody, and whom shall I trust?" This Dr. Riemann inserts in the body of
the text. In a foot-note he calls attention to a letter found among Thayer's posthumous
papers to the author from Gerhard von Breuning in which occur the words: "Caspar
held a respected position in the public service. But how did it come that Rósgen

Seyfried, whose acquaintance with Beethoven ripened just at this time into intimacy, and who in 1802–'05 had the best possible opportunities for observation, beheld the relations between the brothers with far less jaundiced eyes than Ries. He says:

Beethoven was the more glad to choose joyous Vienna for his future and permanent home since two younger brothers had followed him thither, who took off his shoulders the oppressive load of financial cares and who were compelled to act almost as guardians for the priest of art to whom the ordinary affairs of civil life were as strange as strange could be.

At that time Seyfried, like Ries, was ignorant of the circumstances detailed to Wegeler and Amenda and in the testament; but the admirable selection of words in the closing phrase will strike all who have had occasion to read Beethoven's countless notes asking advice or aid in matters which most men would deem too trivial for even a passing word in conversation. The specifications of Ries in his charges against Kaspar will not long detain us. The story of the quarrel over the disposition of the Nägeli Sonatas may stand in all its ugliness and with no comment save the suggestion of the possibility that Kaspar's word as Ludwig's agent may have been pledged to the Leipsic publisher. The one really specific charge of Ries is the one on page 124 of the "Notizen":

All trifles, and many things which he did not want to publish because he thought them unworthy of his name, were secretly given to publicity by his brother. Thus songs which he had composed years before his departure for Vienna, became known only after he had reached a high degree of fame. Thus, too, little compositions which he had written in autograph albums were filched and published.

By "trifles" Ries, of course, here refers to the "Bagatelles, Op. 33, par Louis van Beethoven, 1782," as the manuscript is superscribed, published in the spring of 1803. The manuscript itself proves Ries to be in error. The words "par Louis van

warned my father to warn Ludwig not to trust Caspar too much in respect of money matters because he had a bad reputation; and then, Ludwig having told Caspar that he had received the warning from Steffen, Caspar demanded from my father to know from whom he had received the warning; and when my father refused because he had promised Rösgen on his word of honor not to betray him, Caspar rudely pressed my father, publicly delivered letters containing abuse and threats to the porter of the Court Council of War, etc., and—that my father, calling Ludwig a gossip, was long estranged from him until the letter of reconciliation came (in 1804)." Breuning's utterances in his book "Aus dem Schwarzspanierhause" are of similar import. There are evidences that Breuning was convinced that Carl's character was bad, but is more lenient in his judgment of Johann, whom he charges only with greed and miserliness. Of course, all this material was in the hands of Thayer, who must have weighed it in making up his defence of the brothers.

Beethoven" are in a hand unlike anything known to the present writer from Beethoven's pen. This fact, together with a something not easily described in the appearance of the notes, suggests the idea that this copy of the "Bagatelles" was made by Kaspar, and compiled, except No. 6 and perhaps one other, from the compositions of Beethoven in his boyhood. But the corrections—the words *Andante gracioso, Scherzo Allegro, Allegretto con una certa espressione parlante*, etc., written with lead pencil or a different ink, are certainly from Beethoven's own hand; also, in still another ink, the thoroughly Beethovenish "Op. 33." No one can mistake that. This work most assuredly was never "secretly given to the public."[1]

The only Album composition known to have been published in those years is the song with variations, "Ich denke dein"; and this Beethoven himself had offered to Hoffmeister before it , was printed by the Kunst- und Industrie-Comptoir.

The "songs" referred to by Ries can only be those of Op. 52. The original manuscript, having disappeared, neither refutes nor confirms his opinion. It is, however, exceedingly doubtful that Beethoven's brothers would have dared give an opus number to a stolen publication. *A priori* Ries is more likely to be in error here than in regard to the "Bagatelles." Now, the only contemporary criticism upon the latter which has been discovered, is a single line in Moll's "Annalen der Literatur" (Vienna, 1804): "Deserve the title in every sense of the word." Upon the "Song with Variations" no notice whatever has been found. But, Opus 52 was received by the "Allgemeine Musik-Zeitung" of August 28, 1805, in this style; *Opera* 47 and 38 having been duly praised, the writer continues:

Is it possible that No. 3 of these eight songs is from the pen of this composer, admirable even in his vagaries? It must be, since it is. At least his name is printed large on the title-page, the publisher is mentioned, the songs were published in Vienna where the composer lives, and, indeed, bear his latest *opus* number. Comprehend it he who can—that a thing in all respects so commonplace, poor, weak and in great part ludicrous should not only emanate from such a man but even be published.

And more like this, illustrated by copying "Das Blümchen Wunderhold." These citations suggest an obvious explanation of

[1]Dr. Frimmel is of the opinion that in this criticism Thayer was hasty and premature. In reproducing two *facsimiles* of portions of the Bagatelle in question ("Beethoven Jahrbuch" II, 1909) he says: "The apparent contradictions disclosed by these manuscripts led Thayer to question the authenticity of the autograph. It may safely be said that a later consideration of the matter would have led Thayer to change his mind; he would also surely have corrected his statement that Ries had reference to the Bagatelles Op. 33 in his 'N' (p. 124). Nottebohm knew the manuscript, which was once in the possession of Johann Kafka, well and never expressed a doubt as to its genuineness."

Ries's mistake, namely: Beethoven, mortified, ashamed, angry, purposely left him to believe that he was innocent of the publication of these compositions.   It was one of the advantages of having Kaspar in Vienna, that the responsibility of such false steps could be shifted upon him.   Those who are predetermined not to admit in Beethoven's character any of the faults, frailties and shortcomings of our common human nature, will of course censure this explanation.   Let them propose a better.[1]   Finally: In the paragraph upon the efforts of Beethoven's brothers to keep all of the composer's friends away from him it is easy to read between the lines that it was Ries himself who oft "was rebuked for his good-nature and frankness," which of itself to some extent lessens the force of the charge.   But it is best met by the first half of the Will, or testament, which, with the confessions to Wegeler and Amenda, as above said, open to our knowledge an inner life of the writer studiously concealed from his protégé.

In this solemn document, written as he supposed upon the brink of the grave, Beethoven touches upon this very question. We learn from his own affecting words, that the cause of his separation from friends lay, *not* in the machinations of his brothers, but in his own sensitiveness.   He records for future use, what he cannot now explain without disclosing his jealously guarded secret.   That record now serves a double purpose; it relieves Kaspar and Johann from a portion of the odium so long cast upon their memories; and proves Ries to be, in part at least, in error, without impugning his veracity.   It is very probable Ries never saw the will.   Had he known and carefully read it, the prejudices of his youth must have been weakened, the opinions founded upon partial knowledge modified.   He was of too noble a nature not to have gladly seen the memories of the dead vindicated—not to have been struck with and affected by the words of his deceased master: "To you, brother Carl, I give special thanks for the attachment you have displayed towards me of late."

Pass we to another topic.

On frequent occasions (says Ries), he showed a truly paternal interest in me.   From this source there sprang the written order (in 1802), which he sent me in a fit of anger because of an unpleasant predicament into which Carl van Beethoven had gotten me.   Beethoven wrote:

[1]Differences between the statements made here and some of those in Chapter VI are explained by the author's later inVestigations.

"You do not need to come to Heiligenstadt; I have no time to lose."
At the time Count Browne was indulging himself with pleasures in
which I was taking part, he being kindly disposed towards me, and was
in consequence neglecting my lessons.

That Beethoven, during the summer when his vocations were
interrupted by the dark hours in which the "will" was produced,
could have no time to lose in those lighter days when the spirit
of labor was upon him is clear from the surprising list of compositions written and published in this year.

The works which were developed were the three Violin
Sonatas, Op. 30; the first two of the three Pianoforte Sonatas, Op.
31; the two sets of Variations, Op. 34 and 35; the "Bagatelles,"
Op. 33, and (the chief work of the year) the second Symphony,
D major, Op. 36. The works which came from the press were the
Pianoforte Sonatas, Op. 22, 26 and 27, Nos. 1 and 2; the Serenade,
Op. 25; the Septet, Op. 20; the Quintet, Op. 29; the Rondo in G,
Op. 51, No. 2; the transcription for strings of the Pianoforte
Sonata in E, Op. 14, No. 1; the Variations for Violoncello and
Pianoforte on "Bei Männern welche Liebe fühlen," dedicated to
Count Browne; the six Contradances and six Rustic ("Länd-
rische") Dances. There were thirteen performances of the ballet
"Prometheus." Moreover, it is at least remotely possible that
the two large works which were played together with the Symphonies in C and D at Beethoven's concert on April 5, 1803—viz.: the
Pianoforte Concerto in C minor, Op. 37 and the Oratorio "Christus
am Ölberg," Op. 85—were not so far advanced in all their parts
that they, too, may have occupied the attention of Beethoven in
the winter of 1802–03.

For nearly all the works completed in 1802, studies are to be
found in the sketchbook described in full by Nottebohm,[1] which
covers the period from the fall of 1801 to the spring of 1802;
like the majority of the sketchbooks, it contains themes and studies
which were never worked out. "Overlooking the sketches which
cross each other," says Nottebohm, "and putting aside all that is
immaterial, the compositions represented in the book which were
completed and are known, may be set down chronologically as
follows:

"Opferlied," by Mathisson, first form.
Scene and Aria for Soprano: "No—non turbarti."
Three of the Contradances.
Bagatelle for Pianoforte, No. 6 of Op. 33.
Last movement of the Symphony in D major.

[1]"Ein Skizzenbuch von Beethoven," Breitkopf und Härtel, Leipsic, 1865.

Five of the six "Ländrische Tänze."

Terzetto, "Tremate, empj, tremate," Op. 116.

First and second movements of the Sonata for Pianoforte and Violin in A major, Op. 30, No. 1.

Last mo emen of the Sonata for Pianoforte and Violin in A major, Op. 47. t

Sonata for Pianoforte and Violin in C minor, Op. 30, No. 2.

Bagatelle for Pianoforte, No. 5 of Op. 119 (112).

First movement of the Sonata for Pianoforte in D minor, Op. 31, No. 2 (the first sketch only).

Sonata for Pianoforte and Violin in G major, Op. 30, No. 3.

Last movement of the Sonata for Pianoforte and Violin in A major, Op. 30, No. 1 (the theme had been designed before).

Variations for Pianoforte in E-flat major, Op. 35 (preparatory work).

Variations for Pianoforte in F major, Op. 34 (only the first hints).

Sonata for Pianoforte in G major, Op. 31, No. 1 (not complete).

To which may be added as occurring early in the book, the theme of the Larghetto of the Symphony in D (here for horns), out of which eventually grew the Trio in the Scherzo. A curious remark on one of the pages seems to be a memorandum for a piece of descriptive music: "Marital felicity, dark clouds upon the brow of the husband in which the fairer half unites but still seeks to dispel."

The evident care taken by the composer at this period to make the opus numbers really correspond to the chronological order of his works, is a strong reason for concluding that the Violin Sonatas, Op. 30, were completed or nearly so before he removed to Heiligenstadt. Even in that case, what wonderful genius and capacity for labor does it show, that, before the close of the year, in spite of ill health and periods of the deepest despondency, and of all the interruptions caused by his ordinary vocations after his return to town, he had completed the first two Sonatas of Op. 31, the two extensive and novel sets of Variations, Op. 34 and Op. 35, and the noble Second Symphony!—all of them witnesses that he had really "entered upon a new path," neither of them more so than the Symphony so amazingly superior to its predecessor in grandeur and originality. This was, in fact, the grand labor of this summer.

The three Sonatas for Pianoforte and Violin are dedicated to Czar Alexander I of Russia, who is said to have given command that a valuable diamond ring be sent to the composer. Lenz could find no record of such an incident in the imperial archives. The sketches show that the movement which now concludes the "Kreutzer" Sonata (Op. 47) was originally designed for the first of the three, the one in A major; and that for the

Adagio of the second, in C minor, Beethoven, assuming that he already associated the theme with the work, first contemplated using the key of G.

The three Sonatas for Pianoforte, Op. 31, are without dedication. W. Nagel connects them, or one of them, with the following extraordinary letter to Hoffmeister:

Vienna, April 8, 1802.

Are you all ridden by the devil gentlemen that you propose *such a sonata* to me?

At the time of the revolutionary fever—well—such a thing might have been very well; but now—when everything is trying to get back into the old rut, Buonaparte has signed the concordat with the Pope—such a sonata?

If it were a *Missa pro sancta Maria a tre voci*, or a Vesper, etc.—I would take my brush in hand at once—and write down a *Credo in unum Deum* in big pound notes—but good God, such a sonata—for these days of newly dawning Christianity—hoho!—leave me out of it, nothing will come of it.

Now my answer in quickest tempo—the lady can have a sonata from me, and I will follow her plan in respect of æsthetics in a general way—and without following the keys—price 5 ducats—for which she may keep it for her own enjoyment for a year, neither I nor *she* to publish it.

At the expiration of the year—the sonata will be mine to—i. e., I shall publish it, and she shall have the privilege—if she thinks it will be an honor—to ask me to dedicate it to her. . . .

Now God keep you gentlemen.

My Sonata is beautifully printed [*gestochen*, i. e., engraved]—but it took you a pretty time—send my Septet into the world a little quicker —for the crowd is waiting for it—and you know the Empress has it and there are (scamps) in the imperial city as well as the (imperial court) I can vouch for nothing—therefore make haste.

Herr (Mollo) has again recently published my Quartets but full of faults and *Errata*—in large as well as small form, they swarm in them like fish in the sea, there is no end of them—*questo è un piacere per un autore* —that's pricking music with a vengeance, in truth my skin is full of prickings and rips because of this beautiful edition of my Quartets. . . .

Now farewell and remember me as I do you. Till death your faithful

L. v. Beethoven.

An engagement which Beethoven had obtained from Count Browne for Ries was one that gave him leisure to pursue his studies, and he often came to Vienna and Heiligenstadt for that purpose. Thus it happens that the "Notizen" also contribute to the history of these Sonatas. Ries writes:

Beethoven had promised the three solo sonatas (Op. 31) to Nägeli in Zurich while his brother Carl (Caspar) who, unfortunately, was always meddling with his affairs, wanted to sell them to a Leipsic publisher.

There were frequent exchanges of words between the brothers on this account because Beethoven having given his word wanted to keep it. When the sonatas (the first two) were about to be sent away Beethoven was living in Heiligenstadt. During a promenade new quarrels arose between the brothers and finally they came to blows. The next day he gave me the sonatas to send straight to Zurich, and a letter to his brother enclosed in another to Stephan von Breuning who was to read it. A prettier lesson could scarcely have been read by anybody with a good heart than Beethoven read his brother on the subject of his conduct on the day before. He first pointed it out in its true and contemptible character, then he forgave him everything, but predicted a bad future for him unless he mended his ways. The letter, too, which he had written to Breuning was very beautiful.

The first two Sonatas (G major and D minor) appeared in the spring of 1803, as Op. 29, in Nägeli's "Répertoire des Claveci-nistes" as *Cahier* 5 (the third followed soon after as Op. 33, together with the "Sonate pathétique" as *Cahier* 11). Of *Cahier* 5 Nägeli sent proof-sheets. Ries reports on the subject as follows:

When the proof-sheets came I found Beethoven writing. "Play the Sonata through," he said to me, remaining seated at his writing-desk. There was an unusual number of errors in the proofs, which fact already made Beethoven impatient. At the end of the first *Allegro* in the Sonata in G major, however, Nägeli had introduced four measures—after the fourth measure of the last hold:

When I played this Beethoven jumped up in a rage, came running to me, half pushed me away from the pianoforte, shouting: "Where the devil do you find that?" One can scarcely imagine his amazement and rage when he saw the printed notes. I received the commission to make a record of all the errors and at once send the sonatas to Simrock in Bonn, who was to make a reprint and call it *Edition très correcte*. In this place belong three notes to me:

1. "Be good enough to make a note of the errors and send a record of them at once to Simrock, with the request that he publish as soon as possible—day after to-morrow I will send him the sonata and concerto."

2. "I must beg you again to do the disagreeable work of making a clear copy of the errors in the Zurich sonatas and sending it to Simrock; you will find a list of the errors at my house in the Wieden."

3.   "Dear Ries!

"Not only are the expression marks poorly indicated but there are also false notes in several places—therefore be careful!—or the work will again be in vain. *Ch'à detto l'amato bene?*"

The closing words of the second note show that the matter was not brought to an end until late in the spring of 1803, after Beethoven had removed into the theatre buildings An-der-Wien. After the Sonatas became known in Vienna Doležalek asked Beethoven if a certain passage in the D minor Sonata was correct. "Certainly it is correct," replied the composer, "but you are a countryman of Krumpholz—nothing will go into that hard Bohemian head of yours."

A circumstance related by Czerny, if accepted as authoritative, proves that two of the three Sonatas were completed in the country. "Once when he (Beethoven) saw a rider gallop past his windows in his summer sojourn in Heiligenstadt near Vienna, the regular beat (of the horse's hoofs) gave him the idea for the theme of the Finale of the D minor sonata, Op. 31, No. 2:

The six Variations in F on an Original Theme, Op. 34, dedicated to the Princess Odescalchi, were probably composed immediately after the Variations in E-flat, Op. 35. In the midst of the sketches for the latter (in the Kessler sketchbook) two measures of the theme are noted and the remark appended, "Each variation in a different key—but alternately passages now in the left hand and then almost the same or different ones in the right." The two sets of Variations and the Quintet, Op. 29, were sold to Breitkopf and Härtel in October, 1802. In a letter which the publishers received from the composer on October 18, 1802, Beethoven writes:

I have made two sets of Variations of which the first may be said to number 8, the second 30; both are written in a really entirely new style and each in quite a different way. I should very much like to have them published by you, but under the one condition that the honorarium be about 50 florins for the two sets—do not let me make this offer in vain, for I assure you you will never regret the two works. Each theme in them is treated independently and in a wholly different manner. As a rule I only hear of it through others when I have new ideas, since I never know it myself; but this time I can assure you myself that the style in both works is new to me.

A more interesting letter received by Breitkopf and Härtel on December 26, 1802, relates to the same subject. It demands insertion in full:

Instead of the noise about a new method of V(ariations) such as would be made by our neighbors the Gallo-Franks, like, for instance, a certain Fr. composer who presents fugues *après une nouvelle Méthode*, it consisting in this that the fugue is no fugue, etc.—I nevertheless want to call attention to the fact that these V. differ at least from others, and this I thought I could do in the most unconstrained and least conspicuous manner by means of the little prefatory note which I beg of you to print in the small as well as the large V., leaving it for you to say in what language or how many languages, since we poor Germans are compelled to speak in all tongues.

Here is the prefatory note:

Inasmuch as these V. differ materially from my earlier ones I have, instead of designating them merely by number, 1, 2, 3, etc., included them in the list of my *greater musical works*, and this also for the further reason that the themes are original.

The author.

N.B. If you find it necessary to change or improve anything you have my entire permission.

That by the "large variations," whose number (30) Breitkopf and Härtel seem to have called in question, Beethoven meant his Op. 35, is made plain by a third letter running as follows:

Vienna, April 8, 1803.

I have wanted to write to you for a long time, but my business affairs are so many that they permit but little correspondence. You seem to be mistaken in your opinion that there are not as many variations (as I stated) only it would not do to announce the number as there is no way of telling how in the large set three variations are run into each other in the Adagio, and the Fugue can certainly not be called a variation, nor the Introduction, which, as you may see for yourself, begins with the bass of the theme, then expands to 2, 3 and finally 4 parts, when the theme at last makes its appearance, which again cannot be called a variation, etc.—but if this is not clear to you, send me a proof-sheet along with the manuscript as soon as a copy is printed, so that I may be guarded against confusion—you would do me a great favor if you would omit from the large variations the dedication to abbé Stadler and print the following, viz.: *dediées* etc. *À Monsieur le Comte Maurice Lichnowsky;* he is a brother of Prince Lichnowsky and only recently did me an unexpected favor, and I have no other opportunity to return the kindness, if you have already engraved the dedication to abbé Stadler I will gladly pay the cost of changing the title-page, do not hesitate, write what the expense will be and I will pay it with pleasure, I earnestly beg you to do this if you have not sent out any copies—in the case of the small variations the dedication to Princess Odescalchi remains.

I thank you very much for the beautiful things of Sebastian Bach's, I will preserve and study them—should there be a continuation of the pieces send them to me also—if you have a good text for a cantata or other vocal piece send it to me.

In spite of Beethoven's warning, Op. 34 was printed without
the proof having been read by him; this provoked another letter
calling attention to a large number of errors in the publication,
of which Beethoven promised to send a list. He also expressed
a fear that the "large variations" would also be faulty, the more
since his own manuscript had been put into the hands of the
engraver, and asked that the fact that the theme was from his
ballet "Prometheus" be indicated on the title-page, if there were
still time, offering, as in the case of the dedication, to pay the cost
of the change. Again he begged to be permitted to correct a
proof copy—a request which was ignored in this instance, as it
had been in the first. The result was a somewhat gentle protest
in another letter (October, 1803), in which Beethoven offered the
firm the Variations on "God save the King" and "Rule Britannia,"
the song "Wachtelschlag" and three Marches for the Pianoforte,
four hands. The conclusion of the letter, with its postscript, has
a double value—as an exhibition of Beethoven's attitude towards
the criticism of his day and as a contribution to the debated
question touching the illicit printing of some of his early compositions. We quote:

> Please thank the editor of the M.Z. ("Musikzeitung") for his kind-
> ness in giving place to the flattering report of my oratorio in which
> there is so much rude lying about the prices which I have made and I
> am so infamously treated, which is I suppose an evidence of impartiality—
> for aught I care—so long as this makes for the fortune of the M.Z.—
> what magnanimity is not asked of the true artist, and not wholly without
> impropriety, but on the other hand, what detestable and vulgar attacks
> upon us are permitted.
> Answer immediately, and next time another topic.
>   As always your devoted
>   L. v. Beethoven.
>
> N.B. All the pieces which I have offered you are entirely new—since
> unfortunately so many unlucky old things of mine have been sold and
> stolen.

It was through the printing of the letters to Breitkopf and
Härtel that the fact became known that Beethoven originally had
intended to dedicate the Variations in E-flat to Abbé Stadler.
The Rondo in G, which was announced by Hoffmeister and Kühnel
on March 19, 1803, was published in connection with the Rondo in
C which had already appeared in 1798, as Op. 51, Nos. 1 and 2. It
was originally dedicated to Countess Guicciardi, but Beethoven
gave her the Sonata in C-sharp minor in exchange for it and inscribed the Rondo to Countess Henriette Lichnowsky. This would

seem to indicate that it was finished before the Sonata, probably in 1801. Nottebohm has proved in his study of the Kessler sketch-book that the sixth of the "Bagatelles," in D major, had its origin in 1802, when Beethoven was at work on the second Symphony.[1]

[1]Dr. Riemann thinks that Beethoven originally wrote "1802" on the autograph, and that subsequently he, or somebody else, changed the 8 into a 7 and the 0 into an 8. (See the *facsimile* in Frimmel's "Beethovenjahrbuch" of 1909); yet the German Editor finds suggestions of Beethoven's latest style in the "Bagatelles" and calls attention to the fact that Beethoven detected intimations of No. 5 in the set Op. 119 in the Kessler sketchbook. Dr. Riemann's conclusion is thus worded: "If Ries in his 'Notizen' meant these 'Bagatelles', he was surely in error. Beethoven's complaint to Breitkopf and Härtel in the letter of October, 1803, 'since unfortunately so many unlucky old things of mine have been sold and stolen,' cannot possibly have referred to them. Beethoven himself thought highly of these 'trifles', as is shown by his anger at Peters's depreciation of Op. 119. It is very likely that Ries meant the Two Preludes in all the Keys (Op. 39), which may have been surreptitiously published."

END OF VOLUME I